ARYAN AND NON-ARYAN IN INDIA

THE UNIVERSITY OF MICHIGAN
CENTER FOR SOUTH AND SOUTHEAST ASIAN STUDIES

MICHIGAN PAPERS ON SOUTH AND SOUTHEAST ASIA
Number 14

ARYAN AND NON-ARYAN IN INDIA

Edited by
Madhav M. Deshpande
and
Peter Edwin Hook

Center for South and Southeast Asian Studies
The University of Michigan
Ann Arbor
1979

Library of Congress Catalog Card Number 78-60016

ISBN 0-89148-014-5
Center for South and Southeast Asian Studies

ISBN 0-89720-012-8
Karoma Publishers, Inc.

Printed in the United States of America

PREFACE

The history and mechanisms of the convergence of ancient Aryan and non-Aryan cultures has been a subject of continuing fascination in many fields of Indology. The papers in this volume are the fruit of a conference on that topic held in December 1976 at The University of Michigan, Ann Arbor, under the auspices of the Center for South and Southeast Asian Studies. The expressed object of the conference was to examine the latest findings from a variety of disciplines as they relate to the formation and integration of a unified Indian culture from many disparate cultural and ethnic elements. Reading them one will notice how often questions posed by one discipline lend themselves to the methodologies or discoveries of another. It is to be hoped that the publication of these essays will help stimulate further progress in the interdisciplinary approach to the study of Indian civilization and to the study of cultural convergence in other parts of the world.

The editors wish to express their gratitude to the contributors, who were prompt in submitting the final versions of their papers and to the Center for South and Southeast Asian Studies of The University of Michigan for having funded both the conference and the publication of these papers.

CONTRIBUTORS

A. L. BASHAM is well known for his books on the history of ancient India, among them *The History and Doctrines of the Ājīvikas, Studies in Indian History and Culture*, and above all *The Wonder That Was India.* He has recently edited *A Cultural History of India*. The holder of a Ph.D. from the University of London, he was professor of the history of South Asia in the School of Oriental and African Studies of that university for many years. He is now professor and chairman of the Department of Asian Civilizations at the Australian National University.

GEORGE L. HART, III, took a Ph.D. in Sanskrit from Harvard University. His dissertation has been published by the University of California Press under the title, *The Poems of Ancient Tamil: Their Milieu and Their Sanskrit Counterparts.* A book of translations from Sangam Works will be published in 1979 by Princeton University Press. He is currently an associate professor in the Department of South and Southeast Asian Studies at the University of California, Berkeley.

PETER E. HOOK holds a Ph.D. in linguistics from the University of Pennsylvania. He is currently an associate professor in the Department of Linguistics at The University of Michigan. His book *The Compound Verb in Hindi* has been published in the Michigan Series in South and Southeast Asian Languages and Linguistics, Center for South and Southeast Asian Studies, The University of Michigan, Ann Arbor. He is presently writing a pedagogical work entitled *The Syntactic Structures of Hindi.*

COLIN P. MASICA holds a Ph.D. from the University of Chicago where he is currently an associate professor in the Department of South Asian Languages and Civilization. His book *Defining a Linguistic Area: South Asia* was published by the University of Chicago Press in 1976. He also coauthored, with A. K. Ramanujan, an article entitled "Phonological Typology of the Indian Linguistic Area," which appeared in *Current Trends in Linguistics*, vol. 5.

THOMAS R. TRAUTMANN holds a Ph.D. in history from the University of London. Currently he is Professor of History at The University of Michigan. His first book was *Kauṭilya and the Arthaśāstra: A Statistical Investigation of the Authorship and Evolution*, E. J. Brill, Leiden, in 1971. Since that time he has published articles on kinship patterns in India and is currently working on a book entitled *The Frontiers of Dravidian Kinship*, which is outlined in this volume.

DAVID W. McALPIN holds a Ph.D. from the University of Wisconsin and is currently an assistant professor in the Department of South Asian Regional Studies at the University of Pennsylvania. His research interests include historical and comparative linguistics, generative phonological theory, and Dravidian linguistics. He is currently developing further evidence for the genetic relationship between Elamite and Dravidian on which he has published articles in *Language* and *Current Anthropology*.

MADHAV M. DESHPANDE holds a Ph.D. in oriental studies from the University of Pennsylvania. He is currently Associate Professor of Sanskrit in the Department of Linguistics at The University of Michigan. His book *Critical Studies in Indian Grammarians I: The Theory of Homogeneity [Sāvarṇya]* was published in 1975 in the Michigan Series in South and Southeast Asian Languages and Linguistics. His book *Semantics in Classical and Medieval India* will appear in the same series, and his monograph *Sociolinguistic Attitudes in India: An Historical Reconstruction* has just been published by Karoma Publishers, Ann Arbor, in the series *Linguistica Extranea.*

FRANKLIN C. SOUTHWORTH holds a Ph.D. in linguistics from Yale University and is currently Professor of South Asian Linguistics at the University of Pennsylvania. He is known for his book *Spoken Marathi* which he coauthored with Naresh Kavadi. His *The Student's Hindi-Urdu Reference Manual* was published by the University of Arizona Press, 1971. He has also coauthored, with Chander J. Daswani, *Foundations of Linguistics* which was published in 1974 by the Free Press. He has written numerous articles on linguistic archaeology and sociolinguistics and has recently been engaged in developing a new approach to the study of the relationship between ethnic diversity and linguistic variation as they have developed over the past three millennia in South Asia.

CONTENTS

ARYAN AND NON-ARYAN IN SOUTH ASIA

A. L. Basham
Australian National University

The term Aryan is not often heard nowadays except in the ancient Indian context, and after its misuse by Germanic demagogues in the 1930s this is not surprising. It may have philological relationships with words in non-Indian Indo-European languages, but I understand that modern comparative philologists have recently cast some doubt on several of these (e.g., Irish *Eire*, German *Ehre*, Latin *arare*). The only relative of this Indian word whose kinship is practically certain is the Old Persian *Airiya* (Modern Persian *Īrān*). We may thus safely assert that a powerful group of Indo-Iranians in the early second millennium B.C. called themselves by something like this name. The branch which entered India were the Aryans par excellence.

The Aryans are popularly imagined as tall, upstanding, comparatively fair-skinned nomads, tough and aggressive, riding through the northwestern passes in their horse-drawn chariots and striking terror in the conservative and sedentary non-Aryans of the Indus Valley. The view propagated by the late Sir Mortimer Wheeler[1] that they destroyed the cities of the Harappa culture is now less popular since the theories of Raikes and Dales,[2] but still the Aryans figure in most standard histories of India as a martial, positive people, the antithesis of the priest-ridden "Dravidians" whom they overwhelmed and upon whom they imposed their culture.

The cultural history of India after the Aryan invasion has been commonly interpreted as the process of the fusion of Aryan and non-Aryan elements over a period of three thousand years. In the last century this process was sometimes interpreted as a kind of degeneration—the vigorous, extroverted invader from the steppes steadily losing his lively adventurous character under the influence of subtropical and tropical conditions and through the admixture of alien blood and the absorption of alien ideas. This picture of the history of India still sometimes appears in a rather modified form, though in the present century there has been among Indologists an increasing realization that the nineteenth century view of ancient India as a land where attention was mainly directed towards mystical gnosis and *mokṣa* ("plain living and high thinking")[3] is not wholly borne out by the sum of the evidence.

The data for the earlier racial history of India, especially since the entry of the people who called themselves Aryans, is not wholly satisfactory. This is particularly the case because, owing to the Aryans' custom of cremation, which also affected the peoples whom they conquered and absorbed, skeletal remains are rare in northern India from about 1000 B.C. onwards. Nowhere have the remains of a skeleton been discovered about which it might confidently be said: "These are the bones of a member of the tribes whose priests composed the hymns of the *Ṛg Veda*"; and the same is largely true of later generations. Our knowledge of the early interaction of Aryan and non-Aryan in South Asia must still depend mainly on the evidence of language and literature, studied in the light of archaeology and of the present-day ethnological situation.

It is well known that the subcontinent contains three major ethnic types, which are nowadays frequently termed Proto-Australoid, Palaeo-Mediterranean, and Indo-European. The two latter are considered by modern ethnologists as branches of the widespread "Europoid" or "Caucasoid" type. It is equally well known that there are three major linguistic groups in India—Munda, Dravidian and Indo-Aryan. While a one-to-one relation between the three social types and the three language groups is obviously belied by the facts, it is tempting to link them in their origins. According to this theory, the Munda languages represent the speech of the earliest inhabitants of India, whose ancestors have been in the subcontinent perhaps since Palaeolithic times; the Dravidian languages were introduced by Palaeo-Mediterranean migrants who came to India in the Neolithic period, bringing with them the craft of agriculture; while the Indo-Aryan languages were obviously brought by the Aryans in the second millennium B.C.

Though this interpretation may be oversimplified, the evidence now seems strong enough to show with fair certainty that of the three language groups the Dravidian and the Indo-Aryan were brought to India by migrants, the former considerably earlier than the latter. Arguments in favor of the South Indian Peninsula being the original home of the Dravidian language family, very popular with Tamil scholars at one time, cannot resist the weight of the evidence, both archaeological and linguistic. The hypothesis of Caldwell, the father of Dravidian philology and linguistics, that there is a remote relationship between the Dravidian and Finno-Ugrian groups, put forward over a hundred years ago,[4] and long discredited or ignored, was revived around the time of the Second World War by Burrow.[5] It has since steadily gained support, and countertheories have connected Dravidian with Asianic and Basque[6] (Lahovary) on the one hand, and Elamite (McAlpin) on the other. The last theory, discussed by its author in the pages of this volume, is particularly convincing, and Elamite seems to be the closest relation to the Dravidian group, though the relationship established by McAlpin need not wholly invalidate those of earlier scholars. The various theories, taken together, point to a group of agglutinating languages, widespread from the Mediterranean to the borders of the Indian subcontinent in prehistoric times. Of these, the Proto-Dravidian ancestor of the modern Dravidian group was the most easterly member.

If there should be still any doubts as to the strength of this evidence, it is reinforced by the phenomenon of Brahui, a Dravidian language, in the remote northwest of the subcontinent. Brahui can only be satisfactorily explained as a linguistic fossil, the last remnant of numerous Dravidian languages spoken in protohistoric times in the area of what is now Pakistan. Moreover, though the attempts of numerous scholars to read the Harappa script have not yet produced a fully convincing interpretation, there is at least sufficient evidence, from the several analyses of the syllabary which have already been made, to show that it is more consistent with an agglutinating language than with an inflected one.

Further significant evidence of the early presence of Dravidian languages in the northwest of South Asia, and evidence of a very convincing type, emerges from recent studies of the language of the *Ṛgveda,* and of other Vedic texts which form the earliest surviving literary evidence of the Aryans in India. A brief history of the theories concerning Dravidian influence on Indo-Aryan languages has been given by Kuiper, who has traced the theory that the retroflex consonants of Sanskrit are due to the influence of indigenous languages back to the heroic days of Indology, when Pott first adumbrated it in 1833.[7] Dravidian influence on classical Sanskrit was generally admitted, but admitted only as a substratum, and its influence on Vedic was generally taken as negligible. Only a very few scholars, such as Emeneau and Burrow, who combined deep knowledge of Dravidian and Indo-Aryan languages, were willing to admit any significant influence of Dravidian on the earlier strata of Sanskrit.

A monumental lecture by Kuiper, delivered at Ann Arbor in 1965 and since published in article form,[8] put the study of Dravidian influence on Vedic Sanskrit on a different footing. Kuiper showed that Dravidian had influenced not only the phonology and vocabulary of even the earliest stratum of the Veda, but also its very sentence structure. The work of Emeneau and Burrow, on the one hand, and that of Kuiper, on the other, has been further developed by Southworth in a very important paper in this volume; and it is to be noted that, with due caution, the last scholar even sees the possibility of

Dravidian influence on Indo-Iranian, the hypothetical language spoken by the two peoples calling themselves Aryan before they were divided into Indian and Iranian branches.

Southworth's work has been furthered by McAlpin's establishment of a relationship between Dravidian and Elamite, a theory which seems, at least to a nonspecialist, thoroughly convincing, and which, it is quite clear, brings a new dimension to the study of Dravidian origins. We have not yet heard the reaction of the other specialists to McAlpin's theory, but at least he seems to have finally given the coup de grâce to the view that Dravidian is a language family indigenous to India. Since Caldwell's day innumerable relationships have been suggested between Dravidian words and those in a variety of languages ranging from Basque and Berber, through Hungarian and Finnish, to Etruscan, Hurrian, and now Elamite. No doubt many of these equivalencies are incorrect; but if only one tenth of the total are well-founded, this is enough to prove that the Dravidian languages began outside India and found their way into the subcontinent via the northwest, as Indo-Aryan did later.

We must not, however, infer from this that all linguistic and other evidence points to a neat Aryan-Dravidian polarity in the protohistoric situation in India. There is no definite evidence that Munda languages were ever spoken in the northwest of the subcontinent, though, if we are to take the famous Mohenjo-daro dancing girl as evidence, Proto-Australoid racial elements seem to have been present there. Southworth has shown, however, that, in all probability, in addition to Indo-European and Dravidian, a third language family was present in that area and influenced the vocabulary of the other two. This hypothesis, based on lexical evidence, is strengthened by the survival of vestigial languages such as Burushaski, not clearly affiliated to any other group, in the remote valleys of the Pamirs and the Hindu Kush.

Indeed, recent research shows that the racial and linguistic situation in the northwest at the dawn of history was very complex, and over the past fifty years the simplified picture of the tall, comparatively fair, charioteering Aryans bringing civilizations to a land of insignificant dark-skinned barbarians has been completely destroyed by archaeology and linguistics. Though the distinction between *ārya-varṇa* and *dāsa-varṇa* in the *Ṛgveda* is still emphasized in many books on the subject, it has also been noted that some evidence from that text points to occasional non-Aryan patronage of Vedic sacrifices or of the Brahmins who performed them.[9] Already in this early period the term *ārya* was beginning to lose its original racial connotation, which it retained more definitely in Iran.

This does not imply, however, that it became meaningless. The invaders of

India who called themselves Aryans brought with them a great body of tradition and custom–religious, social and cultural–together with a language or group of languages which became the ancestor of almost all the languages of North India. This Aryan heritage was adopted and adapted in varying measure by all the races of India, until by the time of the Pāli canon the term *ārya* had, in common speech, come to mean something sharing the characteristics of a number of English words such as "good," "moral," "gentlemanly," and "well-bred," and seems to have lost nearly all the sense of race which went with it in the time of the *Ṛgveda.*[10] The polarity of *ārya* and *mleccha* in classical Sanskrit seems also to have had very little purely racial content, at least by the time of the *Mānava-dharma-śāstra*, which contains implicit provisions for the incorporation of foreigners into the Aryan community,[11] a process which seems to have been going on steadily since the days of the *Ṛgveda.* What excluded the *mleccha* was his evil habits rather than his race.

The polarity of Aryan and Dravidian which has been made much of in recent generations seems to have meant very little in earlier times. Even in the time of Manu, Dravidians were acceptable as Aryans if they performed the necessary penances and rituals.[12] From the Pallava period onwards, if not before, it seems that, in the eyes of northerners, respectable people of Dravidian speech, if they followed the Brahminic norms, were classed as Aryans, irrespective of their pigmentation and of certain irregular customs which are taken note of and provided for in the Dharmaśāstras. Indeed the Dravidians themselves borrowed the word *ārya*, and it survives in Tamil to this day in its colloquial form (*aiyar*), as a moderately respectful term of address. Incidentally, the Prakrit form *ajja* seems to have been used similarly by the early Jainas, with little more content than the contemporary English "mister," as a title of respectable Jaina laymen.[13]

In our study of Aryan and non-Aryan in India, we are not in search of racial survivals. There is no question here of tracing how a tall, upstanding, extroverted race of Proto-Nordics was corrupted and polluted by the blood of darker subtropical peoples to become the contemporary Indians, and I am sure none of the organizers of this conference had anything like this in mind. Rather, we are tracing the progress and development of ancient Indo-European cultural and religious traditions, already much modified in their Indo-Iranian form, under the impact of new geographical and climatic conditions and through the influence of the different, and probably more highly developed, traditions of the indigenous peoples whom the bearers of "Aryan" culture encountered as they slowly expanded from the Panjab eastward to the Ganga delta and southward to Kanyākumārī. In the very earliest stages of the process the main agents of that cultural expansion may have been martial bands of pioneers, but for most of the last two and a half millennia they were rather Brahmins and ascetics, the latter including heterodox Buddhist and Jaina monks. And the content of the Aryanism which they propagated differed significantly from period to period, as at each stage the original Indo-European heritage became more deeply modified by other influences. In fact, in the India of the past the word *ārya* must have connoted something a little different in every century, as the "Aryans" spread further in space and time from their original base in the northwest.

The papers in this volume throw important new light on this process in many of its aspects. They form an invaluable contribution toward the clarification of one of the most persistent problems of South Asian cultural history, and I am highly honored by the privilege of being allowed to introduce them.

NOTES

1. Wheeler's theory was propounded in several books and articles, e.g., *The Indus Civilization*, supplementary volume to the Cambridge History of India, 3rd ed. (Cambridge: Cambridge University Press, 1968), pp. 126-34.
2. R. L. Raikes, "The End of the Ancient Cities of the Indus," *American Anthropologist* 65(1963):655-59, 66(1964):284-99); "The Mohenjo-Daro Floods," *Antiquity* 38 (1965):196-203; *Water, Weather and Archaeology* (London: Baker, 1967); G. F. Dales, "Harappan Outposts on the Makran Coast," *Antiquity* 36(1962):86-92; "New Investigations at Mohenjo-Daro," *Archaeology* 18(1965):145-50; "The Decline of the Harappans," *Scientific American*, May 1966, pp. 93-100.
3. Radha Kumud Mookerji, *Hindu Civilization* (Bombay: Bharatiya Vidya Bhavan, 1950), p. 82.
4. Robert Caldwell, *A Comparative Grammar of the Dravidian or South Indian Family of Languages* (London: Harrison, 1856), pp. viii, 528; 3rd ed. rev., J. L. Wyatt and R. Pillai, eds. (London: Kegan Paul, 1913; reprint Madras, U. P., 1956), pp. xl, 640.
5. T. Burrow, "Dravidian Studies," *Bulletin of the School of Oriental and African Studies* 9(1937-39):711-22; 10(1940-42):289-97; 11(1943-46):122-39, 328-56, 595-616; 12(1947-48):132-47, 365-96.
6. N. Lahovary, *Dravidian Origins and the West* (Calcutta: Orient Longmans, 1963), passim, especially pp. 347-74.
7. August Friedrich Pott, *Etymologische Forschungen*, I, no. 1(1833):88f., II, no. 1 (1836):19, *teste* Kuiper (in the article mentioned below), p. 82, n. 2.
8. F. B. J. Kuiper, "The Genesis of a Linguistic Area," *Indo-Iranian Journal* (The Hague) 10(1967-68):81-102.
9. The direct evidence is in fact slight. In one hymn (viii, 46, 32) the Dāsa Balbūtha and another person called Tārukṣa are said to have given a hundred unspecified gifts to a *vipra*, presumably the author of the hymn, Vaśa Aśvya. The verse is not without obscurities:

   Śataṁ dāse Balbūthe vipraḥ Tārukṣa ā dade/te te
   Vāyav ime janāḥ madaṁtīndragopā madaṁtī devagopāḥ//

   The verses preceding this one make mention of the great generosity of a certain Pṛthuśravas to the poet, and in this penultimate verse of the hymn his other benefactors are remembered as an afterthought. The fact that the second half of the stanza has plural verbs, and not dual or singular ones, indicates that the poet wishes to commemorate three benefactors–Pṛthuśravas, Balbūtha, and Tārukṣa. Balbūtha is definitely a *dāsa*, but corruption has been suggested (for references see Macdonnell and Keith, *A Vedic Index of Names and Subjects* [London: Murray, 1912; reprint Delhi: Motilal, 1958], s.v. Balbūtha). This single instance, in which Balbūtha's contribution was evidently much less than that of Pṛthuśravas, is hardly sufficient to base any theory on. This may well be a case of an influential non-Aryan on the way to full incorporation in the Aryan fold, under the influence of an enterprising priest. We cannot tell how far this process had already gone at the time or how many of the rājās with Aryan names were in fact wholly or partly indigenous by blood; but *varṇa* divisions appear to have been by no means rigid during the period of the *Ṛgveda,* and the Aryanization of non-Aryan chiefs is definitely attested in later periods in both India and Southeast Asia. These facts, taken in conjunction with the linguistic evidence, suggest that the blood of even the higher-class Aryans had received considerable admixture with that of the indigenous peoples at the time of the composition of the text.

A further interesting case is provided by *RV* vi, 45, 31-33. Here, appended to a lengthy hymn to Indra, occur three verses in honor of a certain Bṛbu who "stood as the seniormost head of the Paṇis" (*ádhi Bṛbúḥ Paṇīnā́m várṣiṣthe mūrdhánn asthāt,* v. 31). He is praised for his thousand gifts to the singer, said to be Śaṃyu, son of Bṛhaspati (*yásya....bhadrā́ rātíḥ sahasríṇī,* v. 32). The last of these three verses (v. 33) is at first sight obscure: *Tat su no víśve aryá ā sádā gṛṇaṃti kārávaḥ Bṛbúṃ sahasradā́tamaṃ sūríṃ sahasrasā́tamaṃ*. Here with Sāyaṇa, we must take *aryá*, the plural of *arí* and subject of the sentence, in its rarer *Ṛgvedic* meaning as 'a faithful or devoted or pious man' (Monier Williams, s.v.). All such worthy poets (*kārávaḥ*) sing the praise of Bṛbu, the giver of a thousand gifts. (*Sahasrasā́tāmaṃ* is virtually a synonym of *sahasra-dā́tamaṃ.*)

The nature of the Paṇis and their relations with the Aryans are very obscure and have been the subject of much theorizing (for references see Macdonnell and Keith, s.v.). They are referred to once each in the *Ṛgveda* as *dāsas* (v.34.5-7) and *dasyus* (vii. 6.3). They were the objects of much hostility, but the evidence suggests that some of them, such as Bṛbu, came to terms with the invaders. Since they figure in some passages as wealthy traders, it is tempting to suggest, with D. D. Kosambi (The Culture and Civilisation of Ancient India [London: Routledge and Kegan Paul, 1965], p. 80), that they were survivors of the Harappa culture.

10. "The early Buddhists had no such ideas as we cover with the words Buddhist and Indian. *Ariya* does not exactly mean either. But it often comes very near to what they would have considered the best in each." (T. W. Rhys Davids and William Stede, *The Pali Text Society's Pali-English Dictionary* [London: Pali Text Society, n.d.], s.v. *ariya.)* The enormous Trenckner *Critical Pali Dictionary* (Copenhagen: Royal Danish Academy, 1929-48), vol. 1, s.v., though it gives many valuable citations, misses this insight into the overtones of the word in Buddhism.

11. Manu (x. 21-23) gives lists of *vrātya* tribes and peoples descended from each of the three Aryan classes. Those of the brahmin and *vaiśya* groups are comparatively unimportant castes and tribes of the times, but kṣatriya *vrātyas* comprise Jhallas, Mallas, Licchavis, Naṭas, Karaṇas, Khasas and Draviḍas. Of these the Mallas, Licchavis and Khasas dwelt in the lower slopes of the Himalayas or the adjoining plain, while the Draviḍas were obviously in the south of the subcontinent. Jhallas, Naṭas and Karaṇas appear to have been professional castes, not tribes. Later (x. 43-44), Manu gives a further list of kṣatriya tribes who, through neglect of the priests and their rites, had fallen to the status of Śūdras. These are: Pauṇḍrakas, Coḍas, Draviḍas, Kāmbojas, Yavanas, Śakas, Paradas, Pahlavas, Cīnas, Kirātas and Daradas. This is an extension of the earlier group, probably including all the important peoples known by the author to be dwelling somewhere near the borders of Āryāvarta. They, too, would have been classed as *vrātyas*. It is well known how loosely racial names such as Yavana and Śaka came to be used. Thus, it was possible for almost any non-Aryan who had wealth and

influence to find a brahmin who would supervise the rituals and penances necessary to induct him into the Aryan order. As *patitasāvitrīka* Aryans they would, according to Manu (xi. 192), perform three *kṛcchra* penances in order to obtain the right to initiation. This penance involved nine days of partial fasting, followed by three of complete abstention from food. (For variations see P. V. Kane, *History of Dharmaśāstra* [Poona: B. O. R. I., 1953], vol. 4, pp. 132-33. In vol. 2, part 1 [1941], pp. 376-92, Kane reviews the provisions for the restoration of the *patitasāvitrīka* in other texts.)

12. See note 11, above.

13. H. T. Seth, *Pāia-sadda-mahaṇṇavo*, 2nd ed. (Vārāṇasī: Prākṛta-grantha-pariṣad, 1963), s.v. *ajja*.

THE NATURE OF TAMIL DEVOTION

George L. Hart, III
University of California, Berkeley

Bhakti is inextricably entangled with the notion of sin that the bhakta has, for that is the source of his fear before God, his desire to reach Him, and of his desire to attain a sinless state through devotion. So prominent is this consciousness of sin among the Tamil bhakti poets that one can scarcely read more than one or two of their poems without coming across some reference to the debased state of the poet. As Appar says, "My clan is evil, my qualities are evil, my intentions are evil. I am big only in sin...."[1] On the other hand, the awareness of sin is notable for its almost complete absence in premedieval North India. Wendy O'Flaherty writes, "There are some striking exceptional examples of a true sense of sin and repentence in [classical] Hinduism: some Rig-Vedic hymns to Varuṇa, some poems of Tamil Saivism, and a [Sanskrit] verse still recited by many sophisticated Hindus today: 'Evil am I, evil are my deeds.' But these are outweighed a thousandfold by instances of sin regarded as the fault of God or nature. Evil is not primarily what we do; it is what we do not wish to have done to us. That evil that we do commit is the result of delusion *(moha)* or deception (*māyā*); and it is God who creates these delusions and deceptions."[2] Of course, scholars of Tamil have always been aware of the prominence of guilt and sin in Tamil literature and Tamil culture, but those who have discussed it have been heavily influenced by Judeo-Christian notions. Perhaps for this reason, I have not encountered extensive analysis of the Tamil notion of sin in any of the scholarly literature on Tamil bhakti, either in a Western language or in Tamil. Writers seem to assume that the subject is self-evident and to pass it by for what they deem to be more important subjects. This paper will be concerned with pointing out the mistake of these scholars: it will suggest that the Tamil notion of sin is quite different from the Judeo-Christian notion and that, as a result, Tamil devotion is different in fundamental and important ways from its Western counterparts.

If the Tamil bhakti poets differ from classical North Indian writers in having a conception of sin, they also differ because of the conception of sacred power that they inherited from pre-Aryan Tamilnad. Indeed, their indigenous religion is quite different from that of the Vedas, the *Upaniṣads*, or the *Gītā*. To put the matter simply, the ancient Tamils—and this is still true in much of

South India—believed in the sacramental character of life: anything associated with the production or ending of life was felt to contain a potentially dangerous power. No doubt this conception and the manifestations that it showed were determined largely by the agricultural society in which the ancient Tamils lived: their lives depended upon the rains to produce the fertility of the fields; they could not know from one year to the next whether they would survive. In any event, whatever the reason, the powers that were thought to surround life and death were considered capricious and dangerous; it was thought that they should be controlled and bounded. There were three agents whom this power especially touched and who were thought to be especially dangerous. The first was woman: as the source of human fertility, woman was considered extremely powerful and, under certain conditions, quite dangerous. Thus there was developed an elaborate edifice of conduct, rules, and customs, whose purpose was to confine woman in a structure of order so that the power she possessed would itself be ordered. To this end, a woman was supposed to be chaste, controlled, soft-spoken, to stay outside in a hut when menstruous, and, I have argued, to marry her cross-cousin.[3] The second was the low-caste person whose daily tasks brought him into some form of contact with death. Thus the leather worker, the drummer (who officiated at funeral rites), the barber, the washerman, the fisherman, and others were charged by their contact with death or dead substances and had to be segregated from other people lest they pass their charge on to others who did not possess their special fitness to receive it. At the same time, the low-caste person possessed great power with regard to the sacred: it was he who would become possessed, dance, and foretell the future; he who would drum to the king at special occasions and who would drum during battle; he who would sing songs to the king to endow him with fitness and enable him to keep away dangerous forces.[4] The final agent of the sacred, and the most important for this paper, was the king. His was the task of conducting battle; indeed, he was not simply to sit behind his troops and conduct them but, rather, was supposed to be in the forefront of killing, becoming covered with wounds and personally killing enemy kings. The king was no ordinary person, for had he been he could not have borne the charge that so much killing entailed. Rather, he was set apart, charged with a power that, kept under control, was able to insure the fertility and prosperity of his kingdom, but that, out of control, led to catastrophe.[5] So important is the person and position of the king in the indigenous religion of South India that Peter Claus, who has studied the Tulu people of South Kanara, has used the phrase "the cult of the king" to describe their religion.[6] The development of bhakti is the history of the North Indian gods and the Brahmins finding a place in this indigenous religion. Of the elements that characterize this religion, the role of the king and the indigenous notion of sacred power are of pre-eminent importance in the development of bhakti.

One important characteristic of the indigenous South Indian religion is that it was not concerned with other-worldly places or figures. Indeed, it appears to have had virtually no mythology and no coherent notion of another world. Rather, everything was oriented around human beings: the sacred was something experienced by human beings in the course of their daily life that became present in people or in everyday things (the king, a menstruous woman, a drum, a pariah). Power was not something summoned from another world, such as the gods in the *Ṛgveda*; it was immanent in the things one comes into contact with every day.

This aspect of the indigenous religion was of enormous importance when the North Indian gods were imported and had to find a place in South India, for in order to be accessible to South Indians, the new gods had to fit into the indigenous human perspective. This entailed many changes and developments, but we can discern two that are of especial importance. First, the new god was modeled on and assimilated to the king. The temple was called *kōyil*, the house of the king (and earlier the name of the king's palace); many Tamil terms for the North Indian god first meant king or still can mean either king or god; the temple is constructed like a palace; and the deity is treated like a king, being awakened in the morning by auspicious music, getting married, and receiving many of the same ceremonies as the human king. Indeed, Claus suggests that in Tulunad North Indian deities were identified with the king's ancestors.[7] In ancient South India when a king died, a stone was erected to him that was supposed to house his spirit, which could then be easily propitiated and even consulted. There is some evidence that in later times these stones became identified with North Indian gods.

An important consequence of the human character of the indigenous religion was the belief that the god somehow inheres in the idols that are worshipped and the transfer of the places of residence and influence of the Northern gods from the other world (Kailāsa, Vaikuṇṭha) to their temples. One of the great paradoxes of Tamil religion is that the bhakta worships, at the same time, Śiva or Viṣṇu plus a particular manifestation of the god–Naṭarāja at Cidambaram, for example. Clearly, even though one worships the same Viṣṇu at a small temple and at Tirupati, the gods at the two places are not thought to be identical, for pilgrims travel thousands of miles and undergo great hardship to worship Vēṅkaṭēśvara, rather than simply remaining content to worship at a smaller, more accessible shrine. Moreover, in each temple, the god has a special history: he is a different *person* in a very real sense at Tirupati than he is at Ramesvaram. In other words, while the theory of Tamil religion has kept the northern ideal, the practice has adhered to the indigenous model, which demands that gods be modeled after human kings.

At this point, an interesting and, I believe, hitherto unnoticed fact regarding the identification of the northern god and the king may be brought out. One of the first manifestations of Tamil bhakti—and indeed of bhakti in all of India—is the songs of the Nāyaṉmārs and the Āḻvārs. The four most important Śaiva poets (Ñāṉacampantar, Cuntarar, Appar, and Māṇikkavācakar) and many of the Vaiṣṇava poets would go from temple to temple singing to the god in residence and worshipping him. Many of their hymns are the actual verses they sang to a god in a particular place. The *Tēvāram* is, in fact, usually arranged according to the particular temple whose god is being addressed. This procedure of the bhakti poets is, I believe, modeled on the practice of bards and poets in earlier times, who would go from the court of one king to another, sing to the king, and receive some sort of recompense. The life of such poets is described in *Puṟanāṉūṟu* 47:

> The life of suppliants like us
> is discovering benefactors,
> going like birds across many wastelands
> thinking nothing of the long distances,
> singing as well as we can
> with tongues that form words imperfectly,
> rejoicing at what we receive,
> feeding our families,
> eating without saving anything,
> giving without holding back,
> and suffering for the king's good favor....

There are many poems put into the mouths of low-caste bards and drummers in which they are journeying from the court of one king to another. One of the most common of such conventions in ancient Tamil is the *āṟṟuppaṭai*, in which one bard tells another he meets on the road that he should visit a certain king to become rich. Perhaps a century after the bulk of the *Puṟanāṉūṟu* was composed, that is to say, about the third century A.D., the *Tirumurukāṟṟuppaṭai*, one of the *Pattuppāṭṭu*, was written. In that work, those in spiritual need are counseled to go to the god Murukaṉ, just as in the earlier examples of this genre, bards suffering from physical want were advised to go to a certain king: the god had already begun to assume the characteristics of the king. In about the sixth century, Śaiva and Vaiṣṇava poets began to go from one temple to another singing the praises of the god at each temple in imitation of the example of the earlier bards and poets. In their poems, the god at each shrine is often conceived to be a king—for example, Māṇikkavācakar describes the lord at Kōkaḻi as *"Kōkaḻi eṅ kōmāṟku,"* that is, "our king of Kōkaḻi."[8] Like the earlier Sangam poems, the songs of the Nāyaṉmārs and Āḻvārs are each in a particular *paṇ* (an ancient Tamil *rāga*). In both literatures, there are *akam* poems that describe love between man and woman, the chief difference being that in the hymns, the male lover is meant to be identified with God. In later Tamil, such genres as the *piḷḷait tamiḻ*, which describes the childhood of the hero, can be written both to a king and a god.

As has been suggested above, the indigenous Tamils believed that power comes from the taking of life. It is for this reason that the indigenous gods—who were for the most part the spirits of dead heroes and *satīs*—were worshipped with blood and sacrifices. Indeed, even today the indigenous gods are worshipped by killing cocks, buffaloes, and other animals. Human sacrifice existed in ancient times among the Tamils and until the nineteenth century among some Dravidian tribes.[9] It needs to be stressed that the taking of life was thought to be extremely dangerous, as the spirit of the dead somehow remained behind as a force that could produce chaos and misfortune. Thus, blood sacrifice was undertaken only under the most ordered circumstances, where the forces unleashed could be contained, and only when it was deemed necessary to satisfy some especially powerful god who would not be content without it. When the new gods came, their position was ambivalent. On the one hand, they were concentrations of power and had to be treated in the same way as the indigenous sacred powers; on the other hand, they shared the Brahminical conception that power comes from purity and hence, as the Brahmins interpreted indigenous power as impurity, they had to be kept carefully isolated from such powers. The reason for this is twofold: first, the indigenous priests were of the lowest class, and the Brahmins could not model their role after them (though even today there is considerable confusion between the roles of the untouchables and the Brahmins in some areas of South India);[10] second, and more important, indigenous sacred power was closely associated with death, since many of the gods worshipped were simply spirits of dead heroes or *satīs*. Thus, the new gods had a difficult order to fill. They had to retain their "purity"—that is, they had to remain entirely separate from the dangerous forces that pervade the South Indian countryside—but, at the same time, they had to be accepted as sacred and efficacious.

The result was a paradox that has not been fully studied or worked out. Indeed, Pfaffenberger has shown that in northern Ceylon, different gods play very different roles in the system and that a pilgrimage deity like Murugan at Kataragama has a nature quite different from that of the orthodox Brahminical deity in a village. Most of what is known about sacred power concerns those gods in South India who were the objects of pilgrimage. Such gods invariably have detailed mythological histories narrated in *sthalapurāṇas*, many Tamil examples of which have been studied in detail by David Shulman. What he finds is that in many temples the shedding of blood plays an important role with regard to mythological origins. "The modes of revelation," he writes, "are described in a large corpus of myths, in which the sanctity of the site is demonstrated by its association with a series of sacred substances: water, milk, *amṛta*, seed, blood. The final element, the blood of the divinity, is attached to the series despite the impure associations of blood in classical [Sanskrit] sources; its necessary appearance in the myths of origin of the shrines appears linked to an underlying concept of sacrifice."[11] This must be so, I believe, because for the ancient Tamils all sacred places were made so by sacrifice. The taking of any sort of life entails a release of power. Should the life that is taken be especially potent—that of a king, warrior, or *satī*—then the power released is so strong that the place of the release becomes "sacred" for all time, and rites must be undertaken to keep the power under control.[12] It is not surprising that the northern god must follow this southern model, and that in the *sthalapurāṇas* describing the establishing of their temples sacrifice is a necessary element. Nor is sacrifice limited to the beginning of a temple. The northern gods, like their indigenous counterparts, can be motivated through a sacrifice of life or life force. Thus Shulman writes, "....when the chariot of the Paḷḷis was arrested at Kāñcī, the sacrifice of a woman pregnant with her first child induced Kāmākṣi to make the chariot move again."[13] Another revealing story is that of Kaṇṇappar, who tears out his eyes to gratify Śiva.[14] Similarly, Ciṟuttoṇṭar sacrificed his only son to Śiva and actually cooked the child and served his flesh to the god.[15] Even today, it is customary to influence a god by the sacrifice of some substance closely connected with life. Devotees may shave off their hair, a substance thought to be impregnated with the power of the life force. They may fast for a day each week, thus giving up the substance that makes life possible; or they may shed their blood by walking on nail-studded sandals or performing the Kāvaṭi ceremony.

On the other hand, the new gods had to be kept inviolate from actually being touched by powerful, danger-impregnated objects or people. Indeed, one of the most important attributes of the deity both in Śaiva and Vaiṣṇava dogma is *nirmalatvam,* freedom from taint—the strict purity of all that comes into contact with the god. Low-caste people must not be allowed into the temple; the garlands must be kept pure and clean; only the Brahmins who have scrupulously observed all rules of purity (i.e., of not allowing themselves to be in contact with dangerous substances or people) may come near the god. In other words, it may be admissible to sacrifice some life-impregnated substance to the deity, but the hair that is sacrificed would, should it actually touch the deity, result in great danger for all concerned. Untouchables may have roles to play in certain ceremonies to the northern gods, but they may not come into the temple and approach the deity.[16] Clearly, a new principle is at work here. Indigenous deities were and are propitiated by the lowest castes, who often serve as priests. In ancient times, liquor and blood were offered to the *naṭukal*, or hero stone, and to the king's drum, which was deemed to contain a god. And even today, the indigenous deities are propitiated with blood.

Pfaffenberger has discerned three kinds of temples in northern Ceylon: the indigenous, the Āgamic, and the pilgrimage. The indigenous temple is characterized by blood sacrifice and the cult of possession. It is similar to the temples to Murugan described in Sangam literature. The Āgamic temple occupies the other extreme. The Āgamic god is, for want of a better word, pusilanimous: the least infraction of order will send him fleeing away, leaving the temple an empty shell. The purpose of the Āgamic temple is to symbolize and stand for social order in a way that leaves little room for argument—for elaborate ritual has great persuasive power. The patrons of the temple receive two benefits: first, their social standing is enhanced, for only a very "pure" person can successfully build and operate an Āgamic temple; second, they receive a "salubrious field" of *aruḷ*, or grace, which is passed on in attenuated form to all (pure) people who worship in the temple. Pfaffenberger found that virtually no one went to Āgamic temples with any important devotional purpose or concrete boon that he wished to receive from the god. Indeed, the Āgamic temples are in no way bhakti temples: any display of devotion in them is condemned as untoward and uncouth.

The gods who are the objects of bhakti are hybrid deities: like Murugan at Kataragama, they combine both indigenous characteristics of power and untaintedness. They often possess (Vēṅkaṭēśvara); they are propitiated by sacrifice of substance in some form, unlike the Āgamic deities; they can be approached by the impure and sinful; but their priests are Brahmins and they must be kept pure. It is interesting that even though some Āgamic forms are followed by the bhakti temples, Pfaffenberger's informants were adamant that such temples were not Āgamic. Curiously, pilgrimage temples like Kataragama are thought to be even more dangerous than indigenous shrines. Kataragama is in an inaccessible place far removed from Jaffna or other civilization. The only temple in Jaffna that has similar power to remove sin is on a long spit of land surrounded on three sides by water. Similarly, Srirangam is on a river islet–a place thought to be fitted for the release of dangerous power even in Sangam times[17] –while Tirupati is on a moutain. It is interesting that one devotee who visited Kataragama, inspired by the ideal of brotherhood that he observed at that temple, wished to build a similar temple in Jaffna. The reaction of the general public was one of horror and outrage: a temple like Kataragama would not only be unsuitable in a city such as Jaffna; it would be dangerous. At a *bhajana* in Madras city, Singer was told that the power of bhakti worship to make caste distinctions disappear during the worship was dangerous, like fire.[18]

There is only one kind of bhakti god whose temple is found in the city in northern Ceylon, and this may constitute a fourth type of temple: the king's patron deity. Thus, when, in the nineteenth century, Nāvalar proposed that as part of his reform of Hindu temples the Nallūr Kantacāmi Kōyil be made Āgamic, people vehemently opposed his request. The reason is that an Āgamic deity has no real power, either to forgive sins or bring fertility. A hybrid deity such as Murugan at Kataragama or Skanda at Nallūr does.

In order to make sense of this proliferation of different types of temples, it is best to begin by considering the most different: the indigenous and the Āgamic. The difference between these two temples is shown clearly by the conduct of the god when confronted with dangerous power. The indigenous god is not himself threatened by such power, but threatens its bearer. Thus, a Sangam poem mentions that menstruous women tremble in the temple of Murugan.[19] On the other hand, the Āgamic gods are themselves threatened by dangerous power. Pfaffenberger asked an informant what would happen if an orthodox temple were polluted. He was told that the god would leave and the temple would become an empty shell. Whenever a woman in the neighborhood had given birth (thus unleashing dangerous forces) and whenever certain festivals were celebrated, Paṟaiyaṉ drummers would surround the Āgamic temple and drum. This was, Pfaffenberger was told, a way of soaking up the faults or sins (*kuṟṟams*) that were flying around so that they would not enter the temple and cause the god to leave.[20]

It follows that there is something about the space surrounding an Āgamic deity that will not tolerate the presence of the indigenous sacred. There is a boundary around the god into which the taint of death must not be allowed to enter. This is done by carefully restricting entry to those who are undeniably "pure." By a curious circular logic, the Āgamic temple has the ability to confer prestige by showing the "purity" of its builders and trustees for everyone to see; but it can have no real sacred power, for nothing wrong or disordered can be allowed to enter its premises. It cannot put right anything that is wrong, dispel any sins, grant any wishes. It exists as a viable sign and symbol of social order and prestige. This type of temple may be quite ancient, for in *Akanāṉūṟu* 220 the breasts of the heroine are said to be as hard to get to see "as the well-guarded tall post, its middle tied with a rope, of the sacrifice completed in Cellūr, a place of undying [sacrificial] fires, by the one with an axe who, striving, cut down the race of warriors [i.e., Paraśurāma]."

Thus, there is an extreme contrast between the indigenous temple and the Āgamic temple. In the indigenous shrine, dangerous gods and spirits are propitiated with blood and life sacrifice by men who themselves are touched by dangerous sacred power and are of the lowest castes. Their aim is mostly negative–to cajole the god into remaining inactive or to get him to go somewhere else. Sometimes their ceremonies include prophesying, but this appears to be secondary to the propitiation of the god. In the Āgamic temple, the god is totally divorced from sacred power: even the slightest taint of such power will force him to go elsewhere. His chief function is to grant prestige to those associated with the temple by affirming their purity, that is, their untaintedness by sacred forces. Those connected with the temple must, in turn, refrain from contact with indigenous temples and from other manifestations of sacred power (such as menstruous women and widows). Should such men become tainted–and, living in the world, they inevitably do–then they must purify themselves before entering the Āgamic temple again.

Clearly, these two temples leave unsatisfied a primary need: neither is able to function in a positive way to grant the wishes of worshippers, and neither is able to change the state of its worshippers in a positive way. True, each of these functions is accomplished to a small degree by the indigenous temple, but the notions surrounding such temples are so overwhelmingly negative–that is, concerned with getting rid of dangerous powers rather than with summoning benevolent ones–that the indigenous temple can hardly be said to satisfy the more profound religious needs of its devotees. Nor does either of these temples give much scope for a personal, one-to-one relationship of the devotee with the god. Rather, both treat the worshipper as part of a group–his caste, his village, his family.

It is the bhakti temple, I would suggest, that treats the worshipper as an individual, grants his wishes, and changes his state. The bhakti temple is analogous to the Āgamic temple in one important way: the deity must be kept pure (though, unlike the Āgamic temple, it is the worshippers who suffer if purity is not maintained, not the deity). Like the Āgamic god, there is something about the space around the bhakti deity that will not allow the presence of the indigenous sacred: there is a boundary beyond which the taint of death cannot enter. But while the Āgamic deity is unable to tolerate this taint, the bhakti god is able, under certain conditions, actually to dispel it. This, I submit, is the great function of the bhakti god for the devotee: to create a way out of the indigenous system. If the devotee merely enters into the sacred boundary, he is able to leave behind the dangerous and impure charge that he inevitably has acquired, though only if he is utterly sincere and possesses profound devotion. Indeed, he need merely think with devotion of the god, recite a sacred song to him, or put on some sacred ash to achieve this effect. This is put quite eloquently in a Tamil version of the *Śrīraṅgamāhātmyam*:

> When you sneeze, when you cough, when you yawn, when you spit, when a disease happens to your body, when you associate with sinners, when you say a false word, when you speak in accord with sinners, then if with cleanliness of the three organs–the body, [the mind, and speech]–you say with concentration, "Ranga!" then no danger will happen to you....And what is more, even if someone is a thousand yojanas away, if he thinks of that holy place, that great man and the ancestors in his line going back to the 21st generation will become persons of merit [*puṇṇiyavāṉkaḷ*], all the sins they did in former births having departed.[21]

To the Tamil, sin is not merely the failure to follow the golden rule or the failure to live up to the code of ethics promulgated by the *Tirukkuṟaḷ*. Sin is, at least in its most rudimentary form, something far more tangible: it is the state of being charged through contact with death. It should be stressed that this can take many forms; but sin is a state of infection, which itself leads to death. Nor is this state of infection something that applies only to one individual. Pfaffenberger found in northern Ceylon that the possession of a person by the spirit of someone who had died tainted all who were closely related to that living person. Similarly, the bhakti poets sometimes say that not only are they evil, but their clan also is evil.[22] Of course, sin is not this simple, for it depends not only upon the taint of death, but also upon the entire net of disorder that is thought to be connected with death. The world exists in a balance between disorder and order, that is, between irruptions of death and places in which power is contained and under control. So fragile is this balance that any breaking of order inevitably invokes the forces of disorder and causes a failure of fertility. Sin is not merely the simple state of being tainted by death (though this is an important element in it); it is any transgression against the order that holds off the forces of infertility and death. This order was manifold, as shall be seen. The one generalization that can be made about it throughout South India is that it was extremely rigorous, involving virtually everything a person does. In Kerala, the notion of caste order became so extreme that an elaborate system was developed regulating just how close one caste could come to another. Clearly, such order cannot be kept in any human situation, no matter how hard one tries. Thus, there is need for an agency that can do what human beings cannot: the bhakti god keeps perfect order within his temple and his temple is a place where death cannot come. Indeed, the temple, and by extension even the city in which the temple is found (and which the god as king rules), is free of sin. Māṇikkavācakar sings, "The city of Uttarakōcamaṅkai is celebrated by men of devotion as the city of Śiva on earth."[23]

The nature of sin in South India is clarified by Shulman's observation that in South India a sin never disappears. A man may be cleansed of sin by worshipping god, but the sin remains in the world as potent as ever, ready to cling on to someone or something else.[24] The plot summary of a modern Kannada novel says, "The sin that someone did goes around someone else. Whom did the fruit of the sin done by Saraḷa kill ...?[25] The sin in this case is like a ghost or spirit that hovers around ready to attach itself to someone who is vulnerable. That is why the *Srīraṅgamāhātmyam* counsels extreme care when one sneezes or otherwise exposes one's saliva, for at that moment a spirit may enter the mouth and take possession of a man. In the story of Makāpātakaṉ in the *Tiruviḷaiyāṭaṟpurāṇam,* the sin is literally the ghost of the father of the great sinner, whom he has killed, and which follows him, attempting to keep him away from Śiva temples (how different the northern story of Paraśurāma, who suffers no ill consequences at all from killing his mother).[26] The sin need not be a ghost. In his novel *Putra*, Ramamirutham puts in literary form the belief that a curse uttered with enough malice actually takes on form and pursues its victim.[27] But whatever the sin may be, it is in some sense a tangible force released by the breaking of the system of order that must exist in order to insure the fertility of the earth and of the family. The temple of a bhakti god has the power to remove the sins that cling to each devotee, provided only that he be totally sincere and devoted. It may be that many of the great pilgrimage temples of South India and Ceylon–Tirupati, Srirangam, Kataragama–are located in uninhabitable places for this very reason: the area around them is full of cast-off sins that would be dangerous if the temples were in a populated area.[28]

One of the most extreme manisfestations of bhakti in South India was the Vīraśaiva sect, whose members espoused the concept of the *jaṅgama*, the body as temple with the linga worn on the devotee's chest as deity, as opposed to the *sthāvara*, the stationary temple in which most bhakti sects worship. Basavaṇṇa writes (in A. K. Ramanujan's translation):

The rich
will make temples for Śiva.
What shall I,
a poor man,
do?

My legs are pillars,
the body the shrine,
the head a cupola
of gold.

Listen, O lord of the meeting rivers,
things standing [*sthāvara*] shall fall,
but the moving [*jaṅgama*] ever shall stay.[29]

It seems to me that this institution of the *jaṅgama* can be understood in terms of the power of the god in the bhakti temple to release sins. What the Vīraśaiva devotee wishes to do is to keep himself within the sacred boundaries of a temple. So long as the devotee wears the linga (i.e., the deity) around his neck and so long as he is sincere and devoted enough to remain a movable temple, he can never go out into the world and has nothing to fear from the sins and offenses against order that others in South India have to contend with. This is, I feel, the explanation of the extreme social behavior of the early Vīraśaivas, who attempted to marry a Brahmin woman and a pariah man (something no other bhakti sect has ever done to my knowledge). Not content with their status of being immune to infractions against order that are inevitable in everyday life in South India (a status that others would have willingly tolerated), they felt obliged to demonstrate the virtue of their new religion in the most extreme and shocking terms they could imagine. Unfortunately for them, their religion was not proof against temporal forces, and they were severely punished by the king for their behavior, which must have appeared as extremely dangerous to all outside their sect.

Bhakti, then, was developed as a logical response to indigenous ideas in South India regarding the ordering of the cosmos. In the precarious balance of forces in which South Indians lived and live, it was natural to believe that the proper balance depended upon maintaining the correct order in society and in individual life. Of course, all societies have believed this to some extent. What distinguishes the culture of South India is the length to which it carried this belief, until virtually every act a man could do was in some way governed by a proper order. Society itself became minutely divided into classes and castes as nowhere else in the world. Even the arts were not immune from the passion and craving for order. The oldest Tamil literature is divided into many categories, each with its proper musical mode, characters, situations, locations, times, and landscapes. In Telugu, it was thought that if the syllable *da* occurred in the fifth syllable of a poem, it would kill someone.[30] What these examples portend (and many more could be adduced) is that the expedient adopted in South India, more than anywhere else, to control the fickle and capricious forces of nature was order and its correlate, fitness.

Not only is it impossible, because of human frailty, to keep perfectly such a complex and rigid system of order, but there are contradictions built into the very system that make it something that cannot be observed. On the one hand, the system of order relies upon the notion of being tainted, or charged: one must be extremely careful to keep intact all of the boundaries around oneself to keep away dangerous forces. For this reason, one must keep his wife chaste, keep untouchables out of his house, be careful not to eat tainted food or with tainted people, and observe a whole host of other restrictions. It does not take much insight to see that these restrictions dictate against many basic concerns of human morality: they are concerned with the selfish task of protection, not with the ethical work of helping others. There is, moreover, an innate contradiction in this plethora of restrictive rules: their avowed purpose is to enable one to live a prosperous life, yet their observance leads to a life of selfishness and worry. Thus, there arose a new dimension to the concept of order: that it depended not only upon restrictive boundaries being observed, but also upon the selfless disregard of boundaries in acts of generosity. The highest moral imperative for the Tamils is generosity; the darkest stigma, that of the miser.

This mentality is well exemplified in *Puṟanāṉūṟu* 50, in which, as the colophon says, "Mōcikīraṉār sings Cēramāṉ Takaṭūreṟinta Peruñcēralirumpoṟai who, when Mōcikīraṉār climbed on the bed of the royal drum [which had been taken out to be given a bath] in ignorance, did not commit the mistake [of executing him], but took up a chowrie and fanned him until he awoke." Here, even though the poet has compromised the sacred power and order of the king by tainting his drum, the proper response of the king to preserve the order around him is not to kill the poet, but to treat him as a guest with respect:

> Before they brought back from its bath
> the fearful drum that thirsts for blood,
> its black sides lined by leather straps
> and adorned with a sapphire-like garland
> of the bright eyes of long peacock feathers
> and with golden-shooted *uḻiñai*,
> unknowing I climbed upon its bed
> which was covered with soft flowers
> as if the froth of oil had been poured upon it.
> Yet you stayed the edge of your sword that cuts in half.
> Just that was sufficient for all of Tamil land to know of it.
> But you were not satisfied with only that.
> You approached me,
> and raising your mighty arm that resembles a concert drum,
> you fanned me and made me cool.
> Did you do that act, mighty lord,
> because you have heard and understood
> that except for those whose fame here spreads over the broad earth,
> no one can stay there in the world of high estate?

Similarly, in *Kuṟuntokai* 292, King Naṉṉaṉ is censured for killing a girl who unwittingly ate a mango fruit from his tutelary tree and thus compromised his kingly fitness. Here, the mother of the heroine, who refuses to sleep lest her daughter go out to meet her lover, is compared to the wicked king:

> A bright-faced girl went to bathe
> and ate a green fruit
> brought by the water.

For that crime
Naṉṉaṉ refused nine times nine elephants
and a doll her weight in gold,
but had her killed.
May mother go to unending hell
like him
who killed a woman,
for remembering how a guest came one day
with a smiling face,
she does not sleep
like a city under attack
by its enemies.

This dilemma between generosity and taintedness permeates all of Tamil culture. Ramanuja is supposed to have sent his wife away after she foiled his attempt to eat from the used leaf of a man whom he regarded as his teacher, but who was a non-Brahmin. Ciṟuttoṇṭar, a Śaiva saint who vowed to feed every Śaiva devotee who came his way and never to eat unless in the company of another devotee, is supposed to have cooked his own son and served him to a devotee to satisfy his vow. Yet even though Ciṟuttoṇṭar is irremediably tainting himself and his guest by killing and serving a human being, he is careful to keep from polluting the food he serves. The solution to the dilemma between generosity and taintedness does not lie in choosing one over the other, but in reconciling the two in a way that is emotionally and psychologically satisfactory. As with Ciṟuttoṇṭar, the solution need not be a rational one.

At the center of the Tamil social order was the king. It was he upon whom all social order ultimately depended, he who embodied in their most extreme forms the paradoxes and dilemmas of Tamil society. As the poems cited immediately above indicate, the king and his paraphernalia had to be protected from taint very carefully. A verse from Kampaṉ indicates that men were supposed to address the king with their hands before their mouths, lest some of their saliva fall upon his person.[31] At the same time, the king should manifest generosity of spirit, so that in *Puṟanāṉūṟu* 235, Auvaiyār has a low-caste bard describe the king with the words, "With his hand fragrant with orange blossoms, he would stroke my head which stank of flesh." Indeed, more than anyone else in the society, the king had to observe the injunctions of untaintedness and of generosity; even today, the higher one's status in Tamil society, the more restricted his life must be and the more he must avoid becoming tainted. It is also true that the higher one's status, the more he is expected to be kind and generous.

Thus, in a society for which there exists a dilemma between generosity and taintedness, it is the king who experiences this dilemma in its most extreme manifestation. Indeed, it is not merely generosity that the king must show forth; he must be just. In the *Cilappatikāram* when the Pandyan king learns that he has executed Kōvalaṉ unjustly, he falls down dead. This points up the extreme vulnerability of the king to the need for order, and it stands in stark contrast to the king's ability to remain untainted by killing on the battlefield and to protect others from becoming tainted by such killing. Nor is this the extent of the king's ability to resist the forces of disorder. Again and again, the ancient poems describe the king's realm as a place where omens of disaster do not mean anything because of the power of the king, and they describe how the king is able to ignore personal omens because of his power.[32] Of course, these poems are meant to show the exceptionality of the kings they address, but it is still true that a strong enough king can resist the forces of disorder and of taint by virtue of his position and power. Once more we have a paradox: the figure who is most vulnerable to disorder is also the one who is proof against disorder that others could not prevail against. Indeed, the king possesses an aura that is thought to illumine his entire kingdom and to keep disorder from it. This is described in several poems; I will quote *Puṟanāṉūṟu* 22 here.

Young, strong elephants
sway, standing at their posts....
Nearby, pouring out rays
like the moon in the sky
is a white garlanded umbrella. In its shadow
men with no swords at their sides sleep peacefully.
Huts in rows, built of soft sugarcane
and roofed with fine paddy plants,
give an air of ever-new brilliance
like a festival ground.
The broad field resounds with noise
and the incessant thumping of pestles pounding mortars.
Wearing green *tumpai* leaves whose tips sway,
men, carried away, seethe in the wild *kuravai* dance
like waters moving in flood.
Such is the wide camp you rule,

a place that needs no guarding,
O killing lord of those on lofty Kolli mountain,
who make full the families of those who join you
with tribute given abjectly by enemy kings....
We heard the land ruled by Māntarañcēralirumpoṟai
is like the world of paradise.
We came, and saw to our delight, great one.
You are never indolent.
With your army that assaults enemy lands,
you act so that rice is in abundance,
and you never relent in your efforts.

For the king, keeping order does not in any sense involve an escape from the dilemma of Tamil society, even though the king is able in some sense to protect others from some of the consequences of that dilemma. Rather, the king, even more than others, must balance concern with taint with morality; he must sit astride the horns of the dilemma never inclining to one side. That is the real lesson of the above poems about the royal drum and about the tutelary tree. The poets are not suggesting that the king become oblivious to his own need to be insulated from tainted forces, but rather that the king must not become so obsessed with his need for insulation that he allows the need for generosity to be forgotten or eclipsed.

It is a curious but extremely important fact that the higher a man's position in the society, the more restrictions he must observe, and the more closely he must imitate the king in keeping a precarious balance between fundamentally opposed forces. Indeed, this is the ultimate meaning of the process that Srinivas has mistakenly called Sanskritization in the belief that all classes were merely imitating the Brahmins.[33] The fact is that a man's position in the society is determined to a major extent by the degree to which he is able to insulate himself from tainting forces and, at the same time, observe the dictates of generosity. One cannot attain high status and respect without achieving both of these contradictory goals, and this is the reason why the lives of those who have status and prestige in the society appear so much more restricted than the lives of the lower classes.[34] It so happens that the Brahmins are particularly notable in their zeal to insulate themselves from taint. Yet, because their position has demanded that they observe the exigencies of being untainted over the social requirements of generosity, their respectability is not fully acknowledged by all in the society. On the other hand, the higher-caste non-Brahmins may have found it easier to be generous than the Brahmins, but they could not keep themselves as untainted as the Brahmins, and so their status could never clearly surpass that of the Brahmins.[35] In all periods of Tamil history, the king was acknowledged as the paragon, superior to Brahmins, non-Brahmins, and everyone else in the society in both sacred and secular terms by virtue of the fact that he was the ultimate model of order and the most important source of order for the entire kingdom. If a Brahmin or high-caste non-Brahmin strayed from the dictates of order, that fact concerned only him and those close to him. If the king did so, his entire kingdom would suffer the consequences.

It is important that the king was in a real sense a solution to the dilemma for many in his kingdom. As long as the king was able to balance the needs of untaintedness and generosity in his own person, those living in the shadow of his parasol were absolved to some extent from having to do likewise. Of course, the solution was only a partial one, but there is no question that the king did have such a function. Yet, if he was the chief agent of order and harmony, there were others. Early Tamil speaks again and again of the *cāṉṟōṉ*, the great and noble man. The word itself is from the root *cāl*, to be suitable, to be full. It would seem to denote a person who is harmonized, someone who has successfully balanced the various contradictory demands of order. This ideal is eloquently expressed in *Puṟanāṉūṟu* 182:

> This world is
> because even though they receive the gods' ambrosia,
> some will not drink it savoring its sweetness alone;
> they do not bear rancor;
> they are not indolent even though they fear what others fear;
> for fame they will give even their lives,
> but if it brings blame, they will not take it,
> even though they might have the world;
> they are not indifferent;
> and, even though they are so great,
> they do not spend their exertions for themselves
> but strive for others.
> This world is because these men are.

When the northern gods came to Tamilnad and modeled their role after that of the king, they assumed the dilemmas of the king as well. First of all, they had to remain untainted while possessing power to shield others from taint and danger, and second, they had to reconcile the demands of remaining untainted with the requirement that they be models of generosity and morality.

The first of these dilemmas has resulted in deities of different sorts in northern Ceylon: on the one hand, there is the Āgamic deity, who remains perfectly untainted but is almost powerless to influence the world and can, indeed, be forced to flee by the presence of dangerous powers. This sort of deity was not a successful hybrid, and virtually no one approaches him for vows or for the getting rid of sin. More successful was the bhakti god, such as Murugan at Kataragama (or Vēṅkaṭēśvara at Tirupati), who has to be kept isolated from taint, but who nevertheless deals in dangerous substances such as blood, hair, and various kinds of vows. The parallel of this god with the king is striking: just as the king is surrounded by an aura of ordered power that protects his kingdom, the god in his temple is surrounded with an aura that can cause the sins of sincere devotees to depart.

The second dilemma assumed by the bhakti gods is the need to be at once untainted and an upholder of ordered boundaries and at the same time generous and a crosser of boundaries. Thus, we find the story, almost bizarre to an outsider, of Tiruppāṇāḻvār, who, born in one of the lowest castes, was not allowed inside the temple but who nevertheless worshipped the god from outside. The god finally came to the saint, who never actually entered the temple, and allowed him to merge with him. Or, even stranger, the story of Ciṟuttoṇṭar, the Little Devotee, who committed what would appear to be the most impure act imaginable by serving his own son to Śiva masquerading as an ascetic, all the while taking care that the meat not be polluted by such things as hair.[36] Indeed, throughout the bhakti literature of Tamil, we find this contradiction: the god who must be guarded from taint lest his worshippers be destroyed by the power unleashed, and the god who disregards taint only if his worshipper shows extreme devotion. Ultimately, this dilemma reflects an almost universal experience of God: that he is both fearful and loving.[37] But this formulation of the nearly universal paradox is characteristically South Indian.

It is striking how fully the nature of the bhakti god in Tamilnad mirrors the nature of the king. As I have shown above, this is no coincidence or quirk of fate: the bhakti god was modeled upon the king in both his large and small details. Chief among these is the god's power, which is able to dispel taint and sin, yet which depends upon the god's being isolated from taint. As with the king, it is only the wholly devoted servant of the god who has access to his powers of protection and banishing sin. This complex of elements produced a religion characterized by extreme devotion, consciousness of sin and guilt, and an acute awareness of the holy as a source of both fear and love.

NOTES

1. Tirunāvukkaracu Cuvāmikal, *Tēvāram* (Śrīvaikuṇṭam: Śrī Kumarakuruparaṉ Caṅkam, 1961), p. 621.
2. Wendy O'Flaherty, *The Origins of Evil in Hindu Mythology* (Berkeley and Los Angeles: University of California Press, 1976), chap. 1, sec. 3.
3. George L. Hart, III, "Some Aspects of Kinship in Ancient Tamil Literature," in *Kinship and History in South Asia*, ed. Thomas R. Trautmann, Michigan Papers on South and Southeast Asia, no. 7 (Ann Arbor: Center for South and Southeast Asian Studies, 1974), pp. 29-60.
4. George L. Hart, III, *The Poems of Ancient Tamil: Their Milieu and Their Sanskrit Counterparts* (Berkeley and Los Angeles: University of California Press, 1975), pp. 13-18, 31-36, 86-93.
5. Ibid., pp. 81-137.
6. Peter Claus, "The Cult of the King in Ancient Tulunadu," an unpublished paper.
7. Ibid.
8. *Tiruvācakam*, 48.1.
9. Henry Whitehead, *The Village Gods of South India* (Calcutta: Oxford University Press, 1921), pp. 82-87.
10. In "Pilgrimage and Traditional Authority in Tamil Sri Lanka"(Ph.D. dissertation, University of California, Berkeley, 1977), Bryan L. Pfaffenberger reports that several high-caste non-Brahmin informants suggested that Brahmins are like pariahs. One said, "They are our servants....Why should they not be included with our Barbers and Washermen? " (p. 97). Several other informants told Pfaffenberger, "Brahmins and Paṟaiyars are like two sides of the same slipper." (p. 99).
11. David Dean Shulman, "Tamil Mythology: An Interpretation of a Regional Hindu Tradition" (Ph.D. dissertation, School of Oriental and African Studies, University of London, 1976), p. 482.
12 George L. Hart, III, *The Poems of Ancient Tamil*, pp. 25-26, 42-43, 82, 90-93, 121.
13. David Dean Shulman, "Tamil Mythology," p. 62.
14. G. U. Pope, *The Tiruvācagam* (Oxford, 1900), pp. 141-145 n.
15. George L. Hart, III, "The Little Devotee: Cēkkiḻār's Story of Ciṟuttoṇṭar," to appear in a Festschrift for Daniel Ingalls.
16. Tiruppāṇāḻvār, a man of the low Pāṇaṉ caste, never entered the temple to Vishnu. He became a Vaiṣṇava saint by worshipping the god from outside the temple.
17. George L. Hart, III *The Poems of Ancient Tamil*, pp. 24-25, 89.
18. Milton Singer, "The Rādhā-Krishna *Bhajanas* of Madras City," in *Krishna: Myths, Rites, and Attitudes*, edited by Milton Singer (Chicago, 1968), p. 127.
19. *Puṟanāṉūṟu* 299.
20. Pfaffenberger, "Pilgrimage and Traditional Authority," p. 174.
21. *Śrīraṅka Mahātmiyam* (Madras: R. G. Pati Company, n.d.), pp. 11-12.
22. Tirunāvukkaracu Cuvāmikaḷ, *Tēvāram*, v. 9, p. 621.
23. *Tiruvācakam*, 19.3.
24. David Dean Shulman ("Tamil Mythology," pp. 382-85) writes, "For the shrine comes to represent an escape from the closed universe, with its ever-recurring cycles of time, creation and destruction, life and death, evil and its exigencies; the shrine stands as a

kind of absolute outside temporality, not subject to its laws–hence the shrine's survival of the flood of destruction. Worship at the shrine frees one entirely from evil." He cites the *Tiruvāṉaikkāppurāṇam*, in which a Pandyan king inadvertantly kills a Brahmin: "The king's *brahmahatyā* still stands waiting for him, at the eastern gate, where it receives offerings of salt and spices. Complete safety exists only inside the shrine." It would appear that the sin has been identified with the spirit of the Brahmin, which, because he was killed unjustly and was a man of power, is especially dangerous.

25. S. Rājaratnam, *Ondē Dāri athavā Sādhujī* (Bangalore: Rēkhā Prakāsana, 1970), p. iii.

26. George L. Hart, III, trans., "The Dispelling of the Great Sin," to appear in an anthology on the Oedipal myth edited by Lowell Edwards; taken from Parañcōtimuṉivar, *Tiruviḷaiyāṭaṟpurāṇam, Kūṭaṟkāṇṭam* (Madras: Tirunelvēlit Teṉṉintiya Caivacittānta Nūṟpatippuk Kaḻakam, 1965), pp. 123-41.

27. Lā. Ca. Rāmāmirutam, *Putra* (Madras: Vācakar Vaṭṭam, 1965).

28. It is conceivable that royal temples (such as the temple at Nallūr and the Mīṉākṣi temple in Madurai), which also have the power to remove sin, are not dangerous because of the close association of the god and the king, who has the power to render sin safe because of his power of ordering. It is true that all bhakti gods were modeled upon the king. The realm of the god in the pilgrimage temple, however, is restricted to the boundary of the temple, while the realm of the god in the royal temple extends to the entire kingdom.

29. A. K. Ramanujan, *Speaking of Śiva* (Baltimore: Penguin Books, 1973), p. 88.

30. For this information, I am indebted to Velcheru Narayanarao.

31. *Kampar Iyaṟṟiya Irāmāyaṇam, Āraṇiya Kāṇṭam* (Annamalainagar: Annamalai University Press, 1964), vol. 2, v. 3180, pp. 20-21. The commentator remarks, "It is the custom of those who do tribute to great kings to stand without weapons, wearing their upper garments [around] their waists, covering their mouths [with their hands], and, shrinking, to say what they need to say." The dilemma between duty and morality is a universal one, and is especially acute in India. The *Bhagavadgītā* gives an ancient North Indian solution to the dilemma: in all situations, one must choose duty and transfer the fruit of one's actions to God. If duty conflicts with what appears to be moral, then duty should be chosen. In South India, the solution was not so simplistic: one had to satisfy both requirements of the dilemma.

32. *Puṟanāṉūṟu* 20, 68, 105, 117, 124, 204, 384, 386, 388, 389, 395, 397.

33. M. N. Srinivas, *Religion and Society among the Coorgs of South India* (London, 1952).

34. Joan P. Mencher once told me that during her research in Kerala, people of the lowest castes considered that they had a much better time than their high-caste counterparts, whose lives were much more restricted.

35. This is, of course, not to suggest that Brahmins are ungenerous, but rather that their strict adherence to the rules of orthopraxis makes it more difficult for them to be generous and outgoing than it is for others. The novel *Tiyāka Pūmi* by Kalki, himself a Brahmin, opens with a scene in which some pariahs who have been flooded out of their homes wish to take refuge in the Brahmin part of the village, there being no other place for them to go. In spite of the urging of one or two of the more enlightened Brahmins, the strictures of orthopraxis carry the day and the harijans are refused admittance.

36. George L. Hart, III, "The Little Devotee."
37. See Rudolf Otto, *The Idea of the Holy* (Oxford, 1923).

THE MARRIAGE OF HEROINES AND THE DEFINITION OF A LITERARY AREA IN SOUTH AND CENTRAL ASIA

Peter Edwin Hook
The University of Michigan

The diffusion of literary features from one culture to another is far from being a novel concern of those who study the origin and development of literary traditions. Examples abound: from the direct and deliberate importation of Western literary genres into the traditional literatures of the post-Colonial world to the poorly understood but striking resemblances in literary practices that may be observed among the Tuaregs today and the troubadours of medieval Europe.[1] The diffusion of Indian literary motifs and genres into Southeast Asia is too well-known to require comment. More recently George Hart has achieved substantial progress in outlining the progressive Dravidianization of the literatures of Indo-Aryan speaking peoples.[2] But to my knowledge no attempt has been made to conceive of such examples as instances of literary diffusion comparable with and perhaps even correlatable with the diffusion of linguistic traits across "genetic" lines. That is, to my knowledge, no one has considered whether it may be possible to define a *Literaturbund* whose extent and the process of whose formation may be compared to the extent and formational history of some one or other of the various *Sprachbunde* isolated by linguistic geographers. The present paper is such an attempt.[3]

The objective and procedure of this attempt is modeled on Colin Masica's pioneering work on the systematic definition of a linguistic area.[4] Traits which seem somehow peculiar to Indian literature are selected and plotted on a map until literatures exhibiting contrary or "different" traits are encountered. There are, of course, many problems with and limitations on such an endeavor which render its findings much less certain and much less comprehensive than is Masica's demonstration of the South (and Central) Asian linguistic area, not the least of which is the definition of a literary trait and its opposite; and, of course, it is much easier to get a global idea of the characteristics of a language or to determine whether or not a given feature is to be found there than it is to achieve the same degree of acquaintance with the literature of a given culture. While many linguistic traits have a mutually exclusive character that makes the classification of the languages in which they are found quite easy, it is hard to find literary traits that have the same convenient "either-or" property. Thus, it should be obvious that what follows is a preliminary sketch of an experimental study leading to the most tentative of conclusions. I present it here in a form which I hope will be reckoned to be frank, clear, and easily accessible to disconfirmation if such is to be its fate.

Since this study presupposes the procedures and objectives of Masica's work, it might be well to examine his method and findings briefly. As traits characteristic of Indian languages, Masica chose the following:

1. The predominance of word orders in which the direct object precedes the verb rather than following it. Thus, in Hindi one says *raam ne siitaa ko dekhaa* 'Ram Sita saw' rather than 'Ram saw Sita'.
2. The morphological causative. To express the idea "She had the gardener cut the hedge," rather than add a separate verb meaning HAVE, CAUSE or MAKE, in Indian languages one adds an affix to the verb 'cut' to form a new but visibly related verb having the meaning 'make cut' or 'cause to cut'. Thus, the causative of the Hindi verb *kaaTnaa* 'to cut' is *kaTaanaa* 'to cause (someone) to cut'.
3. The so-called conjunctive participle or gerund. This is a nonfinite verb form which is much used in Indian languages where English would usually use 'and'. Thus, while the English speaker will say "go and see," the speaker of an Indian language is most apt to say 'going see' (*jaa-kar dekho* in Hindi) or even 'seeing come' (*dekh-kar aao* in Hindi). Of course, other languages such as English have constructions analogous to the conjunctive participle, but they are both more prevalent and less restricted in Indian languages (for example, they are freely used in imperatives in Hindi but not in English).
4. The compound verb. This is a construction in which the semantically most important or "main" verb is followed by another from a restricted set of items that normally mean GIVE, TAKE, GO, THROW, LEAVE, etc. As members of the compound verb, however, these items appear to lose most of their lexical content and play an auxiliary modifying role, the exact formulation of which need not detain us here.[5] An example from Hindi: the noncompound *DhUURhnaa* 'to look for' alternates with the compound *DhUURh lenaa* (literally: 'look for' plus 'take') which has the meaning 'to find'.
5. The dative-of-subject construction. If the subject of an English sentence is the experiencer of a state rather than the doer of an action, there is a strong

tendency in Indian languages to treat that subject as an indirect object. Thus, while in English we say "I am hungry" or "I have to go," in Hindi one says 'to me is hunger' or 'to me is to go' (*mujhe bhuukh hai* and *mujhe jaanaa hai*).

Masica shows that these five features are to a greater or lesser degree characteristic of Indian languages belonging to three different genetic stocks or families: the Indo-Aryan, the Munda, and the Dravidian.[6]

The truly novel question that Masica then poses (and the question I believe to be his greatest contribution to the study of the linguistic area) is this: Do these five features which are characteristic of Indian languages define a strictly Indian linguistic area? Do they define the languages of India as sharply different from the languages of areas adjacent? To answer this question, Masica began searching for each of these five traits in languages spoken in ever widening circles of territory adjacent to India and did not stop his search until he came to a language in which the given trait could be definitely shown not to exist. The results of this search are shown schematically in figure 1.[7]

From figure 1 it is clear that the traits selected by Masica do not define an Indian linguistic area distinct from neighboring regions. Nor is it a case of randomly distributed features happening to coincide in India. Rather, India appears on the map as the southern lobe of a greatly extended linguistic area that runs from South Asia through Central Asia and ends in Northeast Asia. The language families connected in this way include Indo-Aryan, Dravidian, Munda, some Tibeto-Burman, Altaic, Uralian, Korean, and Japanese. These findings, it goes without saying, will be of great interest to Indologists of every stripe. They not only pose the obvious question of what implications they have for the prehistory and formation of Indian civilization, but suggest that research in a number of other fields might be profitably directed toward the search for affinities between South and Inner Asia, especially in archaeology and anthropology.[8]

One of the problems I faced in my investigation of India as a literary area is the fact that a good deal of the world's literature has as its most ancient source some Indian model which was deliberately translated and adapted to the language and culture of the borrowing group.[9] Often such "consciously diffused" material re-enters the mode of orally transmitted folk literature in a milieu thousands of miles from its original home.[10] Rather often it takes on divergent forms that depend on the beliefs and literary traditions of the receiving people: a glance at the transformations undergone by the Rāmāyaṇa in its peregrinations about Southeast Asia is enough to convince one of that. The presence of such divergences in theme, motif, or treatment is, of course, good evidence for the noncongruence of underlying literary structures; but the absence of such divergences can be given no clear interpretation—perhaps the adapters chose to let alien elements stand, or perhaps there is a basic similarity in literary tradition because of which the imported material is not felt to be alien. It is hoped that by examining literary traditions for similarity of motif where there is no manifest influence of one tradition on another through direct and conscious literary borrowing we can elude the problems posed by ambitious travelers, curious kings, and efficient translators. Thus, with one or two deliberate exceptions, I have restricted myself to a consideration of what is as near as I can determine literature of local origin. In addition, I have selected a constellation of traits or motifs which strike me as somewhat more archaic and unconscious than others I might have chosen, less amenable to conscious manipulation, more deeply cathected in the collective belief and value structure of a given culture. And, finally, I have looked for the expression (or nonexpression) of these motifs in what are, or seem to be, works of universal appeal in a given place, works with which everyone is acquainted regardless of the level of his formal education or social rank, works of which a knowledge is presupposed, even obligatory, in a person who claims membership in the group which gave them birth.

The motifs I have chosen focus on marriage and the relations between hero and heroine, both before and, where relevant, after their wedding. Specifically, the questions I have asked are these:

1. Do the hero and the heroine get married?
2. Who takes an active role in making the marriage possible: the hero? the heroine? or both?
3. Does the heroine love the hero: at all? for a time? throughout the entire period of the story?

I selected these questions because it seems to me (and has seemed to others)[11] that the answers Indian literature gives to them are somewhat unusual: assuming that there is a hero and a heroine in an Indian story, they almost always get married; the heroine often shows a great deal of initiative in bringing their marriage about; and her fidelity to the hero or the hero's memory is unwavering throughout the course of the story. As I hope to show presently, most of that portion of Asia adjacent to India gives very different answers to these questions. But first I shall illustrate the Indian portion of the thesis.

In the story of Nala-Damayanti[12] the hero and heroine fall in love and exchange their vows through the good offices of a messenger swan. At the time of Damyanti's *swayamwara*[13] the gods try to fool Damayanti into choosing one of them by resembling Nala down to the last detail. It is Damayanti's presence of mind that leads her to make a *satyāgraha* (to demand true behavior of the gods on the basis of her own devotion to *dharma* [right conduct]), which forces the gods to reveal their true identities. She then is able to recognize Nala, and the two are married. Later her husband proves to be quite a cad. He gambles away his rights to the Nishadan kingdom to a brother and then slinks off into the forest where he abandons Damayanti as she lies sleeping under a tree. In spite of Nala's fecklessness and treachery Damayanti remains faithful to him and goes to great pains to get herself reunited with him. Through her ingenuity Nala is found. He rejoins her, regains his rights to the kingdom, abdicates in favor of a son and spends his final years with Damayanti wandering in the forest as a *sādhu*. The story is marked by the pluck, activeness, and devotion of the heroine especially as these qualities stand in contrast to the strange passiveness that comes upon the hero at times.

Savitri-Satyavan[14] is another story of pan-Indian popularity. Savitri, who possesses a strange radiance which frightens off suitors, is finally given permission by her father to go out looking for her own husband. She discovers Satyavan supporting his aged parents by working as a woodcutter in the forests. Although she and her father are warned by Narada (the omniscient messenger god) that she will enjoy marital happiness only for the brief period of one year if she marries Satyavan, Savitri insists on her choice. When the year is up, and Yama, the god of death, comes to take Satyavan away to the underworld, Savitri follows along behind. There she is able to fool Yama into giving her the standard blessing of fruitfulness (*śatam sutānām...bhaviṣyati... tava!* 'You'll have a hundred sons.' *Mahābhārata* 3.281.45) But how can she, a chaste woman, be fruitful except through the good offices of her husband? Yama is forced to relinquish Satyavan.

In both the story of Damayanti and of Savitri the power of the heroine to take an active role in courtship and later to protect her husband and her marriage derive from the power she comes to possess through her chastity and devotion. Although the following is not well-known in North India and thus not as universal in India as the first two, I give a synopsis of it here as one of the most dramatic expressions of the moral power of woman that I have encountered in Indian literature. Kovalan and Kannaki[15] are the children of rich merchants in ancient Tamilnadu whose marriage is arranged by their families. Kovalan after a short period of marital bliss with Kannaki takes up with a famous and beautiful dancer, Madhavi. The languishing Kannaki, in accordance with the *dharma* of the faithful wife, makes no complaint but waits patiently for Kovalan to return to her. He finally does so after having squandered the family fortune on Madhavi. In order to regain his wealth Kovalan decides to set out with Kannaki for Madurai where he will sell one of her jewel-filled anklets to obtain capital to set up as a merchant. At Madurai he is framed by the king's goldsmith who has himself stolen the queen of Madurai's anklet. Believing the goldsmith's story that the thief has been found in the market attempting to fence the stolen anklet, the king orders his guards to go to the market, summarily execute Kovalan, and recover the missing anklet. When Kannaki hears what has happened she rushes to the palace and curses the king for having strayed from the path of *dharma*. When she shows the king and queen that the anklet they have recovered is not the one they had lost, they both fall down dead on the steps in front of their thrones. Kannaki leaves the palace and calls on the gods to punish the people of Madurai as she walks through the streets of the city. She then plucks off her left breast and throws it down. The torn breast ignites a conflagration which destroys the entire city. Kannaki shortly thereafter rejoins Kovalan in heaven.

In all these stories: (1) the hero and heroine do marry; (2) where possible, the heroine takes an active role in making and maintaining the marriage (she chooses him; she discourages his rivals; she forgives him, rehabilitates him, or saves his life); (3) her attitude toward him is absolutely monogamous: she is unswervingly faithful to him even upon his death. (In this light it is instructive to examine an adaptation for the Marathi stage of Ibsen's play *A Doll's House*. In *A Doll's House*, the heroine Nora becomes convinced that her husband Helmer is not worthy of her love and leaves him to return to her hometown and build an independent life for herself. The Marathi play *Kulawadhu*[16] could hardly be considered a version of *A Doll's House* if it did not retain at least this element of Ibsen's plot. But Rangnekar, the adapter, does not allow the least possibility of unchaste behavior to Bhanumati, the heroine. She does leave her husband, but she leaves him to go off and live with *his* parents!)

At this point we might ask if the stories of Damayanti and Savitri (and yet others: Sita, Shakuntala, etc.) simply represent one among several different types of treatments of the heroine in Indian literature or whether they in some way provide an exhaustive archetypal structure for stories of India-wide appeal that involve women. That is, can we claim that marriage and fidelity characterize the fate of the Indian heroine in the same way that first subject, then object, and finally verb characterize the order of words in a sentence in an Indian language? The answer depends of course on the absence of counterexamples. There are apparent counterexamples of three sorts. I believe it is possible to dispose of these on one ground or another.

First, there are a number of culturally important and entrenched stories, such as Hir-Ranjha and Sohani-Mahiwal, in which the marriage of the hero and heroine does not take place. However, I think it is important that these stories are associated with northwest India (particularly Panjab) and thus can be interpreted as a territorial extension of the Perso-Arabic treatment of the heroine into those areas of India closest to and most deeply affected by the Perso-Arabic world (whose treatment of the heroine we shall examine in more detail presently). In the same way, certain modern heroines such as may be found in the works of Mohan Rakesh[17] can be accounted for as the result of the (remarkably shallow) diffusion of Western literary models.

Second, there are numerous examples from traditional "story-literature" that appear to disconfirm my hypothesis. For example, in a number of stories in the *Vetālapañcaviṃśati* we find married women who are not faithful to their husbands.[18] Collections such as this and the *Kathāsaritsāgara* at one time enjoyed immense popularity in India.[19] Nevertheless, the heroines in these stories seem to have left little trace on the collective consciousness. They are not known by name to the ordinary person. They are not alluded to in ordinary conversation. In short, they have not received ratification as cultural archetypes.

The third counterexample, perhaps the most difficult to deal with, is the story of Radha. Not only does she fail to marry Krishna, but she is unfaithful to her husband into the bargain. It can be argued, of course, that since her husband is in no way the hero of the story, this second point is not relevant. Moreover, I am informed[20] that in later versions of the story she is made to marry Krishna. However, these are tergiversations. The correct interpretation of the story of Radha is as a deliberate departure from the culturally established norm. The story of Radha's love for Krishna accumulates its power from its context: without Savitri, Damayanti, Sita, and Shakuntala in the background, Radha's trysts with Krishna become negligible amatory escapades. The erotic and adulterous behavior of Radha that strikes us as introducing a dissonant mundanity into the depiction of man's transcendent relation to God has quite a different effect in a literary tradition where every heroine is unswerving in her devotion to duty and her fidelity to husband-hero. It follows, of course, from this that there can be only one Radha.

Now let us turn our attention to the literatures of Central Asia. My statements concerning the treatment of love, marriage, and the heroine in Central

FIGURE 1

THE MASICAN LINGUISTIC AREA

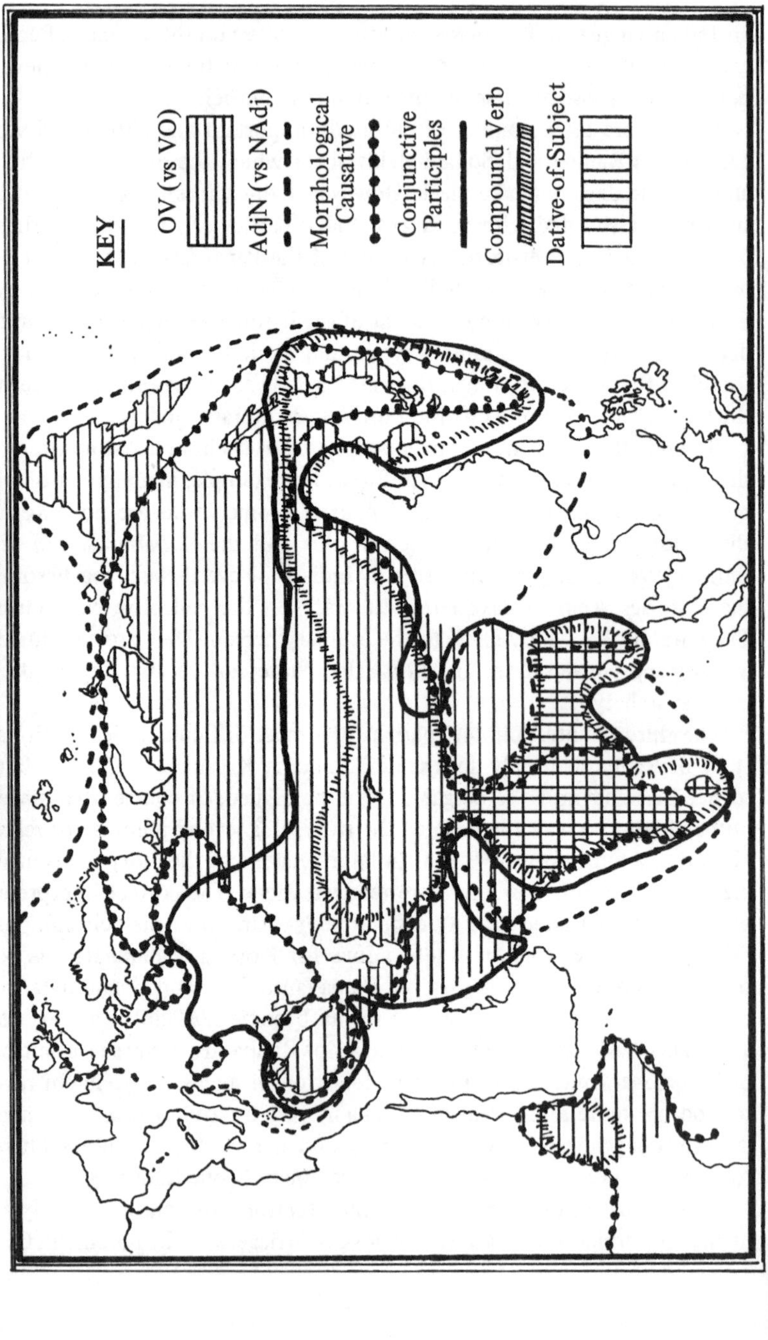

Asian literature must, of course, be considered extremely tentative. I am unable to read any of it in the original and only a very small portion of it has been reduced to writing. It is, of course, impossible in such circumstances to hope for any exhaustive conclusions. Even so, the material I have been able to examine at second and sometimes third hand is striking in the extent to which it exhibits motifs comparable to those found in the stories of Damayanti, Kannaki, and Savitri.

The nomad herders of Central Asia, be they of Altaic or Mongol affiliation, until very recent times possessed a tradition of oral epic poetry that would rival and perhaps even surpass that of ancient India before the great epics Mahābhārata and Ramayana were committed to writing. For example, the Kirghiz epic *Manas* contains some 250,000 verses in each of the two full versions that have been recorded. This is only a part of the epos based on a single genealogy.[21] The professional reciters (*bakshy* or *akin*)[22] of these epics had enormous repertoires: one of them was found to be able to recite any one of seventy works.[23] Improvisation plays a great part in the performance which is accompanied by some form of musical instrument (*jädigän*, *domra*, *kobuz*, *dutara*)[24] and often lasts all night.[25]

In the stories of Damayanti and Savitri it is the intervention of the heroine that is responsible for the success of the suit and marriage. The active participation of the heroine in bringing about her own marriage is a recurring motif in Central Asian epics and saga. In the Kazakh poem *Kyz Zhibek*, Zhibek the heroine marries a petty chieftain named Tulegen against the will of her father who has betrothed her to Bekezhan. Tulegen is killed by Bekezhan's henchmen shortly after his marriage to Zhibek. He is succeeded by his younger brother Sansyzbay who, according to Turkic custom, is expected to seek his elder brother's widow's hand. (The Turks, like many groups both modern and ancient in India, practiced *niyoga* or the levirate.)[26] Again, she has been promised to someone else by her father, but hearing of Sansyzbay's approach she takes one of the unwanted suitor's horses and flees across the steppe to join her first husband's younger brother.[27]

The Buryat are a Mongol people living near the shores of Lake Baikal. In their myth of the origin of the Angara, the river that drains Lake Baikal into the Yenisey, the warrior Yenisey falls in love with the lovely Angara and, like Nala in the story of Nala and Damayanti, sends her messages via birds. Angara's mother arranges her marriage to an unwanted suitor, Prince Irkut. Angara is warned of Prince Irkut's approach by the messenger birds. She escapes from her mother's yurt and runs away to join her lover Yenisey in the north.[28]

The most intense expression of the resourceful heroine that I have encountered is in the Kazakh poem *Kozy Körpösh*. The hero and heroine are betrothed before birth by their fathers. But, as the hero's family is later reduced to poverty, the heroine's father decides to renege and arranges for her to marry a local chief. Meanwhile, the hero, disguised as a beggar, meets the heroine and wins her love. His rival attempts to kill the hero but is himself killed by the heroine who then marries Kozy (the hero).[29] (In the version of a neighboring group, the hero is killed by his rival who is in turn killed by the heroine. She then commits suicide and falls dead on the hero's body.)[30]

The theme of restoration to life of the dead is not uncommon in the epics and saga of Central Asian peoples (as might be expected in an area where, until quite recently, all spiritual life was centered on the shaman or shamanka). Given the general intellectual superiority of the women depicted in this literature[31] it is not surprising to find them restoring a sick or wounded husband to health. This ability sometimes partakes of the supernatural: in the first part of the Kirghis epos *Manas*, the hero is slain by the Kalmucks and then revived by his wife Kanykai.[32] In the Sagai epic *Altyn Pyrkan* the hero, during his childhood, is restored to life by a woman whom he later marries after overcoming her in a wrestling and archery match.[33]

In the Kazakh epic *Er Sain*, the hero is an only son born to parents of advanced age. He grows up to be a precocious and very successful warrior, but is finally killed by an overwhelmingly superior force of Kalmucks (Mongols under the tutelage of China). When the news of his death reaches his wife Ayu Bikesh, she first vows to remain faithful to him as a widow; then, impelled by intuition, she rides out over the steppe with a pair of horses and the pelt of a white bear given to her by her mother. Riding day and night she finally discovers the body of her husband Er Sain by a poplar tree at the top of a hill (important shamanistic symbols). She laments:

> Do you see how playful is my glance?
> Do you see how beautiful is my face?
> Why are you lying cold, my husband?

Then she carries him on her shoulder to a spring, washes his wounds, and applies fat from the white bear skin. He is restored to life.[34]

As far as I am able to tell, the power of such heroines to protect their husbands or restore them to life is not explicitly linked in Central Asian literature to their chastity and fidelity in the fashion that may be observed in South Asian literature.[35] However, marriage of the heroine, her resourcefulness, and her faithfulness seem to be characteristic. Nora Chadwick, one of the first Westerners to turn serious attention to this literature, is led to remark:

> Perhaps the most striking feature of the poems is their preoccupation with marriage. The marriage of the hero forms the climax in most cases. Even apart from this the feminine interest is very strongly represented throughout the poems. The dénouement is very frequently brought about by women, and they are undoubtedly more gifted, both intellectually and spiritually, than their husbands and brothers.[36]

The similarity of Central and South Asian heroines and the similarity of the treatment of marriage in Central and South Asian literatures is thrown into strong relief by an examination of corresponding themes in the literatures of adjacent areas in the Middle East and Southeast Asia.

This examination is perhaps the most important and the most difficult part of this essay: it is the quest for negative data. To uphold the hypothesis of South and Central Asian literary affinities, it is necessary to show that the presence of the aggressive and faithful heroine somehow distinguishes the literatures of these places from other places. Since it was not possible for me to review the literature of the entire world or even of that part of Eurasia that Masica covers in his discussion of India as a linguistic area, I have had to content myself with a brief look at a few of the works of those areas nearest to South Asia: the Near East, Tibet, Burma, Thailand, Cambodia, and Vietnam. Even discounting for such a reduction in the scope of the investigation, the results must still be considered extremely tentative. It is much easier to be confident about the existence of a theme in a nation's literature than about its absence.

In Perso-Arabic literature, love is usually a source of unhappiness and tragedy. It rarely leads to marriage. In the Arabian story of Leili and Majnun, the love of the hero and heroine is hampered by their belonging to different tribes. Although Majnun's father makes an attempt to obtain Leili's father's consent to the marriage of their children, the latter refuses. Majnun begins to wander in the desert, demented by his love for Leili who is eventually married to somebody else. Although she loves Majnun, sends him messages, and refuses to consummate her marriage with the unwanted Ibn Salam, she is not willing to meet Majnun even after Ibn Salam dies, until the required two-year mourning period is past. When at last they do meet, it becomes clear that

Majnun has progressed in his insanity beyond any hope of recovery. He is unable to speak and flees from Leili into the desert. She dies shortly after and is buried. Majnun comes to her grave and dies from beating his head against her tombstone. His bones are laid to rest with hers.[37]

The native Persian stories that we have been able to examine resemble the story of Leili and Majnun in gross outline. The heroine is either already married to someone else at the time she meets the hero (as in Farhad and Shirin) or is married against her will to someone else later (as in Valeh and Hadijeh).[38] Although the heroine may write to the hero or give him some other indication of her feelings, she is unable to bring herself to brave the opposition of family or society by running off with him. These themes not only leave little room for the motif of the aggressive bride and protecting wife but are to some extent opposed. They reach their most intense form in classical Persian and Indo-Persian poetry where the affections of the hero are displaced to a beloved of the same sex or to a prostitute. Love is typically unrequited or quickly withdrawn. Woman is seen, if at all, as a heartless destroyer.[39]

Turning to regions east of South and Central Asia one finds an oral tradition of heroic poetry and saga similar to that of the Turks of Central Asia in Tibet. The hero of Tibetan epic literature is Gesar of Ling (a region in Eastern Tibet) who defeats his people's enemies, throws off the yoke of Hor, and protects the institutions of Buddhism in Tibet. The story is permeated with magic and the supernatural. The motif of the messenger bird is found in an extreme form: the raven who comes and announces to Gesar's uncle that he shall ascend the throne is none other than Gesar himself, whose ability to change form is of great importance to his victories. Gesar is the child of an aged father (Singlen). His mother is Singlen's servant, a Nagi princess who is brought to Tibet from under the sea. The epic makes it appear that she conceives Gesar after drinking a magic potion provided by the gods, a motif not unknown in Indian literature.[40]

But in its treatment of the heroine, the tale of Gesar of Ling departs most decidedly from Central and South Asian literary patterns. Gesar obtains his bride Sechang Dugmo without the least participation on her part as a prize for winning a race. Her role in the marriage is one of complete passivity until, in Gesar's absence, she is carried off by Kurkar, King of Hor and enemy of Ling. She falls in love with this man and has a child by him. Eventually Gesar kills both Kurkar and Sechang Dugmo's son. She, it seems, is forgiven, for we find her at his side when he dissipates his earthly form in order to regain the world of the gods at the end of the epic.[41]

I have had much difficulty in attempting a characterization of the treatment of marriage and the heroine in Burmese literature, a literature which is very much in the shadow of India. Most of the synopses which I have seen are of works which have roots in either Sanskrit or Pali literature. Moreover, there is a confusing mixture of opposite treatments of the heroine within the works of individual authors or adapters: viz., the plays *Paduma* and *Waythandaya* of U Pon Nya. In the first, the hero, a prince sent into exile with his wife, has her drink his own blood to save her from death by thirst as they wander in the forest. They finally encounter a man without arms or legs with whom the heroine falls in love. She pushes Prince Paduma off a cliff and carries the man away in a basket. Paduma lives, regains his kingdom, and one day recognizes his wife, whom he banishes from his realm along with her helpless lover. In the second, written at the instance of the women of the court who were outraged by the first, the heroine follows her husband into exile and faithfully looks after him and their children.[42]

Although Thailand, too, lies in the shadow cast by Sanskrit and Pali literature, it has managed to preserve one very popular *sep'ha* or folk epic which up until the nineteenth century was transmitted orally and has since provided subject matter for Thailand's greatest poets.[43] This is the story of *K'hun Chang K'hun P'hen*. The plot revolves around the life of the heroine Wan T'hong, who is unable to make up her mind as to which of two men, known to her since childhood, she prefers to live with. One, K'hun P'hen is handsome and a heroic warrior; the other, K'hun Chang, is ugly and bald (since childhood), but rich. The heroine marries one, runs off to the other, returns to the first, returns to the second, and so on, until the uproar she causes becomes such that the king decides to have her executed.[44]

The literature of Cambodia remains nearly inaccessible to those who do not know Khmer. I am informed[45] that "official" or court literature is heavily influenced by Indian models, especially the Ramayana. Sita is taken as the ideal heroine in literature destined for the upper class. It is possible that autochthonous traditions were quite different. In the story of Neang-Kakey, the king is visited each week by a krouth[46] with whom he plays chess. The krouth falls in love with the king's favorite, Neang-Kakey, who connives at his abduction of her. Kotonn, friend of the king, suspects the krouth, and, turning himself into a flea, hides under the krouth's wing when the latter departs after his weekly chess game. Neang-Kakey is discovered in the krouth's palace by Kotonn who has no difficulty in seducing her. When the krouth learns of this second treachery, he loses interest in Neang-Kakey. She is returned to the palace of the king, who has her chained and set adrift on a raft. She perishes among the waves and monsters of the deep.[47]

In *Kim-Van-Kieu*, the "national poem of Viet-Nam"[48] the heroine Thuy-Kieu betroths herself to Kim-Trong. While the latter is away, Thuy-Kieu's father and brother are arrested on false charges. A large sum of money will secure their release. Thuy-Kieu agrees to marry a wealthy merchant for the required sum. She makes her younger sister promise to marry Kim-Trong in her place. Too late, she discovers that she has actually sold herself into prostitution. There follow a number of further vicissitudes, which include Thuy-Kieu's unwitting destruction of a popular warlord who rescues her from prostitution. She finally encounters Kim-Trong who has married her younger sister. A symbolic marriage is performed, and Thuy-Kieu lives out her days in complete chastity in the house of Kim-Trong as his second wife.[49]

If I may be forgiven what may well turn out to be a most premature schematization, the differences among the literatures of (1) the Near East, (2) South and Central Asia, and (3) Southeast Asia with respect to the treatment of the heroine and her marriage may be characterized in terms of the occurrence or nonoccurrence of the marriage of hero and heroine and the presence or absence in the heroine of faithful sentiments or behavior toward the hero. In the Perso-Arabic tradition their marriage usually does not occur. In the Southeast Asian examples I have examined, a marriage usually occurs but the heroine for one reason or another is not able to maintain her fidelity to the hero throughout. In Central Asian literature, and certainly in South Asian literature, there is both a marriage and purely monogamous behavior on the part of the heroine until the end of the story. Whether such a characterization will stand up to further reading in the literatures concerned remains to be seen. If it does, it will add one more strand to the bundle of prehistoric affinities that appear to link the cultures of South and Central Asia.

NOTES

1. See Chadwick 1940: 650, 666-67.
2. Hart 1975.
3. It was first presented at the spring meeting of the South Asia Colloquium of the Pacific Northwest on the campus of the University of Washington, Seattle, Washington, in March 1975. It was presented again at a South Asia Committee brownbag at the University of Hawaii sometime late that year. What improvements its successive revisions show owe much to the comments and criticisms of earlier hearers. Much of the basic information on the literatures of Southeast Asia was collected *viva voce* from Professors Alton Becker and William Gedney of the University of Michigan and Professor Philip Jenner of the University of Hawaii. I am most grateful to these individuals for their patience and encouragement and for having shortened my search for the data which I considered relevant to my thesis. I wish to assure the court, however, that they were witnesses, not accessories, to the crime.
4. Masica 1976, a revised version of Masica 1971. As there are certain highly speculative but very exciting ideas in Masica 1971 which do not appear in Masica 1976 (especially in the concluding chapter), I recommend them both to the interested reader's attention.
5. For discussion of the functions of the compound verb (in opposition to the non-compound verb), see Hook 1974, 1978, and forthcoming, and Schiffman 1969 (for Tamil); Hacker 1958, and Pořízka 1967-69 and 1972.
6. I speak of greater or lesser degrees because the case for the presence of each of these five traits is not equally well made for the languages of each of these three families. For example, Masica 1976 offers no evidence for the presence of the compound verb in Munda; and except for the Southern Munda Parengi (see Aze, p. 279) no such evidence appears to be available in the literature on Munda.
7. Figure 1 is derived from map 7 ("Selected Distributions Superimposed") in Masica (1976:180).
8. Some of the features whose investigation seems promising in the light of Masica's findings are: (1) indications of an ancient pan-Siberian cult to the Mother Goddess *Umay* (see Nahodil 1968:462-63, and Tekin 1968:235, 268); (2) the connection of woman's breast and fire in South India *and* Siberia (see Hart 1975:104-6, and Nahodil, p. 466); (3) startling resemblances in the iconographies of Lord Shiva and Erlik Khan, ruler of the Turkic underworld (Chadwick 1969:163-64); (4) the survival of shamanistic traits in ancient (as well as modern) South Indian religious practice (Hart [p. 16] mentions the resemblance of the traditional royal *muracu* drum to that of the Siberian shaman: the drums in both areas were sacrificed to with blood and were made of wood from a tutelary tree which in turn represented the connection of both Siberian shaman and ancient Tamil king with the sacred realms); (5) the resemblance of the practice among certain Siberian groups (such as the Sagay) of building little houses around and offering food and drink to gravestones of ancestors (Diószegi 1968:80) to the complex of practices surrounding the *naṭukal* of Ancient Tamilnadu (Hart, pp. 82, 93); and (6) the recognition and worship of the *svayambhū* (the *seite* or "found" idol) by the Lapps (Manker 1968). Of course, many of these features are of too pervasive an occurrence among archaic peoples all over the world to be sufficient in themselves for the demonstration of prehistoric contacts or affinities among

the peoples of ancient South and Central Asia. But in the light of Masica's work it seems to me that they all deserve to be looked into by scholars of the disciplines concerned.

9. Benfey's famous study of the worldwide diffusion of the *Pañcatantra* comes to mind. See Lanman 1959:312-15.
10. For discussion of the factors governing the "re-entry" of imported literary motifs into local oral traditions, see Riftin 1974:75-76.
11. See, for instance, Spratt 1966.
12. Related in the *Mahābhārata*, Araṇyakaparvan, pp. 50-78.
13. The free choice of a husband from among a group of contending suitors. This method of making a match was frequent with daughters of royalty.
14. Related in *Mahābhārata*, Araṇyakaparvan, pp. 277-82.
15. Related in Iḷaṅkōvaṭikaḷ 1965. For a synopsis see Hart 1975:104-7.
16. I know this play of Rangnekar's only from a phonograph recording.
17. For instance, Nilima in Rakesh's *andhere band kamre* or Savitri in his play *aadhe adhuure*. (The first of these has been translated by Carlo Coppola under the title *Lingering Shadows* [New Delhi: Hind Pocket Books, n. d.]. The second has been translated by Steven Poulos and Ramanath Sharma in *Journal of South Asian Literature* 9, nos. 2,3:203-67.
18. For instance, in story no. 21. Gnomic verses abound that trivialize and belittle the affections of women in general. Śloka 1 of the Nītiśataka is a famous example.
19. van Buitenen 1959: introduction.
20. Madhav Deshpande, personal communication.
21. Chadwick 1969:29ff.
22. Distinctions are discussed in Zhirmunsky 1969:327ff.
23. The Uzbek Pulkanshair. See Zhirmunsky 1969:325.
24. Chadwick 1940:22-23.
25. Chadwick 1969:214.
26. See Manu 9:59-70. Some discussion in Hart 1959:114ff.
27. Chadwick 1969:52.
28. Diószegi 1968:23-24.
29. Radlov 3:261-97.
30. Sobolev 1940:74ff; Chadwick 1940:46.
31. Chadwick 1969:128.
32. Chadwick 1969:158. There is, as far as I know, no connection between this name and that of Kannaki, the heroine of the Shilappadikaram.
33. Chadwick 1969:110-11.
34. Sobolev 1940:44.
35. Hart 1975:97ff discusses the protective power of the chaste woman at some length. He cites a modern manifestation of it in a Malayalam novel, *Chemmeen*, written by Thakazhi S. Pillai: "This wide-open sea contains everything, my child. Everything. Why do you think all the men who go out there come back safely? It is because of the women at home who lead clean lives. Otherwise the currents in the sea will swallow them up. The lives of the men at sea are in the hands of the women on shore.... The strength and wealth of the fisherman lie in the purity of his wife" (Hart, p. 101).
36. Chadwick 1940:106.

37. Atkinson 1894.
38. Mahomed and Rice 1903.
39. See the discussion of the sociopsychological causes for this attitude in Russell and Islam 1968:117ff.
40. A similarly supernatural potion figures in the story of the conception and birth of Ram and his brothers.
41. Narrated in David-Neel and Yongden 1959.
42. For a more detailed synopsis of these plays see Aung 1937:78-81, 96-99.
43. This particular *sep'ha* was rendered by a committee of poets including the great Sunt' hon P'hu (1786-1855) at the instance of King P'huttaleutla early in the nineteenth century and further perfected during the reign of King Mongkut (circa 1860).
44. A synopsis can be found in Schweisguth 1951:207-9.
45. By Professor Philip Jenner of the University of Hawaii (personal communication).
46. I understand from Professor Hiram Woodward, Jr., of the University of Michigan that a krouth is both conceptually and linguistically related to *garūḍa*, the giant bird that serves as a vehicle to Vishnu.
47. The story is related in Pavie 1969:3-23.
48. See the introduction to Le-Xuan-Thuy's English translation in Nguyen-Du (1968).
49. See Nguyen-Du 1968:428, fn. 245.

REFERENCES

Atkinson, James. 1894. *The Loves of Lailī and Majnún. A Poem from the Original Persian of Nizámi.* London: David Nutt.

Aung, Maung Htin. 1937. *Burmese Drama*. Oxford: Oxford University Press.

Aze, Richard F. 1973. "Clause Patterns in Parengi-Gorum." In *Patterns in Clause, Sentence and Discourse in Selected Languages of India and Nepal*, Part I. Edited by R. L. Trail. Norman, Oklahoma: Summer Institute of Linguistics.

Chadwick, Herbert M., and Nora K. 1940. *The Growth of Literature*. Vol. 3. New York: Macmillan Co.

Chadwick, Nora K. 1969. *The Epic Poetry of the Turkic Peoples of Central Asia*. In Chadwick and Zhirmunsky, pp. 1-268.

Chadwick, Nora K., and Victor Zhirmunsky. 1969. *Oral Epics of Central Asia*. Cambridge: Cambridge University Press.

David-Neel, Alexandra, and the Lama Yongden. 1959. *The Superhuman Life of Gesar of Ling*. London: Rider.

Diószegi, Vilmos. 1968. *Tracing Shamans in Siberia*. Translated from the Hungarian by A. R. Babó. Anthropological Publishers.

———, ed. 1968. *Popular Beliefs and Folklore Tradition in Siberia*. Bloomington: Indiana University Publications.

Hacker, Paul. 1958. *Zur Funktion einiger Hilfsverben im Modernen Hindi*. Mainz: Akademie der Wissenschaften und der Literatur.

Hart, George. 1975. *The Poems of Ancient Tamil*. Berkeley and Los Angeles: University of California Press.

Hook, Peter Edwin. 1974. *The Compound Verb in Hindi*. The Michigan Series in South and Southeast Asian Languages and Linguistics, no. 1. Ann Arbor: Center for South and Southeast Asian Studies.

———. 1978. "The Hindi Compound Verb: What It Is and What It Does." In *Readings in Hindi-Urdu Linguistics*. Edited by K. S. Singh. New Delhi: National Publishing House, pp. 129-46.

———. Forthcoming. "Some Uses for Probabilistic Conceptualizations of Dialect Space." In *Spoken and Written Language in South and Southeast Asia*. Edited by H. H. van Olphen. Austin: University of Texas, Dept. of Asian and African Language and Literature.

Iḷaṅkōvaṭikaḷ. See Shilappadikaram.

Lanman, Charles. 1884. *A Sanskrit Reader*. Cambridge: Harvard University Press.

Mahābhārata. 1941. Vol. 3. Edited by Sukthankar et al. Poona: Bhandarkar

Oriental Research Institute.
Mahomed, Mirza, and C. Spring Rice. 1903. *The Story of Valeh and Hadijeh.* London: Duckworth and Co.
Manker, E. 1968. *"Seite" Cult and Drum Magic of the Lapps.* In Vilmos Diószegi, ed., pp. 27-40.
Manu. 1884. *The Ordinances of Manu.* Translated from the Sanskrit by Arthur C. Burnell. London: Trübner and Co.
Masica, Colin P. 1971. "A Study of the Distribution of Certain Syntactic and Semantic Features in Relation to the Definability of an Indian Linguistic Area." Ph.D. dissertation, University of Chicago.
———. 1976. *Defining a Linguistic Area: South Asia.* Chicago: University of Chicago Press.
Nahodil, O. 1968. "Mother Cult in Siberia." In Vilmos Diószegi, ed., pp. 459-77.
Nguyen-Du. 1965. *Kiều.* Traduit du Vietnamien par Nguyễn Khắc Viên. Hanoi: Éditions en Langues Étrangères.
———. 1968. *Kim-Vân-Kiều.* Translated by Lê-Xuân-Thủy. Saigon: Nhà sách Khai-trí.
Nitiśataka of Bhartṛhari. 1959. In *Bhartṛhari-śataka-trayam,* edited by D. D. Kosambi. Singhi Jain Series, no. 29. Bombay.
Pavie, Auguste. 1969. *Les Douze Jeunes Filles ou l'Histoire de Néang Kakey.* Institut Bouddhique, Mission Pavie Indochine.
Pillai, Thakazhi S. 1962. *Chemmeen.* Translated by Narayana Menon. Bombay: Jaico Publishing House.
Pořízka, Vincenc. 1967-69. "On the Perfective Verbal Aspect in Hindi." *Archív Orientální* 35:64-68, 208-31; 36:233-51; 37:19-47, 345-64.
———. 1972. *Hindština-Hindī Language Course.* Prague: Státní Pedagogické Nakladatelství.
Propp, V. I. 1928. *Morphologie du Conte.* Translated by M. Derrida et al., 1970. Paris: Seuil.
Radlov, Vasilij V. 1866-1904. *Proben der Volkslitteratur der Türkischen Stämme Südsibiriens und der Dsungarischen Steppe.* St. Petersburg: Eggers and Co.
Riftin, B. L. 1974. Особая ролъ Индии в литературных связях Востока и Запада. In Типология и Взаимосвязи Средневековых Литератур Востока и Запада. Москва: Наука. Стр., 68-116.
Russell, Ralph, and Khurshidul Islam. 1968. *Three Mughal Poets.* Cambridge: Harvard University Press.
Schiffman, Harold. 1969. "A Transformational Grammar of the Tamil

Aspectual System." Ph.D. dissertation, University of Chicago.
Schweisguth, P. 1951. *Etude sur la Littérature Siamoise*. Paris: Imprimérie Nationale, Adrien Maisonneuve.
Shilappadikaram of Prince Ilangô Adigal. Translated by Alain Daniélou. New York: New Directions.
Sobolev, Leonid. 1940. Песни Степей: Антология Казахской Литературы. Москва: Гос. Изд. Художественная Литература.
Spratt, Philip. 1966. *Hindu Culture and Personality: A Psychoanalytic Study*. Bombay: Manaktalas.
Tekin, Talât. 1968. *A Grammar of Orkhon Turkic*. Uralic and Altaic Series, no. 69. Bloomington: Indiana University Publications.
Thompson, Stith. 1955-58. *Motif-Index of Folk Literature*. Rev. and enl. ed. 6 vols. Copenhagen: Rosenkilde and Bagger.
van Buitenen, J. A. B. 1959. *Tales of Ancient India*. Chicago: University of Chicago Press, Phoenix Books.
Vetālapañcaviṃśati of Jambhaladatta. Edited and translated by M. B. Emeneau. New Haven: American Oriental Society.
Zhirmunsky, Victor. 1969. *Epic Songs and Singers in Central Asia*. In Chadwick and Zhirmunsky, pp. 269-339.

ARYAN AND NON-ARYAN ELEMENTS IN NORTH INDIAN AGRICULTURE

Colin P. Masica
University of Chicago

1.1. The original inspiration for this paper came from a monograph of Wilhelm Brandenstein, published in 1936 and entitled *Die erste "indo-germanische" Wanderung.*[1] In this monograph, Brandenstein tried to establish, on the basis of semantic consistencies in the vocabulary shared and not shared between Indo-Iranian and the rest of Indo-European, that the ancestors of the Indo-Iranians left the primitive Indo-European community prior to its more general dissolution, and incidentally, prior to its acquisition of agriculture. The latter conclusion he based on (1) the almost total absence of agricultural (as distinct from pastoral) terms common to Indo-Iranian and the other languages, and (2) the retention in Indo-Iranian of exclusively nonspecific, presumably older meanings for some common roots and stems that developed agricultural meanings in "later" Indo-European.

For example, Vedic *ajraḥ* means simply 'open area, a plain' and bears no trace of the meaning 'arable field' that shows up in its non-Indic cognates (e.g., Gk. *agros*, Lat. *ager*, *agricola*, Ger. *Acker*, *Ackerbau*), although other languages do retain traces of an older meaning unconnected with agriculture (Gk. *agrios* 'wild'). Similarly, Old Indic *parśāṇah* has only the meaning 'cleft or fissure in the ground; chasm (i.e., from natural causes)', while many of its non-Indic cognates have developed the meaning 'plowed furrow' (Lat. *porca,* Welsh *rhych,* OHG *furuh,* Eng. *furrow*). The Indo-European root **se(i)-* has two meanings, 'hurl' and 'sow'. The latter is reconstructed from European words for 'sow' and 'seed' (Lat. *serō, sēmen,* Ger. *Samen,* Russ. *s'ejat', s'emia*). Only derivatives of the former are present in Indic:[2] *sāya(ka)* 'arrow, missile', *sēnā* 'missile, dart, spear' (only later, 'army' [Monier-Williams 1899: 1246]).

In these and other cases Brandenstein argues for the historical priority of the more general meaning on the basis of logical priority. That is, 'sow' could have developed out of 'throw', 'furrow' out of 'natural cleft', and 'arable field' out of 'open area', but not the other way around. Indic, of course, has developed words for 'field' (*kṣētra*), 'furrow' (*sītā*), and 'sow' (*vapayati*), but these are from different roots and are therefore not part of an Indo-European semantic inheritance in the same sense—which, again, is Brandenstein's point.

All this was merely prerequisite to Brandenstein's main purpose, which was to establish that there were two stages of Indo-European unity ("early" and "late," respectively, with and without the Indo-Iranians) and to ascertain an appropriate geographical location and lifestyle for each. Although his conclusions in these matters may not stand up in every detail today,[3] their general thrust is not that wide of the mark represented by the best present-day consensus. He put the "early" Indo-Europeans in the southeastern outliers of the Urals and adjoining steppes and identified their economy as based primarily on a rather primitive pastoralism. He was not the first to advocate what has been called the "steppe homeland" (that honor goes to Otto Schrader in 1890), but that hypothesis has been in disfavor, especially in German-speaking Central Europe and especially among philologists from the 1930s until quite recently. The North German plain, perhaps extended eastward to include the lower Vistula valley, was a strong favorite instead.

Brandenstein (and Schrader) have been vindicated first of all by archaeology. There is only one archaeological culture that is a candidate for identification with the Indo-Europeans (Gimbutas 1970:156; Goodenough 1970: 254; Littleton 1973:28-29; Childe 1926), namely, the Separate Grave, Tumulus, or, as Gimbutas has christened it, the *Kurgan* culture. Recent and continuing excavations combined with new dating methods have indicated the early center of dispersion of this culture to be the lower and trans-Volga steppe of northwestern Kazakhstan together, perhaps, with the northern Caucasus, a conclusion in substantial agreement with Brandenstein (Gimbutas 1970; Littleton 1973). From this staging area, the culture begins to spread westward (west of the Don, according to Gimbutas [p. 174], the Kurgan people appear in the archaeological record as intruders) beginning, perhaps, as early as the middle of the fifth millennium B.C. (latest calibrated radiocarbon dates being far earlier than had been thought), overcoming or infiltrating more advanced European neolithic farming cultures, and eventually (third millennium) reaching the Rhine before later descending to the Mediterranean. (It also—significantly for our purposes—expanded eastward as far as the Yenisei, southward across the Caucasus, and southward also around the Aral Sea toward India.) This, too, accords with Brandenstein's surmise of a move westward by the "later" Indo-European community and the picking up of the agricultural vocabulary common to the European branches of Indo-European from a non-Indo-European source.

A few philological skirmishes remain to be fought, but here, too, the battle is beginning to go in the same direction. A notable milestone has been the demolition of the "beech line" argument, vital to the North German plain hypothesis, by Friedrich (1970:112), who pointed out that a species of beech (*Fagus orientalis*) very similar to the European one (*Fagus silvatica*) is common in the Caucasus.

What is particularly original about Brandenstein, however, and what recent investigators have largely ignored, is his hypothesis of two stages of Indo-European "unity" as explanatory of some of the differences between Indo-Iranian and the rest of the family. This neglect may be partly because the movements of the Indo-Europeans seem now to have been manifold and complex. Although this in itself would not preclude a prior break with the Proto-Indo-Iranians, features other than agricultural and environmental vocabulary shared by Indo-Iranian with only certain other Indo-European groups (i.e., the *satem* languages) obviously pose problems (though not insoluble ones)[4] for such a hypothesis. It may also be due to focus of interest on the fate of European branches of the family, rather than on what may have been happening to the Indo-Iranians.

In one respect at least, Brandenstein's theory has to be modified. The archaeological evidence seems to indicate that the Proto-Indo-Iranians did not move out first, as Brandenstein has suggested, but rather last, having remained in the staging area after the others had left (Littleton:29-30). This, however, does not preclude the possibility of a breach of contact between these stay-at-homes and those who had departed for the west, with the result that the former did not share in the agricultural discoveries of the latter. The breach would have been reinforced by the fact that when the Proto-Indo-Iranians did move, it was in a different direction, taking them farther out of range.

It is also possible, of course, that most of any agricultural vocabulary (whether acquired or inherited) shared by the Indo-Iranians and their Indo-European relatives may have been lost by the former through atrophy as they developed into something closer to true pastoral nomads during the later stages of their wanderings and entered regions inhospitable or unfit for agriculture (Gimbutas:177; Gryaznov 1969:97ff, 237), although this is more difficult to reconcile with the apparent fact of "semantic stages" in such items as *ager/ajraḥ*.

1.2. What interests us in all this is its implications for India. If the invading Aryans did not bring the elements of agriculture with them from the Indo-European homeland (for whatever reason), then where did they get them? From what sources–from which earlier (or later) groups–were such elements incorporated into the ultimate Indian socioeconomic and cultural synthesis effected by the Aryans and their successors? That is the question, rather than Brandenstein's hypothesis as such, that is the focus of this paper.

I propose to pursue it here primarily through the linguistic (that is, the etymological) evidence. (Analogous questions naturally arise with regard to sources of agricultural terms in the western Indo-European languages, which to some extent have been pursued, particularly with regard to Greek [see Mellaart 1975:282]). I propose, moreover, to begin the investigation with the ultimate product of the historical process deposited in the modern language rather than with Sanskrit. There are several reasons for this. First, the process of assimilation, as represented even by traditional Indian agriculture as we know it, was a continuing one and not necessarily complete with Sanskrit. (The question thus becomes not *where and with whom the beginnings of Indian agriculture lie*—a question in any case wrongly put because it begs the question of complexity—but, rather, *where the various elements in the developed complex of Indian agriculture come from* and, specifically, *what the history of words can tell us about this*.) Second, there is really no Indian agriculture as such, but a group of related regional complexes differing in important details, including inventories of cultivated plants. Sanskrit, being a supraregional language, incorporates terms relating to various regional features. Many of these may have been used on a regional basis in Sanskrit also. There is no way of ascertaining this directly except by a long and complex analysis based on the geographical provenance of Sanskrit texts, which itself is often uncertain. A more reliable, though indirect, route to this information would seem to lie in the observation of the differing fallout in the various modern languages as evidence. Third, Sanskrit was, to an important extent, an artificially cultivated language with many literary synonyms. There is no way of knowing which of these was in actual use, except, again, through their descendants or lack of them in the living languages.

For all of the above reasons, but especially the second, as well as to make the problem more manageable, I shall confine myself in this initial essay to northern India and to its main language Hindi-Urdu as the take-off point. The several regional complexes must be studied separately before their common features can be understood.

1.3. First, however, a word of caution regarding the trickiness of such lexical evidence. Borrowing words from another language is only one, if indeed the most straightforward, of the methods a language may employ when faced with new terminological needs. It may also (1) coin a new (descriptive) term out of its own elements (e.g., Anglo-Indian *custard apple*); (2) extend or transfer the meaning of a term it already has (as the English term "corn" 'grain' became the designation for 'maize' in America); and (3) translate a foreign term into its own morphemes (perhaps a more sophisticated and learned device, exemplified by Russian *m'ezhdu-narodnyy* for "international," 'between-people-ish'). Borrowing itself, moreover, usually involves some degree of both phonetic and semantic modification. The former may go to the extent of complete phonological reinterpretation of a foreign item according to native meaningful elements (as in the oft-cited English colloquial example of "sparrowgrass" from "asparagus"). In such a case, obviously, it may be difficult to identify an item as borrowed, except on the grounds of known history or semantic absurdity–the latter always a risky criterion, since genuine creations may be equally capricious to our understanding–however reasonable they seemed at the time. The same caveat applies to seemingly implausible semantic leaps between cognates. Etymologists must make and do make such judgments, but they necessarily involve a large dose of subjectivity.

We can probably safely exclude the modern device of using acronyms (*NEFA, kolxoz*), but one never knows. Even less likely is another theoretical possibility, the invention of completely new morphemes. This appears to have been rarely used until the commercial product-naming of modern times, although seventeenth century "gas" is perhaps the most famous example (not, however, a pure one since it is said to have been suggested by "chaos"). It still ranks far behind the other devices, but we should not rule out the possibility that at some unthinkably remote period it may have been more productive.

In only two of the above cases does the new item clearly point to a foreign origin for the item or process involved: borrowing, when the nativizing phonetic disguise has not been too successful, and descriptive coinages actually referring to a foreign origin, of the type "Chinese cabbage" or "India mustard."

Thus, in English, while we might be able to tell from the words alone that, e.g., the potato, the tomato, tapioca, tobacco, and chocolate were of Amerindian origin, we would not be able to tell this, without other evidence, from the American English names for corn, squash, peanuts, rubber, pineapple, peppers, and many varieties of beans. In the case of corn, beans, pineapple, and peppers, old words have been transferred to new but analogous objects. (In the case of pineapple, the analogy seems to have been one mainly of shape, the word having originally referred to what we now call pinecones. In the case of peppers, reapplying, incidentally, what came as a borrowing via the classical languages from India, the analogy may have been pungency.)

In the cases of peanuts and rubber, a new word has been formed (or a specialized meaning evolved) out of native elements. In the case of squash, a truly borrowed word has been made to look English.[5]

All of these processes have been abundantly at work in Indo-Aryan also. An example of the transferring of an old word to a new but analogous object is the Hindi word for potato, *ālū*. Just as American English "corn" bears a name that hearkens back to Indo-European antiquity (**gr̥-nóm*),[6] also *ālū* goes back through Sanskrit to the same,[7] despite the fact that this Peruvian or Chilean plant was not known in India before the late sixteenth century.[8] The word had previously been applied to various other edible roots and tubers, particularly *Amorphophallus campanulatum*, a species of taro, the latter still an alternative meaning in Hindi.[9] The process of descriptive coinage is exemplified by Hindi *ajmod* 'parsley', from Sanskrit *ajamoda*, from *ajah* 'goat' plus *mōda* 'delight' equals 'goat's delight'. On the other hand, this may be a popular etymology of the sparrowgrass type. A more certain example is *ratālū*, from Sanskrit *raktālū*, from *rakta* 'blood; red' plus *ālū*, referring to a yam of red or purplish color.

As for the third process, making a borrowed word look native, this was unfortunately the special forte of the old Sanskrit lexicographers. Aided by a precocious discovery of the laws of sound change and the assumption that all languages were corruptions of Sanskrit, they were able not only to turn Prakrit and Modern Indo-Aryan forms "back into" Sanskrit but also to manufacture plausible-looking Sanskrit out of material that had never been Sanskrit. This was quite in accord with the function of Sanskrit as the great linguistic clearinghouse of the new cultural synthesis built on diverse peoples, but it complicates our task here. All the great languages of culture perform this integrative function to some extent,[10] but probably in none was it carried out so deliberately and on such a massive scale. (It is true that Sanskrit efforts to disguise foreign items, or, more likely, just to make them phonologically intelligible, are often not entirely successful; to the practiced eye the words still do not "look Sanskrit" in characteristic groupings and sequences of consonants and vowels. This is a whole study in itself, however, and is not a criterion we can fruitfully apply here.)

This means that the occurrence of a word in "Sanskrit" tells us little. It may be late and artificially Sanskritized, particularly if it is attested only in the lexicons. It may not have been actually used in Sanskrit, but merely collected from somewhere by an enterprising lexicographer or subject-specialist. It is therefore necessary to note attestation of the word in the earliest texts, pondering their (frequently uncertain) dates and natures (e.g., not only the lexicons but also medical treatises such as those of Caraka and Suśruta may involve collections of exotica); see whether it can be connected with a Sanskrit root; and, finally, search for cognates in the rest of Indo-European or elsewhere. It is not a requirement that the word be connected with a root, of course; there are many native words in Sanskrit as in all languages that cannot be analyzed, despite the remarkable degree of transparency of Sanskrit in this respect. In the case of unanalyzable words without cognates in Indo-European, however, we are dependent on the chance availability of evidence of specific non-Aryan origin—either in the form of historical (textual) evidence, which is largely lacking for many of the language families concerned, or in the form of greater analyzability or phonological plausibility in terms of a known non-Aryan system.

If the use of a "native" word is no guarantee that the referent is indigenous, then does the use of a foreign word at least indicate that the referent is foreign? Not necessarily. Occasionally the foreign name of a new variety or special aspect of an object may replace an older native generic name, either by generalization or by replacement of the older referent itself. The older term may linger in a restricted meaning. For example, in English, for most purposes, the older Germanic 'dove' has been replaced by the French 'pigeon', originally apparently referring to the domesticated rock pigeon but now the accepted term for all birds of this kind, wild or domestic. Another example is the adoption in Eastern Europe of some form of Germanic *plug* for 'plow' along with an improved version of the instrument, while the older word for 'plow' (e.g., Russ. *ralo*) now refers either to a part of the plow or to the primitive plow only—at any rate, the older word did not succeed in accommodating the new version. In some of these cases (including that of the plow), the question may well arise of whether it is proper to equate the glosses of the old and new terms merely on the basis of the abstracting perspective of English when it is likely that the two terms embodied quite distinct perceptions for the users of the language. In what sense are the old and new referents truly "the same"? (In both cases cited above, it may be admitted that at least some cultural change was involved, along with the change in terminology.)

Common internal semantic developments also affect the data. These include replacement of older terms by diminutives, pejoratives, and other terms of originally restricted application. An example is the replacement of the older word for 'goat', Sanskrit *ajaḥ* (with Indo-European affinities), by *bárkara*, the term for 'kid'. Seemingly greater semantic shifts, for example, of *uṣṭra* from 'buffalo' (*Ṛgveda*) to 'camel' (*Mahābhārata*), also occur in Indo-

Aryan as in all languages.

Despite these qualifications, the history of words can tell us a great deal—if not necessarily about the ultimate origins of this or that domestic animal, plant, tool, or practice, at least about cultural history. For instance, although the cultivation of tea was introduced by the British from China in the mid-nineteenth century (*Imperial Gazetteer of India:* vol. 3, p. 56) and the drink propagated in much of the country within living memory, the Hindi term for it, *cāy* (rather than, i.e., *ṭī*, used in several South Indian languages), indicates a prior acquaintance with it in northern India from the direction of Persia.

1.4. It is not just the single item and its history that interest us here, however, fascinating as these may be. Taking a cue from Brandenstein, we are interested in the broader cultural historical trends possibly discernible when the etymologies of a large number of them are sorted out and collated with semantic fields.

Despite many unsolved problems, and numerous disagreements among the experts, we now have available enough lexicographical and etymological tools to make such an attempt worthwhile (in this as well as in other fields). These include Turner's *A Comparative Dictionary of the Indo-Aryan Languages* (1966, 1969), Mayrhofer's *Kurzgefasstes etymologisches Wörterbuch des altindischen* (1956-1972),[11] Pokorny's *Indogermanisches etymologisches Wörterbuch* (1959), Buck's *A Dictionary of Selected Synonyms in the Principal Indo-European Languages* (1949), Burrow and Emeneau's *A Dravidian Etymological Dictionary* (hereafter cited as DED), and Zide and Zide's "Proto-Munda Cultural Vocabulary" (1976), as well as an accumulation of articles on individual items by Bloch, Burrow, and others.

My purpose here is thus not to find new etymologies but to make use of those that others have found. The "method" accordingly includes the following: (1) ascertaining the etymology of the Hindi term, if given by Turner; (2) ascertaining the relationship, Indo-European or otherwise, of Turner's ancestral Sanskrit term according to Mayrhofer; (3) checking further with Pokorny and/or Buck if this seems desirable; and (4) checking suggested Dravidian etymologies (usually of the Sanskrit ancestral term, sometimes directly of the Hindi term or of Turner's reconstructed Modern Indo-Aryan or Middle Indo-Aryan terms) in the DED and Munda etymologies in Zide and Zide. (Here a special caution is necessary, as both Turner and Mayrhofer have relied on Kuiper's earlier work [e.g., *Proto-Munda Words in Sanskrit* (1948)] for indications of possible Munda or Austroasiatic etyma as has Burrow [1955/59] in *The Sanskrit Language*. According to N. Zide, a great many, if not most, of these were not well-founded and are now repudiated by Kuiper himself. A word cannot be ascribed to "Munda," or for that matter to "Dravidian," merely on a hunch, if there are no Munda or Dravidian correspondences.) When a term is missing from Turner, Platts' *A Dictionary of Urdu, Classical Hindi, and English* (1960) will often have suggestions, but these must be used with caution as many of Platts' etymologies (or etymological speculations) do not seem to be accepted by Turner, Mayrhofer, and other later authorities. Words of Persian origin are not dealt with by Turner, nor are they always completely obvious. Platts' work, as well as some of the more modern Hindi dictionaries, gives indications of some but not all of these. Words of Persian origin, as well as any unexplained words, should in any case be checked with Persian dictionaries. I have used several, but have found that, for this purpose, there is no substitute for Steingass (1892).

The long history of Indian, and particularly North Indian, contact with Iran, with whose language Indo-Aryan is closely cognate, in fact constitutes a general complication in this investigation. It is not just a matter of the deep imprint of Persian culture during the eight centuries of Muslim domination of the North[12] but also of the dimmer ages before that, stretching back to the period of Indo-Iranian unity. After the separation of the two peoples (or rather, of their main cultural streams, since there was always an interconnecting web of transitional peoples in the mountains of the northwest), contact was only intermittently intense but included periods involving Iranian expansion into the subcontinent as well as periods of Indian expansion far to the northwest. Modern Persian borrowings into Hindi or Urdu are generally more readily identifiable, although there is sometimes a question of a word originally borrowed by Persian from Sanskrit returning with the earmarks of Persian. It may be more difficult to identify Iranian loanwords from an earlier period, however, because of the closer linguistic relationship as well as the partial overlap of territories (and therefore of characteristic environments), particularly when the Sanskritizers have been at work. We would like to identify them, as all Iranian developments after the period of Indo-Iranian unity constitute for present purposes another "foreign," therefore in a narrow sense "non-Aryan," input, albeit from a kindred Indo-European culture. Here it must not be overlooked that Iranian culture, in the course of its separate development after the Indo-Aryans had gone their separate ways, absorbed and integrated its own distinctive non-Aryan elements which would be part of its later bequests to India.

Before any of these questions arise, however, there is an important prior step—that of identifying the Hindi terms to be investigated *and their referents*. In retrospect, perhaps the best thing to do—rather daunting in its time requirements–would be to comb the dictionaries entry by entry. Not having that much time at my disposal, I have deferred that thorough an investigation till another day and attempted a shortcut to an initial significant sampling through such works as the Indian Council of Agricultural Research's *Handbook of Agriculture*, Grierson's *Bihar Peasant Life*, and Watt's *A Dictionary of the Economic Products of India*. Such works only provide the initial impetus, perhaps in a crudely Englished spelling and wrongly glossed, for a phase of intensive detective work with Hindi and Urdu dictionaries, both monolingual and bilingual. Resort to the latter is necessary because Hindi-Hindi dictionaries often give only a gloss such as 'a kind of grain' or 'a vegetable'. We would like to be more specific than that! The monolingual dictionaries never give international botanical names. On the other hand, even when the bilingual dictionaries are more specific, they sometimes disagree among themselves. This lack of agreement (which sometimes is no doubt due to regional variations) obviously poses a problem, but even more frequent are those problems posed by inadequate glossing or no entry at all. I have followed, in my final selection, the rule of thumb of not including any item unless at least two sources agree on it–which is not so say that every item included is thereby adequately glossed. I have allowed repeated references to persuade me even if they are all in disagreement or vague.

There are hundreds of agricultural terms, many of them no doubt regionally restricted, that simply do not find their way into dictionaries at all. Such is the case even with many terms in Grierson's *Bihar Peasant Life*, regarding which he also gave up. There is no remedy for this situation here. This is not meant to be a dialect geography. Although these terms would have obvious relevance to the present study and might well affect its conclusions, the uncertainty as well as lack of explanation (etymological or botanical) surrounding them dictates that they be left out of consideration at this time. I have consulted informants but have not launched a full-scale survey on this basis. Stray references and afterthoughts have sent me scurrying back to the chain of dictionaries and reference works again and again in pursuit of an elusive completeness, but this process has had to be resolutely brought to a halt. The study may be said to rest on terms of fairly standard and cross-regional (in North India) reference, therefore, for which lexicographic entries exist.

One area of special difficulty has been that which I had naively expected would bring order to the confusion at a single stroke–that of scientific botanical nomenclature. While it is possible and indeed probable that lexicographers not well versed in botany have applied some of these Latin terms inaccurately–and they certainly disagree alarmingly among themselves–it seems also to be true that the nomenclature and the classifications themselves have been revised more than once, sometimes quite extensively, over the period covered by the lexicographical works consulted. I had begun to despair of ever finding a key to this labyrinth when I stumbled on one, or what seems to be one, and I am adopting it as such–the tenth revised edition (1972) of Robert Zander's *Handwörterbuch der Pflanzennamen*. It contains the latest international agreements and terminological revisions, along with fairly extensive cross-reference to formerly used names and classifications. It is not quite complete in some areas of interest to us, although nearly so, and unfortunately it is in German (making the vernacular equivalents of the entries less immediately useful–a more encyclopedic German-English dictionary than I have readily at hand being required to decipher some of them), but it has been a big help. I have revised all of the botanical nomenclature in accordance with Zander where it has been possible to establish the equivalences. Where this has not been possible (because of absence of entry or of cross-reference in Zander) the Latin name as found in the sources has been given in quotes.

1.5. Kinds of evidence other than the linguistic-etymological obviously also have a bearing on the problem of the sources of Indian agriculture. These include:

1. Archaeological and especially paleobotanical evidence for types of economy and technology in a certain time and place and for the presence of particular domestic animals and cultivated plants; for the establishment of priority, not only data from the subcontinent is needed but also data from neighboring and possible source areas (i.e., including the hypothetical Indo-European homeland). Despite more and more accurate methods of dating–first carbon 14 and now its refinement by calibration with tree-ring dates–not everything is beyond dispute in these fields. Archaeologists challenge one another's identifications (especially of minute plant remains), as well as dates and interpretations. There is, in addition, the broader question of whether an animal or plant found at a site is domesticated/cultivated or wild (that is, hunted or gathered) and of what constitutes "domestication."
2. Literary evidence (that is, written records), which may be divided into two kinds, internal and external. The latter would include accounts of observant travelers and newcomers, written in languages foreign to India. (This may present problems in the writer's identification of Indian exotica and/or in his transcription of their names.) They have the advantage of close datability and localizability. Among those relevant for North India

are the accounts of Megasthenes, Hsüan Tsang, Ibn Batuta, and the Emperor Babur. (That acute and accurate observer, Alberuni, was, unfortunately for our purposes, more interested in the humans of Hindustan, and their ideas, than in its fruits and vegetables.) The other category comprises the texts of the Indian literary tradition. Allchin (1969*b*:327-28) remarks that the archaeological evidence so far tends to support the accuracy of the literary record: no mention in early texts means no presence at the early sites. At the same time, we might expect both kinds of literary record, domestic and foreign, to fail to mention some items, especially the humble foodstuffs of the poor. The occurrence of many items only in pharmaceutical catalogs and lexicons and not in earlier texts may be simply due to the fact that beans and spinach are not what high drama or philosophy are made of, or it may reflect a genuine lateness of arrival on the scene. (There is a subtype of literary evidence–*historical* evidence as he would call it–exemplified by someone like Berthold Laufer. By historical evidence he appears to mean not mere mention, but actual discussion, in an ancient text of a product's introduction into a country by a certain agent at a certain date, and the like. China abounds in documents of this kind, but in India they are almost nonexistent before the advent of the Muslims. Thereafter, this kind of evidence is important in India as well, however, down through the British period.)

3. Botanical, paleozoological, and geographic evidence pertaining to the area or areas of domestication of various animals and cultivated plants; that is, the area of distribution (or former distribution, especially in the case of animals) of wild forms, or, if only a domestic or cultivated form is known, of ancestral forms, where these can be established through cytogenetic studies. Here it is important to distinguish primary wild distributions from escapes from cultivation, feral animals, or other secondary distributions by man (e.g., as a weed in his fields). According to one very influential theory (that of Vavilov) the number and distribution of *cultivated varieties* is also of prime importance in establishing sites or centers of domestication.
4. Another kind of evidence, inadequately dealt with here, is the anthropological–the role of an item in the folklore, custom, and ritual of a culture. The subject is fascinating but tricky and must be approached with extreme care and avoidance of premature generalization. It seems plausible that integration into the above-mentioned complexes should mean great antiquity for an item, and lack of such integration its recent introduction, but this is by no means always the case. India shows a remarkable capacity to weave a foreign item into its fabric of legend and ritual very quickly.

Examples are the coconut, according to Basham (1954:193-94), "a comparatively late innovation from Southeast Asia...not mentioned in early sources," and yet playing a key role in popular Hindu ritual, and, more recently, the custard apple (*Annona squamosa*), a native of Mexico and hence presumably introduced in post-Columbian times, yet bearing at least in some parts of India the appellation "Sītā's fruit" (*sītāphal*) and associated in the popular mind with Sītā's nourishment during her exile in the forest with Rāma. Despite such examples, there is probably a limit, a minimum required lapse of time before new items are even accepted as articles of food (put by Watt [1893: vol. 6, p. 3] at no less than fifty years), let alone integrated into folklore and ritual. Some types of ritual (i.e., Vedic) are probably more conservative than others that give a deceptive appearance of primeval timelessness.

1.6. Several larger questions are necessarily involved on the margins of our topic: the homeland and economy of the Indo-Europeans as already touched upon; the origins of pastoralism; the origins–single or multiple–and history of Old World agriculture; the priority of plant and animal domestication; the priority of planting or sowing; the settlement and prehistory of India and its early relations with other areas.

A special issue is one of definitions: "What constitutes 'agriculture'?" For some (e.g., Ho 1975:373), the planting activities characteristic of Southeast Asia (and other tropical areas) are "horticulture," not "agriculture": the latter must involve the raising of cereal crops in large fields and the operation of sowing. Some would go further and require the use of some kind of plow and draft animals.

A related question is that of the distinctions to be made between plants developed versus merely improved by man, between those improved and those merely propagated, and between those propagated and those merely "protected." This entails a scale or cline running all the way from maize, remote from any wild ancestor; hybrid forms such as polyploid wheats; and yams, which have lost the ability to propagate themselves; to various nuts and berries not far removed from the gathering stage. (From this point of view even the tomato is not fully "domesticated" and quickly reverts to the wild.) I shall sidestep these issues here and cast my net wide so as to include, potentially, any plant systematically utilized in the culture to meet man's needs for food, fiber, and certain other purposes (but excluding the medicinal). The different types of utilization can then later be correlated with etymological types to reveal any significant patterns.

There is also, among many methodological issues, the question of the legitimacy of the identification of archaeological "cultures" with known later ethnic groups.

The following main conclusions, deriving from the work of specialists in the ancillary fields mentioned in 1.5 and answering some of the above questions, have a bearing on the general problem of agriculture in India:

1. The primitive Indo-Europeans (or the early Kurgan people) lived mainly by stockbreeding (Gimbutas:157; Littleton:26), especially of cattle and horses, although sheep, goats, and pigs were also known; there is no possibility of their originally domesticating any of these except the horse, which is a late domesticate and could well have come from the Indo-European homeland region (Gimbutas:158; Isaac 1970:93); the spread of the horse is everywhere associated with Indo-European peoples (Drower 1969); and the great numbers of horse bones at early Kurgan sites suggest that at first it was eaten. (For the pig, see 3.10 below.)
2. It is sometimes added that the early Indo-Europeans, being semisettled and not true pastoral nomads, also engaged in simple agriculture; this is based on the find of a few flint sickles as well as grindstones, pestles, and saddle-querns in Kurgan sites north of the Black Sea, and on the existence of the root **ar-* 'plow'; however, the sickles, etc., prove only that grain was utilized—it may have been wild grain; the citation of the root **ar-* again ignores Brandenstein's point in that it is not found in Indo-Iranian (or Anatolian) and therefore possibly is not truly *Proto*-Indo-European; it is generally admitted that "agriculture," if it existed, was very limited (Gimbutas: 171); linguistically, there are many Indo-European terms for cattle but few for grain or grain products; archaeologically, aside from the above-mentioned primitive tools, only a few millet grains have been found in late sites.
3. On the other hand, in the northwestern part of India, prior to the Aryan invasions, there existed the Harappan civilization, based on the extensive cultivation of *wheat and barley* (Fairservis 1975:18).
4. There is, however, no comparison in age of Harappan or pre-Harappan agriculture (third millennium B.C.) with that of the Near East (at least seventh millennium at many sites; beginning possibly in the eighth or ninth millennium, or even earlier at some Palestinian and North Mesopotamian sites: [Mellaart:23-26, 50, 66; Fairservis:391; Isaac:31]).
5. An important area in the later phases of the Near Eastern Neolithic explosion, and the probable area of development of bread wheats and of sheep

and goat domestication, still prior to Harappa, was the region from Afghanistan to southern Central Asia, northwestern Iran, and into Turkey, athwart the Aryan route to India.

6. Meanwhile, a quite different agricultural complex, based on *rice* cultivation, was coming to maturity in the eastern Ganges valley early in the first millennium B.C., that is, considerably later than the Harappan wheat complex and also after the coming of the Aryans; while some of its components point to Southeast Asian affinity, present archaeological evidence indicates that the settlers themselves, who initiated the larger-scale production techniques, were from western India (Fairservis:351-52).
7. Eastern India or adjacent regions of Southeast Asia have been considered the likely home of cultivated rice, particularly since Vavilov, but there was little archaeological evidence to back this up until recently; the earliest finds in the subcontinent were from western India in late-Harappan and contemporary (second millennium B.C.) sites (Lothal, Ahar, Navtadoli); there was a question also whether some of these represented cultivated or wild rice (Vishnu-Mittre 1973:6); Fairservis (p. 380) asserted that by Buddha's time (sixth century B.C.) rice "may have had hardly a thousand years of cultivated history." However, excavations at Chirand in Bihar have yielded domestic rice in strata estimated by Vishnu-Mittre at between 2500 and 3500 B.C. (Vishnu-Mittre:3). Ho (1975:61-73), however, claims priority for China on the basis of finds dated to 4000 B.C. and earlier, abundant reference to wild progenitors along with cultivated rice in earlier Chinese literature (since consciously eliminated, as competitors, from much but not all of the country), and complex rice nomenclature in Chinese. The basis of this is disputed by Watson (1969*b*:398-99). Rice was not introduced to Japan until the second century B.C. (Watson 1969*b*: 397).
8. The long-standing assumption of the diffusion of agriculture in the Old World from one Near Eastern center was challenged by Vavilov's theory of multiple centers of domestication (translated in *Chronica Botanica* 1949-50:vol. 13, pp. 1-6) and challenged further by Sauer's theory of a Southeast Asian fishing-planting cradle for them all (1952:24ff). Many were persuaded, but the former was challenged on ecological-historical grounds (Isaac:52-53) and the latter on archaeological grounds: archaeological evidence from the Near East is far older (in continuous sequence from the Natufian of the twelfth millennium B.C.) and movement of ideas and techniques from Southeast Asia to the Near East would stand alone "against the general flow of the cultural current" in the opposite direction

(Isaac:52-53). To objections that climatic conditions have not been as favorable to preservation of evidence in the tropics as in the dry Near East, Isaac (p. 36) counters that sites in between, via which any influences from Southeast Asia must have passed to reach the Near East (by which I assume he must mean India) are favorable to such preservation and have been excavated, "many of them down to sterile ground," without revealing any such evidence. It would seem obvious, however, that neither Southeast Asia nor India has been excavated to the extent of the Near East, under which circumstances the argument, from lack of evidence, loses some of its weight.

9. The contention of extreme Near Eastern diffusionists is that not only rice domestication but even yam cultivation is the result of the eastward migration of Near Eastern grain-raising peoples (Isaac:55, 65).

10. A new dimension to the argument has been provided by the reports of Gorman (1969, 1970) and Solheim (1970, 1972) on finds at Spirit Cave, Thailand, and other Southeast Asian sites, indicating plant domestication from the tenth millennium B.C. and rice cultivation by the fifth millennium (along with early bronze and even iron), and by Benedict's case (1967) for the borrowing of these cultural terms by Chinese from Thai. More recent excavations have brought additional evidence to light (Arlene Zide, personal communication). Some, however, doubt either the dates or the identifications. J. R. Harlan (Director of the Crop Evaluation Laboratory and professor of plant genetics at the University of Illinois), consulted by Ho (1975:372), comments:

> "If the material was really well preserved one could surely tell a pea from a palm and *Vicia* from *Phaseolus*. The other problem is a strange association of tropical plants with cool-temperature plants adapted to Mediterranean climates (*Pisum* and *Vicia*). The almond also seems out of place along with very tropical species such as *Areca* and *Aleurites*. I do not know of a large-seeded *Phaseolus* in that part of the world, but the material might have been Dolichos (?). The pea/palm suggests the material was an unidentified round seed, but perhaps not much more could be said than that. The case of cultivated plants is based primarily on the leguminous grains, and these are the most suspect of the identifications."

Ho concludes, "What an unbiased scholar can deduce from the reported plant material is intelligent food-gathering–a far cry from agriculture." The Spirit Cave finds and their interpretation aside, there remains a case for agriculture in the area by the fifth millennium B.C. which is significant in its own right.

11. While these battles for priority rage beyond India's frontiers, Vishnu-Mittre (16,1) soberly concludes that the plant economy of ancient India is largely of foreign origin (western Asian, African, Central Asian, and Southeast Asian). "In view of their belated appearance around 2700 B.C., or even if the date is stretched to 3000 B.C., one would be ill-advised to look for the origins of cultivated plants here, as long before this work elsewhere has established that many of our cultivars had already been domesticated and by about this time they were on the way toward diffusion or radiation from the centres of their origin."

12. There remains the question of pastoralism. The old notion, going back to classical antiquity, that the sequence of human development was from hunting to herding to farming, has given way, on the whole, before archaeological and distributional evidence showing that pastoral nomadism is a late development, a kind of spin-off of specialists from mixed farming-stockbreeding cultures as the herds got too large and needed more pastures, that it is everywhere dependent on agriculture and does not develop otherwise among hunters (in, e.g., Australia or North America–reindeer herding being a late and specialized development), and that domestication of herd animals (as against dogs and pigs) was an achievement of sedentary farmers, generally preceded by plant domestication (Isaac:6, 15; Goodenough:258-59). This prevailing view was challenged by Carleton Coon, who claimed that finds of herd animal remains in South Caspian caves (1951/53) without plant evidence indicated herding prior to harvesting of grains. Others are doubtful about the data, or claim that the sites can be interpreted as seasonal camps of herders associated with grain-raising cultures, especially since the affinity of the other artifacts is with the Levant rather than with the steppes. The consensus is that both the distribution of the main herd animals (excluding horses) and the techniques of animal husbandry (including the plow, wagon, etc.) indicate that the complex is to be associated not only with farmers but specifically with Near Eastern farmers, and there is no question in particular that cattle were originally domesticated by farmers (Isaac:46-48). Recent indications that the Natufians of Palestine may have attempted to herd gazelles has a marginal bearing on the priority of plants versus animals (does it indicate simultaneity?) but not on association with sedentary groups.

13. This question has been broached because it has a bearing on the origin of the Indo-Europeans. If stockbreeding groups are specialized offshoots of farming societies, of which farming societies could the Indo-Europeans (or, one should say, the *pre*-Indo-Europeans) have been offshoots? There are two possible candidates, both extensions of the Near Eastern farming complex: the southeast European and the Central Asian. Goodenough prefers the former on the grounds of the present aridity of the Trans-Caspian area; this requires him to reject Gimbutas' interpretation of the archaeological data. Gimbutas (p. 157) assumes different climatic conditions–warmer and wetter. Such conditions, indeed, would have prevailed during the Atlantic period (ca. 5500-3000 B.C. [Friedrich:23]; these dates may have to be moved back along with everything else as a result of tree-ring calibration dating). Littleton (p. 30) emphasizes the fact that the Indo-Europeans were latecomers, adding that "their culture, though unique in many important respects, was in large measure ultimately derived from economic and technological patterns that were several thousand years old in the Near East." If we accept the Indo-Europeans, thus, as specialized offshoots of the older farming culture, the question may have been one of reacquisition from different sources of an agricultural vocabulary that had atrophied rather than of exposure to it for the first time. A few fragments of the earlier stratum may have survived, complicating the picture.
14. Such relearning is not unheard of, in language or in technology. A real possibility in India itself according to Vishnu-Mittre (pp. 15,16), unless gaps in the record are somehow filled in, is the disappearance of various cultivars from the scene and their reintroduction from outside–more than once. We shall have occasion to return to this important point.

2.0 The Tabulated Etymological Data. Leaving more detailed questions for section 3, let us at this point present the data immediately involved in our particular approach. The following conventions are used in the tabulation:

1. For ease of reference, the Hindi terms are presented in the order of the Nāgarī alphabet under each of thirteen topical headings ("Cereals," "Pulses," "Roots," etc.), but numbered consecutively throughout. Cross-references are alphabetized but not numbered.
2. For ease of typing, the transcription uses /n̲/ for nasalized vowels, the appropriate nasal consonant (/n/ or /m/) for *anuswār* on short vowels. This also produces a more readily recognizable word, as does the use of both

/v/ and /w/ according to environment.

3. These transcriptions are followed, in the case of plant names, by the standardized Latin names according to Zander, if obtainable, and by equivalent outmoded Latin names, as found in the sources, in parentheses.
4. Under "Sources," the first Sanskrit etymon given is Turner's unless otherwise indicated. Starred forms given first (as against starred Indo-European and other forms, given later) are likewise Turner's reconstructions on the basis of Modern Indo-Aryan forms (those not actually occurring in Sanskrit or Middle Indic, though often resembling the latter). Final opinions as to the source of the Sanskrit are generally Mayrhofer's, unless otherwise indicated. Personal speculations are rarely offered, but when given are always *preceded* by a question mark.
5. Abbreviations of Sanskrit texts follow Turner's (or Monier-Williams') conventions. These and other abbreviations are as follows:

@	– according to;
AA	– Austroasiatic;
Akk	– Akkadian;
An	– Austronesian;
Apast.	– Āpastamba;
ApSr.	– Āpastamba's *Śrautasūtra*;
Av.	– Avestan;
AV	– *Atharvaveda*;
B	– Burrow 1959;
BhP	– *Bhāgavata Purāṇa*;
Bhpr.	– *Bhāvaprakāśa*;
BHSk.	– Buddhist Hybrid Sanskrit;
Buddh.	– Buddhist literature;
comm.	– commentary;
cw.	– compare with;
DED	– *Dravidian Etymological Dictionary*, by T. Burrow and M. B. Emeneau;
Dhatu.	– *Dhātupāṭha*;
Em.	– Emeneau;
Gaut.	– Gautama's *Dharmaśāstra*;
Gk.	– Greek;
Goth.	– Gothic;
GrS	– *Gṛhya Sūtra*;
GrSrS	– *Gṛhya and Śrauta Sūtra*;

H	–	Hindi;
HCar.	–	*Harṣacarita*;
Hariv.	–	Harivaṃśa;
Heb.	–	Hebrew;
HJ	–	*Hobson-Jobson*, by Col. Henry Yule and A. C. Burnell;
HSS	–	*Hindī Śabdasāgar*, by Syāmsundardās;
Kalid.	–	Kālidāsa;
Kan.	–	Kannada;
Kathas.	–	*Kathāsaritsāgara*;
Katy.	–	Kātyāyana;
KatySr.	–	Kātyāyana *Śrautasūtra*;
Kaus.	–	*Kauśikasūtra*;
Kav.	–	Kāvya literature;
Kol.	–	Kolami;
L	–	found only in Sanskrit lexicographical works, not in texts;
Lat.	–	Latin;
Latv.	–	Latvian;
Lith.	–	Lithuanian;
M	–	Mayrhofer;
MaitrS	–	Maitrāyaṇī Saṁhitā;
Mal.	–	Malayalam;
MBh.	–	*Mahābhārata*;
MGk.	–	Modern Greek;
MIA	–	Middle Indo-Aryan;
Mn.	–	*Mānava Dharmaśāstra*;
MW	–	Monier-Williams;
n.	–	neuter gender;
Nep.	–	Nepali;
NIA	–	Modern Indo-Aryan;
NyayaS	–	*Nyāya Sūtra*;
onom.	–	onomatopoetic;
OPers.	–	Old Persian;
OSl.	–	Old Slavic;
P	–	Pokorny;
Pan.	–	Pāṇini;
Pancat.	–	*Pañcatantra*;
Pancom.	–	Pāṇini commentary;
Pers.	–	Persian;

Pkt.	– Prakrit;
Pl.	– Platts;
Przyl.	– Jean Przyluski (as cited by Mayrhofer);
Ram.	– Rāmāyaṇa;
RV	– *Ṛgveda*;
SadvBr.	– Ṣaḍviṃśa Brāhmaṇa;
SankhGrh.	– *Sāṅkhāyana Gṛhyasūtra*;
Sant.	– Santali;
SB	– *Śatapatha Brāhmaṇa*;
Stn.	– F. Steingass, *Comprehensive Persian-English Dictionary*;
Susr.	– Suśruta;
T	– Turner;
Ta.	– Tamil;
TandBr.	– *Tāṇḍya Brāhmaṇa*;
Te.	– Telugu;
TS	– Taittirīya Saṁhitā;
VarBr.	– Varāhamihira's *Bṛhatsaṁhitā*;
VLat.	– Vulgar Latin;
VS	– *Vājasaneyi Saṁhitā* (White Yajurveda);
WP	– Walde-Pokorny;
Yajn.	– Yājñavalkya;
*	– reconstructed form, not attested;
?	– origin unknown;
??	– doubtful.

ETYMOLOGICAL DATA

Hindi Term	Latin Term for Botanical Items	English Equivalent	Source of Hindi Term
2.1 Cereals and Cereal Products			
1. ANĀJ	–	'grain'	Skt. *annādya-* 'food' (AV), fr. rt. *ad-* 'eat' = IE
2. ĀṬĀ	–	'flour'	Skt. *aṭṭa-* 'food, boiled rice' (L)= Sktized non-Aryan? (M). Some see, despite late (14th c.) attestation, a lone Indian representative of *IE *ar_2- 'grind', (Gk. *aléō* 'grind', Pers. *ārd* 'flour') = ? Sktized Iranian loanword?
3. KAṈGNĪ	*Setaria italica*	'foxtail millet'	*Skt. kaṅgu(nī)-* (NyayaS), fr. ? ?, cf. Gk. *kénkhros*
4. KUṬKĪ	*Panicum sumatrense (P. miliare)*	'little millet; *kutkī*'	Skt. *kuṭakā-* (in Varma; not in M or MW); cw. *kuṭaka-* 'a kind of tree' (Kaus), MW? , fr. ? ?
5. KODOṈ	*Paspalum scrobiculatum*	'kodra millet'	Skt. *kōdrava-* (MBh.), fr. ? ?
6. KHĪL	–	'puffed rice'	cw. H *khilnā* 'to swell', fr. *khiḍ- (T)
7. GEHŪṈ	*Triticum aestivum; T. durum*	'wheat'	Skt. *gōdhū́ma-* 'cow smoke' (= pop. etym.?) (VS); cf. Pers. *gandum*; confined to Indo-Iranian
8. CAPĀTĪ	–	'thin flour cake'	Skt. *carpaṭī* (L), fr. *carpaṭa-* 'palm of hand; thin flour cake' (L), cw. **carpa-* 'flat'; cf. *parpaṭa-* 'a thin cake made of rice or pease-meal and baked in grease' (L), MW;

9.	CĀ(Ṇ)WAL	*Oryza sativa*	'rice(husked)'	@ Pl., fr. Persian = ? Persianized? , cf. *-t-*; fr. Drav.? M? **cāmala/cāvalā*, fr. Drav.(Bloch)? cf. Ta. *aval* 'pestled rice', Kol. *cavli* 'mortar'
10.	CENĀ/CĪNĀ	*Panicum miliaceum*	'common millet'	Skt. *cīnaka-* (Hemadri), fr. *cīnā-* 'China'(Mn.)
	janerā (E.), see *junhār*			
11.	JUNHĀR	*Sorghum cernuum (S. vulgare, Andropogon sorghum, Holcus s.)*	'sorghum, great millet, jowar'	Skt. *yavanala-* (Susr.); @M, fr. *yavana-* 'foreign, Western'
12.	JWĀR/JUWĀR	" "	" "	(anal. **yavākāra-* 'barley-shaped'? [T,MW]); see no. 11
13.	JAU	*Hordeum vulgare*	'barley'	Skt. *yáva-* 'barley', fr. 'grain'(RV), fr. *IE **yewo-*
14.	DHĀN	*Oryza sativa*	'rice(unhusked or as crop)	Skt. *dhānyá-* 'rice'(Susr.), fr. 'grain'(RV) = IE
15.	BĀJRĀ	*Pennisetum glaucum (P. typhoideum)*	'pearl or bulrush millet'	**bājjara-*, fr. ? ?
16.	BHĀT	–	'boiled rice'	Skt. *bhaktá-* (n.) 'food'(RV), rt. *bhaj-* 'partake', fr. IE
17.	MA(Ṇ)ṚŪA	*Eleusine coracan(a)*	'finger millet, ragi'	Skt. *maḍaka-, maṭṭaka-* (L), fr. ? ?
18.	MAKĀĪ/MAKKĀ	*Zea mays*	'maize, Amer. corn'	Skt. *markaka- 'Ardea argala'*(L), fr. ? ?
19.	MAIDĀ	–	'white flour; fine flour'	fr. Pers.
20.	ROṬĪ	–	'bread'	Skt. *roṭikā-* (Bhpr.), fr. ? ?
21.	LĀĪ/LĀWĀ	–	'parched rice'	Skt. *lāja-* (VS), not in M; fr. ? ?
22.	SĀṆWĀṆ	*Echinochloa frumentacea (Panicum frumentaceum)*	'barnyard millet, sawa-millet'	Skt. *śyāmāka-* (VS), fr. *śyāma-* 'black, dark' (? fr. IE)

Hindi Term		Latin Term for Botanical Items	English Equivalent	Source of Hindi Term
23.	SŪJĪ	–	'farina, semolina'	**sūjjī* **sōjjī* (in most NIA vernaculars), fr. ? ?
24.	SELĀ	–	'rice parboiled in the husk'	Pl.: prob. Skt. *śāli-* 'rice' (MBh.), fr. ? ?
25.	SĀL	*Oryza sativa*	'rice (growing)'	Skt. *śāli-* 'rice' (MBh.), fr. ? ?
26.	SEVAIṆ	–	'vermicelli'	Skt. *sevikā-* (BhP) = Skt-ized NIA? , "*Junge Kulturwortsippe*" (M)
2.2	*Pulses*			
27.	ARHAR/ARHAṚ	*Cajanus cajan* (*C. indicus*, *C. bicolor*)	'purple-veined pigeon pea'	Skt. *adhakī́* (Susr.)? cf. *ādhaka-* 'a measure of grain' (Pan.); rel. of H to Skt. (T) and origin of Skt. (M) unclear
28.	UR(A)D	*Phaseolus mungo* (*P. radiatus*, *Dolichos pilosos*)	'black gram'	**uḍidda*
	kisārī, see *khesārī*			
29.	KULTHĪ	*Dolichos biflorus*	'horsegram'	Skt. *kulatthikā-* (Susr.), Zide and Zide (1976:1313): probably fr. Munda **kodaXj*; vs. M (vol. 1, pp. 237, 565): dissim. fr. **kulakkha*, fr. Drav. **kolakku*; cf. DED 1790
30.	KHESĀRĪ	*Lathyrus sativus*	'chicklingvetch'	**k(h)esārī*; T: cf. *kṛsará*

				'dish of rice, peas, etc.' (MBh.)? ; not cw. *kḗsara-* 'hair' by T or M
31.	G(A)WĀR/GUĀR	*Cyamopsis tetragonoloba* (*C. psoralioides*) (*Dolichos fabaeformis*)	'cluster bean'	Pkt. *govālī* 'kind of creeper'; Skt. *gopālī* 'kind of cucumber' (L), cw. ? *gopālá-* 'cowherd'?
32.	CANĀ	*Cicer arietinum*	'chickpea, (Bengal) gram'	Skt. *caṇa(ka)-* (MBh., Susr.) 'not satisf. expl.' (M), Drav.? cf. Te. *senagalu, Parji* cenaya
33.	CAULĀ (CAULĪ?)	(*Dolichos sinensis*) = *boṛā* *Cicer arietinum* = *caṅā* (Panjab, Bengal) *Vigna sinensis s.* = *lobiyā*	'kind of bean'	"*Desī*" (HSS)
34.	TU(W)AR/TOR	*Cajanus cajan* = *arhar*? (*Cajanus indicus flavus*) (*Cytisus cajanus*)	'yellow pigeon pea'	Skt. *tubarī* (L), prob. fr. Drav., cf. Ta. *tuvarai*
35.	DĀNĀ	–	'grain; seed'	fr. Persian
36.	DĀL	–	'split pulse'	*_dāla_ 'splitting', cw. *dāra-* 'rent, hole', *dārayati* 'rends asunder', fr. IE
37.	PHALĪ	–	'pod'	fr. *phal* 'fruit' (q.v.)
38.	BĀKLĀ	a. *Phaesolus vulgaris* *(Faba sativa)* b. *Vicia faba*	'haricot bean, navy bean, pole bean' 'broad bean, Euopean bean'	fr. Persian, fr. Arabic *bāqlā*
39.	BESAN	–	'gram flour'	Pkt. *veṣana* 'cumin seed; pea flour', fr. Skt. *vēsana-* 'flour of a particular vegetable product'(Bhpr.)

	Hindi Term	Latin Term for Botanical Items	English Equivalent	Source of Hindi Term
40.	BOṚĀ	(*Dolichos sinensis*)	'kind of bean'	Skt. *barbaṭa-/varvaṭa-* (L), fr. Drav.? ; cf. Te. *bobbara* = 'uncertain' (M)
	bhaṭnās (HSS), see *bhaṭmāṣ*			
41.	BHAṬMĀṢ	*Glycine max*	'soybean'	/? *bhaṭ-*, cw. *bhuṭ-/bhoṭ-* 'Bhutan; Tibet'? + *māṣa-* 'bean'; cf. Ho 1975:60
	bhaṭwaṇs, see *bhaṭmāṣ*			
42.	MAṬAR	*Pisum sativum*	'common garden pea'	**maṭṭara*
43.	MAŚŪR(Ī)	*Lens culinaris* (*L. esculenta, Cicer lens*)	'lentil'	Skt. *masū́ra(kā/ikā)-* (VS), "probably non-Aryan" (M)
44.	MĀŚ/MĀṢ/MĀH	*Phaseolus mungo* (=*urd*), (etc.)	'black gram'	Skt. *māṣa* 'bean' (RV); cf. Pers. *māsh* 'vetch, pea'; "probably a wandering culture-word" (M)
45.	MŪṆG	*Phaseolus aureus* (*P. mungo*)	'green gram, moong, mungo beans'	Skt. *mudga-* (VS), "no convincing explanation" (M)
46.	MOṬH	*Phaseolus aconitifolius*	'kind of kidney bean, Germ. *Mattenbohne*'	Skt. *mukuṣṭha* (L, BHSk.), fr. ??, M: cf. Mundari *mugi*
	rahar(ī), rāhari, see *arhar*			
47.	RAH(I)LĀ	*Cicer arietinum* (=*canā*)	'gram, chickpea'	**rahala* 'a kind of pulse'
48.	LOBIYĀ	*Vigna sinensis sinensis* (*V. catiang*)	'cowpea, blackeyed pea'	fr. Pers. *lūbiyā*
49.	SEM	a. *Dolichos lablab* b. *Vicia faba* (=*bāklā*) c. *Phaseolus vulgaris*	'field bean' 'broad bean' 'haricot bean'	Skt. *śaimbya* (Katy Sr. comm.); cw. *śimba* 'pod, legume' (Susr.), prob. non-

		(*P. magnus*)		Aryan (M); Drav. ?

2.3. Roots, Bulbs , and Tubers

50.	ARUĪ/ARVĪ	*Colocasia esculenta* (*C. antiquorum, Arum colocasia*)	'arum, taro, Indian yam'	Skt. *ālukī-* (BhP) 'species of root', fr. *ālu-* 'root of *Amorphophallus campanulatum*' (L), fr. IE **ālu-* 'edible root'
51.	ĀLŪ	a. *Solanum tuberosum* (*S. esculentum*)	'potato'	Skt. *ālu(ka)-* (L); see no. 50
		b. *Amorphophallus campanulatum* (*Arum campanulatum*)	'telinga potato'	
52.	KACĀLŪ *(=aruī?)*	*Colocasia esculenta*	'a kind of arum or taro'	H *kac-* 'crude'? + *ālū*
53.	GANDNĀ	*Allium porrum*	'leek'	fr. Pers.
54.	GĀJAR	*Daucus carota*	'carrot'	Skt. *gārjara-* (L); cw. *garjara-* 'a kind of grass' (L)? ; neither attested in lit., origins unclear
55.	GHUIYĀṆ *(=aruī?)*	—	'a kind of yam or taro'	? ?
56.	CUKANDAR	*Beta vulgaris*	'beetroot'	fr. Pers. (HSS:1012); *čukundur*, *čug̱hundur* (Stn.: 397a, 396a)
57.	ZAMĪNKAND (-QAND)	*Amorphophallus campanulatum*	'telinga potato' 'a kind of sweet potato'	fr. Pers. *zamīn* 'ground' + H *kand* 'bulbous root',or + Arab.-Pers. *qand* 'sugar candy'
58.	PIYĀJ/PIYĀZ	*Allium cepa*	'onion'	fr. Pers.
59.	MŪLĪ	*Raphanus sativus*	'radish'	Skt. *mūla-* 'radish' (Mn.), 'root' (RV), non-Aryan? ;

	Hindi Term	Latin Term for Botanical Items	English Equivalent	Source of Hindi Term
				cf. Ta. *mula* (DED 4105), Sant. *mula*; Korean *mu* 'radish'
60.	RATĀLŪ	(*Dioscorea sativa*) (*Typhonium frilobatum*)	'potato-yam'	Skt. *raktālu* '*Dioscorea purpurea*' (L); *-ka* (Susr.). fr. *rakta-* + *ālu* = 'red tuber'
61.	LA(H)SUN/ LAHSAN	*Allium sativum*	'garlic'	Skt. *laśuna-* (Gaut.), fr. ? ? , could be *IE because of *-una-* (M)
62.	ŚAṈKHĀRU/ ŚAṈJHĀLU	*Pachyrrhizus erosus* (*P. angulatus*)	'yam-bean'	? Skt. *śaṅka-* 'conch'? + *ālu* 'tuber'
	śankhakand, see *śankhāru*			
63.	ŚAKARKAND/ SAKARKAND/ ŚAKARQAND	*Ipomoea batatas* (*Convolvulus batatas*)	'sweet potato'	H *sakar/śakar* + *kand* = 'sugar root' (see commentary to this section, 3.3)
64.	ŚALGAM/ ŚALJAM	*Brassica rapa*	'turnip'	fr. Pers. *shalgham*
	sāṉk, see *śankhāru*			
65.	SUTHNĪ/SŪTHNĪ	*Dioscorea bulbifera* "*Dioscorea fasciculata*"?	'another kind of yam'	? ?
66.	SŪRAN	*Amorphophallus campanulatum* ("*Arum campanulatum*")	'giant or elephant's foot taro' (?)	Skt. *sūraṇa-* 'telinga potato' (MW) (HCar., Susr.), fr. ? ?
67.	ŚIMLĀ ĀLŪ	*Manihot esculenta* (*M. utilissima*)	'manioc, cassava, tapioca'	H 'tuber from Simla'

2.4. *CUCURBITS*

68.	KAK(A)ṚĪ	*("Cucumis utilissimus")*	'kind of cucumber; long melon; vegetable marrow'	Skt. *karkaṭī* (L); cf. *karkaru* 'kind of gourd', fr. IE? (WP)
69.	KAD(D)Ū	*Lagenaria siceraria (L. vulgaris, Cucurbita lagenaria)*	'calabash; bottle gourd; SPD: a gourd or pumpkin'	Pl.: prob. Skt. *kaṭu-* 'sharp, bitter' (@T, RV; @MW, MBh.); M: prob. fr. Pkt. **kṛt* 'cuts' = IE; but cf. Drav. (DED 952), e.g., Ta. *kaṭu- (-pp-, -tt-)* 'throb with pain, be pungent; bitterness, pungency'; cognates in all Drav. languages (Brahui *kẖarēn*, Malto *qaṟqe*, etc.)
70.	KARELĀ/ KARAILĀ	*Momordica charantia*	'bitter gourd'	Skt. *kāravēlla* (Susr.); "probably non-Aryan plant name" (M)
71.	KUṈDARŪ	*Coccinia cordifolia*	'ivy gourd'	Skt. *kunduru* 'olibanum' (VarBr.), fr. *kunda-* 'jasmine', fr. ? ?
72.	KUMHṚĀ/ KOṈHṚĀ	*Cucurbita pepo*	'pumpkin; squash'	MIA *komh-* fr. non-Aryan (prob. AA); also yields (Neo-)Skt. *kuṣmāṇḍha-* 'pumpkin gourd' (MBh.) = *Benincasa hispida* (*B. cerifera*)
73.	KHARBŪJĀ/ KHARBŪZĀ	*Cucumis melo*	'muskmelon'	fr. Pers.
74.	KHĪRĀ	*Cucumis sativus*	'cucumber'	Skt. *kṣīraka* 'name of a

Hindi Term	Latin Term for Botanical Items	English Equivalent	Source of Hindi Term
			fragrant plant' (L); cw. *kṣīra-* 'thickened milk' (RV), fr. ? ?
75. GHIYĀ = *kaddū*?	*Lagenaria siceraria*?	'bottle gourd; pumpkin'	NIA, fr. ? ?
76. GHIYĀTURAĪ/ GHIYĀTORĪ	?	'sponge gourd' (Bulcke)	H *ghiyā* 'gourd' + *torī* 'gourd'
77. CICIṆḌĀ/ CICIṚĀ	*Trichosanthes cucumerina, var. anguina* (*T. anguina*)	'snake gourd'	Neo-Skt. (16th c.), fr. NIA, fr. ? ?
78. ṬIṆḌĀ	("*Diospyros melonoxylon*") See commentary, 3.4	'round gourd, squash melon'	Skt. *tinduka-* ('*Diospyros embryopteris*'), fr. ? ?
79. TARBŪJ/ TARBŪZ	*Citrullus lanatus* (*Cucurbita citrullus*)	'watermelon'	fr. Pers.
80. TOMṚĀ	*Lagenaria siceraria*	'dried bottle gourd'	Skt. *tumba-* (Susr.), fr. AA ?
81. TURAĪ/TORAĪ	*Luffa acutangula*	'ribbed or ridged gourd'	**tōrī* 'gourd'
82. PARWAL	(*Trichosanthes dioeca*)	'pointed gourd'	Skt. *paṭōla* (Susr.), fr. Drav. (B)
83. PEṬHĀ	*Benincasa hispida*	'ash gourd'	? ?
84. PHŪ(Ṇ)Ṭ	(*Cucumis momordica*)	'kind of melon which bursts when ripe'	cw. Skt. *sphuṭ-* 'burst', fr. IE
85. LAU(K)Ā/-Ī	*Lagenaria siceraria*	'bottle gourd'	Skt. *alābu* (AV, Susr.), fr. AA

2.5. Other Vegetables, Including Greens

Hindi Term	Latin Term for Botanical Items	English Equivalent	Source of Hindi Term
86. AMBĀṚĪ	*Hibiscus cannabinus*	'rozella, red sorrel, Deccan hemp'; also 'hogplum'	Skt. *āmrātaka-* 'hogplum' (MBh.), fr. *amla-* 'sour'
87. KARAMKALLĀ	*Brassica oleracea capitata*	'cabbage'	fr. Pers. *karamb* 'cabbage'

	(=bandgobhī)			+ *kallā* 'head'
88.	KĀF(I)RĪ MIRC *(=simlā mirc)*	*Capsicum annuum (C. grossum)*	'bell pepper, capsicum'	fr. Pers. *kāfirī* 'infidel' + H *mirc* 'pepper'
89.	KĀSNĪ	*Cichorium endiva*	'endive, escarole'	fr. Pers.
		Cichorium intybus	'chicory'	
90.	KĀHŪ	*Lactuca sativa*	'lettuce'	fr. Pers.
	kobī, see *gobhī*			
91.	GOBHĪ	"*Elephantophus scaber*" (Pl.)	'a medicinal herb'	(Neo-?) Skt. (no Pali or Pkt.) *gōjihvikā* 'cowtongue' (Susr.)
	(a) BANDGOBHĪ	*Brassica oleracea captiva*	'cabbage'	fr. Pers. *band* 'closed' + *gobhī*
	(b) PHŪLGOBHĪ	*Brassica oleracea botrytis*	'cauliflower'	fr. H *phūl* 'flower' + *gobhī*
92.	CŪKĀ/COKĀ	*Rumex vesicarius* (*R. montanus*)	'Indian sorrel'	Skt. *cukra-* 'sour, sharp to taste' (Susr.), "name of var. sharp-tasting plants, e.g., sorrel" (L); late deriv. fr. **kuc-* 'draw together, pucker'?
93.	CAULĀĪ	*Amaranthus paniculatus*?	'(tender) amaranth'	**catūrāji* 'having four lines' ? ; HSS: *cau* 'four' + *rāī* 'seed'
	(a) LĀL C.	*Amaranthus tricolor?* (*A. polygamus, A. polygonoides*)	'red amaranth'	
94.	ṬAMĀṬAR	*Lycopersicon lycopersicum*	'tomato'	fr. English
95.	TARKĀRĪ	–	'general term for *vegetables*'	fr. Pers. *tarah* 'potherbs',

Hindi Term		Latin Term for Botanical Items	English Equivalent	Source of Hindi Term
				fr. *tar* 'fresh, tender'
96.	PĀLAK	*Spinacea oleracea*	'spinach'	Pkt. *pālakkā* 'kind of spinach', fr. Skt. *pālakyā*, 'leafy beet' (*Caraka*, L), fr. ? ?
97.	POĪ	*Basella alba* (*B. rubra*)	'Malabar spinach, M. nightshade, Indian spinach'	Skt. *pōtikā, pautikī* (Susr.), *pūtikā* (L) '*Basella*', fr. ? *pūtīka* 'plant used in place of Soma' (SB), fr. ? ; cf. *pūti-* 'purification', *pūtika-*, 'foul, stinking'? ; Iranian cognates
98.	BATHUĀ	*Chenopodium album*	'lamb's-quarters, pigweed, goosefoot'	Skt. *vāstuka-* (Susr.); cw. *vāstu* 'site of house' (IE) = 'yard-weed'?
	bilāetī baigan, see *tamāṭar*			
99.	BAI(Ṉ)GAN	*Solanum melongena*	'eggplant'	fr. MIA (Pali) *vātiṅgaṇa* (L); probably a non-Aryan plant name" (M)
100.	BHAṆṬĀ	*Solanum melongena*	'eggplant (round variety)'	Skt. *bhaṇṭākī* (L); same origin as above (M)
101.	BHIṆḌĪ	*Abelmoschus esculentus* (*Hibiscus esculentus*)	'okra, ladyfinger'	Skt. *bhiṇḍā-* (Pancat., L), fr. ? ?
102.	MAKO(Y)	a. *Solanum nigrum*	'common or black nightshade'	PL.: prob. Skt. *mārkava-;* M: *Eclipta prostrata,* fr. ? ? (see

		b.*Physalis peruviana*	'Cape gooseberry ground-cherry'	commentary, 3.5)
103.	MARSĀ	*Amaranthus caudatus*? (*A. gangeticus, A. oleraceus*)	'Gangetic amaranth'	Pl.: Skt. *mārṣa/mariṣaka-*; M: 'a worthy man'? ?
	māṭ(h), see *marsā*			
104.	REWATCĪNĪ/ REBANDCĪNĪ	*Rheum rhaponticum, R. emodi, R. ribes, R. palmatum*	'rhubarb'	fr. Pers. *revand/rivand* 'rhubarb' + *cīnī* 'Chinese'
105.	SABZĪ	–	'general term for *vegetables*'	fr. Pers. *sabz* 'green; fresh'
106.	SAH(I)(Ṉ)-JAṈ(Ā)	*Moringa oleifera* (*M. pterygosperma, M. hyperanthera*)	'drumstick tree, horse-radish tree'	Skt. *śōbhāñjana* (MBh.); cw *?śōbhā-* 'splendor' + *? añjana* 'ointment'
107.	SĀG	–	'general term for *pot-herbs, greens*'	Skt. *śaka-* (GrS); cw. IE? (Lith. *šėkas* 'freshcut fodder, etc.')
108.	SINGHĀṚĀ	*Trapa natans* (*T. bispinosa*)	'water chestnut'	Skt. *śṛṅgāṭa* (L)/*-ṭi* (Susr.)/*-ṭaka* (MBh.); "unclear, probably foreign" (M)
	simlā mirc, see *kāfirī mirc*			
109.	HĀLIM *(=caṉsur)*	*Lepidium sativum* (Pl., HSS)	'garden cress' (HSS and BHK: plant whose seeds are used in medicine)	@HSS: "Deśī"

2.6. Oilseeds, Fibers, Dyestuffs, Stimulants, and Intoxicants

110.	APHĪM/AFĪM	–	'opium'	Pl.: Skt. *ahi* 'snake' + *phena* 'froth, saliva' (L, also MW), or *a-* 'neg.' + *phena* = 'frothless' (L, MW); vs. Pers. which is *afyūn*
111.	ALSĪ (=*tīsī*)	*Linum usitatissimum*	'linseed'	Skt. *atasī* 'flax' (Susr.); cw. *ataśa-* 'bush' (RV), fr. ? ?

Hindi Term	Latin Term for Botanical Items	English Equivalent	Source of Hindi Term
112. ĀL	*Morinda citrifolia*	'a root from which a red dye is obtained'	**allā*
113. KAPĀS	*Gossypium herbaceum*	'cotton (plant, or in pod)'	Skt. *karpāsa* (Susr.), prob. from AA (M)
114. KAPŪR	*Cinnamomum camphorum*	'camphor'	Skt. *karpūra-* (Susr.) prob. fr. AA (M); MW derives from *kṛp-* 'mourn'
115. KUSUM	*Carthamus tinctorius*	'safflower'	Skt. *kusumbha-* (Susr.); 'saffron' (L), fr. ? ?
116. KHASKHAS	*Papaver somniferum*	'poppy seed'	fr. Pers. *xasxāsh*; but cf. H *khas-khas* 'dry rattling sound'–onom.)
117. KHAIR	*Acacia catechu*	'catechu (ingredient in *pan*)'	Skt. *khadira-* (RV); cw. ? *khādati* 'chews'?
118. GĀ̱NJĀ (see also *bhā̱ng, san*)	*Cannabis sativa*	'cultivated hemp'	Skt. *gañjā-* (L), fr. Sumerian? (T)
119. TAMBĀKŪ	*Nicotiana tabacum*	'tobacco'	evid. via Persian (see commentary 3.6.)
120. TĀṚ	*Borassus fl. bellifer* (*B. flabelliformis*)	'toddy-palm, palmyra'	**tāḍa*, fr. *tāla*, fr. *hintāla* 'marshy date plam' (Hariv.) ? ; but cf. Drav. (Kan.) *tāṛ* (Te.) *tāḍu*, etc. (DED 2599)
121. TIL	*Sesamum indicum* (*S. orientale*)	'sesame'	Skt. *tila-* (AV)"not a satisfactory explanation, perhaps non-Aryan" (M)
122. TĪSĪ, see *alsi*			
123. TOṚĪ/TOṚIYĀ	*Brassica rapa silvestris*	'mustard/rape-seed (for oil)'	**trōṭikā-*; cf. *truṭi* 'small cardamom' (L)? ; cw. *truṭati* 'breaks, splits' = non-Aryan @M

	nariyal, see "Fruits and Nuts," 2.8.			
124.	PĀN	*Piper betle*	'betel leaf'	Pali *paṇṇa*, fr. Skt. *parṇa-* 'wing, feather, leaf' (RV); cw. IE **per-* 'fly'
125.	POSTĀ	*Papaver somniferum*	'opium poppy; poppy capsule'	fr. Pers. *pūst* 'skin, rind, shell'
126.	BINAURĀ/ BINAULĀ/ BINOLĀ	*Gossypium herbaceum*	'cotton seed (esp. as food for cattle)'	**vīnōpala*? , fr. **vīna* 'woven' + *úpala* 'stone' ? ? ; @Pl.: fr. *vaṅga* 'Bengal' + *guḍaka/golaka* 'ball'
127.	BHĀṈG	*Cannabis indica*?	'wild hemp; leaves of hemp'	Skt. *bhaṅgá-* (AV); "a perhaps very old culture-word" (M)–Indo-Iranian ? IE?
128.	MAHUĀ	*Bassia latifolia*	'mahua'	Skt. *madhuka-* (SankGrh.), fr. *madhu* 'honey' (RV), fr. IE
129.	MEṈHDĪ/ MEHAṈDĪ	*Lawsonia inermis* (*L. alba*) *Melaleuca viridiflora*?	'henna' 'myrtle'	Skt. *mēndhī/-ikā* (L), fr. ? ?
130.	MŪṈGPHAḺĪ (= *vilāetī mūṉg*)	*Arachis hypogaea*	'peanut, groundnut'	fr. H *mūṉg* 'kind of pulse' + *phalī* 'pod'
131.	RŪĪ	–	'cotton wool (carded and cleaned)'	**rū-a*, fr. /**rūca*; cw. Pkt. *ruṁcai* 'cards cotton'? ; cw. **rōñc-* 'crush, press in' ?
132.	REṈṚ (*=aṉṛaṛ*)	*Ricinus communis*	'castor-oil plant'	Skt. *ēraṇḍa-* (Susr.); "foreign" (@M)
133.	LĪL/NĪL	*Indigofera tinctoria*	'indigo plant'	Skt. *nīla-* 'dark, blue, black' (RV); @M prob. fr. **nī-* 'sparkle, shine' (cf. *nayanam, netram* 'eyes'), w. IE cognates
134.	SAN	*Crotalaria juncea*	'fiber hemp'	Skt. *sáṇá-* (AV, SB); "old culture-

	Hindi Term	Latin Term for Botanical Items	English Equivalent	Source of Hindi Term
		(also *Cannabis sativa*)	'Bengal hemp'	word" (M); fr. IE? Uralic? Drav.? (B)
135.	SARSOṈ	*Brassica rapa*? *Sinapis alba alba*?	'mustard (incl. oil)'	Skt. *sarṣápa-* (SadvBr.); "a non-IE culture-word" (@M), despite Pers. *sipandān*, Gk. *sinā́pi*, Germ. *Senf*, etc.; Burrow: Austronesian-Austroasiatic; "others skeptical"
136.	SUPĀRĪ	*Areca cathechu*	'betel nut'	**suppāra*
137.	SŪTĪ	–	'cotton (cloth)'	'made of thread', fr. Skt. *sūtra-* 'thread' (AV), fr. IE **siu* 'sew'
2.7. Citrus				
138.	KHAṬṬĀ (= *galgal*? BHK)	*Citrus aurantium*?	'the bitter or Seville orange'? 'wild orange'?	H *khaṭṭā* 'sour'
139.	GALGAL	*Citrus medica sarcodactylis* (*C. medica citron*)	'citron' (Bul., SPD) 'kind of lemon (SPD vol. 2)'	? cw. Skt. *gal-* 'drip, swallow' ?
140.	CAKOTARĀ (= *mahā-nīṃbu, bātāvī-nīṃbu*)	*Citrus maxima* (*C. decumana*)	'pomelo, shaddock'	? ?
141.	JAMBĪR	*Citrus limon* (*C. medica limonum*)	'lemon'	Skt. *jambhīra-* (L, Buddh.); "non-Aryan" (M)
142.	TURANJ	*Citrus medica sarcodactylis* (*C. medica citron*)	'citron' (@Bul., Pl., Miller); @Pl. also 'orange'; @BHK = *cakotara*	fr. Pers. *turunj* 'citron'; @Pl., this is from Skt. *taraṅga-* 'wrinkle, wave' via Arabic (? ?)
143.	NĀRANGĪ (NĀRANJ)	*Citrus sinensis* (*C. aurantium*)	'sweet orange (tight-skinned)'	Skt. *nāraṅga-* (Susr., L, etc.); "probably a vernacular expression" (M); @ Caldwell, Kittel, Gundert: fr. Drav. *nāram* 'fragrant' + *kāy* 'unripe fruit'

144.	NĪM̱BŪ/NĪM̱Ū/ NĪM̱BU	*Citrus aurantifolia*	'(sour) lime'	Skt. *nimbūka-* (L), fr. NIA? , fr. AA or AN? (M) (Drav. also fr. AA or AN)
	(a) *pahāṛī nīm̱bu* (= *jambir*)		(lemon)	H *pahāṛī* 'pertaining to the Hills' + *nīmbu*
	(b) *baṛā nīm̱bu* (= *jambīr*)		(lemon)	H *baṛā* 'large' + *nīmbu*
	(c) *bātāvī nīm̱bu* (= *cakotarā*)		(pomelo)	H *bātāvī* 'pertaining to Batavia (Jakarta) in Java'
	(d) *mahānīmbu* (= *cakotarā*)		(pomelo)	H/Skt. *mahā-* 'great' + *nīmbu*
	(e) *mīṭhā nīm̱bu* (= *mausambī*)	*C. limetta*	(sweet lime)	H *mīṭhā* 'sweet' + *nīmbu*
145.	BIJAURĀ (BHK = *bījapūr*)	?	@Bul. 'citron' @BHK, 'a citrus the size of a large orange'	? cw. H *bījār, bijālā* 'abounding in seeds' (Pl.); or ? cw. Bijapur, Deccan ?
146.	MUSAMMĪ/ MAUSAMBĪ *(=mīṭhā nīm̱bu)*	*Citrus limetta* (*C. Medica limetta*)	'sweet lime'	fr. "Moçambique"
	līmū, līmbū, see *nīm̱bu*			
147.	SANTARĀ/ SAṈGTARĀ	*Citrus sinensis v.* (also ?) *C. deliciosa* *C. reticulata*	'loose-skinned orange' 'tangerine' ? 'mandarin orange' ?	via Pers. *sangtarā*, ult. fr. *Cintra*, the "Rock of Lisbon" famous for this variety in the Middle Ages

2.8. Other Fruits and Nuts

148.	AKHROṬ/ AXROṬ	a. *Juglans regia* b. *Aleurites moluccana* (*A. triloba*)	'(Persian) walnut' 'country walnut or candlenut'	Skt. *akṣōṭa* (Susr., Kalid.); non-Aryan (Iranian ?) (M)
149.	ANGŪR	*Vitis vinifera*	'grape'	fr. Pers.
150.	ANJĪR	*Ficus carica* (*F. oppositifolia*)	'fig'	Skt. *añjīra-*, but also = Pers. *anjīra*; M: an Iranian loanword (in Skt.); T: Hindi, prob. direct fr. Pers.

Hindi Term		Latin Term for Botanical Items	English Equivalent	Source of Hindi Term
151.	ANĀR	*Punica granatum*	'pomegranate'	fr. Pers.
152.	AMRŪD, see also *bihī*	*Psidium guajava* (*P. pyriferum, P. pomiferum*)	'guava'	fr. Pers. (= 'pear')
153.	ĀṚŪ (= *saftālū*)	*Prunus persica*	'peach; nectarine'	**āḍu*; T: perhaps cw. an **arduda*, cw. Pahlavi *ālūd* 'plum' (T:1103)
154.	ĀT(Ā) (= *sītāphal, sarīfā*)	a. *Annona squamosa*	'custard apple'	fr. Mexican *ahate/até* prob. via Filipino *ate* (HJ:285)
		b. *Annona reticulata*	'sweetsop; bullock's-heart'	
155.	ĀLŪCĀ	*Prunus domestica* (*P. ovalifolia*)	'plum'	fr. Pers. *ālučah* 'kind of berry, small plum', dimin. fr. *ālū* 'plum'
156.	ĀLŪBĀLŪ	a. *Prunus cerasus*	'(sour) cherry'	fr. Pers.
		b. + *Prunus ceracifera* ?	'cherry plum; myrobalan'	
157.	ĀLŪBUKHĀRĀ	*Prunus domestica*	'dried plum, prune'	fr. Pers. *ālū* 'plum' + *Buxārā* 'city in Central Asia'
158.	ĀM(B)	*Mangivera indica*	'mango'	Pkt. *amba* fr.Skt. *āmra* (MBh.,SB)
159.	ĀMLĀ	*Phyllanthus emblica*	'emblic myrobalan'	Skt. *amlaka-*
160.	IMLĪ/AMLĀ	*Tamarindus indica*	'tamarind'	Skt. *āmlā/āmlīkā* (L) Nos. 158, 159, 160 app. fr. Skt. *amla-* 'sour, bitter' (Mns), fr. IE (Lat. *amārus*, etc.)
161.	KAṬAHAL	*Artocarpus heterophylla* (*A. integrifolia*)	'jackfruit'	fr. Skt. *kaṇṭakaphala* (L) = 'thorn' + 'fruit'
162.	KĀJŪ	*Anacardium occidentale*	'cashew'	prob. fr. Portuguese (fr. Amer-indian)
163.	KIŚMIŚ	–	'raisin (dried grape)'	fr. Pers.
164.	KELĀ	*Musa paradisiaca* (*M. sapientum*)	'banana'	Skt. *kadala(ka)/-i* (MBh.,Susr.); prob. AA (M)
165.	KAITH(Ā)	*Limonia acidissima* (*Feronia elephantum*)	'wood apple'	Skt. *kapittha-* (MBh.);@M "prob. Drav.; however, Ta. *veḷḷil*, Mal.

				viḻā, Kan. *beḷala*, Te. *velāga* (DED 4535) show no connection with this; Drav. appears to be source (T:9248) of Skt. *bilva-*, name of a related species, also often translated 'wood apple'; see *bel*, no. 180
166.	KHAJŪR	a. *Phoenix dactylifera* b. *P. sylvestris*	'date' 'wild date'	Skt. *kharjūra-* (TS,Kathas), fr. ?
167.	KHŪBĀNĪ	–	'dried apricot'	fr. Pers. *xūbānī*
168.	CĪLŪ	*Prunus armeniaca*	'apricot'	? ?
169.	ZARDALU	*Prunus armeniaca*	'apricot'	fr. Pers. *zard* 'yellow' + *ālū* 'plum'
170.	JĀMUN/JĀMAN	a. *Syzygium jambos* (*Eugenia jambolana*) b. *Syzygium cumini* (*Syzygium jambolanum*)	'rose apple' 'jambolana plum'	fr. Skt. *jambu-* (Kaus.); *jambula* (L); (M) "probably non-Aryan"
171.	DĀKH	*Vitis vinifera*	'raisin; grape'	Skt. *drākṣā* (Hariv.); "late, isolated" = loanword? (M); others have attempted var. IE deriv. incl. **drā-* 'run' (= 'running vine' [Buck:534, 379], or **deregh* 'thorn' (!) (WP Vol. 1, p. 862) or **derayk(es)* 'berry; cornel cherry' (WP Vol. 1, p. 803); all doubtful (@M)
172.	NĀRIYAL	*Cocos nucifera*	'coconut'	Skt. *nālikera-* (Susr.,MBh.), fr. Drav. *nari* 'fiber' + *kēli* 'coconut palm' ? (Bloch)
173.	NĀSPĀTĪ/ NĀŚPATI	*Pyrus communis*	'pear'	fr. Pers.

	Hindi Term	Latin Term for Botanical Items	English Equivalent	Source of Hindi Term
174.	PAPĪTĀ (= *eraṇḍ-kharbūzā*) (= *papaiya*: this term is only local @BHK)	*Carica papaya*	'papaya'	? ? (H/Skt. *eraṇḍ* 'castor-oil plant' + Pers. *kharbuza* 'melon')
175.	PISTĀ	*Pistacia vera*	'pistachio'	fr. Pers.
176.	PHAL	–	'general term for *fruit*'	Skt. *phala-* (RV), quite possibly fr. Drav. (Ta. *pal̤am* 'ripe fruit' [DED3299]); cw. genuine Drav. variants and derivatives (Te. *paṇḍu* 'to ripen') or Skt. *phulla-* 'expand, burst'
177.	BĀDĀM	*Prunus dulcis* (*Amygdalus communis*)	'almond'	fr. Pers.
	a. pahāṛī bādām	a. *Corylus colurna*? b. *Corylus avellana*	'cobnut' 'hazelnut'	H *pahāṛī* 'pertaining to the Hills' + *bādām*
178.	BER	*Ziziphus jujuba* (*Zizyphus*)	'jujube'	Skt. *badara-* (VS); "probably non-Aryan plant name" (M)
	bīl, see *bel*			
179.	BIHĪ (= *amrūd*)	a. *Cydonia oblonga* b. *Psidium guajava*	'quince' 'guava'	fr. Pers. (mod. *behī*)
180.	BEL	*Aegle marmelos*	'wood apple (offered to Shiva)'	Skt. *bilva-* (AV), fr. Drav. (DED 4535)
	mahuā, see "Oilseeds and Intoxicants"			
181.	MEVĀ	–	'general term for dried fruit'	fr. Pers. *mīvah* (mod. *miveh*) 'fruit'
182.	RĪṬHĀ	*Sapindus saponaria* (*S. detergens*)	'soapnut'	Skt. *ariṣṭa* (Yajn., Mn.); cw. RV *ariṣṭa-* 'unhurt'? (T)
183.	LĪCĪ	*Nephelium "litchi"*	'lichi'	Chinese *li-chi*
184.	ŚAFTĀLŪ/ SATĀLŪ	*Prunus persica* (= *āṛū*?)	'peach; nectarine'	fr. Pers. (*shaft* 'rough' + *ālū* 'plum')

185.	ŚARĪFĀ (= *āt*)	*Annona squamosa*	'custard apple'	fr. Pers. *sharīfā* 'noble', @HSS 3286 fr. Skt. *srīphal* or *sītāphal*
186.	SĪTĀPHAL	*Annona squamosa*	'custard apple'	H/Skt. 'Sita's fruit'
187.	SEB	*Malus sylvestris*	'apple'	fr. Pers. *sīb*

2.9. Spices, Herbs, and Condiments

188.	AJAMOD(Ā)	*Petroselinum crispum* (*P. sativum*)	'parsley'	Skt. *ajamoda*, fr. *aja-* 'goat' + *mō-da* 'delight' = pop. etym.; cf. *ajāji* 'cumin'; cw. *yavānī* 'ajowan' (T: 152; Susr.)
189.	AJWĀIN/ AJWĀYAN/ AJWĀN	a. *Trachyspermum ammi* (*Carum copticum*) (*Ptychotis ajowan*)	'ajowan' ('a species of lovage with flavor of carroways')	Skt. *yavānī* 'a kind of bad barley' (Pancom.), *'ajowan'* (Susr.), fr. *yavana-* 'Westerners' (M, T, Pl.)
		b. *Apium graveolens v. dulce*	'celery' (Ayk.)	
190.	AD(A)RAK (also = *ād*)	*Zingiber officinale*	'fresh ginger'	Skt. *ārdraka-*, fr. *ārdra-* 'fresh, moist', fr. **ard* 'flow, dissolve' (Susr.)
191.	ILĀYCĪ	a. *Elettaria cardamomum* (*Alpinia cardamomum*?)	'Ceylon cardamom'	@M: Pers. *alāčī* (because of the Turkish suffix *-čī*) is the source of the H (and Nep.) word; the Pers. presum. fr. Skt. *ēlā* (Susr.), in turn fr. Drav. (T, M, Em.)
		b. *Alpinia officinarum*? (*A. stricata*?)	'round cardamom'	
		c. *Amomum repulaga*?	'Java cardamom'	
192.	ĪKH(w)/ŪKH(e)	*Saccharum officinarum*	'sugar cane'	Skt. *ikṣu-* (AV), fr. ? ?
193.	KABĀB CĪNĪ	*Piper cubeba*	'cubebs'	Pers. *kabābah* (fr. Aryan) + *čīnī* 'Chinese'
194.	KESAR	*Crocus sativus*	'saffron'	prob. Skt. *késara-* 'hair'; cw. VLat. *caesariēs* 'hair', not certain (M)

Hindi Term		Latin Term for Botanical Items	English Equivalent	Source of Hindi Term
195.	KUMKUM	*Crocus sativus*	'saffron'	Skt. *kuṅkuma* (Susr.); "culture-word" (M); *if* not Semitic (Akk. *kurkanū*, Heb. *karkōm*) fr. same unknown source as Gk. *krokos* and the Semitic words
	khaskhas, see "Oilseeds and Intoxicants"			
196.	KHĀṆṚ	–	'unrefined sugar'	Skt. *khaṇḍu* 'sugar', prob. fr. Drav. (DED 1490?)
197.	GUṚ	–	'jaggery, molasses'	Skt. *guḍa-* (Katy.); cw. *guḍa* 'globe, ball'? ; cw. M *gola-* 'prob. Drav.'; but ? cf. *gurguṛ* (H onom.) 'bubbling noise'
198.	CĪNĪ	–	'white (refined) sugar'	fr. Pers.? , *cīnī* 'Chinese'
199.	ZĀFRĀN	*Crocus sativus*	'saffron'	fr. Pers., fr. Arabic *za'farān*
200.	JĀYPHAL	*Myristica fragrans* (*M. moschata*)	'nutmeg' (= seed)	Skt. *jātī-* 'mace, nutmeg' (Susr.) + *phala-* 'fruit' (*jātī*, fr. ? ?)
201.	JĀVITRĪ (= *jāepatrī*)	*Myristica fragrans*	'mace' (seed covering)	Skt. *jātīpattrī* (Bhpr.), fr. *jātī* + *páttra-* 'wing feather' (VS) > 'leaf, petal' (KatySr.)
202.	JĪRĀ	*Cuminum cyminum*	'cumin'	Skt. *jīraka* (Susr.); prob. Iran. loanword, **zīraka*, Pers. *zīrah* (M lex. and late texts)
203.	DALCĪNĪ/ DARCĪNĪ	"*Cinnamomum iners*" *C. aromaticum*? *C. zeylanicum*	'cinnamon'	fr. Pers. *dārčīn* (= *dār* 'tree' + *čīn* 'China', or ? fr. *dārū* 'medicine'?
204.	DHANIYĀ	*Coriandrum sativum*	'coriander'	Skt. *dhānaka* (Bhpr.), *dhāneyaka* (MBh.), fr. ? *dhānā-* 'grain, seed'
205.	PIPALĪ (PĪPLĀ)	*Piper longum*	'long pepper' (long pepper *plant*)	Skt. *pippali* '*Piper l.*' (Ram.); 'berry' (AV), fr. *pippala* 'berry, esp. of *Ficus religiosa*' (RV); cognate

				with *pīpal* (tree); "prob. non-Aryan" (@M)
206.	PUDĪNĀ/PODĪNĀ	*Mentha piperita*? (*M. sativa*)	'mint'	fr. Pers.
207.	MARUVĀ	a. *Majorana hortensis* (*Origanum marjorana*)	'marjoram'	Skt. *maruva-* (L); @M: "a culture-word that belongs with Gk. *amā́r-akon*, probably loanword from 3rd('Indo-Mediterranean')source"
		b. *Ocimum "pilosum"*?	'basil-like plant'	
		c. *Artemisia vulgaris*?	'mugwort'	
208.	MIR(I)C = *kālī mirc*	*Piper nigrum*	'(black) pepper'	Skt. *marīca-* (Apast., Ram.); @M: likely AA loanword (Mon *mrāk*, Khmer *méréć*, etc.); also found in Drav. (Ta.) *miḷaku*)
	(1) *lāl mirc*	1. *Capsicum frutescens* 2. *Capsicum annuum* (ssp)	'(dried red) chillies'	H *lāl* 'red'
	also called *lankā mirc*			
	(2) *harī mirc*	*Capsicum annuum* (ssp)	'green chillies (before ripening and drying)	H *harā* 'green'
209.	METHĪ	*Trigonella foenum-graecum*	'fenugreek'	**metthi* (L?), fr. Drav. (Ta.) *mēti* (DED4161)
210.	RĀI (= *toṛī*? , see "Oilseeds")	a. *Brassica juncea juncea* b. *Sinapis alba*? (*S. ramosa, S. Chinensis*)	'small-seeded mustard'	Skt. *rajika-* (Susr.), fr. ? ?
211.	LAUṈG	*Syzygium aromaticum* (*Eugenia caryophyllata*)	'cloves'	Skt. *lavaṅga* (Kav.); Indonesian loanword (B)
212.	SAK(K)AR/ ŚAK(K)AR	– –	'(granulated) sugar'	Skt. *śarkarā* 'grit, gravel' (IE) + similar Mon-Khmer word for 'sugar', contam.
213.	SOĀ/SOWĀ	a. *Anethum graveolens* (*Peucedanum gr.*)	'dill'	
		b. *Foeniculum vulgare* (*Anethum sowa*)	'fennel'	

Hindi Term	Latin Term for Botanical Items	English Equivalent	Source of Hindi Term
214. SAUṈF	a. *Anethum graveolens* (*Peucedanum gr., A. sowa*) b. *Pimpinella anisum*?	'anise, fennel'	both nos. 213 and 214 fr. Skt. *śatapuspa-* 'having 100 flowers' (MBh.); *'Anethum'* (Susr., L)
215. HALDĪ	*Curcuma longa*	'turmeric'	Skt. *haridrā* (Kaus.), fr. *hari(t)* 'yellow, green', fr. IE **ĝhel-* 'yellow, green, grey, blue' (P:429; WP, vol. 1, pp. 624ff; Buck:1059)
216. HĪNG/HING	*Ferula assa-foetida*	'asafoetida'	Skt. *hiṅgu* (BhP, MBh.); Pers. also *hing*

2.10. Domestic Animals

217. ŪṈṬ	'camel'	Skt. *úṣṭra-* 'camel' (MBh.); but 'buffalo' (RV), fr. IE **wes-* 'be moist'
218. GADHĀ	'donkey'	Skt. *gardabhaka-* (RV) 'the crier'? (rt. **gard-* 'to cry')
219. GĀY/GĀĪ	'cow'	Skt. *gāvī* (fem. pattern), fr. **gāvā*, fr. **gāva-* 'ox', fr. *gava-* compounding form of *gṓ/gaúh* 'ox; cow', fr. IE **gʷōus*
220. GHOṚĀ	'horse'	Skt. *ghōṭaka-* (Pancat.), fr. *ghōṭa-* (ApSr.); in Pali *'poor* horse' (T:4516); allegedly fr. Drav. (Ta.) *kutirai* (DED 1423); but there are cogent objections to this; Ḥock refers to Turk.and MGk. cognates; ?cf. also Skt. *ghoṭate* 'barter, exchange' (MW: 377c)
221. BAKRĀ	'goat'	Skt. *bárkara* 'goat' (L), fr. 'kid, lamb' (ApSr.), imitative? ; cw. 'bleat' IE
222. BACHṚĀ	'calf'	Skt. *vatsatará* 'young bull or goat before weaning or copulation' (TS); cw. *vatsá* (see no. 224)
223. BACHEṚA	'colt'	
224. BĀCHĀ	'calf'	Skt. *vatsá* 'calf, child' (RV), i.e. 'yearling'; cw. *vatsa* 'year' (L); cf. *samvatsam* 'for one year' (RV)=IE (Gk. *étos*, Lat. *vetus*, Lith. *vẽtušas*)
225. BATTAK	'duck; goose'	fr. Pers. *batax*
226. BAIL	'ox'	**balilla*; cw. *balín* 'strong' (RV), fr. *bála-* 'strength', fr. Drav. (@B); Ta. *val*, Kan. *bal*? (DED4317); but M connects with IE (Lat. *dēbilis*, Gk. *apophōlos*)

227.	BHEṚ	'sheep'	Skt. *bhēḍra-* 'ram' (L); *bheḍa, bheṇḍra, meṇḍha* (L)=prob. non-Aryan, perhaps AA (cf. *m/bh* alt.); cf. Sant. *meṛom* 'goat'; Przyl.: fr. **meḍra*
228.	BHAIṈS/MHAIṈS	'water buffalo'	Skt. *mahiṣa* 'great, powerful' = *mahiṣo mṛgāṇām* 'great one of the beasts'; or *mahiṣi* 'buffalo cow', fr. 'chief queen' (RV)
229.	MURGĪ	'hen'	fr. Pers. *morgh* 'a bird, a fowl' fr. OPers. *murgh*, Av. *meregha*; cognate w. Skt. *mṛga-* 'quadruped' (*not* 'bird'); Iranian forms = 'bird'; origin of both Indic and Iranian uncertain; no IE cognates (except possibly Gk. *amorbós* 'shepherd')
230.	MEMNĀ	'kid; lamb'	onom., fr. 'bleat of lamb or kid' "*meme*"
231.	SĀNṚ	'bull'	Skt. *sāṇḍa-* 'uncastrated' (MaitrS, TandBr., GrSrS); *sa-* 'with' + *āṇḍa* 'testicles' (AV)
232.	SŪAR	'pig'	Skt. *sūkará* 'boar', fr. IE **sus*
233.	HĀTHĪ	'elephant'	Skt. *hastín* 'elephant' (AV) = 'having hands' = Aryanization of *karin/karabha-* (non-Aryan) 'elephant', by assoc. of *kar-* element with Skt. *kará-* 'hand' thence with *hastá* 'hand'

2.11. Products of Domestic Animals

234.	AṆḌĀ	'egg'	Skt. *āṇḍa-* 'egg' (RV), 'testicle' (AV), fr. Munda? (Kuiper), fr. IE? ; but "old comp. with OSl. *jędro* 'kernel, testicle' now given up on phonol. grounds" (M vol. 1, p. 26), = ? ?
235.	ŪN	'wool'	Skt. *ū́rṇā* (RV) = *IE (Lat. *lāna*, Goth. *wulla*, etc.)
236.	KHĀL	'hide'	Skt. *khalla* 'leather, leather garment' (L); possibly Munda? (Kuiper), = ? ?
237.	GHĪ	'clarified butter'	Skt. *ghṛtá* (RV), fr. rt. **ghṛ-* 'trickle' = IE; cf. Irish *gert* 'milk'
238.	CAMṚĀ (= *cām*)	'leather'	Skt. *cárman-* 'hide, skin' (RV) = IE, prob. fr. **ker-* 'cut, separate'
239.	CARSĀ	'raw oxhide'	**carassa-* (but see no. 238)
240.	CHĀCH	'buttermilk'	**chācchī*, ? ?
241.	DAHĪ	'curd'	Skt. *dádhi* (RV); cw. IE (+ irreg. decl. = old word); redupl. fr. *dháyati* 'sucks' (irreg.), also fr. IE
242.	DŪDH	'milk'	Skt. *dugdhá* (AV); cw. rt. **duh-* 'to milk' (*dṓgdhi*, etc. [RV]); but IE (exact?) cognates uncertain outside Indo-Iranian (M); cf. "daughter," etc.

	Hindi Term	English Equivalent	Source of Hindi Term
243.	MA(K)KHAN	'butter'	Skt. *mrakṣaṇa-* 'ointment, oil' (Susr.), 'rubbing in ' (Dhātu), rt. **mrakṣ-* 'rub'; possible Iranian cognates; others not mentioned
244.	MALĀĪ	'cream'	H, cw. 'scum' (Pl.:1063); cf. *mal* 'dirt, sediment', fr. Skt. *mála-* 'dirt' (AV), fr. IE
2.12. Names of Tools and Implements			
245.	KUDĀLĪ	'kind of hoe'	perhaps fr. Drav.; cf. Kan. *guddali* 'hoe', *guddu* 'to hoe'
246.	KHURPĀ	'(blade of) hoe'	Skt. *kṣurapra* 'sharp-edged' (BhP), 'sort of hoe' (L), rt. **kṣur-* 'scrape' = IE
247.	CAKKĪ (= *cākī*)	'quern, (hand) mill'	Skt. *cakrī* 'wheel' (RV), fr. *cakrá-* 'wheel' (RV), fr. IE (Gk. *kýklos*, English *wheel*)
248.	JŪĀ (= *jūh*)	'yoke'	Skt. *yugá-* (RV) = IE
249.	JUĀṬH	'yoke'	Skt. *yugá-* + *kāṣṭhá-* 'wood' (prob. IE, but not suf. expl.)
250.	JOT(Ā)	'ropes which go around the bullocks' necks'	Skt. *yoktra-* 'thong, halter' (RV), 'tie of yoke to plow' (L); **yuj*, **yu* fr. IE
251.	DARĀṈTĪ	'sickle'	fr. Panjabi (T:6260), fr. Skt. *datra/-i* (RV), **da-* 'cut' = IE cognate Iranian forms
252.	NĀṈGAL/ LĀṈGAL	'plow'	Skt. *lāṅgala-* (RV); found in Drav., NMunda and Korku (not in SMunda), Mon-Khmer, Austronesian, Iranian dial. of Lar; fr. AA? (@B, Kuiper; Zide doubtful); 'plow with metal point' (Bloch)
253.	PHĀL	'plowshare'	Skt. *phāla-* (RV); cw. Pers. *supār* 'plow'; rel. to **phal-* 'burst', doubtful; Drav.? (Master); **spāla*? (cf. Pers.); "infl. by Munda or Drav. to account for early *ph-*" (T:9072)
254.	SŪP	'winnowing basket or fan'	Skt. *śū́rpa-* (VS), fr. Drav.@B, noted in M, but no likely candidates in DED
255.	HAL (= *har*)	'plow'	Skt. *halá-* (MBh.); @B and Kuiper, der. fr. *lāṅgala-* (which is attested much earlier) by removing the "Austric prefix" **lāṅ-*

256.	HAN̲SUĀ	'sickle or reaping-hook'	T: fr. Skt. *áṁsiya* 'belonging to the shoulder' (RV), fr. *áṁsa* 'shoulder' (RV), from IE
257.	HEN̲GĀ (BHK: = *paṭelā*)	'harrow' (BPL:7; Bul:287)	? ?

2.13. Other Terms Connected with Agriculture

258.	KUĀN̲	'well'	Skt. *kū́pa-* 'hole, hollow, cave' (RV), 'well' (L); cw. Gk. *kýpē*; Asia Minor origin?
259.	KŪN̲Ṛ	'furrow'	? cw. H *koṛnā* 'dig up'? , fr. Skt. **kuṭ-* 'break'; ? cw. Drav. 'plowshare'? (DED 1785)
260.	KHAL	'threshing floor'	Skt. *khala-* (RV, AV), fr. Drav. (B; DED 1160)
261.	KHARĪF	'autumn-harvested crops'	fr. Pers. *xarīf*, fr. Arabic
262.	KHET	'field'	Skt. *kṣētra-*, fr. rt. **kṣi-* 'dwell' (IE)
263.	TALĀU/TĀLĀB	'tank, reservoir'	Skt. *taḍāga-* (GrS, MBh.), fr. ? ? ; cf. Drav. *taṭa-* 'obstruct, dam up' (DED 2460; B); cf. also Pers. *tālāb* (? cw. *tall* 'hillock, mound of earth' + *āb* 'water'?)
264.	PŪLĪ/PŪLĀ	'sheaf'	Skt. *pūla-* (Sutras), fr. ? ? ; cf. Latv. *pùlis* 'heap'? ; Munda (Kuiper)? ?
265.	PHASAL/FASAL	'harvest; crop; season'	fr. Pers., fr. Arabic *faṣl* (**f-ṣ-l* 'to separate, divide')
266.	BĀWLĪ	'large masonry well with steps leading down to the water'	@ Pl. and HSS fr. Skt. *vāpa/vāpi/vāpī́* 'large pond or tank' (Mn., Epics, etc.) + dim. *-ḍī* or *lī*; but ? cf. Pers. *bāvlī* 'large well' (Stn.:153); (M questions connection of *vāpī* with OSl. and Hittite forms)
267.	BĪJ	'seed'	Skt. *bīja-* (RV), fr. Drav.? (B; DED 4485, 4428)
268.	BONĀ	'to sow'	Skt. *vap-* 'strews, scatters, sows' (RV); no other IE occurrences
269.	BHŪSĀ	'straw, chaff'	Skt. *busa-* 'chaff, rubbish' (Kaus.); cw. **bussa* 'defective'? , (fr. ? ?)
270.	RABĪ	'spring-harvested crops'	fr. Pers. *rabī* 'spring; spring harvest', fr. Arabic

Hindi Term	English Equivalent	Source of Hindi Term
271. ROPNĀ/ROṈPNĀ (cf. *rop* 'seedling')	'to plant; transplant'	Skt. **rupati* 'pierce, make holes, plant'; cf. *ropayati* 'plants' (MBh.) *ropa* 'hole', rt. **rup-* 'pierce'; cw. IE 'break, etc.' (M)
272. LUNNĀ	'to reap, harvest'	Skt. *lunā́ti* = IE (M: Iranian, Lith., Germ.; perhaps also Gk., Lat. *lyō, luō* 'loose')
273. SĪTĀ	'furrow'	= Skt. *sītā*, fr. **sī* (Indic only) 'draw a straight line' (M); @Pokorny, fr. IE **sē* 'sow'

3.0. Commentary on the Data. A chastening warning from Berthold Laufer (1919:206) may serve as an appropriate preface to this section:

> In point of method, de Candolle has set a dangerous precedent to botanists in whose writings this effect is still visible, and this is his over-valuation of purely linguistic data. The existence of a native name for a plant is apt to prove little or nothing for the history of the plant, which must be based on documentary and botanical evidence. Names, as is well-known, in many cases are misleading or deceptive; they constitute a welcome accessory in the chain of evidence, but they cannot be relied upon exclusively. It is a different case, of course, if the Chinese offer us plant-names which can be proved to be of Iranian origin.

Although our interest here is not so much in the "history of the plant" per se as in the use made of it (or of animals and tools) in various cultures, such history is among the nonlinguistic data that it is appropriate to consider as we ponder the linguistic data. Nonlinguistic data may well have a bearing on doubtful etymological points, just as etymological data may throw some light on the history of an item. I propose to examine some relevant features of both in this section, as they affect, reinforce, or contradict one another, in terms of the categories of the etymological data given in section 2. These details logically follow upon the preliminary generalizations of 1.6 (1-14) and precede the general conclusions of section 4.

3.1. *Cereals.* There are two striking things initially: the absence of any Indo-European cereal names except for barley, which originally meant 'grain in general', and the transference of certain other Indo-European words for 'grain in general' or 'food' to the new cereal; rice. To be sure, other, non-Aryan words are also applied to rice in one or another of its forms (*cāwal, lāī, lāwā, sāl, selā, khīl,* etc.), but only the first of these may be called a basic term. It may very well be Dravidian. Here it should be noted, however, that rice is older by at least a millennium (perhaps by two) in the North Indian archaeological record than it is in the South Indian, indicating a diffusion of its cultivation from North to South (Vishnu-Mittre:17,4). In the Ganges valley it is, moreover, the only grain found (Allchin 1969*b*:327), whereas in the peninsula there are finds of millet reported, possibly predating it. The Sanskrit word *vrīhi* has left no descendants in Hindi. With regard to *sāl* and *selā* (cf. the Persian word *shālī* 'unhusked rice'), rice cultivation had spread to Iraq by 500 B.C. (Isaac:66).

The group of words for wheat and its products (flour, bread, etc.) are peculiar in being both unexplained and shared, in several cases, with Iranian. Since this is the area (North Iran/Afghanistan) where bread wheats are thought to have originated (Zohary 1969:61ff) from a hybrid of emmer (*Triticum dicoccum*) and 'goat-face grass' (*Aegilops squarrosa*), is it too much to suspect a source in some unknown pre-Indo-European neolithic language of the region?

At least eight millets are of economic importance in India: *Echinochloa frumentacea, Eleusine coracana, Panicum miliaceum, Panicum sumatrense, Paspalum scrobiculatum, Pennisetum glaucum, Setaria italica, and Sorghum cernuum,* in Hindi *sāṉwāṉ* or *sāwā, maṉṛuā, cenā, kuṭkī, kodoṉ, bājrā, kaṉgnī,* and *junhār* or *juwār*. Of these, only two of the lesser ones, *Paspalum* and *Panicum sumatrense*, are definitely thought to be of Indian origin (Sauer:78; he also mentions a third, 'jungle rice' or *Echinochloa colonum*, for which I have no Hindi equivalent, and comments, "It is a poor lot; something seems to be missing or lost.") The first of these has been identified in first-millennium B.C. sites in peninsular India.

Panicum miliaceum (common millet or broomcorn) and *Setaria* (foxtail millet) were of very early cultivation (pre-5000 B.C.) in both Europe and China (Sauer:75; Renfrew 1969:165-66,168; Burkill 1962:259,267; Ho 1975:57-61); *Setaria* was also anciently cultivated in Mexico (ca. 3800B.C.), preceding maize. Some authorities (e.g., Vavilov) credit China with the former; *Setaria* is so widespread it could well have been domesticated in several places independently. Burkill thinks that Central Asia would afford a site for dispersion, explaining the distribution of both. In any case, the Hindi and Sanskrit names of *Panicum miliaceum* (*cenā/cīnaka*) clearly record association with China as far as northern India is concerned. Textual references to the name of *Setaria* (Sanskrit *kaṅgu*) as a '*mleccha* word' (Gotama, Nyāyasūtra 2,56: in Mayrhofer 1956:vol. 1, p. 138) and its congruence with Greek *kenkhros* probably indicate a borrowing from the west. Zide and Zide (p. 1303) have reconstructed a Proto-Munda word for *Setaria*, **(h)oXy*, but this would appear to have no bearing on the Sanskrit and Hindi words. *Echinochloa frumentacea* or barnyard millet (*sāwā*) is thought to be a Chinese or Japanese domesticate (Sauer:76). All three of the above are ancient beer grains. None is reported from archaeological sites in the subcontinent, at least as yet.

The more important millets–*Sorghum (jowar), Pennisetum* (pearl or bulrush millet, *bājrā*), and *Eleusine* (finger millet or *ragi*)–are generally all held to be of African origin (Burkill:270; Sauer:77; Allchin 1969*b*:327; Ho 1975: 381-83), primarily on botanical and especially cytogenetic (i.e., rather than archaeological) grounds. They also appear late in the Indian archaeological record and primarily in southern India. Allchin (1969*b*:325) says that "firm" evidence for all three dates only from the beginning of the Christian era. Vishnu-Mittre adduces earlier finds; particularly significant are evidences of *Sorghum* at Ahar in Rajasthan about 1500 B.C.(coming later than rice at that site, however). None of them are mentioned in Sanskrit literature (except for reference to *Sorghum, yavanala*, in Suśruta's medical treatise early in the Christian era) or incorporated into more than a local ritual complex, despite their great importance as staple crops in large sections of later India. (This stands in contrast with the great importance of millet–*Panicum*–in Chinese literature and ritual.) The word *yavanala* is interpreted as derived from *yavana* 'foreign, Western'. The suggested etymon **yavakara* 'barley-shaped' apparently is not actually attested, only reconstructed from words like *jwār*. *Sorghum* is believed to have reached China as well as India from Africa via the "Sabaean lane" (South Arabia), thence in the case of China via Inner Asia (Burkill:267; Ho 1975:381). In this connection, its Uzbek name is of some interest: *jokhari* (Matley 1967:125). Possibly a Sanskrit borrowing, of course, but, as we have seen, the form in /r/ is not attested in Sanskrit.

The earlier association of most of the millets with South India in the archaeological record (with the significant exception of the Ahar finds), and their continuing greater importance there suggests a movement the reverse of that of rice–this time from South to North, and with it perhaps a movement of terms. Unfortunately, the Dravidian terms do not in the least resemble the Hindi ones: *bājrā* versus Ta. *kampu, maṟruā* versus Ta. *kēppai, kodoṉ* versus Ta. *varaku* (but *jwār* and Ta. *coḷam* may relate?).

Megasthenes (late fourth century B.C.) mentions "much millet" grown, presumably in northern India. Of what sort is not clear without consulting the Greek text, if then, but it is likely to have been *Setaria* or *Panicum*, as these were familiar to the Greeks, and sown, as he mentions, in the rains (as is *kodoṉ*). Megasthenes mentions another crop, *bosmoron*, unidentified and possibly a cereal (McCrindle 1877:32,55).

Maize or American corn presents an intriguing problem both botanically and etymologically. Despite its undoubted New World origin, a number of authorities now hold that it was present in parts of Asia before Columbus (Isaac : 75fn, attesting Robert Heide-Geldern 1958, *Anthropos* 54:361-402). It has been particularly associated with interior hill peoples. Thus, in China it was first brought to the attention of the imperial court not by coastal people in touch with foreigners but by tribesmen from the southwestern interior (Ho 1975:381). This may be merely a matter of the rapid filling of an ecological niche–too dry for rice, too hot and wet for wheat, more productive than millet. In China, as often elsewhere, the new grain was dubbed a kind of *Sorghum* (which the plant, at any rate, closely resembles): *shu-shu/yü-shu-shu* (Ho 1975:381), cf. Korean *ok-su-su* (in both cases, 'jade sorghum').

In India there is archaeological evidence for maize from at least the fifteenth century (Allchin 1969*b*:326). The alleged Sanskrit etymon of Hindi *makkā/makāī*, namely *markaka* (Turner:9879)–lexical only–is glossed as *'Ardea argala'* in Turner, following Monier-Williams. This, it turns out, is a species of *bird*. There are similar words *markaṭa* 'spider; monkey' and *markaṭaka* 'a species of grass', the latter allegedly yielding only the dialectal Shina word *mʌkʌṛi* 'large millet'. Is a Sanskrit source for either of these necessary or at all likely? Or have we here another pseudo-etymology, invoking a familiar device–(C)C- > -rC- –to bring foreign words within the Sanskrit pale?

A less common Hindi word for maize, *bhuṭṭā* (Platts:182), recalls a Bengali word for the millet *Panicum miliaceum* indicating (according to Dimock, cited by Ho 1975:60; Platts, of course, gives a supposed Sanskrit etymon *bhṛṣṭikaḥ*) introduction via the Himalayan foothills (*Bhutan, Bhotia* 'Tibetan')–cf. the southwestern Chinese tribesmen at the Ming court.

This is intriguing, but does not help us with *makkā*. In closing we should cite the Central Asian term *mäkkä-jokhari* (Allworth et al., 1967:126) *'mäkkä-*sorghum', which suggests *makkā* may be adjectival (< Mecca?).

3.2. *Pulses.* The absence of any Indo-European pulse names is even more complete, extending even to Indo-European derived forms. The sole exception seems to be the word *dāl* itself, not the name of a variety but referring to a way of preparing pulses (and, of course, the Persian borrowing *dānā* 'seed', cognate with Sanskrit *dhānya-* 'grain'). Yet, as is well known, pulses are a vital staple of the Indian diet. They are also among the oldest plants to be utilized and cultivated by man (although it is not always easy to distinguish gathered from cultivated seeds in archaeological deposits: paleobotanists seem to rely on the relative size of the seeds). The pulses cultivated in India originate in the Near East, Africa, China, and the Americas, in addition to India itself. It might help order a confused field if we discussed them under those headings.

1. Pulses domesticated in India: *Phaseolus mungo (urad), Phaseolus aureus (mūng), Dolichos biflorus (kulthī), Phaseolus aconitifolius (moṭh)*, and

probably *Cyamopsis tetragonoloba (guār)* (Burkill:275-76; Hedrick 1972: 224). These are found first in peninsular archaeological sites (e.g., Navtadoli, Paiyampalli), and not as early as several of the Near Eastern pulses discussed in the next section (Allchin 1969*b*:326). Later, *mūng* and *kulthī* turn up about 1100 B.C. at Noh in Rajasthan (near Agra) (Vishnu-Mittre:8). Vishnu-Mittre suspects early finds of *kulthī* in South India to represent wild beans. Most of the names are opaque. Turner speculates that *mudga* and *mukuṣṭha* (the same as *mūng* and *moṭh*) are somehow connected. Zide and Zide have reconstructed a plausible Proto-Munda etymon for *kulthī* which could also be Dravidian according to Mayrhofer. It is much more a South Indian than a North Indian crop (Indian Council of Agricultural Research:192), hence its frequent appellation *Madras* horsegram. For *guār*, in addition to the usual Sanskrit etymon, cf. Kannada *gōri (kāyi)* (DED 1846). Sauer (p. 79) and Burkill (p. 275) credit India with a fourth *Phaseolus* species domestication, identified by the latter as *P. calcaratus*. Zander refers this to the new taxon *P. pubescens*, identified as *Reisbohne*, 'rice bean'. So far I have been unable to match this up with any Hindi term (although there are some extra ones lying about). Perhaps *Dolichos lablab (sem)* is also an Indian domesticate (Burkill:276).

2. Pulses domesticated in the Near East: *Pisum sativum (maṭar), Pisum arvense* (also *maṭar? maṭarā, maṭarī?*), *Lathyrus sativus (khesārī), Cicer arietinum (canā), Lens culinaris (masūr), Vicia faba (bāklā)*—that is, the pea, field pea, chicklingvetch (or vetchling or grass pea), chickpea (or gram), lentil, and broad bean (or vetch). This group contains both the oldest (*Pisum, Lathyrus,* and *Lens*) and some of the more recent (*Cicer, Vicia*) of the legumes cultivated in India. Significantly, the area of domestication of the former subgroup is thought to be in the areas of southwest Asia closest to India, that is, eastern Iran and Afghanistan; that of the latter two is further away, closer to the Mediterranean. The earliest legumes found in India (at Chirand in Bihar, about 2500 B.C., according to Vishnu-Mittre) are these southwest Asian types, not the Indian varieties discussed in the preceding section. In the Indus valley, only *Pisum* has been found. The inference seems justified that the example of cultivated legumes brought by the settlers from southwest Asia provided the stimulus for the domestication of local varieties, unless contrary new evidence is forthcoming. (That from Thailand, as we have noted, is particularly doubtful in this area, and in any case concerns *Vicia*, not Indian pulses.)

The more recent introduction of *Vicia* and *Cicer* (the latter shortly before the turn of the Christian era, according to Allchin [1969*b*:326], versus the sixth millennium B.C. in Anatolia) seems to be reflected in the variability of their names, in contrast with the more ancient group. Thus *Cicer*, now certainly the *dāl* par excellence of northern India, greatly exceeding all others in acreage, is called *rahilā* and *caulī* as well as *canā*. *Vicia faba* seems to have no name exclusively its own, being called *sem* (also applied to *Dolichos lablab*), *bāklā* (also applied to the American *Phaseolus vulgaris*), and according to Aykroyd "chastang," a term I cannot find reference to elsewhere. Its place in India, indeed, seems marginal (in contrast with its deep penetration into European and Mediterranean folklore, cf. "Jack and the Beanstalk").

3. Pulses domesticated in Africa: *Cajanus cajan* (*arhaṛ* and *tuar* varieties) and *Vigna sinensis (lobiyā)*, that is the pigeon pea (or Angola pea) and the cowpea (or black-eyed pea). Neither of these is mentioned among the archaeological finds. The foreign (Persian, but ultimately Sumerian, according to Burkill, p. 270) name of *lobiya* plus the use of other names (e.g., *boṛā, caulā*) for it, in contrast with the apparently Dravidian name of *tuar*, suggest that *Vigna* (formerly called *Vigna catiang*) came later than *Cajanus* and also suggest that *Vigna* passed via the Sabaean Lane to the Middle East before reaching India, whereas *Cajanus* somehow came directly to South India. (*Cajanus* also passed from India to Malaysia during the period of Hindu contact [Burkill:278].) Sauer (p. 77) also credits Africa with *Dolichos lablab (sem)*.
4. Pulses domesticated in the Americas: India has not proven very receptive to the American legumes, despite their alleged superior qualities (productivity, large-seededness, etc.) (Crosby 1972:170ff), perhaps because it already had a surfeit of them. In this it stands in contrast with other areas of the Old World. In India, North India was less receptive than South India. *Phaseolus vulgaris* (variously called the haricot, French, or kidney bean) is cultivated, but called by names also applied to the European (broad) bean (*Vicia*) and to *Dolichos lablab*—that is, *bakla* and *sem*. I can find no Hindi terms for the Mexican scarlet runner bean (*Phaseolus multiflorus*), said to be cultivated in India (Watt: vol. 6, pt. 1, p. 186), nor for the lima bean (*Phaseolus lunatus*), the cultivation of which appears to be confined to the South (where it is known as the "duffin bean," after a Mr. Duffin who is said to have introduced it from Mauritius [Hedrick:419], and thence as the "double" bean). Platts gives a term for it, *kharsambal*, labeled 'Dakkini', which appears to be the same as one given in Watt (vol. 6, pt. 1, p. 187)—*kursumpulle* or *-pullie*.

5. Pulses domesticated in China: the only one of relevance here is, of course, the soybean, *Glycine max* (actually a Manchurian domesticate). It is of recent introduction, though cultivated longer in the eastern Himalayan foothill country, which may be reflected in its name *bhaṭmās* (*bhat-* equals *bhoṭ-* 'Tibetan, Bhutanese'?). Another Chinese bean (Sauer:76), the "velvet bean," *Mucuna hassjoo*, is reported (Indian Council of Agricultural Research:313) to be a very successful recent introduction to the Panjab. It is not clear what names are applied to it locally.
6. It is worth adding here that no pulse is reported as domesticated from Southeast Asia. Those presently grown there seem to be of Indian, Chinese, or New World origin (or transmission).

3.3. *Roots, Bulbs, and Tubers.* Esculent roots–yams and aroids–are especially associated with the Vavilov-Sauer "Old Planter" agriculture (or horticulture) of Southeast Asia, but in every region local varieties–often inedible or poisonous without elaborate preparation–seem to have formed an important food resource for early man. In Indian markets I am sure we have all seen, amid the red chillies and marigolds and brilliant green vegetables, these piles of unattractive and ill-shaped objects, often quite large, of uncertain affinity. Hindi apparently does not have an especially rich vocabulary in this area (Bengali and other east coast languages seem likely to be richer), and the literature (both botanical and lexicographic) is extraordinarily confused. I have done the best I can with it for the time being, but have not sorted out matters to my complete satisfaction (or, no doubt, to the reader's) by any means. More work is necessary, but some of the confusion may indeed be a fact of the language. It seems to be common all over the world, among scientists (e.g., ethnographers) as well as in the popular mind. When it is considered that the nomenclature of plants as different as the potato (*Solanum tuberosum*, nightshade family) and the sweet potato (*Ipomoea batatas*, morning glory family) has become hopelessly confused in the course of the spread of these two cultigens from their South American home (the Peruvian name of the latter–*batata*–being applied to the former–Peruvian *papa*–in many languages), it is small wonder that various species of yams (*Dioscorea*) have been confused with each other and with taros (*Colocasia*) and other aroids (*Amorphophallus, Alocasia*, etc.). It is also expecting too much to expect the popular mind to keep straight what botanists themselves have had trouble sorting out. At this point, I can say only the following:

1. The Indo-Europeans seem to have had a word (**ālū-*) for an esculent root

(possibly the source of the Latin word for onion, *allium*) which on arrival in India was applied to a local aroid, the 'telinga potato' (*Amorphophallus*), and in derived form (*ālukī*) to one or more *Colocasias* (taros). Later it was transferred (or extended) to the newly introduced potato.

2. The major cultivated yams (according to Alexander and Coursey 1969), of mainland Southeast Asian origin, namely *Dioscorea alata* (the "greater yam") and *Dioscorea esculenta* (the "lesser yam"), are said to be widely cultivated in India (perhaps in Bengal and the South?), but do not show up among the glosses for Hindi yam words. As noted above, however, these do not seem to be accurate–failing to distinguish, among other things, yams from taros. *Sūrana* is identified as a yam by Allchin (1969*b*:327), although its glossing by Monier-Williams (1086b,1246a) as *Amorphophallus* 'telinga potato', by Platts (697b) as *Arum campanulatum*, and by Chaturvedi and Tiwari (1975:829b) as 'elephant's foot' (cf., Alexander and Coursey:406) would indicate synonymy with *ālū* (and with *zamīnkand*). Similarly *ghuiyāṉ* is called both a yam and a taro (no Latin names given). On the other hand, *suthnī* seems to be unambiguously the 'aerial yam', *Dioscorea bulbifera*. The term 'potato yam' is applied both to the latter and to *ratālū*, identified as *D. sativa, D. purpurea, Typhonium trilobatum*– terms I have been unable to collate with the later botanical terminology.
3. The names of most of the cool weather root crops–'turnip', 'beet', 'onion', and 'leek' (not, however, 'carrot')–are of Persian origin. It may seem odd that the onion should have a foreign name, since it is seemingly such a necessary ingredient in Indian cuisine. It is primarily Indian cuisine of a special type in which it has this role, however–i.e., Mughalai (Muslim) cuisine, and regional cuisines strongly influenced by the latter, e.g., the Panjabi. In a number of orthodox Hindu circles, especially those distant from this influence, the onion is still regarded with suspicion. Hsüan Tsang noted in the seventh century that onions (and garlic) were grown and eaten by few persons and these were "expelled beyond the walls of the town" (Beal 1906:vol. 1, p. 88)–perhaps a reference to untouchables. Onions surely were not called *piyāz* then, a name they received when introduced from above by later ruling circles. A relic of an older name may exist in some regions or social strata. (The onion originates in Central Asia.)
4. The variations in the name of the sweet potato show interesting processes at work. The standard form now seems to be *shakarkand*; *sakarkand* would be purer Hindi. Urdu standards of elegance led to the substitution of Persian *shakar* for vernacular *sakar* 'sugar', however, and once this was done,

a similar process, reinforced by semantic association (however illogical), substituted Arabic *qand* 'loaf sugar' (itself ultimately via Persian from Sanskrit *khaṇḍa/khaṇḍu* 'candied sugar'–in turn possibly Munda according to Mayrhofer [vol. 1, p. 300]) for Hindi *kand* 'bulbous root' (from Sanskrit *kanda-*, probably from Dravidian, [cf. DED 984]), all etymological strands in the subcontinent thus joining forces to name this American import. A different result is reported by Grierson (p. 250) from North Bihar–*lamkā aluā*–the "*alu*" of Lankā. The sweet potato incidentally is another American cultigen that is believed to have crossed the Pacific before Columbus (or Magellan).

5. The tuberous-rooted legume *sankhālū (Pachyrhizus)*, the 'yam-bean', although widely cultivated, does not occur wild in India (Imperial Gazetteer of India).
6. Alexander and Coursey (p. 411) say Indian literary evidence for yams dates from the sixth century A.D. Allchin (1969*b*:327) says it dates from the first or second century A.D.

3.4. *Cucurbits.* Melon seeds are found both in Harappan sites (Fairservis: 304) and in Kurgan sites north of the Black Sea associated with the Indo-Europeans (Gimbutas:161), but Hindi words for melons are recent Persian borrowings. Melons flourish in Central Asia but do not do well in the climate of India. Evidence suggests that successive invaders from the former region have tried to introduce them at various times. Hsüan Tsang mentions them in the seventh century (Beal:vol. 1, p. 88), but Ibn Batuta says only that they were imported in dried form from Khwarizm in the fourteenth (Husain 1953: xxxviii) and Babur complained of their absence in India in the sixteenth (Leyden and Erskine, trans., *Memoirs*, rev. King, vol. 2, p. 241). Abul Fazl says that Akbar introduced their cultivation in the seventeenth century (Ayn:vol. 1, p. 74, quoted in Leyden and Erskine:vol. 2, p. 235fn).

Other *Cucurbitaceae* have fared better in the subcontinent. Indeed, some authorities (Sauer:79; Watt 1889-93:vol. 2, p. 633; Laufer [1919:301] cites de Candolle, Engler, and Watt but is not quite convinced himself) credit India with the domestication of the cucumber itself (*Cucumis sativus*); others favor the Near East. The Hindi name *khīrā* is puzzling in terms of its alleged Sanskrit etyma (Turner:3697), 'a fragrant plant'<'thickened milk'. Laufer suggests, instead, Persian *xiyār* 'cucumber' (cf., Mill'er 1953:204b), with a common metathesis (*dāūd*>*dādū*, etc.)–surely a much simpler explanation!

On the other hand, a number of cultivated cucurbits are undoubtedly of Indian origin: *Trichosanthes cucumerina anguina (ciciṇḍā* 'snake gourd'*)*,

Trichosanthes dioeca (*parwal* 'pointed gourd'), *Coccinia cordifolia* (*kundarū* 'ivy gourd'), *Momordica charantia* (*karelā* 'bitter gourd'), *Luffa acutangula* (*turaī* 'ridged gourd'), *Luffa aegyptica* (*ghiyā* 'dishcloth gourd'), and probably also *Benincasa hispida* (*peṭhā* 'ash gourd') (Sauer:79; Burkill:276,278; Hedrick:341). The *Luffas* are widely cultivated in Africa as well as throughout southern and eastern Asia. All of the aforementioned have appropriately un-Aryan (but unexplained) names.

The bottle gourd (*Lagenaria siceraria*), one and possibly more of whose Hindi names (*lauā, tomṛā, tumbā*) have an Austroasiatic etymology, is of ancient (pre-2000 B.C.) cultivation in Europe, Africa, and even the Americas (Burkill:271; Isaac:74). Sauer thinks its origin may be in the *western* Indian borderlands and Burkill seems to credit Africa, but these words point eastward as far as India is concerned.

There is a slight problem with the identification of Hindi *ṭiṇḍā*. It is given by Bulcke (1968:274) as 'round gourd' and by the Indian Council of Agricultural Research (p. 401) as 'Indian squash-melon' under "Cucurbitaceous crops." Prasād, Sahāy, and Śrīvāstav (532b) define it as 'a fruit which is used as a vegetable'. My colleagues C. M. Naim and K. C. Bahl confirm that it is a small round green cucurbit used as a vegetable. However, Chaturvedi and Tiwari (p. 261), Platts (359a), and Turner (5814), in defining it (the first two sources as 'a kind of vegetable'), give the taxon *Diospyros melanoxylon*. This is the ebony tree, which bears a small resinous fruit like an apricot–in Sanskrit *tinduka* or *tindukī*. Aykroyd (1956:68) gives only "tinda" with a botanical name, *Citrullus vulgaris*, once applied (Hedrick:169; Zander:177) to the watermelon (now *C. lanatus*). There is another *Citrullus* species, however, *C. colocynthis*, of African origin and the source of the drug colocynth (classified as a poisonous plant by Zander), regarding which Hedrick (p. 169) notes that "in India, according to Vaupell, there is a sweet variety which is edible and cultivated." (Bhargava's *Dictionary* [p. 219], generally avoided but consulted here in desperation, offers unhelpfully 'a vegetable like a cabbage'.)

Some confusion arises from the loose application of the English word *pumpkin* to various cucurbits in India, including the bottle gourd. True pumpkins and squashes (genus *Cucurbita*) are all natives of the New World (Sauer:66-69), though cultivated varieties seem to have existed in the Asian tropics before Columbus. *Cucurbita pepo*, which has established itself in India, is known by the term *kumhṛā*, apparently transferred from *Benincasa hispida* (Turner:3374). Another name is *halwā kaddu*.

3.5. *Other Vegetables.* Of these, tomatoes, cabbages, cauliflower, and bell peppers, as their names ('foreign eggplant', 'Simla pepper', etc.) partly belie, are of recent European introduction, confined at the end of the nineteenth century to the vicinity of European settlements (hill stations) and cantonments (Watt 1889:vol. 1, pt. 1, pp. 533-35; vol. 2, p. 139; vol. 5, p. 100). Regarding cabbage and cauliflower, the transference of names from a medicinal plant, and the Persian name *karamkallā*, should also be noted. The okra or "ladyfinger" (*Abelmoschus esculentum*, formerly *Hibiscus–bhiṇḍī*) is generally agreed to be of African origin (Hedrick:302). (*Okra* and its synonym *gumbo* are among the few African words in American English.) An alternative Hindi name is *rām-turaī* 'Ram's gourd'(Yule and Burnell 1968: 84; Grierson:255)–always suspect (cf., *sītāphal*). The name *beṇḍi* is widespread in South India but is not considered to be Dravidian. On the other hand, India is credited with the eggplant or "*brinjal*" (*Solanum melongena*) (Burkill:276; Sauer:79; Watt [vol. 6, pt. 3, p. 259] disagrees).

The drumstick or horseradish tree is a peculiarly Indian food plant whose roots serve as a substitute for horseradish but whose long pods are used as a vegetable; the leaves and flowers are also eaten. The Sanskrit name *śōbhañjana* looks suspiciously like a popular etymology (cf., *gō-dhūma*). The Dravidian name (Mal. *muriṅṅa*, Ta. *muruṅkai*) is quite different, but is the source of the Latin name (*Moringa oleifera*, formerly *pterygospermum*) as well as of another Sanskrit name *muraṅgī, muruṅgī*, represented in Hindi by *munagā* (Turner:10209). This seems to be a less common name than *sahijan, saiyan*, etc. (Grierson:256; Prasād, Sahāy, and Śrīvāstav:1089c). According to Turner it is also represented by *mūṉgā*, although *The Student's Practical Dictionary, Hindi-English*; Chaturvedi and Tiwari; Prasād, Sahāy, and Śrīvāstav; and Grierson all give the latter as meaning only 'coral'. The word is found in Platts, however, marked "dialec." It is confused with the pulse *mūng* (cf., Platts:1095a).

The water chestnut, *Trapa natans*, is an extremely old cultigen, once widely used in Europe (e.g., by the Swiss lake-dwellers). It is still common enough in Kashmir (Isaac:55). The Indian variety (cf., Grierson:246) seems to accord with the prehistoric European species rather than with the Chinese/Southeast Asian species (*Trapa bicornis*).

Greens were among the earliest plants utilized by man (Burkill:250-51). Many have been "ennobled" by domestication; others are still utilized in a wild or semiwild state (e.g., nettles) or represent weedy escapes from early cultivation (e.g., lamb's-quarters or *Chenopodium album* [Isaac:18; Hedrick: 450]). Some are relatively late domesticates–e.g., spinach, not earlier than the sixth century A.D. (Laufer 1919:392-98). Often, greens were cultivated for their roots (beet and turnip) and seeds (mustard and fenugreek) also, and some Hindi items that can be classed as greens will be found under those categories here. The importance of greens in the Indian diet is indicated by the fact that the Hindi words for 'vegetables' (*sabzī, tarkārī*) seem originally to have indicated 'greens, potherbs' (likewise, of course, British English *greengrocer*). (A fact harder to account for in this country of vegetarians is that both words are Persian.)

According to the Indian Council of Agricultural Research (p. 400) nearly twenty kinds of greens are grown in India (presumably in addition to those that are merely gathered, and not including cabbage and cauliflower, which are discussed under another category). Aykroyd (pp. 62-64) lists thirty-one kinds of greens but includes, besides cabbage, such things as soybean leaves, chickpea foliage, and carrot tops, while omitting several important North Indian crop plants. (Coriander, fenugreek, and parsley, here classed with herbs and spices, are probably fairly included.) Of other greens, endive, lettuce (also known as *salād*), and kale (*karamsāg*) have Persian-derived names and seem to be Near Eastern domesticates. The latter is also true of garden cress (*Lepidium*) and of spinach, which bear opaque names (*hālim, pālak*), the latter formerly assigned to the leafy beet. On the other hand, purslane (*Portulaca oleracea*), which has both a Persian-derived name (*kulfā* from Pers. *xurfah*) and a Sanskrit-derived one (*loniyā* from Skt. *lavaṇikā* [in Platts, but not in Monier-Williams], compare with *lavaṇa* 'salt'), is sometimes referred to as being of Indian origin.

The two armaranths (*marsā* and *caulaī*) and Indian spinach (*Basella*) or *poī* also seem to have opaque names, despite the attempts to explain *caulaī*. Some of the amaranths are New World domesticates, but I have been unable so far to collate the old and the new botanical terminology in order to find out which.

The sorrels (*ambāṛī, cokā*) have Sanskrit-derived descriptive names relating to their sources. The latter (two species may be involved) is cultivated from India to Europe (Hedrick:513-14); the former may be an Indian plant (Hedrick:302). Only the word for 'greens' in general (*sāg*) seems to be truly Indo-European. The lowly *Chenopodium*, *bathuā*, may bear an old name, however.

The Chinese *pak-choi* creeps over the Himalayas as *"bhutia rai"* (Burkill: 262), 'Tibetan mustard'.

The problems encountered in checking the reference of the item *makoy* are so extraordinary that they are best relegated to an appendix.

3.6. *Oilseeds, Fibers, Dyestuffs, Stimulants, and Intoxicants.* These categories have been grouped together in the tables to avoid undue repetition in cross-referencing because they overlap a good deal. That is, cotton and flax furnish both fiber and oil, hemp a fiber and an intoxicant, the poppy and the mahua blossom an oil and an intoxicant, and so forth. I shall try to sort them out again for purposes of this discussion.

1. *Oilseeds.* The basic oilseed is obviously *Sesamum* (*til*), which has given its name to oils in general (*tel*). It is found at Harappan sites (Fairservis:304; Vishnu-Mittre:5) and mentioned in early Sanskrit texts (*Atharvaveda, Mānava Dharmaśāstra*). Some would credit India with its domestication (Vishnu-Mittre:18; cf., Indian Council of Agricultural Research:236 and Allchin 1969*b*:327; and Western classical authors such as Pliny, cited by Laufer 1919). Others (Burkill:270; Sauer:77, 82; Laufer 1919:290; and Darlington 1969:67) attribute the plant to Africa; this is the prevailing view. Few (e.g., Isaac:56) credit the Near East with it, despite the antiquity of references to it there (from ca. 2350 B.C. in Sumerian records, according to Burkill, who concludes that the Harappans, in any case, did get it via the Near East, probably Sumer). The antiquity of *Sesamum* in the Near East has, however, been challenged by the paleobotanist Helbaek, who claims that literary references to it—local and classical—before the Islamic period actually refer to linseed (Hoffner 1974:126). (The Chinese for a long time confused the two oilseeds, both imports from Iran, under the common name 'Iranian hemp' *hu ma* [Laufer 1919: 289ff].) In that case India would appear to have been the transmitter rather than the receiver. Helbaek's view itself has been challenged, however (*JAOS* 88 [1968]:112-19). In the medieval Arab world sesame oil was used mainly in Iraq, olive oil in Syria, and turnip and radish oil in Egypt (Ashtor 1975:131).

Two other oilseeds are ancient in the Indian archaeological record—linseed (*atasī*) and mustard (*Brassica juncea* according to Allchin and therefore *rāī* rather than *sarsoṉ, Brassica campestris* [Indian Council of Agricultural Research:230; cf. Burkill:262]). Both are Near Eastern domesticates, but while the mustard is found at Chanhu-Daro in the Indus valley, the linseed is from the Deccan (Navtadoli), the only oilseed discovered there (Allchin 1969*b*:324, 326).

An African oilseed, *Ricinus communis* (the castor-oil plant, Sanskrit *ēraṇḍa-*, Hindi *reṇṛ*) is also held to be ancient, probably pre-Aryan, in India by Burkill (p. 275) on the basis of comparative linguistic and literary evidence, but I can find no confirmation of his assertion that the name is "Vedic." Mustard, however (*sarson*/Sanskrit *sarṣapa*) is mentioned in the later Vedic literature. Burrow's suggestion of an Austronesian/Austroasiatic etymology for the word does not square well with the botanical history of the plant, which points toward colder regions (Burkill:262). The poppy is probably a later arrival as an oilseed, but hemp (*Cannabis*) may have been an early source of oil for the Aryans (Burkill:275).

The coconut is not an important source of oil in northern India. Other oilseeds include Niger seed (*Guizotia abyssinica*), important in Madhya Pradesh, and black nettle (*Perilla frutescens*), an intruder from China in the northeast, but for these I can find no Hindi names. I almost left out the peanut! India is the world's number one producer of this New World import (Indian Council of Agricultural Research:220) descriptively named (*mūṉgphalī, vilāetī mūṉg*).

2. *Fibers and dyestuffs.* Laufer (1919:293) says that, as linen was the chief plant fiber of the ancient Mediterranean, so hemp (*Cannabis sativa*) was the main plant fiber of ancient China (cf. also Ho 1975:81). The early Aryans apparently passed close enough to China to come under the latter influence (Burkill:275); 'hemp-as-fiber' (Skt. *śaṇa*) is one of their earliest-stratum material culture-words. In the same way, India has been the land of cotton, from at least the time of the Harappans down to the present day. Isaac (p. 72) credits pre-Aryan India with the domestication of cotton. Sauer (p. 78) credits it with the development of cotton as a fiber plant, but suggests cotton was first domesticated in Africa (Ethiopia) for its seeds. In any case, it does not come from Southeast Asia (though it was established there at a fairly early date by Indian colonists), making an Austroasiatic etymology for Hindi *kapās*/Sanskrit *karpāsa* suspect. The latter is apparently based on "prefixless" forms in Southeast Asian languages (Burrow 1955:378)–but isn't it possible that these languages analogically reinterpreted a long foreign word as having a prefix, which in fact it did not have, to make it conform to their system? (We know this has happened elsewhere, e.g., in Swahili, where Arabic *kitabu* has the plural *vitabu* on the analogy of other singular/plural *ki-/vi-* prefixes. Non-Arabic words have even been given Arabic "broken" plurals.) On the other side of the matter, the word is of strangely late attestation in Sanskrit for such a basic article of life in India. There is also the word *karpaṭa* 'rag' (source of Hindi *kapṛā* 'cloth'), alleged (Turner:2871) to contain the same "prefix," also late. This could mean that Sanskrit was actively borrowing basic culture-words from Austroasiatic speakers (presumably in India) as late as the turn of the Christian era (despite the fact that "cotton" must have been a new element of life for the Aryans to contend with at least a millennium earlier). Alternatively, it could have somehow just been passed

over in the texts.

It has been held (Laufer 1919:294) that flax was cultivated in both ancient India and Iran solely for oil, never for fiber (oil presumably being a more ancient use). Discovery of spun fibers used to string beads in a Deccan site (Chandoli) of about 1400-1200 B.C. (Allchin 1969*b*:326; Vishnu-Mittre:8) throws some doubt on this, however.

Among dyestuffs we have dealt only with four–indigo, safflower, henna, and *Morinda citrifolia (āl)*, the first possibly Indo-European and the others unexplained. Laufer (1919:370,324,338) is my main source on these. He credits India with indigo and apparently safflower, but thinks henna was brought by the Muslims. Saffron and turmeric (here under "Spices") are also dyestuffs. Laufer (pp. 320-21) suggests the former reached India from Sasanian Iran, but he and Sauer (p. 26) credit India with the latter.

3. *Stimulants and intoxicants.* Tea and coffee have been omitted as either very recent introductions to northern India or, in any case, not part of its agricultural economy (Imperial Gazetteer of India:56,63) except indirectly through the tribal migrants who work in Assam. The case is quite different with tobacco, which, according to Watt (vol. 5, p. 353), has "probably the widest range of any economic plant." Introduced by the Portuguese around 1605(Imperial Gazetteer of India:49),it overcame official attempts by the Emperor Jahangir to stop its spread (and interdiction by the Sikhs and other religious groups) to become not only a crop of such importance that India ranked third in world production in 1966 (Indian Council of Agricultural Research:276) but also "one of the commonest weeds" (Watt 1886:353). Its commercial production is centered in Coastal Andhra rather than North India, however. It seems always to have kept its foreign (ultimately Amerindian) name and has not been confused with any native plant (unlike other American cultigens). Although ostensibly introduced by the Portuguese, the /m/ seems to indicate that the word reached Hindi through Persian (Persian *tambākū*, Arabic *tambāk*, versus Port. *tabaco*).

Among crops of these categories with deeper roots in the area, it is curious that two out of three ingredients of the betel quid treated here have Hindi names derived from Indo-European. Betel chewing, which reaches out into the islands of the Pacific and apparently centers in Southeast Asia (where evidences of it are reported by Solheim [1970:145] from the Spirit Cave site in northeastern Thailand ca. 9000 B.C.), is, of course, a whole topic in cultural history in its own right. Another local item with a curiously Aryan name is the *mahuā*, whose fermented fleshy blossoms yield a liquor. Another typically Indian source of alcohol, the toddy palm, seems to have a Dravidian name, which is appropriate since it is more at home in the South. The Rajputs are famous for their specialty liqueurs, but I have not gone into this specialized topic.

The grape and wine making are themselves a complicated matter. Though listed in the tables under "Fruit" (2.8), it might be appropriate to discuss it here. The most current Hindi terms, *angūr* and *sharāb* ('wine'), are Persian, and grape cultivation and wine making originated in southwest Asia and have been particularly dear to the Persians. The question is, how old are they in India? It is recorded by Abul Fazl and by the Emperor Babur in his *Memoirs* that organized attempts were made by both Babur and Akbar to introduce grape cultivation (Leyden et al. 1921:235fn, 416-17), and skilled viniculturists were imported for the purpose from Central Asia. Earlier, Ibn Batuta had recorded that grapes were not available in India, save in the form of raisins imported from Central Asia (Husain: xxxviii). The St. Thomas Christians of South India used to soak the latter overnight in water to produce a substitute for sacramental wine. In the seventh century, however, Hsüan Tsang reported that grapes were abundant in Udyāna (the Swat valley, north of Peshawar), and that Kshatriyas drank fermented beverages made from the juice of the grape and from sugarcane, while Brahmins and Buddhist monks drank unfermented beverages made from the same ingredients (Beal:89,119). Watt (vol. 6, pp. 263ff), on the basis of the extensive Sanskrit vocabulary for the plant, its fruit, dried fruit, wine and spirit, and mention in the treatises of Suśruta and Caraka early in the Christian era, concludes that the grape is of considerable antiquity in India. Megasthenes (fourth century B.C.), while recording that wine making was taught to the Indians by "Dionusos" (interpreted as Indra), notes also that they never drank wine except at sacrifices (McCrindle:37,69). (McCrindle suggests this was Soma juice.) What all this amounts to seems to be this: India is on the margins of the grape and wine area. The fruit and its special uses have been introduced from time to time, like melons, but have met with obstacles, probably more cultural than climatic, and cultivation has periodically declined. One such decline can be traced to the orthodox Islamic reaction under Aurangzeb, when the vineyards of Kashmir were ordered destroyed (Watt:vol. 6, p. 261). A relic in Hindi from the ancient period is the word *ḍākh*, referring also to 'raisin', the main form under which the grape was known in the periods when its cultivation languished. (In view of the late occurrence of Sanskrit *drākṣa,* and its unsatisfactory explanations, the existence of the Persian word *tāk* 'grapevine' may be a hint that the first introducers were earlier Persian invaders of the northwest of India, the Achaemenids. Considering the cultural predilections of the two peoples with regard to grapes and wine, we would not expect the Persians to have gotten their word from the Indians.)

Both Rajputs and Persians were fond of opium. Although a rather far-fetched Sanskrit etymon (nonattested) has been proposed for Hindi *afīm*, it is likely that, despite its slightly different shape, it belongs with Persian *afyūn* and other words of Persian origin (*postā, khaskhas*) pertaining to the poppy, a Near Eastern domesticate, and its parts.

Marijuana or hashish is another matter. *Bhāng* does go back to the Vedas, and earlier, and may well have been brought by the Aryans, if not also by their predecessors in the Indus Valley (cf. the word *gānjā*), to India from its Central Asian home (Burkill:298; Laufer 1919:294). The plant is also of ancient cultivation in China (see below under "Fibers"). The first word is shared with Iranian, but not with other Indo-European languages (which did not travel the same Central Asian route). It is not mentioned in archaeological finds in India, however.

3.7. *Citrus.* The genus *Citrus* is native to tropical Asia and Australia (Watt:vol. 2, pp. 333ff). India is credited with the domestication of several varieties (Burkill:276; Sauer:26). The question is–when? *Citrus* are not reported in Indian archaeological deposits. They occur late in Sanskrit (Suśruta, Lexicons, *Bhāgavata Purāṇa*). They were introduced into the Middle East about the tenth century A.D. (Ashtor:134; Hedrick:173). (The flourishing citrus groves that greeted the crusaders in the Levant were unknown in biblical times.)

Regarding individual species, the sweet orange (*Citrus sinensis*) is most often regarded as coming from southern China, as both its Latin name and some of its European vernacular names (e.g., German *Apfelsine*) indicate. The Arabic name *nāranj* (whence English *orange*, via Portuguese *laranja*) is, however, from Sanskrit, not Chinese. Watt (vol. 2, p. 336), Tannahill (1973:164), and others agree that the sweet orange was introduced into India from China (or Indo-China?) early in the Christian era. Hsüan Tsang found them already abundant in the North in the seventh century (Beal:vol. 1, p. 88). Paradoxically, the ancestor of both the sweet orange and the bitter or Seville orange (*Citrus aurantium*), the latter probably the first to reach Europe but not cultivated in India, is supposed to be the wild bitter orange of the Himalayas. Watt suggests that *nāraṅga* was first applied to this bitter orange and later transferred to the sweetened import from the East. The suggestion of a Dravidian source for *nāraṅga* is handicapped by the fact that the tree is a native of the Himalayas, not South India, and that the word appears long after the period of contact with any hypothetical aboriginal Dravidian speakers in the North had ceased. Another possibility would thus be some Himalayan language, but this again runs into the difficulty of late appearance—although conceivably it somehow just did not enter the Sanskrit stream until that time. The tree is also native to the Khasi Hills and probably more easterly Indo-Chinese ranges. The timing of the word's appearance coincides too well with the period of initial contact between India and mainland Southeast Asia for us not to consider a source in that region. Compare also the phonology of a known (island) Southeast Asian borrowing, *lavaṅga* 'clove'. (*Citrus* terminology in Dravidian languages does not appear to be old.)

The central Indian citrus name is clearly *nīmbū/nīmū*, basically the sour lime (*C. aurantifolia* in the new terminology), but used as a base for descriptive names of other species, including *C. limetta* 'sweet lime', *C. limon* 'lemon', and *C. maxima* 'pomelo'. The sour lime may be indigenous; its name is late and probably Austroasiatic (Mayrhofer:vol. 2, p. 166). The pomelo (*C. maxima*) is definitely a post-European import from Java; its name *cakotarā* is unexplained.

Oranges were carried westward to Italy and Iberia by the Arabs in the twelfth and thirteenth centuries and did so well that the variety developed at Cintra in Portugal allegedly sent its name back to India via the Arabs and the Persians as *santarā*. This is the usual story (cf. Yule and Burnell:642-43) but *santarā* refers to the Mandarin orange (Indian Council of Agricultural Research:349), *Citrus reticulata*, whereas the famed oranges of Cintra seem (?) to be *Citrus sinensis*. On the other hand, cf. the English word *tangerine*, from another locality not too far from Cintra. Worth noting also is the common ending *tarā*, cf. *sanTARĀ, cakoTARĀ*.

The place where the lemon originated is unclear. Tannahill (p. 175) suggests Central Asia, and the Indian Council of Agricultural Research (p. 348) confirms that it likes a cooler climate. It does not loom large on the Indian scene. The name *jambīr* (or *jambīrī nīmbū*) may conceivably be connected with that of a noncitrus fruit, the rose apple or *jambu*.

The one citrus with a Persian-derived name, the citron (*turanj*), is also the only one reported from the Mediterranean in classical times (Hedrick:173).

3.8. *Other Fruits and Nuts.* It should occasion little surprise that most of the temperate fruits and nuts (apples, pears, plums, pomegranates, pistachios, grapes, etc.) bear Persian names in Hindi. They are grown mainly in Kashmir and the hill areas of Panjab, Uttar Pradesh, and Himachal Pradesh (although the grape now flourishes in the Deccan). The Mughals did much to promote them. However, they were only among the latest of a series of promoters going back at least to Kanishka, the first century Kushana king (Beal:vol. 1, pp. 173-74). The Modern Persian-derived names, accordingly, must be only the latest in a series of names (some of them borrowed, it is true, from Middle Persian, which complicates the picture, cf. Laufer [1919:407]). On the ultimate origins of these plants themselves (mainly the more hilly margins of the Near East [Burkill:264]) we need not linger, except to note that the peach and the apricot were introduced into Persia itself from China (Laufer 1919:539-40; Isaac:71), a fact betrayed by their purely descriptive names in Persian (and thus Hindi) built on Pers. *ālū* 'plum'–'rough plum' (*shaftālū*) and 'golden plum' (*zardālū*).

Dried fruits generally also have Persian names (*kishmish, ālūbukhārā, khūbānī, mevā*, etc.) and, carried by the ubiquitous *Kabūlīwālā*, found their way to all parts of northern India.

It is interesting that several typically Indian fruits have Aryan-derived names in Hindi–the jackfruit (*kaṭahal* replacing earlier non-Aryan *panasa*), the *mahuā*, the soapnut (*rīṭhā*), the tamarind (*imlī*), the myrobalan (*āmlā*), and most important of all, the mango itself (*ām(b)*). The latter seems clearly cognate with the two preceding and with the Sanskrit word for 'sour'. I am not persuaded of any connection with Dravidian *māṅkāy*; there is no motivation or parallel for the loss of an initial /m/, and the Sanskrit form *āmra* is the only one mentioned by early travelers in the North and borrowed into such languages as Arabic (*anbā*), Persian (*amba*), and Chinese (*an-lo*) (Laufer 1919: 552); for the intrusive /-b-/ –*amB*–cf. *nīmū/nīmbū*. It might seem strange that the queen of Indian fruits is distinguished by such an unflattering title. There is evidence, however, that some of the glory of the mango is due to recent improvements, especially those effected by skilled Muslim arboriculturists set to work by such interested patrons as Babur (who did not think much of the mango as he found it). I owe this suggestion to my colleague C. M. Naim, who points out that many cultural varieties of mango have Persian names in token of this activity and that the technical vocabulary relating to grafting etc.–*kalam lagānā*–is of Persian origin. (This is confirmed by the *Encyclopaedia Britannica*, 1977, vol. 1, p. 330.) Before that, the mango may have been prized mainly for pickling, like its etymological cousin, the myrobalan, still is. (That, perhaps, is a rash statement, but its challenge should be answerable from references to the mango in pre-Muslim Indian literature: here is a small project for someone!)

The remaining indigenous fruits, with unexplained names, are not too impressive a lot: the rose apple and the jambolana plum (both apparently *jāman*), the former "with a delicate, rose-water perfume but dry and hardly worth eathing" (Hedrick:261), the latter "...harsh but sweetish...like a radish in taste" (ibid.); the "resin-flavored" *tendū* (*Diospyros melanoxylon*) or ebony fruit (the name is also applied to its relative, the persimmon, developed in China and recently introduced, *D. kaki*); the two 'wood apples', *kaith* (*Limonia acidissima*), "acid and smelling of rancid butter" (Hedrick:267), and *bel* (*Aegle marmelos*)–this last gets better notices. The banana (or plantain) and its name seem to be originally from mainland Southeast Asia (Burkill:277), though it has been long in India, perhaps since the Harappan civilization (Fairservis:304).

The only fruits reported from archaeological sites (Vishnu-Mittre:8) are the *ber* or jujube (*Zizyphus nummularia*) and the emblic myrobalan/*āmlā* (*Phyllanthus emblica*). Figs, mangos, and pomegranates are also assumed from the Harappan civilization, apparently from seal representations (Fairservis: 304). The fig is little grown in India at present and according to the Indian Council of Agricultural Research (p. 354) never has been. Hsüan Tsang reported it (Beal:163) but Ibn Batuta (Husain:xxxviii) found it missing. The date is likewise mainly a foreign item, to which a word formerly denoting an indigenous wild fruit is applied.

Many fruits widespread in India today are of New World origin. They are often recognizable by their double or triple names–one a descriptive name built on some existing plant name, another a foreign name (usually Amerindian via Portuguese, perhaps with further changes), not always readily recognizable as such. This contrasts with the single names of the indigenous fruits discussed above. Thus the papaya (*Carica papaya*) is *papītā/eraṇḍ-kharbūjā/eraṇḍ-mevā* (literally 'castor-oil watermelon/castor-oil fruit'); the guava (*Psidium guajava*) is *amrūd/bihī/jām* (Dakkini) (the first two names derived from the Persian for 'pear' and 'quince' respectively); the pineapple (*Ananas sativa*) is *anannās/bhuiṉkaṭahal* (literally 'earth-jackfruit'); the custard apple (*Annona squamosa*) is *āt/sharīfā/sītāphal*; and the sapodilla (*Achras sapota*) is *sapoṭa/cīkū* (the first of these names being very common, but studiously ignored by all Hindi dictionaries; the second is noticed by Bulcke and Chaturvedi and Tiwari).

The litchi, now widely cultivated in northern India (Indian Council of Agricultural Research:360), has retained its Chinese name, although many local varieties have been developed.

3.9. *Spices, Herbs, and Condiments.* India is traditionally the land of spices and condiments. Many of them, however, come originally from elsewhere. Quite a number come out of the West, either before the Aryans, with them, or at various periods after them. Most of these, which include especially members of the family *Umbelliferae*, are native to the Near East, particularly Iran. A few of these have Persian names: *jīrā* (cumin), *podīnā* (mint), *khaskhas* (poppyseed). Quite a number have descriptive Aryan names (a circumstance which indicates belated acquaintance, according to Sauer [p. 62] and other scholars): *ajamod* (parsley), *dhaniyā* (coriander), *sowā* (dill or fennel), *saunf* (aniseed), and *ajwāin* (ajowan)–the last (Sanskrit *yavānī*), according to Mayrhofer, containing the same reference to the Western foreigners (*Yavanas*) found in *yavanala* (Hindi *junhār*) 'sorghum'. Several are unclear in their affinity: *maruvā* (marjoram), *rāī* (mustard seed), *hīng* (asafoetida), and *kumkum* (saffron). *Lahsun* (garlic) should probably be included, though it has an outside chance of being Indo-European (the only such item). Laufer (1919:361) regards *hīng* as an ancient Iranian loanword in Sanskrit.

Most likely native to India are fenugreek, cardamom, cinnamon, ginger, turmeric, black pepper (*Piper nigrum*) and long pepper (*Piper longum*). The first of these is a crop of the North but is supposed to have a Dravidian name (*methī*). The rest are associated mainly with South India, although ginger and long peppers are found in the northeast as well. None of these has a Dravidian name except cardamom in part (*ilāycī*<*ēlā*), which, however, filtered into Hindi apparently via Persian. Cinnamon, which actually comes mainly from Ceylon (Sri Lanka), has a Persian name (*dār-cīnī*, corrupted in Hindi to *dāl-cīnī*), which indicates a roundabout acquaintance through China! Ginger and turmeric have Aryan-derived descriptive names. The word for *Piper nigrum* (Sanskrit *marīca*, Hindi *mirc*) is said to be Austroasiatic, although the plant is native to the Malabar coast, far from any Austroasiatic speakers. Our words for pepper derive from the word for *Piper longum, pipalī*, which appears to be an extension of a Sanskrit word for berry (and ultimately the sacred fig or *pīpal* tree), of unclear affinity.

The chili 'peppers' (genus *Capsicum*, not *Piper*) now so intimately a part of the Indian scene are clearly of New World origin (Pickersgill 1969:443-49; Crosby:170ff; Indian Council of Agricultural Research:267; Hedrick:134-36; Yule and Burnell:196), introduced in the seventeenth century. This is belied by their descriptive name, *lāl mirc, harā mirc*, etc. There is no Sanskrit or Persian word for them.

Several condiments reached India from Southeast Asia during the period of overseas contact: cloves (*laung*), nutmeg (*jāyphal*), mace (*jāvitrī*). Also from the island world came *Piper cubeba* "cubebs" whose name (*kabāb cīnī*), however, indicates (especially in its internal syntax) a roundabout journey via China and Iran, like that of cinnamon.

A much earlier arrival from Southeast Asia, evidently the mainland, was the most valuable condiment of them all, sugar. India has been the transmitter of sugarcane to peoples further west, and has thus often been regarded as its source, but botanists (Burkill:277; Laufer 1919:376; Hedrick:515-17) seem to favor Indo-China, and the word *śarkara* (Hindi *sakkar*) is seen as Mon-Khmer. The word for the cane, *ūkh*, is unexplained, but other words relating to sugar making (*guṛ, khā̃ṛ*) seem to be Dravidian. Typically again, the Hindi word for refined or white sugar, *cīnī*, appears to be Persian and to refer to China, cf. *maidā* 'refined flour'. Sugarcane is not reported from Indian archaeological finds, but is early in Sanskrit literature (*Atharvaveda*) (Allchin 1969*b*:327).

3.10/3.11. *Domestic Animals and Their Products.* Since the Aryan invaders are known to have had a predominantly pastoral economy, it is not surprising to find more Indo-European and Indo-European-derived terms in these areas than in any other (about 68 percent, conservatively put). Animal husbandry was not the monopoly of the Aryans in the prehistoric Indian context: the Harappans also had their livestock (Fairservis:179,184), and there were the stockade-building cattle-keepers of the Deccan (Fairservis: 323ff), whose affinities and cultural contributions have yet to be fully assessed. However, the Aryans, in addition to retaining most of their names for familiar animals, tended to bestow their own names on unfamiliar domestic animals of the new country as well (the water buffalo, the camel, the ass, and the elephant–though the last seems to be a partial calque), rather than borrow them–quite different from their attitude toward plants.

Nevertheless, the striking thing is the replacement in the course of the later evolution of Indo-Aryan of many of the older Aryan terms (e.g., of *aja-* 'goat', *avi-* 'sheep', words for 'colt', 'calf', 'kid', 'lamb', and, most important of all, *aśva-* 'horse') with new terms either internally derived or borrowed, typically with an originally diminutive, pejorative, or otherwise specialized meaning. There often seem to be shifts of referents involved. Thus, the Hindi term *bheṛ* 'sheep' is alleged to be Austroasiatic: this would be hard to reconcile with the fact that sheep are in no way associated with eastern Indian or Southeast Asian environments or cultures, but the suggested etymon actually means 'goat' and "the goat is both herd and household animal and is found among people who have none of the other herd animals, but who keep pigs and fowls" (Sauer:92). (It is also possible that Austroasiatic speakers were once much further west, as Hock 1975 claims.)

A similar and greater apparent anomaly is the replacement of *aśva-* 'horse', the animal introduced by the Aryans and deeply associated with their communal rituals, by the non-Aryan term *ghoṭaka-*. Hock (1975:116,fn. 9*a*) joins Bloch in objecting to the Dravidian etymology usually given this word, on the grounds of (1) initial /gh/, (2) horse breeding not being associated at any time with the Deccan, and (3) possible cognates in Turkish and Modern Greek. I have checked the last point, and although I can find no Turkish word that seems to qualify ('horse' is *at* or *beygir*), in Modern Greek, besides *álogo* 'horse', we find *gáidaros* 'ass', which could stand in a relationship with both Sanskrit *ghoṭa-* and Tamil *kutirai*, suggesting a lost Middle Eastern source–or an African one, since Nubia was the site of that animal's domestication (Sauer:93). Domestic asses (and onagers) were known in the Middle East and in the Indus valley before the arrival of the Aryans and their horses (Fairservis:179). The Pali gloss 'poor horse' suggests the process of semantic shift here, perhaps pejorative nicknaming. Hindi *gadhā*/Sanskrit *gardabhaka* 'ass' might well belong here also.

A final irony is the use of a Persian word to designate the primary domestic creature India is generally credited with (Allchin 1969*a*:320; Sauer:32; Fairservis:101)–the chicken (*murgī*). (This is cognate, it is true, with Sanskrit *mṛga* 'quadruped, animal', but 'bird'–the meaning in Persian–is not one of the meanings of the Sanskrit.) Descriptive Sanskrit words (*uṣākala-*, *kṛkavāka-*, etc.) appear to have left no descendants, although the onomatopoeic *kukkuṭa*/*-i* has left the dialectal archaic-poetical Hindi word *kukṛī* (and *kukṛā*) (Prasād, Sahāy, and Śrīvāstav), along with words in a number of northwest frontier languages. A Dravidian word for chicken (Ta. *kōṟi*, Te. *kōḍi*) which may have wandered as far as Greek (*kotta*) and Russian (*kur-itsa*, pl. *kuri*)–although Slavic etymologists would not accept this, preferring to derive it from an onomatopoeic verb–may show up in Hindi *kuḍuk* 'a hen that has ceased laying eggs' (*The Student's Practical Dictionary*:348a; Prasād, Sahāy, and Śrīvāstav:299b).

The Aryan cow and pig survive. There is some dispute as to whether the Aryans kept pigs. Brandenstein was of the opinion that the two Indo-European stems for pigs **sus* and **pork'os* referred to wild and domestic pigs respectively, and since the latter was not found in Indo-Iranian (Eric Hamp informs me that Benveniste has since adduced some tenuous evidence of its existence in Iranian, however), this forms part of his argument concerning the economy of the early Aryans (pig raising presumably demanding, unlike cattle and horse raising, a more settled way of life than he postulated at the first stage). Most Indo-Europeanists today think the two words referred to adult and young pigs, and archaeological evidence also indicates that domestic pigs were known throughout the Proto-Indo-European period, though less numerous in the early phases (Gimbutas:157). It also indicates a less nomadic way of life at the beginning. Something closer to pastoral nomadism (versus stockbreeding) was a feature of a later, specifically Indo-Iranian phase. Opinions differ as to whether domestic pigs diffused from Southeast Asia (Sauer: 31,37), from the Near East (Isaac:85), or were developed in several centers independently, including Europe and China (Ho 1975:103, 109-11). The oldest archaeological evidence is, of course, from the Near East (seventh millennium B.C. at Çayönü in Anatolia [Isaac:32]). In any case, the pig seems to have been known in India well before the Aryan invasions (Allchin 1969*a*: 318-19), and, wherever it came from (east or west), we need not postulate the Aryans driving herds of pigs before them across the Central Asian steppes and deserts. Nevertheless, the pig is known by an Aryan name, not only in Hindi (*sūar*) but as far as Sri Lanka (MSinh. *īrī, ūrā* from OSinh. *suhuru* [Turner:13544]).

The subcategory of animal *products* is at least 80 percent Aryan. This could at least raise the question whether, in spite of the prior occurrence of cattle in India, such uses as, for example, those connected with milking might not in fact be an Aryan contribution. (A contribution, that is, to the Indian scene, or perhaps just to the North Indian scene, but not to humanity in general. There is a fairly extensive Dravidian vocabulary for dairy products, although much of it seems to be descriptive or derived from more general reference, e.g., Ta. *pāl,* Br. *pālh* 'milk; sap of plants, etc.' [DED 3370], although the reverse is also possible, and it is hard to refute the evidence of an irregular verb stem: Ta. *kaṟa-/-pp-/-nt-* 'to milk' [DED 1166]–South Dravidian only, however.) Milking apparently diffused from a single southwest Asian center (Sauer:87) and there are important cattle raising cultures without it (China, Southeast Asia, tropical Africa, etc.). These may have occupied a larger area in 2000-1500 B.C. East African evidence may be relevant to this question, since the zebu cattle there probably came from India at a remote date (Isaac:65). At present the cattle raising peoples (e.g., the Nuer, the Masai) do utilize milk in addition to their well-known utilization of blood (Cranstone 1969:251-52).

3.12/3.13. *Tools, Implements, and Other Terms Connected with Agriculture.* This is obviously the area that could most stand expansion and where my present sample can only be suggestive, the area of what might be called technology and techniques. Investigation of the changing semantics of verb stems in connection with the latter is a particularly delicate matter, very different from the study of *realia*, living or inanimate. Whole sets of technical terms are involved, such as the one of largely Persian origin connected with fruit grafting mentioned above. Nevertheless, even in this small sample a few things stand out. Except for words referring to draft animals and their utilization, words for key agricultural implements (plow, hoe, winnowing basket, threshing floor) and other appurtenances of cultivation (seed, tank, furrow) are mostly non-Aryan, sometimes specifically Dravidian. Implements for reaping grain (wild as well as cultivated?) seem to have Aryan names. Terms relating to the general organization of agriculture (*kharīf, rabī, fasal*) come from Persian and belie North India's debt to the Mughals.

4.0. Conclusions and Suggestions for Further Work. Obviously this study only scratches the surface. I only hope it might lay a foundation for further work, despite its many imperfections and loose ends. It is now much clearer to me in which directions such work might most profitably proceed. In trying to sift through the literature dealing with the kinds of evidence reported in sections 2 and 3 of this paper, I have frequently run into much that is inconclusive as well as seemingly irreconcilable differences of opinion among the experts. There is a great deal of special pleading according to whether one is a Near Eastern diffusionist, a Southeast Asian diffusionist, a believer in multiple origins or an advocate of (or merely specialist in) some other area–or, among etymologists, whether one is an Indo-Europeanist, a Dravidianist, or an "Austricist." Burrow rightly complains (1968:321) of the tendency of older Indo-European scholarship to "resort to tortuous reconstructions in order to find, by hook or by crook, Indo-European explanations for Sanskrit words," even when "perfectly valid etymologies from Dravidian had already been pointed out." Such tendencies are by no means confined to Indo-Europeanists, however. We have noted the earlier overenthusiasm of Kuiper for Austroasiatic. Specialists often wear blinders, as it were. One of the more frequent things encountered is the attempt–perhaps not too surprising in the Indian cultural context, but indulged in by Western scholars as well–to find "by hook or by crook" Sanskrit etymologies for Hindi words for which obvious Persian sources are at hand (e.g., *afīm, khīrā*). Contradictory evidence from other specialties is not disputed or refuted; it is simply ignored.

No doubt when all the arguments with their evidence are aligned, some can be seen to have the better case, but it is often not easy to judge among so many specialist opinions, and perhaps presumptuous to try. Rather than aiming for such omniscience, I would propose as the next phase (along with the expansion of the Hindi base into appropriate specialized areas, and field work–

especially necessary in the area of tools, for we often do not know exactly what we are talking about when knowing might matter) the collection of another kind of evidence, namely the cross-linguistic geographical distribution of agricultural terms and their meanings. The distributions should be traced over languages of all linguistic stocks in the subcontinent (i.e., not just Indo-Aryan) and adjacent areas (e.g., Southwestern and Central Asia, northeast Africa, Southeast Asia) and beyond where necessary. Two types of distributions should be traced: first, the standard terms for given referents; and second, the distribution of cognate terms, whatever their referents (keeping track of the referents, however). The first, ideally, should yield "term areas"; the second (taken with the first) could point to "centers" of at least some term distributions. To trace cognates, of course, linguistic history has to be taken into account: contemporary surface forms may be deceptive (deceptively similar or deceptively different)!

When taken in conjunction with the available etymological, archaeological, botanical, and literary-historical evidence, this type of data may provide keys to some of the riddles and conflicting conclusions produced by that evidence. It would also contribute much to cultural history in its own right.

Allchin (1969*b*:328) actually proposes something similar:

> The new perspectives provided by archaeology hold out great hopes for a reappraisal of other types of evidence. It is evident that much useful work could still be done in plotting the modern dialect names for different species and considering them in a historical light. Such "linguistic palaeontology" is likely to yield useful information, now that the chronological dimensions are beginning to appear.

I am not sure just what he means by "modern dialect names" but I would insist that the plotting must extend outside India, particularly in view of Vishnu-Mittre's warning:

> In view of their belated appearance around 2700 B.C. or even if the date is stretched to 3000 B.C., one would indeed be ill-advised to look for the origins of cultivated plants here (p. 1).

> The plant economy of the Harappans on the whole appears to have been exotic, largely derived from western Asia and

> Africa via Iran....
> The plant economy of the post-Harappan period prior to the Iron Age too is largely of exotic origin; either the plant species had been diffused through the Harappans migrating to other areas...or they were introduced afresh through or via Iran (p. 15).
>
> There is a big gap in our knowledge of plant economy between the Chalcolithic and late Historical cultures since the Iron Age has not yielded much information. If [the gap is real] the reappearance of many cultivars in the early Historical period could be assigned to foreign influences....
> It would thus appear that the ancient plant economy of the Indian subcontinent has been characterized largely by foreign influences from western Asia, Africa, central Asia, etc. The finds earlier to those of Indian rice from Thailand would suggest southeastern Asian influence if proven that the earlier records of rice from that country or elsewhere are indeed of cultivated rice (p. 16).

I shall return to my suggestions later, with proposals as to how they might be made somewhat less daunting. First, however, it is necessary to examine the conclusions that can be drawn from the present paper.

4.1. *Gross Analysis of the Etymological Data.* We must now look at the data overall, strictly from the etymological point of view. Because of the many doubtful etymologies, we cannot be absolutely precise in our statistical breakdown of the data and will have to indicate whether we are being "generous" or "conservative" in our assessments. (Only Hindi forms will be listed. The reader interested in the etymological data is directed to section 2.)

1. *Aryan*—19.4 percent. No more than 20 percent of the Hindi terms treated here (generously assessed, but excluding for this purpose later Persian borrowings) are Aryan-derived.
   a. Only 3.5 percent might be said to go back, in roughly their present meanings, to Indo-European:

anāj 'grain' (Skt. 'food')	*jot(ā)* 'bullock-ropes'
ūn 'wool'	*dahī* 'curds'
gāy 'cow'	*lunnā* 'to reap'

camṛā 'hide, skin'	*sāg* 'greens'
jūā/juāth 'yoke'	*sūar*

Possibly *lahsun* 'garlic' and *san* 'fiber hemp' also belong to this category. The former is very doubtful. The latter is widespread in Indo-European languages (Germanic, Slavic, Greek, Iranian) but regarded as a non-Indo-European loanword, possibly Uralic (Mayrhofer:fasc. 21, p. 292).

b. Another 2.8 percent or so may go back as words, but have altered (specialized or shifted) meanings in Hindi versus Sanskrit, or in later versus earlier Sanskrit:

arvī 'arum' (*esculent root)	*dhān* 'unhusked rice' (*grain)
ālū 'potato' (*esculent root)	*pān* 'betel leaf' (*wing, feather; leaf)
cakkī 'quern' (*wheel)	*bhāt* 'boiled rice' (*food)
jau 'barley' (*grain)	*ropnā* 'to plant' (*pierce, break)

The word *kakṛi* 'long melon' belongs here–if it is really Indo-European.

c. The remaining 13.1 percent seem to be descriptive derivations within Sanskrit. (The distinction between this category and the one above may not always be clear.) It includes many terms for characteristic Indian animals and food plants as well as for later arrivals from the Near East–proving to no great surprise that Indo-Aryan was as up to naming new things from its own resources as the next language. (Those marked with an asterisk show further semantic development in Hindi.)

ajamod 'parsley'	*bacheṛā* 'colt'
ajwāin 'ajowan'	*bathuā 'Chenopodium album'*
adrak 'ginger'	*bhaiṉs/mhaiṉs* 'buffalo'
ambāṛī 'rozelle; hogplum'	*mahuā 'Bassia latifolia'*
ām 'mango'	*ratālū* 'potato-yam'
āmlā 'emblic myrobalan'	*rīṭhā* 'soapnut'
imlī 'tamarind'	*līl* 'indigo'
ūṉṭ 'camel'	*loniyā* 'purslane'
kaṭahal 'jackfruit'	*sāṉṛ* 'bull'
kesar 'saffron'	*sāṉwāṉ 'Echinochloa frumentacea'*
khurpā 'blade of hoe'	*sītā* 'furrow'
**khet* 'tilled field'	**sītāphal* 'custard apple'
khair 'catechu'	**sūtī* 'cotton cloth'

gadhā 'ass' (?)
ghī 'clarified butter'
cūkā/cokā 'Indian sorrel'
cenā/cīnā 'Panicum miliaceum'
junhār 'Sorghum'
dhaniyā 'coriander'
bakrā 'goat'
bachṛā 'calf'
sowā 'dill'
saun̲ph 'fennel; aniseed'
han̲suā 'reaping hook'
haldī 'turmeric'
hāthī 'elephant'

The words *gehūn̲* 'wheat' (*godhūmā* 'cow-smoke'), *sahijan* (drumstick-tree' (*sobhañjana* 'splendor-ointment'), and *afīm* 'opium' (*ahiphena* 'snake-foam') may also belong here, but I strongly suspect false etymologies or morphological restructuring.

2. *Non-Aryan*–80 percent. By definition, the remainder or 80 percent of the terms must be non-Aryan (that is, non-Indo-European). Of course it is not quite that simple because of the problematic status of earlier and later Iranian loanwords and of late descriptive formations within Hindi. The surprising thing is that *only a small proportion of this remainder is either Dravidian or Austroasiatic*, even by generous estimates.
   a. Dravidian (suggested)–9.5 percent

kand 'bulbous root'
kaddu 'bottle gourd'
kudālī 'kind of hoe'
(*kulthī* 'horsegram' [see also 2b])
(*kūṛ* 'furrow')
khal 'threshing floor'
khāṇṛ 'unrefined sugar'
(*guār* 'cluster bean [*Cyamopsis*]')
(*ghoṛā* 'horse') (?)
(*canā* 'chickpea')
(*capātī* 'thin flour cake' [Persianized])
(*cāval* 'husked rice')
(*talāu* 'reservoir, tank')
tāṛ 'toddy palm'
tuar 'yellow pigeon-pea(*Cajanus*)'
(*nārangī* 'orange')
nāriyal 'coconut'
parwal 'Trichosanthes dioeca'

phal 'fruit'
bīj 'seed'
bel 'Aegle marmelos'
boṛā 'Vigna sinensis'

(*mūlī* 'radish')
methī 'fenugreek'

sem 'Dolichos lablab; Vicia faba'
sūp 'winnowing fan'

Several of these are quite doubtful; the more doubtful are put in parentheses. The list nevertheless contains some key terms. To these may be added *ilāycī* 'cardamom' through Persian, but ultimately Dravidian.

b. Austroasiatic (suggested)–5.7 percent

aṇḍā 'egg'
kapās 'cotton'
kapūr 'camphor'
kulthī 'horsegram' (see also 2a)
kelā 'banana'
koṉhṛā 'pumpkin'
tumbā 'bottle gourd'
tomṛā 'dried bottle gourd'
nīmbū 'lime'

**bheṛ* 'sheep'
mirc 'pepper (*Piper nigrum*)'
moṭh 'Phaseolus aconitifolius'
laṉgal 'plow'
laua 'bottle gourd'
sakar 'sugar'
sarsoṉ 'mustard'
hal 'plow'

c. Persian–21.3 percent. In this large category (of varied and often unclear ultimate origin) we shall include a few items, marked (I), apparently borrowed from Middle Iranian rather than Modern Persian. Words will not be so marked, however, which, though borrowed by Sanskrit from Middle Iranian, were reborrowed from Modern Persian by Hindi (e.g., *bādām*). Items marked with an asterisk have undergone important semantic changes.

angūr 'grape'
anjīr 'fig' (I)
akhrot 'walnut' (I)
anār 'pomegranate'
aphīm/*afīm* 'opium'
**amrūd* 'guava'
**āṛū* 'peach'
**ālūcā* 'plum'
ālūbālū 'cherry'
ālūbukhārā 'prune'
ilāycī 'cardamom'
karam 'kale'
karamkallā 'cabbage'
kalam 'graft (fruit)'
kāhū 'lettuce'

tambākū 'tobacco' (Amerind.)
tarkārī 'vegetable'
tarbūj/*tarbūz* 'watermelon'
turanj 'citron'
nāspātī/*nāshpātī* 'pear'
dānā 'seed, grain'
dālcīnī/*dārcīnī* 'cinnamon'
piyāj/*piyāz* 'onion'
pistā 'pistachio'
podīnā/*pudīnā* 'mint'
postā 'opium poppy'
phasal/*fasal* 'harvest; season'
battak 'duck; goose'
bāklā 'Phaseolus vulgaris'
bādām 'almond'

kāsnī 'endive-chicory-escarole'	*bāwlī* 'large well'
kishmish 'raisin'	*(*) bihī* 'quince; guava'
kulfā 'purslane'	*murg̲ī* 'chicken'
kharīf 'rainy-season crops'	**mewā* 'dried fruit'
kharbūjā/kharbūzā 'muskmelon'	*maidā* 'refined flour'
khaskhas 'poppyseed'	*rabī* 'winter crops'
khīrā 'cucumber'	*rewatcīnī* 'rhubarb'
khūbānī 'dried apricot'	*lobiyā* 'cowpea (*Vigna sinensis*)'
gandanā 'leek'	(*shakarqand* [see 4f below])
**cīnī* 'refined sugar'	*sharīfā* 'custard apple'
cukandar 'beet'	*shalgam* 'turnip'
jardālū/zardālū 'apricot'	*satālū/shaftālū* 'peach'
jafrān/zafrān 'saffron'	*santarā* 'mandarin orange' (Pg.)
jīrā/zīrā 'cumin' (I)	*sabzī* 'vegetable'
	seb 'apple'
	hīṉg/hing 'asafoetida' (I)

A characteristic of the Persian loans is the postposed modifier as in *rewatcīnī, kabābcīnī, dālcīnī, karamkallā, ālūbukhārā. Zardālū* 'apricot' and *shaftālū* 'peach' do not follow this rule.

d. Indo-Iranian–3.2 percent. This category consists of a few words common to Indic and Iranian without clear priority and of partly unclear, partly specialized Indo-European origin. Those that seem to go back to Indo-European roots but do not exist as words in other branches of Indo-European are marked (IE). Special meaning shifts in Hindi are marked with an asterisk.

āṭā 'coarse flour'	*phāl* 'plowshare'
gehūṉ 'wheat'	*bhāṉg* 'leaves of hemp'
darāṉtī 'sickle' (IE)	**makkhan* 'butter'
dūdh 'milk' (IE)	**māṣ/māh* 'black gram (*Phaseolus mungo*)'
**poī 'Basella alba'*	

To this category may possibly belong *hing* 'asafoetida' (4c) and *langal* 'plow' (4b).

e. Other Specific Foreign–2.5 percent

āt(ā) 'custard apple' (Amerind.) *līcī* 'litchee' (Chinese)

kājū 'cashew' (Pg.<Amerind.)	*lauṉg* 'cloves' (Indonesian)
ṭamāṭar 'tomato' (Eng.<Amerind.)	*sapoṭā* 'sapodilla' (Pg.<Amerind.)
mausambī/musammī 'sweet lime' (Pg.<Afr.?)	

There are very few of these in Hindi; there seem to be more in coastal Indo-Aryan (Bengali, Gujarati, Marathi). In Hindi these items either have alternate names (see 4f, etc.) or refer to items not grown in North India and known only as imports (*kājū, lauṉg*).

f. Hindi Descriptive Formations–8.2 percent. These typically involve elements from non-Aryan sources. Some seem to be onomatopoetic.

eraṇḍkharbūjā 'papaya'	*bhaṭmāṣ* 'soybean'
kacālū 'taro'	*malāī* 'cream'
kāfrī mirc 'bell pepper (*Capsicum*)'	*mānkand* 'giant taro'
khaṭṭā 'bitter orange'	*mūṉgphalī* 'peanut'
khīl 'puffed rice'	*memnā* 'kid; lamb'
jamīnkand/zamīnqand 'elephant yam'	*lal mirc* 'chillies'
pahāṛī bādām 'cobnut; hazelnut'	*vilāetī baiṉgan* 'tomato'
phalī 'pod'	*vilāetī mūṉg* 'peanut'
phūṇṭ 'bursting melon'	*vilāetī sem 'Phaseolus vulgaris'*
phūlgobhī 'cauliflower'	*shakarkand* 'sweet potato'
bandgobhī 'cabbage'	*simlā ālū* 'manioc'
bijaurā 'citron'	*simlā mirc* 'bell pepper (*Capsicum*)'

g. Unknown–31 percent. The remainder–words of unknown origin–constitutes the largest category in our sample. Category 4d (excluding Indo-European items) should probably be added to it, bringing the "unknown" to 34 percent. In addition, it should be remembered that a significant portion of the suggested Dravidian and Austroasiatic etymologies is uncertain. (In a selection more truly representative of rural life, the proportion is likely to rise. Many items–for example, in Grierson's *Bihar Peasant Life*–were excluded because I could not ascertain their exact referents. The sample is thus skewed in favor of the familiar and the urban–which here largely means Persian.) They may be broken down into three subcategories:

i. Unexplained words–that is, not explained with any degree of satisfaction–which existed in Sanskrit–22 percent. Speculations exist in some cases, of course–here noted in parentheses: (IE), (Drav.), (AA), etc. An asterisk is used to indicate meaning development in Hindi.

**arhar* 'pigeon-pea (*Cajanus*)'
īkh/ūkh 'sugarcane'
kaṉgnī '*Setaria* millet' (cf. Gk.)
kakaṛī 'long melon' (IE?)
karelā 'bitter gourd (*Momordica*)'
kundarū 'ivy gourd (*Coccinia*)'
kuaṉ 'well'
kuṭkī '*Panicum sumatrense*'
kusum 'safflower'
kodoṉ '*Paspalum* millet'
kaith '*Feronia* = mod. *Limonia*'
khajūr 'date'
khāl 'hide'
(*gadhā* 'ass' [Skt. internal der.?])
galgal 'citron'
gāñjā 'hemp'
gājar 'carrot'
guār 'clusterbean (*Cyamopsis*)' (Drav.?)
(*ghoṛā* 'horse' [Drav.?])
canā 'chickpea' (Drav.?)
ciciṇḍa 'snake gourd (*Trichosanthes cucumerine/anguina*)'
caulāī 'amaranth'
jambīr 'lemon'
jāman 'rose apple; jambolana plum'
jāyphal 'nutmeg'

(*) tendu 'Coromandel ebony; persimmon'
dākh 'grape'
**pālak* 'spinach'
piplī/piplā 'long pepper (*Piper longum*)'
pūlī 'sheaf'
ber 'jujube'
besan 'gram flour'
baiṉgan 'eggplant'
**bonā* 'to sow'
bhaṇṭā 'eggplant'
bhiṇḍī 'okra'
**bhūsā* 'straw, chaff'
maṉṛuā 'ragi or finger millet (*Eleusine*)'
(*) makoy 'nightshade; Cape gooseberry'
**makkā/makāī* 'maize'
maruvā 'marjoram'
marsā 'Gangetic amaranth'
masūr 'lentil' (Drav.?)
mūṉg 'green gram (*Phaseolus aureus*)'
meṉhdī 'henna; myrtle'
raī 'small-seeded mustard'
reṉṛ 'castor-oil plant'
roṭī 'bread'
lahsun 'garlic' (AA? IE?)
lāī/lāvā 'parched rice'
san 'fiber hemp' (Uralic?)

jāvitrī 'mace'
tiṇḍā 'round gourd'
til 'sesame'
tīsī/alsī 'flax'
sahijan 'drumstick-tree' (Skt. deriv.?)
sāl 'rice' (Persian?)
singhāṛā 'water chestnut'
sūran 'telinga potato; yam'
selā 'rice parboiled with husks'
sevaiṉ 'vermicelli'

ii. Unexplained words not attested in Sanskrit but reconstructed by Turner from several occurrences in Modern Indo-Aryan–5.4 percent.

āl 'red dyestuff' (**alla*)
urad 'black gram (*Phaseolus mungo*)' (**uḍidda*)
khesārī 'chicklingvetch (*Lathyrus*)' (**kesārī/khesārī*)
carsā 'raw oxhide' (**carassa*)
cāwal/cāṉwal 'husked rice' (**cāmala/cāvala*) (Drav.?)
chāch 'buttermilk' (**chācchi*)
jwār 'Sorghum' (**yavakāra*)
torī 'mustard seed' (**troṭika*)?
dāl 'split pulse' (**dāla*) (cw. IE)
bājrā 'pearl/bulrush millet (*Pennisetum*) (**bājjara*)
binaulā 'cottonseed' (**vīnōpala*?)
bail 'ox' (**balilla*) (IE? Drav.?)
maṭar 'peas' (**maṭṭara*)
rahilā 'chickpea' (**rahala*)
rūī 'cotton wool' (**rūa*)
supārī 'betel nut' (**suppāra*)
sūjī 'semolina' (**sūjjī/sōjjī*)

iii. Unexplained words in Hindi not reconstructed or treated by Turner–3.6 percent.

ghiyā 'dishcloth gourd (*Luffa aegyptica*)'
ghuiyāṉ 'kind of yam or taro'
cakotrā 'pomelo'
cīkū 'sapodilla'
cīlū 'apricot'
papītā 'papaya'

peṭhā 'ash gourd (*Benincasa*)'
sūthnī 'aerial yam'
hālim 'garden cress'
he̱ngā 'harrow'

4.2. *Conclusions from the Overall Etymological Analysis.* A better title for this section might be "Questions Raised."

1. The greatest question is raised by the fact that about one-third of the items treated do not seem to be clearly either Aryan or Dravidian or Munda/Austroasiatic or Persian or of known foreign origin. While it is possible that further work will show a few more of them to belong to one or another of these categories, we have also seen that the list of "unknowns" can be considerably expanded and that all the words already accounted for in the other categories cannot be regarded as secure. A sizable group of words, therefore, seems to point to an unknown language or languages in northern or northwestern India or close by. It seems that I am not the first to notice this. The existence of such an element has been strongly advocated by Burrow (1968:327-32 [originally published 1958]), who refers especially to the work of Koppers on the Bhils:

> It is my opinion that, when all has been done in this direction which can be done, the number of loan-words in Sanskrit, which cannot be explained as either Dravidian or Munda, will remain considerable. It may very well turn out that the number of such words which cannot be explained will outnumber those which can be. This is the impression one gets, for instance, from the field of plant names, since so far only a minority of the...non-Aryan words has been explained from these two linguistic families.... Evidence such as this leads to the conclusion that there must have been several non-Aryan languages or families of languages which exercised an influence on the vocabulary of Indo-Aryan (p. 327).

> The most ancient element in the population of the mountainous region of Central India cannot be identified as either Kol [that is, Munda] or Dravidian. There are quite a number of tribes in the region who can be regarded with

> some plausibility as the pre-Gond and pre-Kol stratum of the population. The Baigas are a well-known case in point (p. 330).

> Thus [Koppers] arrives at a large group of non-Munda and non-Dravidian tribes, scattered over a large area...there is no need to assume that these among themselves necessarily form a united group. Koppers' theory represents a clear-cut break with a common tradition in Indian ethnological studies which looked for either Dravidian or Munda in everything that was pre-Aryan. In the case of Nahali, at any rate, it turns out that it has some linguistic support (p. 331).

> We...have to assume the existence of other pre-Aryan languages and language families to account for the large number of unexplained words in Sanskrit.... What goes for Central India was originally the case no doubt in northern and southern India, and the universal adoption of Indo-Aryan in the North and Dravidian in the South have covered up an original linguistic diversity (p. 332).

It also raises a question, one might add, of the linguistic affiliations of the Harappan civilization. Was it perhaps multilingual? Burrow's argument is based on Sanskrit, but confirmed by Hindi. The non-Dravidian, non-Munda element in the Indo-Aryan lexicon persists, and even grows (cf. Turner's reconstructed items, most of which have a distinctive phonological appearance, it may be noted). Needless to say, not all unexplained items need be attributed to this ancient stratum: some no doubt stem from insufficiently investigated foreign contacts.

2. The Dravidian element, while not large, does loom somewhat larger than the Munda or Austroasiatic element (at least by virtue of inclusion of a number of doubtful items). However, it seems to decline from Sanskrit to Hindi. Though this is not documented here, I could not help noting while researching this paper that many a Dravidian word current in Sanskrit has left no living descendants in Hindi. Either one of its Aryan synonyms has alone survived, or its place is taken by a new Aryan coinage. (An example is the word for 'jackfruit' *panasa*, replaced by Aryan 'thorn-fruit' *kaṭahal*.)
3. The Austroasiatic element is quite small, suggesting, according to Burrow, that "the hypothesis that languages of this family were current much

further west than they are now found" is mistaken. "The evidence as it is so far established would suggest that these languages in ancient times as well as now were situated only in eastern India" (1968:328). Standard Hindi is based on the western dialects. It might be interesting to see if some of the terms in, for example, *Bihar Peasant Life* which have no analogs in Standard Hindi show more Munda affinities than Bengali does. There do, however, seem to be a few significant later accretions to this category, e.g., *nīmbū, kapūr*. It is possible that these come from the period of Indian contact with Mon-Khmer peoples in Southeast Asia rather than from the Kolarians of India proper. The problem is complicated by the fact that many investigators have not differentiated properly between Austroasiatic and Austronesian and label as Austroasiatic items which may be Indonesian.

4. The deep Persian influence on North Indian life is shown even by this study of agricultural vocabulary, although that influence is sometimes thought to be preeminently urban. It would be interesting to examine other semantic areas to determine where Persian influence is strongest and where it is weakest. Although here perhaps skewed by the heavy representation of temperate fruits and vegetables–which, however, are part of the scene in the extensive hill areas of the North–it is underrepresented also by our failure to delve very deeply into technical vocabulary. Although we are discussing "Aryan" versus "non-Aryan" (that is, autochthonous?) elements in Indian civilization, it is clear that, from the medieval period on, a third component must be taken into account that does not easily fit either label.
5. The differential survival of Sanskrit lexical items raises the question of whether they were used with the same frequency in all parts of India. To answer it would require the comparison of different languages on this point.

4.3. *Etymologies and Areas of Origin.* Let us now look at the data in a different way, and see how the etymologies match up with the areas of origin of the items in question, where these are known. This section can be only suggestive, since for many items this is not known, or has been guessed at with the aid of the etymologies themselves. It should also be remembered that it is not only areas of origin that may be involved, but areas through which an item was transmitted to India.

1. *Indian origin.* Of items suspected of originating in India itself, at least ten

have descriptive or derived Aryan names in Hindi (including turmeric, ginger, sorrel, purslane, tamarind, myrobalan, soapnut, jackfruit, mango, and *Bassia latifolia*), plus several terms for rice–if that is of Indian origin–and the names for such local domestic animals as the elephant and the buffalo. Perhaps indigo should be added. One of the names of the drumstick tree and, very insecurely, the names of two of the pulses (horsegram and cluster bean) are or may be Dravidian, along with fenugreek, cardamom (through Persian), the bel fruit, the gourd *Trichosanthes dioeca*, and the toddy palm. To these should be added the names of local tools and features of agricultural engineering–the tank, the Indian hoe, and the winnowing fan. Only the sour lime (if it is indeed an Indian domesticate), pepper, the word "egg," and possibly horsegram are ascribed to Austroasiatic (or Austronesian?). As noted earlier, the chicken now goes by a Persian name. Other Indian items–the millets *Paspalum scrobiculatum* and *Panicum sumatrense*, the pulses *Phaseolus mungo, Ph. aureus,* and *Ph. aconitifolius*–as well as, probably, the cluster bean speculatively ascribed to Dravidian above (*Cyamopsis tetragonoloba*), Indian nightshade, safflower, the rose apple, Coromandel ebony, and perhaps another name of the drumstick tree, the wood apple (*Feronia*), eggplant, Gangetic and other amaranths, and the gourds *Momordica, Coccinia,* and *Trichosanthes cucumerina*–are in the category of "unexplained."

2. *Southeast Asian origin.* Clove, mace, nutmeg, and pomelo came to India from Indonesia; the first has an Indonesian, the rest unexplained names in Hindi. To these the coconut perhaps should be appended; although its ultimate origin may be further afield, Indonesia and Ceylon were no doubt its last stops before reaching India proper: it has been speculated that the Hindi and Sanskrit word is Dravidian, which would represent an obvious final intermediary before coming to the attention of North India.

It is not always easy–or perhaps desirable–to differentiate between mainland Southeast Asian and eastern Indian origin. The area of origin of some important cultivated yams has been shown cytogenetically to be in the vicinity of the upper Irrawaddy and Mekong (Alexander and Coursey: 414): several yams and taros have unexplained names in Hindi. Although the betel leaf and catechu have descriptive-derived Indo-European names, the betel nut itself–like the leaf, part of the Spirit Cave finds (Solheim 1970:145) and therefore very ancient in the region–has an unexplained name. The word for camphor, several words for bottle gourd (*Lagenaria*), the word for banana, and the main word for sugar are Austroasiatic. Other words for various forms of sugar are Dravidian or "unknown." (Although the bottle gourd is distributed worldwide, it may not be amiss to attribute it to Southeast Asia as we are doing here. Southeast Asia seems to be big on bottle gourds. According to Chang (1970), quoted in Solheim (1970), it "figures prominently in the creation myths throughout Southeast Asia and must have been in use in the region since antiquity.") If rice should turn out to be a Southeast Asian domesticate, it may be noted that some of its names are unexplained.

3. *East Asian origin.* It is likewise difficult to differentiate between domestications in southern China and northern mainland Southeast Asia. Prominent here is the sweet orange, which, however, allegedly has a name in Hindi derived from a place-name in Portugal. To this may be added the litchi, retaining a Chinese name, and the persimmon, to which Hindi has understandably extended the word for ebony fruit, a related species. Another name for orange is alleged to be possibly Dravidian. Turning to North Chinese domesticates, the millets *Panicum miliaceum* and *Echinochloa frumentacea*, pak choi (*Brassica chinensis*), and the soybean all have descriptive or derived Aryan names–all except *sāwā̱n* explicitly indicating origin in China or Tibet. There are several kinds of rhubarb, some originating in Siberia and Mongolia, some in the Himalayas, one in eastern Persia and Afghanistan (according to Hedrick, pp. 490-91). I am not sure to which the term *rewatcīnī* refers, but it is a Persian term indicating connection with China. The peach and apricot have Persian names.
4. *American origin.* These for the most part are readily recognizable from their descriptive Hindi names or alternate names: the chili pepper, haricot bean, lima bean, tomato, peanut, papaya, pineapple, bell pepper, sweet potato, etc. The sapodilla, papaya, custard apple, pineapple, tobacco, and tomato also have foreign names or alternate names. The guava, potato, Cape gooseberry or Brazil cherry, and again the custard apple have names extended from native or earlier plants. Only the name for maize is a mystery; one of its alternate names suggests introduction via the eastern Himalayas. The Austroasiatic name for the pumpkin (if this is correct) suggests introduction via Southeast Asia. Neither is unreasonable.
5. *West Asian origin.* This category perhaps should be divided into Iranian-Central Asian and Near Eastern-Mediterranean. Both Persian and unexplained (and a couple of Indo-European) names are found among items of both subcategories. I will not list them all here; they essentially comprise all items not mentioned under the other areas, and make up by far the largest category. A lone Austroasiatic etymon–*sarso̱n*–must either be a mistake or involves a very special history.

6. *African origin.* An important group of plants–plus one animal, the ass–seems to come originally from Africa. Two routes, and possibly a third, are indicated: via the "Sabaean Lane" (South Arabia) and Iran; directly to South India; and via Southeast Asia–if the Austroasiatic etymology of cotton, *kapās*, is to be accepted. Direct contact between Africa and Southeast Asia without the mediation of India was not unknown; the problem is the relative age of cotton in India versus Southeast Asia. The names of *Dolichos lablab*, one variety of *Cajanus*, and one variety of *Vigna* seem to be Dravidian; that of another *Vigna* is Persian–or really much older in the Near East (Sumerian). *Sorghum* and the yam bean may have descriptive Aryan names. Sesame, okra, the castor-oil plant, bajra, ragi, and another variety of *Cajanus* are unexplained.

4.4 *Conclusions from the Areal Analysis.* India has been open to economic contributions from all directions, as well as originating a number on her own. Those from the Near East or Western Asia by far outweigh, in sheer number of items, those from further east, at least in this survey. At the same time, Southeast Asia, aside from its own contributions, seems to have been the route by which a number of American and South Chinese cultivars reached India. On the other hand, certain Southeast Asian, Chinese, and even South Indian items are known to North India via the roundabout route through (China and) Iran. Northeast Africa is a source of items in the Indian economy at least equal to, if not greater than, Southeast Asia. The Aryans themselves brought very little.

4.5 *Suggestions for Further Work.* The proposals for work beyond this preliminary survey made on pages 127-28 can now be focused a bit more narrowly and assigned order of priority. Rather than pursue *all* the terms (and any additional ones) across *all* the languages in and around India–though this may be ultimately desirable–as a first step we could concentrate only on the unexplained category (plus any items already assigned whose explanations are deemed unsatisfactory). If the item clearly comes from one direction rather than another, we could pursue its terminology beyond the borders in that direction only rather than in all directions.

A further key to such simplification is offered by Burkill (p. 275): the *rabī* or cool-weather crops, sown in the autumn, are likely to have come from Western Asia; the *kharīf* or rainy-season crops are likely to come from Southeast Asia, Africa, or India itself.

In tracking down a particular mystery name, specialized terms connected with the cultivation of the crop and its industrial processing (e.g., cotton) might be more indicative of a solution than the bare name by itself. A series of smaller, more manageable projects concentrating on these items is thus in order.

NOTES

1. My thanks to Zbigniew Golab (Professor of Slavic Languages and Literatures at the University of Chicago) for calling my attention to this neglected work and thus provoking this paper. I also wish to thank Norman and Arlene Zide for the loan of some important materials, Herbert Paper for calling my attention to Laufer's *Sino-Iranica*, Rani Fedson for calling my attention to Burrow's *Collected Papers*, and various colleagues for putting up with my pesty questions and idle chatter on this subject. I should have exploited them more.
2. That is, unless we accept the (controversial) derivation of *sītā* 'furrow' from **se(i)*, as Pokorny (1959:890) does. Mayrhofer (1972:vol. 1, pp. 23,472) believes derivation from a root **sī* 'draw a straight line' (not supported by non-Indic material) is more likely, cf. *sīmā* 'boundary'.
3. Particularly doubtful (and quite unnecessary to the main hypothesis) is his conclusion that the staging area for the second, more settled "European" phase of Indo-European semi-unity lay in the Pripet Marshes between present Byelorussia and Ukraine–always merely a refuge area, poor in resources, and incapable of supporting such a population. Similarly doubtful are certain other details, such as the suggestion that the later Indo-Europeans domesticated the pig in the Baltic forests, etc. The advanced Neolithic cultivators of southeastern Europe revealed by archaeology seem to have been unknown to Brandenstein.
4. Continued contact between the Proto-Indo-Iranians and such groups as the Proto-Slavs and Balts–after more westerly groups had moved out–without shared agricultural vocabulary could be explained by the fact that the Slavs and Balts moved *west*, where they could have picked up the refinements of cultivation from the same autochthonous population (or its now Indo-Europeanized remnants) as their predecessors.
5. From Algonquian *askutasquash* 'eaten green', but confusable with the verb *squash* 'crush', from OF *esquasser*, VL **exquassare*, also used as a noun (obs.) 'something easily crushed, esp. an unripe pod of peas' (Webster).
6. That is, the root it appears to relate to, **ĝer-* 'rub, ripen, grow old' and the formant -**no-* go back to Indo-European antiquity. The specific meaning 'grain' is confined to northwest Indo-European (Pokorny:390). The related Sanskrit form *jīrṇa* means simply 'old, worn out, withered' (Monier-Williams:422). This again supports Brandenstein's theory.
7. There is not 100 percent agreement on this point. Brandenstein (p. 67) referring to Walde (p. 90) takes it as Indo-European meaning 'plant with thickened root'. Pokorny (pp. 33-34) accepts it but defines it as 'bittere Pflanze'.
8. Of the South American origins of the potato (*Solanum tuberosum*) there has never been any doubt (Laufer 1938:9), although it spread rapidly in the sixteenth century and in the process often got confused with other spreading American cultigens such as the sweet potato (*batata: Ipomoea batatas*) and even the Jerusalem artichoke (*Helianthus tuberosus*). The date of its introduction to India, probably by the Portuguese, is unknown but seems to be prior to 1700 (Watt 1893:vol. 6, pt. 3, p. 266; Laufer 1938:90-92). It was first resisted by the Hindu population, but had become general among them also by the early nineteenth century–unlike the tomato, whose acceptance took longer.

9. Assuming *Amorphophallus campanulatum, Arum campanulatum*, etc., are indeed different. There is no reference to the latter taxon in Zander, although the genus is a recognized one; cf. *Arum maculatum* "Aronstab", a poisonous plant (Zander 1972: 119).
10. An analogous example from medieval Latin is the word *aurantium* 'orange', from (not underlying) Portuguese *laranja* (mistaking the /l-/ for an article, from Arabic *nāranj* [with /n/-/l/ confusion], from Persian *nārang*, from Hindi, from Sanskrit, etc.) (Yule and Burnell 1968:642). Of course the orange was unknown in the Mediterranean in classical times.
11. Unfortunately, at the time of writing the complete Mayrhofer was not available, as the final two fascicles (25-26, *svápiti* through *hvā-*, plus Additions and Corrections), dated 1974 and 1976, had either not appeared or had not yet reached the University of Chicago Library. *"Mayrhofer"* here therefore means through the entry *svan-* at the end of fascicle 24.
12. That is, dating, not from the Arab conquest of Sind, but from the Ghaznavid occupation of the Punjab in the eleventh century through the demise of the Kingdom of Oudh in the middle of the nineteenth century.

REFERENCES

I. Dictionaries (comparative and language)

Apte, V. S. 1963. *The Student's English-Sanskrit Dictionary*. Delhi: Motilal Banarsidass.

Betteridge, Harold T. 1958. *The New Cassell's German Dictionary*. Rev. ed. New York: Funk and Wagnalls.

Buck, Carl Darling. 1949. *A Dictionary of Selected Synonyms in the Principal Indo-European Languages*. Chicago: University of Chicago Press.

Bulcke, Fr. Camille. 1968. *An English-Hindi Dictionary*. Ranchi: Catholic Press.

Burrow, Thomas, and M. B. Emeneau. 1966 (1961). *A Dravidian Etymological Dictionary*. Oxford: Clarendon Press.

Chaturvedi, Mahendra, and Dr. B. N. Tiwari. 1975. *A Practical Hindi-English dictionary*. 2nd rev. ed. Delhi: National Publishing House.

Iz, Faher, and H. C. Hony. 1952. *An English-Turkish Dictionary*. Oxford: Clarendon Press.

Mayrhofer, Manfred. 1956-72. *Kurzgefasstes etymologisches Wörterbuch des altindischen*. (Vol. 1, 1956; Vol. 2, 1963; fascicles 18-24, 1964-72). Heidelberg: Carl Winter/Universitätsverlag.

Michaelis, H. 1945. *A New Dictionary of the Portuguese and English Languages*. 2 vols. New York: Frederick Ungar.

Mill'er, B. V. 1953. *Persidsko-russkii slovar'*. Gosudarstvennoie izdat'elstvo inostrannykh i natsional'nykh slovar'ei. Moscow.

Monier-Williams, Sir Monier. 1899. *A Sanskrit-English Dictionary*. Oxford: Clarendon Press.

Platts, John T. 1960 (1930; 1884). *A Dictionary of Urdu, Classical Hindi, and English*. London: Oxford University Press.

Pokorny, Julius. 1959. *Indogermanisches etymologisches Wörterbuch*. Bern.

Prasād, Kūlikā; Rajavallabha Sahāy; and Mukundilāl Śrīvāstav, eds. S. V. 2020. *Bṛhat Hindī Koś*. 3rd ed. Vārāṇasī: Jñānamaṇḍal Ltd.

Redhouse, Sir James W. 1974 (1890). *A Turkish and English Lexicon*. Beirut: Librairie du Liban.

Śāstrī, Rāmsarūp. 1957. *Ādarś-hindī-saṁskṛt-koś*. Vārāṇasī: Caukhambā Vidyābhavan.

Steingass, F. 1963 (1892). *A Comprehensive Persian-English Dictionary*. London: Routledge and Kegan Paul.

The Student's Practical Dictionary, Hindi-English. 1949. 8th ed. Allahabad:

Ram Narain Lal.
Śyāmsundardās, ed. 1916, 1919, 1925. *Hindī śabdasāgar (hindī bhāṣā kā ek bṛhat koś)*. Kāśī: Nāgarī-Pracāriṇī Sabhā.
Turner, R. L. 1966. *A Comparative Dictionary of the Indo-Aryan Languages.* Indexes 1969, compiled by Dorothy Rivers Turner. London: Oxford University Press.
Varmā, Rāmcandra, ed. 2014 V. *Saṁkṣipt hindī śabdasāgar*. Kāsī: Nāgarī-pracāriṇī Sabhā.

II. Other references (including alphabetized technical and encyclopedic references):
Alexander, J., and D. G. Coursey. 1969. "The Origins of Yam Cultivation." In Ucko and Dimbleby, pp. 405-26.
Allchin, F. R. 1969*a*. "Early Domestic Animals in India and Pakistan." In Ucko and Dimbleby, pp. 317-22.
———. 1969*b*. "Early Cultivated Plants in India and Pakistan." In Ucko and Dimbleby, pp. 323-30.
Allworth, Edward, ed. 1967. *Central Asia: A Century of Russian Rule.* New York: Columbia University Press.
Anthropological Survey of India. 1961. *Peasant Life in India: A Study in Indian Unity and Diversity.* Calcutta: Anthropological Survey of India Memoir no. 8.
Ashtor, Eliyahu. 1975. "An Essay on the Diet of the Various Classes in the Medieval Levant." In *Biology of Man in History* (selections from *Annales*), edited by Robert Forster and Orest Ranum and translated by Elbory Forster and Patricia M. Ranum, pp. 125-62. Baltimore: Johns Hopkins Press.
Aykroyd, W. R. 1956. *The Nutritive Value of Indian Foods and the Planning of Satisfactory Diets.* 5th ed. Edited by V. N. Patwardhan and S. Ranganathan. Nutrition Research Laboratories, Indian Council of Medical Research, Coonoor. Delhi: Government of India Press.
Basham, A. L. 1959 (1954). *The Wonder That Was India.* New York: Grove Press.
Beal, Samuel, trans. 1906. *Si-yu-ki* [Buddhist records of the western world]. Translated from the Chinese of Hiuen Tsiang (A.D.629). 2 vols. London: Kegan Paul, Trench, Trübner and Co.
Benedict, Paul K. 1967. "Austro-Thai Studies: Material Culture and Kinship Terms; Austro-Thai and Chinese." *Behavior Science Notes* 2:203-44, 275-336.

Bloch, Jules. 1936. "La Charrue Vedique." *Bulletin of the School of Oriental Studies* (London) 8, no. 4:11-18.

Bökönyi, S. 1969. "Archeological Problems and Methods of Recognizing Animal Domestication." In Ucko and Dimbleby, pp. 219-30.

Brandenstein, Wilhelm. 1936. *Die erste "indo-germanische" Wanderung.* Historische Studien zur feudalen und vorfeudalen Welt. Klotho 2: Wien: Verlag Gerold and Co.

Burkill, I. H. 1962 (1951-2). "Habits of Man and the Origins of the Cultivated Plants of the Old World." Repr. in *Readings in Cultural Geography*, edited by Philip L. Wagner and Marvin W. Mikesell, pp. 248-81. Chicago: University of Chicago Press.

Burrow, Thomas. 1959 (1955). *The Sanskrit Language.* London: Faber and Faber.

———. 1968. *Collected Papers on Dravidian Linguistics.* Department of Linguistics publication no. 13, Annamalai University, Annamalainagar, South India.

Cardona, George; Henry M. Hoenigswald; and Alfred Senn, eds. 1970. *Indo-European and Indo-Europeans.* Papers presented at the Third Indo-European Conference at the University of Pennsylvania.

Childe, V. Gordon. 1926. *The Aryans: A Study of Indo-European Origins.* London: Kegan Paul, Trench, Trübner and Co.

Cranstone, B. A. L. 1969. "Animal Husbandry: The Evidence from Ethnography." In Ucko and Dimbleby, pp. 247-64.

Crosby, Alfred W., Jr. 1972. *The Columbian Exchange: Biological and Cultural Consequences of 1492.* Westport, Conn.: Greenwood Press.

Darlington, C. D. 1969. "The Silent Millennia in the Origin of Agriculture." In Ucko and Dimbleby, pp. 66-72.

Drower, M. S. 1969. "The Domestication of the Horse." In Ucko and Dimbleby, pp. 471-78.

Fairservis, Walter A., Jr. 1975. *The Roots of Ancient India: The Archaeology of Early Indian Civilization.* 2nd rev. ed. Chicago: University of Chicago Press.

Friedrich, Paul. 1970. *Proto-Indo-European Trees.* Chicago: University of Chicago Press.

Gimbutas, Marija. 1970. "Proto-Indo-European Culture: The Kurgan Culture during the 5th, 4th, and 3rd Millennia B.C." In Cardona, Hoenigswald, and Senn, pp. 155-97.

Goodenough, Ward H. 1970. "The Evolution of Pastoralism and Indo-European Origins." In Cardona, Hoenigswald, and Senn, pp. 253-65.

Gorman, C. F. 1970. "The Hoabinhian and After: Subsistence Patterns in Southeast Asia during the Late Pleistocene and Early Recent Periods." *World Archaeology* 2:300-320.

———. 1972. "Excavations at Spirit Cave, North Thailand." *Asian Perspectives* 13:79-107.

Grierson, Sir George. 1975 (1885). *Bihar Peasant Life.* Delhi: Cosmo Publishers.

Gryaznov, Mikhail P. 1969. *The Ancient Civilization of Southern Siberia.* Translated by James Hogarth. New York: Cowles Books (Ancient Civilization series).

Hedrick, U. P., ed. 1972 (1919). *Sturtevant's Edible Plants of the World.* New York: Dover.

Ho Ping-ti. 1969. "The Loess and the Origin of Chinese Agriculture." *American Historical Review* 75, no. 1:1-36.

———. 1975. *The Cradle of the East.* Hong Kong: The Chinese University; Chicago: The University of Chicago Press.

Hock, Hans Henrich. 1975. "Substratum Influence on (Ṛg-Vedic) Sanskrit?" *Studies in the Linguistic Sciences* 5, no. 2. Urbana: University of Illinois.

Hoffner, Harry A. 1974. *Alimenta Hethaeorum: Food Production in Hittite Asia Minor.* American Oriental Series, vol. 55. New Haven: American Oriental Society.

Husain, Mahdi, editor and commentator. 1953. *The Rehla of Iban Battuta (India, the Maldive Islands, and Ceylon).* Gaekwad's Oriental Series. Baroda: Oriental Institute.

Imperial Gazetteer of India, vol. 3.

Indian Council of Agricultural Research. 1969. *Handbook of Agriculture.* New Delhi.

Isaac, Erich. 1970. *Geography of Domestication.* Foundations of Cultural Geography series. Englewood Cliffs, N. J.: Prentice-Hall.

Keith, A. Berriedale. 1966 (1920). *A History of Sanskrit Literature.* Oxford University Press.

Krapovickas, A. 1969. "The Origin, Variability and Spread of the Groundnut (*Arachis hypogea*)." In Ucko and Dimbleby, pp. 427-42.

Laufer, Berthold. 1919. *Sino-Iranica: Chinese Contributions to the History of Civilization in Iran, with Special Reference to the History of Cultivated Plants and Products.* Field Museum of Natural History Publication 201. Chicago.

———. 1938. *The American Plant Migration. Part I: The Potato.* Field

Museum of Natural History Anthropology Series, vol. 28, no. 1. Chicago.

Littleton, C. Scott. 1973. *The New Comparative Mythology: An Anthropological Assessment of the Theories of Georges Dumezil.* Rev. ed. Berkeley and Los Angeles: University of California Press.

McCrindle, J. W. 1877. *Ancient India as Described by Megasthenes and Arrian.* London: Trübner and Co.

Matley, Ian Murray. 1967. "The Population and the Land." In Allworth, pp. 92-130.

Mellaart, James. 1975. *The Neolithic of the Near East.* New York: Scribn^r's.

Menges, Karl H. 1967. "People, Languages, and Migrations." In *Central Asia: A Century of Russian Rule*, edited by Edward Allworth. New York: Columbia University Press.

Pickersgill, Barbara. 1969. "The Domestication of Chili Peppers." In Ucko and Dimbleby, pp. 443-50.

Renfrew, J. M. 1969. "The Archeological Evidence for the Domestication of Plants." In Ucko and Dimbleby, pp. 149-72.

Sachau, Edward C., trans. 1962 (1888). *Alberuni's India.* An English edition with notes and indices. Lahore: Government of West Pakistan.

Sauer, Carl O. 1952. *Agricultural Origins and Dispersals.* The American Geographical Society, series two, Bowman Memorial Lectures. New York.

Solheim, Wilhelm G., II. 1970. "Northern Thailand, Southeast Asia, and World Prehistory." *Asian Perspectives* 13 (1970).

———. 1972. "An Earlier Agricultural Revolution." *Scientific American* 226, no. 4:34-41.

Tannahill, Reay. 1973. *Food in History.* New York: Stein and Day.

Tringham, Ruth. 1969. "Animal Domestication in the Neolithic Cultures of the Southwestern Part of the European USSR." In Ucko and Dimbleby, pp. 381-92.

Ucko, Peter J., and G. W. Dimbleby, eds. 1969. *The Domestication and Exploitation of Plants and Animals.* Proceedings of a meeting of the Research Seminar in Archaeology and Related Subjects held at the Institute of Archaeology, London University. Chicago: Aldine.

Vavilov, N. I. 1926. *Tsentry proiskhozhdeniia kul'turnykh rastenii* [Studies on the origin of cultivated plants]. Leningrad.

———. 1949/50. "The Origins, Variation, Immunity and Breeding of Cultivated Plants. Selected writings of N. I. Vavilov." K. Starr Chester, translator. In *Chronica Botanica* 13 (Waltham, Massachusetts).

Vishnu-Mittre. n.d. (1973?). *Changing Economy in Ancient India.* Lucknow: Birbal Sahni Institute of Palaeobotany (mss.).

Waterbolk, H. T. 1968. "Food Production in Prehistoric Europe." *Science* 162:1093-1102.

Watson, William. 1969*a*. "Early Animal Domestication in China." In Ucko and Dimbleby, pp. 393-96.

———. 1969*b*. "Early Cereal Cultivation in China." In Ucko and Dimbleby, pp. 397-404.

Watt, George. 1889-93. *A Dictionary of the Economic Products of India.* 6 vols., reprinted in 10 vols. Delhi: Cosmo Publications.

Yule, Col. Henry, and A. C. Burnell. 1968 (1903). *Hobson-Jobson: A Glossary of Anglo-Indian Words and Phrases, and of Kindred Terms, Etymological, Historical, Geographical, and Discursive.* New ed., edited by William Crooke. Delhi: Munshiram Manoharlal (reprint).

Zander, Robert. 1972. *Handwörterbuch der Pflanzennamen.* Neubearbeitete und erweiterte 10. Auflage von Dr. Fritz Encke, Dr. Günther Buchheim unter Mitarbeit von Dr. Siegmund Seybold. Stuttgart: Verlag Eugen Ulmer.

Zide, Arlene R. K., and Norman H. Zide. 1976. "Proto-Munda Cultural Vocabulary: Evidence for Early Agriculture." *Proceedings of the First International Austroasiatic Conference,* Honolulu, 1973.

Zohary, Daniel. 1969. "The Progenitors of Wheat and Barley in Relation to Domestication and Agricultural Dispersal in the Old World." In Ucko and Dimbleby, pp. 47-66.

THE STUDY OF DRAVIDIAN KINSHIP

Thomas R. Trautmann
The University of Michigan

What is Dravidian kinship? The matter has been much debated of late among anthropologists. A conviction that the problem is essentially a historical one emboldens this historian to transgress the boundaries of what has been anthropology's private demesne, not merely to poach its data but, far worse, to give the landlord some unsolicited advice about what to do with it. Such presumptuousness, I know, is unforgivable; but before fists and stones send me back where I belong, I beg a hearing.[1]

The question of the nature of Dravidian kinship subsumes the concept of the Dravidian, a far from unitary notion. "Dravidian" has a venerable history as a label, and given that in modern times it has been employed in studies of Indian phenomena as diverse as language and temple architecture, literature and systems of land tenure, religion and race, it is hardly surprising that it lacks conceptual consistency from one context to another. Such consistency, however, is both possible and highly desirable for the coordination of the several branches of enquiry into Indian culture. To devise a sound method for the study of Dravidian kinship, therefore, we shall have to begin by going back to basics, the foundation in this case being provided by historical linguistics, whence the modern concept of the Dravidian originates and wherein it remains exceptionally clear and well-defined.

In historical linguistics Dravidian denotes a family of languages believed to be related to one another by common descent from ancestral languages, ultimately from a single apical ancestor called Proto-Dravidian. The relationship between particular Dravidian languages, ancient and modern, is usually called a "genetic" one, but the usage is only metaphoric; there is no presumption of *racial* uniformity and continuity between the ancient and modern speakers of Dravidian languages. What is essentially a genealogical metaphor has its own metaphor, that of the "family tree," which is also invoked to explicate the historical relations between languages. Thus, the contemporary Dravidian languages are related to Proto-Dravidian as twig to trunk, and among themselves as twig to twig, via a common branch. From the tree theory or the genetic model, call it what you will, the broad outlines of a method may be derived; for the tree theory presumes that the Dravidian languages are related not only in *form*, but in *history*, such that formal similarities, systematically compared, are made to yield evidence of the genetic relations of which they are the effects. The calculus of formal similarities and differences feeds content into a scheme of historical classification whose principles are determined by the genetic model. Model and method combine to permit, or rather to require, that for the completion of its task historical linguistics accomplish its most spectacular project: the reconstruction of the unrecorded languages of the past. This model and this method, of course, are not specific to Dravidian linguistics. As far as India is concerned, they serve also to define Indo-Aryan (Indo-Iranian, Indo-European) and Munda (Austroasiatic, Austronesian) language families, concepts coordinate with and opposed to one another, such that no genetic relation between them is assumed, or at best a genetic relationship in a past so remote as to be practically irrecoverable.

All of this is well known, but I will belabor the obvious a bit longer in order to elicit the limitations of the tree theory and to derive from it consequences for extralinguistic study. Tree theory posits the existence of coordinate, discrete language groups which in respect of India are Dravidian, Indo-Aryan, Munda, and perhaps others. If linguistic features were transmitted solely along genetic lines, it would be perfectly possible to study any one of these in ignorance of the others. That is not the case, however; the fact that there are some movements of linguistic features across genetic boundaries makes it necessary to identify, let us say, non-Dravidian features in Dravidian languages for genetic reconstruction to succeed. This entails a knowledge of contiguous non-Dravidian language groups, of Indo-Aryan at a minimum. It implies that the refinement of knowledge concerning Dravidian is contingent upon the refinement of our knowledge concerning Indo-Aryan, Munda, and other non-Dravidian groups.

It has long been recognized that the data which the tree theory discards—the data of nongenetic movements of linguistic features—can much of it be accounted for by nongenetic models, especially as represented by the idea of the wave-like movement of linguistic features in all directions from a center of innovation, such movement being no respecter of genetic boundaries. The methodological activity proper to the "wave" theory is the drawing of isoglosses, and its purpose is to explain what the "tree" theory does not, such as borrowing and dialect formation. Only within a nongenetic framework is it possible to consider India as a linguistic region (Emeneau),[2] or a part of a larger linguistic region (Masica).[3] Creolization (Southworth and others)[4] and retroflexion (Deshpande, this volume; Southworth)[5] are other cross-genetic subjects of interest current among linguists of India.

In truth the tree theory, taken by itself, begins by explaining much but ends by being offensive to common sense and simple observation, for it assumes a movement from unity to diversity which is irreversible and inexorable. But a theory of continual divergence can only proceed by sifting out and throwing away a great deal of the data of language history, such that language history can only be made complete by its complement, a theory of language convergence–and the refinement of either being contingent upon the refinement of each.

All of this is of relevance to the problem of Dravidian kinship, or, indeed, to that of Dravidian culture in general (of which language is a part), because Dravidian is essentially a genetic construct. The linguist's notion of the unbroken genetic transmission of Dravidian languages from past to present rests upon the assumption of an unbroken continuity of Dravidian speech communities through history, the human substratum of the linguistic evidence. Here we have an opening wedge for cultural study beyond the historical linguist's immediate concerns, for it is reasonable to attribute to these historically related communities other common features of social and cultural life, among them literature, religion, and kinship. We have no a priori guarantees, of course, that the various aspects of Dravidian culture in this genetic sense have persisted to the present in the way that language has, so that some features of Dravidian culture will prove difficult to reconstruct, while others must be presumed lost beyond hope of recovery. Furthermore, beyond the task of the reconstruction of aspects of the culture of Dravidians, Indo-Aryans, and the like by specialists looms the problem of the emergence of a synthesizing Indian culture, a problem for which the coordination of specialists' knowledge is essential. The evident fact that the convergence of what must be regarded as pre-Indian cultures (Dravidian, Indo-Aryan) to produce a synthesizing Indian culture has been more limited in some respects, such as language, and more complete in others, such as religion, calls for a theory of Indian social history which can explain this differential convergence. But first things first; a comprehensive enquiry into the history of Indian culture must attend the study of its component parts, of which kinship is our present concern.

The notion of a Dravidian kinship system rests upon the genetic model, which in turn presupposes the historical continuity of Dravidian communities with an ancestral community. These are communities of kinship; and as marriage is a form of communication which requires a common grammar of kinship among its participants, it serves to define the scope and bounds of the communities in question. The empirical units of investigation in the ethnographic present, therefore, are endogamous groups, the local intra-marrying castes or local intermarrying groups of castes.

The Dravidian kinship system is a general, historical entity which can only be known through particular Dravidian systems, local in scope and perceived at particular points in time from the ethnographic and historical record. The analysis of this record presents us with two problems: the problem of distinguishing within the particular kinship systems of record that which is Dravidian from that which is not, and the problem of characterizing the Dravidian kinship system in general by abstraction from the various particular Dravidian kinship systems which are available to inspection.

As to the first problem, that of identifying non-Dravidian elements in the data, we find in practice the need to posit a comparable genetic entity, the Indo-Aryan kinship system, some of whose features have been borrowed by particular Dravidian systems (and were Munda studies more advanced we might find analytic need to posit a Munda kinship system as well). We also find a need to establish the concept of a synthetic Indian culture of kinship which extends across South Asia, and whose units of variation are regional (as, e.g., South Indian, North Indian) rather than genetic (e.g., Dravidian, Indo-Aryan). In respect of distinguishing the Dravidian data from the non-Dravidian, then, we need a hierarchy of concepts, the minimum terms of which are three: the genetic concepts Dravidian and Indo-Aryan, and the synthesizing concept of Indian kinship.

As to the second problem, that of reconstructing the Dravidian system from the many empirical systems, of deriving the general from the particular, however elusive the details of a successful analytic procedure have hitherto been, we may at least say broadly that the methods must be comparative in order to distinguish what is purely local from what is generally Dravidian. The common practice of arbitrarily selecting a particular Dravidian system as a "type case" of the Dravidian, for example, is a practice which is valid only for certain strategic purposes (to which limited ends we will employ it in this paper). It is a point of departure, not a conclusion, a first approximation, not a final statement as to the nature of the Dravidian system of kinship. That can only be known when the components of the entire range of particular Dravidian systems are brought into relation to one another.

This programmatic statement, occasioned by the ahistorical style of current analyses of Dravidian kinship, has grown long enough. The reader is entitled to wonder when we are going to come to cases, and whether the foregoing will prove to have made any contribution to our understanding of them. In the ensuing pages I shall attempt to show that it does make a difference, by sketching the lines along which a historical approach to Dravidian kinship must advance. I shall largely confine myself to the problem of distinguishing the Dravidian data on kinship from the Indo-Aryan and the Indian.

To begin, we need to specify those broad features of the Dravidian and Indo-Aryan kinship systems which serve to distinguish them from one another. We will not go seriously wrong if to this purpose we employ the genealogical language of anthropological typologists and the method of the "type case," using Tamil and Hindi as our examples, so long as it is understood that what follows is a crude approximation adequate only to present purposes. We may say, then, that in respect of the *rules* of kinship, Dravidians are expected to marry their cross-cousins–a class of kin which includes the mother's brother's child and the father's sister's child–and, at the same time, are forbidden to marry parallel kin, including brother and sister, father's brother's child, and mother's sister's child. To view it from another perspective, the children of a brother and sister should marry, while those of two brothers or of two sisters are conceived to be related to one another in the same way as siblings and must not marry. This rule also applies to more remote cousins, who are classified into cross and parallel categories. In most Dravidian systems, with important exceptions, marriage partners must be of the same generation, and the groom must be older than the bride. There are a few additional constraints upon marriage we must pass over.

As to *behavior*, actual marriages among Dravidians conform to rule in a significant degree, though in any empirical setting there are some instances in apparent violation, and a great many marriages between individuals whose prior relationship is unknown. The assessment of the behavioral component of the Dravidian kinship system is fraught with problems of method into which we cannot delve. Very briefly, it is essentially a matter of comparing behavior to the rules of marriage by a statistical analysis of instances of marriage between (1) properly related kin, (2) improperly related kin, and (3) nonkin. This demands extensive genealogical information, as well as knowledge of the indigenous mode of kin classification and the rules of marriage. Past improper marriages muddy the waters of interpretation since they generate contradictory kinship classifications for relatives of the couple, such that in individual cases it is possible to be related properly and improperly at the same time. Finally, an analysis of behavior cannot truly measure degree of behavioral conformity to rule without taking the demographics of each marriage choice into consideration. In this respect, an improper marriage indicates indifference to the rules only if the proper mates were available to the individuals in question, which may not be the case. Such studies have yet to be made.[6]

As to the *conceptual* component of the kinship system we can say that the Dravidian kinship terms correlate well with the rules of marriage. For example, Tamil *māmaṉ* is mother's brother, father's sister's husband, and spouse's father, genealogical relationships which are equated by a presumption that every marriage is between cross-cousins (see figure 1). Of the three genealogical relationships which are merged in Tamil, each pair can be derived directly from cross-cousin marriage. Thus, the mergers MB=SpF and FZH=SpF follow directly from the genealogical definition of cross-cousin marriage, while MB=FZH follows from the presumption that father and mother, having married, are cross-cousins, whence the siblings of one are cross-cousins to the siblings of the other. Indeed, the entire contents of the parents' generation are ordered by this principle, as we will see below.

The Indo-Aryan scheme could not be more different. Hindi *māmā*, almost certainly a cognate of the Tamil word, also means mother's brother, but Hindi has quite separate terms for father's sister's husband (*phūphā*) and spouse's father (*sasur*), and the remaining contents of this generation are differently ordered than in the Tamil. Again, in Hindi the members of ego's generation, cousins of all kinds, are regarded as so many species of *bhāī* and *bahin*, terms which designate one's own brother and sister; cousins are not, as in Tamil, divided into two large categories of cross and parallel, and relatives by marriage are, on the whole, kept distinct from relatives by blood. These remarks, *mutatis mutandis*, apply to Indo-Aryan terminologies generally. In respect of the rules of marriage, the Indo-Aryan system frames these in terms of a notion of *proximity*, a kind of law of prohibited degrees rather like our own: near kinsmen may not marry. In Dravidian, on the other hand, it is not *proximity* but *kind* of relationship which constrains marriageability, i.e., whether parallel or cross. Finally, in respect of behavior, Indo-Aryan systems exhibit in their actual marriages a tendency, quite different from that of the Dravidian system, to marry at a distance from the immediate circle of kin. Thus, sharp contrasts between the Dravidian and Indo-Aryan kinship systems exist at every level: concept or terms, rules, behavior.

Since the underlying notions of our concern–divergent, genetic relationships and nongenetic convergence as they form the concepts of Dravidian, Indo-Aryan and Indian kinship–are historical, the systematic comparison of kinship terminologies seems especially critical, both to determine the extent and kinds of convergence and, within the Dravidian system, to define the system itself in the full range of its particular manifestations. To this end,

FIGURE 1

Tamil and Hindi Kinship Terms for Mother's Brother, Father's Sister's Husband, and Spouse's Father

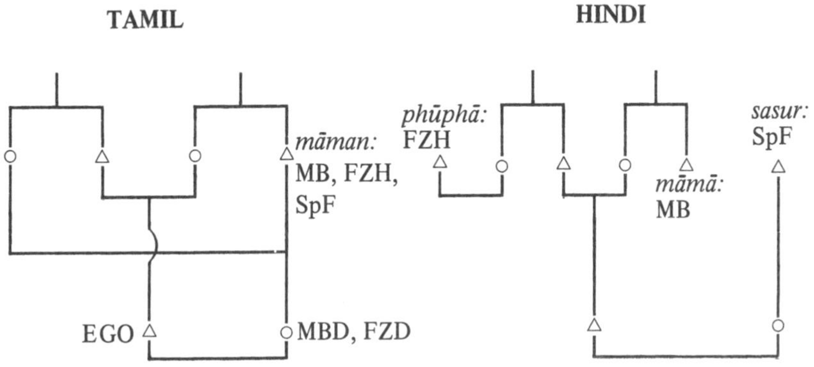

Notation

F = father, M = mother, Pa = parent
B = brother, Z = sister, Sb = sibling
H = husband, W = wife, Sp = spouse
S = son, D = daughter, Ch = child

only the data of contemporary kinship systems will suffice, for it is inherently difficult to find the complete sets of terms which are wanted in texts or dictionaries. I would not so boldly–perhaps foolhardily–have set foot on the anthropologist's turf if the task had already been accomplished by those better qualified to do so. Unfortunately, this is not the case. Comparison of Indian terminologies is as old as Morgan's *Systems of Consanguinity and Affinity*,[7] with which anthropology's most arcane and exclusive preoccupation came into being, forming the pattern for Karve's more recent *Kinship Organization in India*.[8] Both rest upon the genetic model, and both take over from historical linguistics the assumption that the unit of study is the regional language, e.g., Tamil, Marathi, Gujarati, etc. The effect is innocuous in Morgan's data since he collected each set from a single informant; but in Karve we get, for example, a list of "Marathi Kinship Terms" which combines the vocabularies of many informants from many castes and districts.[9] It happens that Maharashtra lies in the frontier zone where two different kinship systems overlap, so that although all her informants were Marathi-speaking, some were Indo-Aryan, others Dravidian in kinship. Caste-specific sets of data cannot be disentangled from her conflated table of Marathi terms, and we cannot therefore use her tables to carry the work forward. The work must be done over, using not the linguistic regions as a whole, but the local community of kinship as the unit of study. A recent, more limited survey by Carter does not have the defect which limits the usefulness of Karve's work, but is marred by a defect of another kind: the assumption of fundamental similarity between Dravidian and Indo-Aryan systems.[10]

The radical differences which distinguish the two kinship systems constitute an inherent obstacle to their complete convergence; a synthetic system cannot be created without altering the fundamental principles of one or both systems. Convergence between Dravidian and Indo-Aryan terminologies can be studied empirically, for their geographical distributions overlap, forming a broad frontier zone where castes of each kinship system live in close proximity, sometimes in the same village. In such settings we generally find a shared lexicon of kinship marking a divergent semantics which can easily be identified as either Dravidian or Indo-Aryan for any given case.

Kathiawar falls within the frontier zone, and analysis of Trivedi's data on the terminologies of the Mer and of Gujarati (unspecified as to caste) of that area may be used in illustration of those effects.[11] Terms for kinsmen in the parents' generation are given in figure 2.

The vocabulary is identical, but the Mer employ only four of the ten Gujarati terms. This is because the semantic categories of the Mer are organized by

FIGURE 2

Gujarati and Mer Kinship Terms, Parents' Generation

Kin Terms	Gujarati	Mer
kākā	FB	FB, MZH
kākī	FBW	——
māsī	MZ	MZ, FBW
māsā	MZH	——
fuī	FZ	FZ, MBW, SpM
fuā	FZH	——
māmā	MB	MB, FZH, SpF
māmī	MBW	——
sasaro	SpF	——
sāsu	SpM	——

(For explanation of abbreviations, see figure 1, p. 159.)

a Dravidian logic which takes systematic cross-cousin marriage as its basis, and, in consequence, their terminology is fundamentally the same as that of the Tamils, in spite of its non-Dravidian lexicon. The groupings of genealogical referents in the Mer terminology may be derived directly from the genealogical representation of Tamil terminology in figure 1, producing the equations MB=FZH=SpF (*māmā*) and FZ=MBW=SpM (*fuī*). The remaining two groups, FB=MZH and MZ=FBW, Mer *kākā* and *māsī* respectively, are also found in Tamil which, however, additionally includes father and mother in these two categories while the Mer have distinct terms for them (*bāpu, māṅ*). The ten Gujarati terms, plus the two terms for father and mother (*bāpu, māṅ*) not given in figure 2, by contrast, are structured both lexically and semantically in a manner fundamentally the same as among other Indo-Aryan systems. In other regions of the semantic field defined by Mer kinship terms the story is very much the same: in semantic structure the system is recognizably Dravidian, and although the influence of environing Indo-Aryan systems is by no means negligible, these influences are largely confined to such surface features as the lexicon.

The situation of Mer is broadly representative of the situation of other Dravidian systems within the frontier zone, to which we may add that the specific details of local attempts to solve the inherently insoluble problem of convergence with Indo-Aryan systems are heterogeneous, varying from place to place such that there emerges no common solution, however limited. It seems to me quite clear that the historical record extends these findings to the past, showing at best a very meager rapprochement between the two systems in general, and their terminologies in particular, in antiquity. For example, Hindi and Gujarati *māmā* and Tamil *māman* are certainly cognates, so widely represented in both Indo-Aryan and Dravidian languages that we are sore pressed to determine the direction of borrowing. But convergent features like this are extremely few and limited, by and large, to surface features which leave the organizing principles of the opposed systems untouched.

A geographical survey of terminological sets delimits a contiguous area, comprising South India and Sri Lanka, within which Dravidian kinship prevails today. The northern limit of this region runs through Orissa and Madhya Pradesh, continuing westward to include much of Maharashtra and part of Gujarat, namely the Kathiawar peninsula. The southern limit of the Indo-Aryan kinship region falls below this, and the two borders together outline the region of interpenetration, the frontier zone whose approximate situation is mapped in figure 3.

Considered in connection with the evidence of language, the historical

FIGURE 3

APPROXIMATE GEOGRAPHICAL DISTRIBUTION OF THE DRAVIDIAN AND INDO-ARYAN KINSHIP SYSTEMS

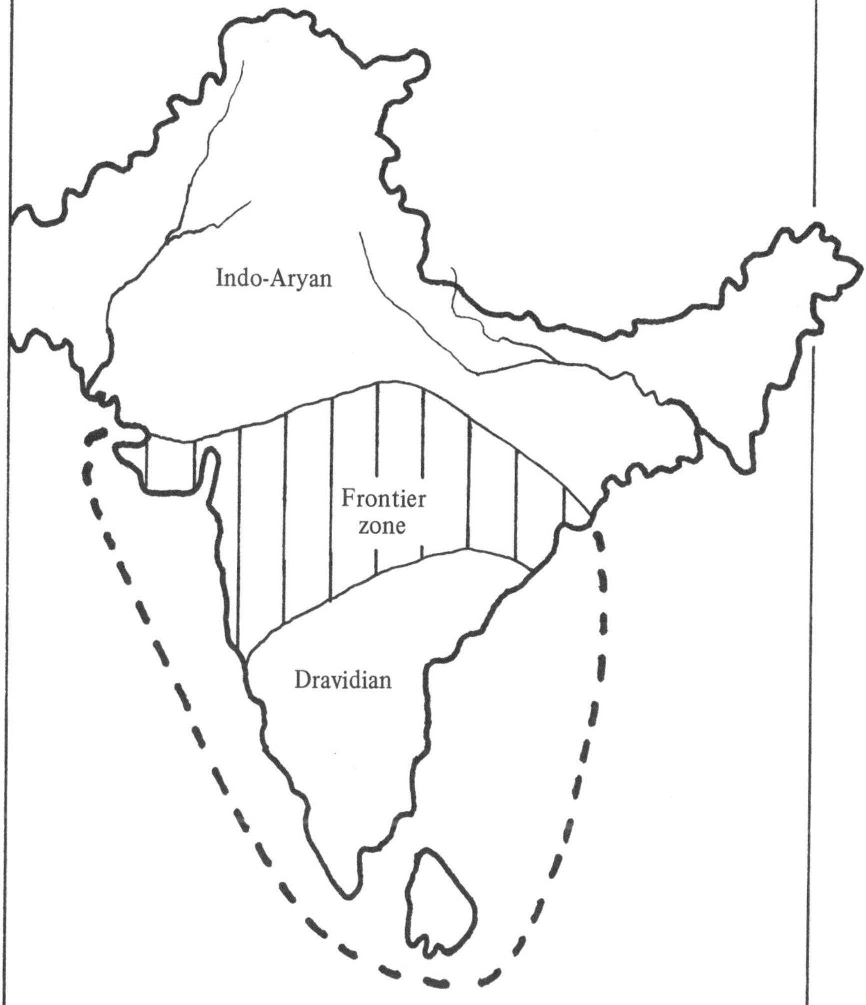

significance of this information is very considerable, for within the Dravidian region there are many communities which are Indo-Aryan in speech while remaining Dravidian in kinship, especially some castes of Gujarat and Maharashtra, as well as the speakers of Konkani and Sinhalese. Indo-Aryan linguistic expansion has proceeded furthest southward down the west coast, and the linguistic map which results shows the contiguous Dravidian region separated from its Brahui outlier by an Indo-Aryan wedge. The evidence of kinship terminologies, however, shows a Dravidian presence all along the west coast up to and including Kathiawar (the data on Brahui terms available at this writing being insufficient for a determination). Evidently, in these areas Dravidian kinship has persisted long after Dravidian language was lost. This evidence tends to support Southworth's view that Marathi and Mahārāṣṭrī Prakrit developed among an ancient Maharashtrian population which was Dravidian in speech.[12] Further, the evidence of terms extends the Dravidian region to the edge of the Indus valley, with whose ancient civilization the Dravidians have often been speculatively connected. Finally, it lends some support to McAlpin's view (this volume) of linguistic affiliation between Dravidian and Elamite and a movement of ancestral Dravidians from Iran into India, continuing down the west coast, prefiguring in broad terms the route of Aryan advance. The geographical distribution of marriage rules and their associated behavioral patterns largely coincides with that of terminologies of kinship.

Instances of cross-cousin marriage in ancient literature must be analyzed in reference to the geographical distribution of the two kinship systems as we find it today. Stories of cross-cousin marriage in ancient Indo-Aryan literatures, whose settings and characters are for the most part North Indian, are particularly critical to the historical study of Dravidian kinship, the more so in that scholars who have commented on these cases, with one or two exceptions, have mistakenly regarded these stories as historically factual and have compounded the error by attributing them to non-Dravidian (Aryan, Munda) systems. These cases then constituted a crux without whose proper resolution the study of the historical record of kinship, I believed, could not progress. Hence, I have surveyed and analyzed these cases in a pair of articles, the burden of which may be illustrated by a single case, that of Ajātasattu and Pasenadi.[13]

In the fifth century B.C., as we learn from the Pali canon, two kingdoms of the middle Ganges region went to war. The older and the larger of the two was Kosala, ruled by Pasenadi. To its east lay Magadha, ruled by the ambitious and ruthless Ajātasattu. Magadha in the next two centuries was to expand into an empire which embraced nearly the whole of the Indian subcontinent. At the time of our story, however, the absorption of Kosala by Magadha lay in the future: in the war to which I refer, Pasenadi of Kosala defeated Ajātasattu of Magadha and then, it would seem, restored amity between the two.

The Pali canon gives us little beyond this by which we may understand the origins of this event. If we consult the postcanonical Pali literature of Sri Lanka, including commentaries and chronicles, however, we find a more elaborate treatment of the war, in the following terms: Pasenadi's sister had been married to Bimbisāra, king of Magadha and father of Ajātasattu, making the two kings brothers-in-law; indeed, one source says that the two kings exchanged sisters, so that they were doubly related by marriage. However that may be, the Kosala princess brought with her a dowry consisting of a village in Kāsi, or Benares, which lay on the border of the two kingdoms. The revenue of this village was a hundred thousand coins, and its purpose was to pay for the Kosaladevi's bath powder. I should explain that we are in the era before the invention of soap and that the particular expression employed indicates that the substance used in its place was a scouring powder made of lime.

Ajātasattu was born of this union, and all our sources agree in giving him a cruel and ambitious character. Too eager for the throne, he killed his father, whereupon his mother died of grief. Pasenadi refused to release the revenues of the Benares village to his sister's son Ajātasattu, whom he regarded as a parricide and a thief. Thus, what I have called "The War of the Bath Powder" broke out between them.

The war was protracted and the fortunes of the antagonists wavered back and forth. But the long and the short of it is that Pasenadi captured his erring nephew together with his entire army (our ecclesiastical sources attributing Pasenadi's success to the military advice of a Buddhist monk). In a magnanimous gesture Pasenadi freed Ajātasattu on a promise of good behavior. To seal the peace he gave the nephew his daughter Vajirā in marriage, and on this daughter he bestowed the very village in Benares over which the two kings had fought to provide for her bath powder! (See figure 4.)

A charming story, but is it true, by any chance? The answer is a decided no, even though historians of ancient India have hitherto been inclined to grant it a certain credence. In order to show that it is not factual, we shall have to show what meaning it had for the audience for whom it was composed.

It will be obvious from what has been said that from the perspective of

FIGURE 4

The Genealogy of Ajātasattu in Postcanonical Pali Literature

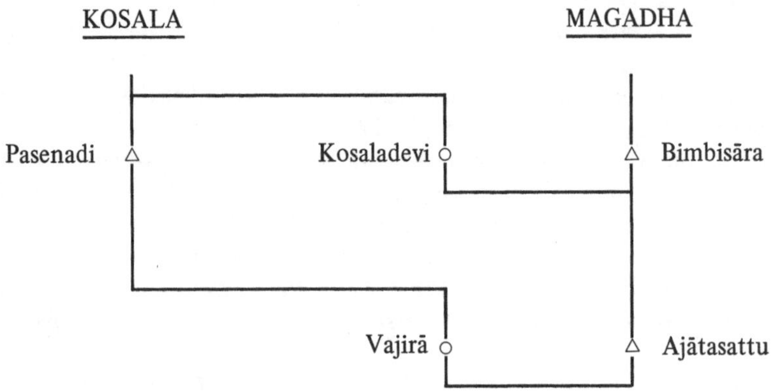

the Indo-Aryan kinship system the story is not only unintelligible, but the marriage of Ajātasattu to his mother's brother's daughter, in which it results, is illicit. If, on the other hand, we read it from a Dravidian point of view it makes excellent sense. The war between Pasenadi and Ajātasattu amounts to the pathology of the mother's brother/sister's son relationship, which ought to be close and amicable, but which in this instance turns into one of conflict. The conflict is resolved and the proper relationship is restored in an ideal way, Dravidian-style, by means of a cross-cousin marriage. The historical event, which was probably a mere border dispute, has been reworked in Dravidian terms. History "as it actually happened" has been sacrificed to structure.

We need only add two other bits of evidence to clinch this conclusion. In the first place the Sinhalese, among whom the Pali chronicles and commentaries were written, are Dravidian in marriage rules and in their terminology of kinship, even though Indo-Aryan in language. In the second place, the Pali canon itself, supported by Jain documents, shows that Ajātasattu's mother was not from Kosala, but rather from another neighboring state, that of Videha. This undermines the entire Ceylonese version of the story, for the two antagonists are now no longer uncle and nephew, and even if Ajātasattu did marry Pasenadi's daughter, she would not have been a cross-cousin. The historical significance of the Ceylonese tale relates not to the events of fifth-century North India at all, but to the social structure of ancient Sri Lanka. It reworks a historical event in a manner which is meaningful to a Dravidian audience, but is no longer factual.

In the articles referred to above, the methods used and the conclusions reached in the analysis of the "War of the Bath Powder" story are generalized through comparable analyses of all other known instances of cross-cousin marriage in Indo-Aryan literature. No such instance proves the existence of cross-cousin marriage in ancient India beyond the northern border of the Dravidian system as we find it today, and almost all of them can be satisfactorily explained by evidence that the writers of the tales in question lived within the present geographical horizon of the Dravidian system and may therefore be presumed to have been themselves Dravidian in respect of kinship. The prevailing view of these cases had been doubly wrong in failing to place them in a Dravidian context and in taking them as factual events. Far from having the character of the behaviorist's data on how individuals actually marry, they are rather emblematic representations of the Dravidian rules of marriage.

The historical record can, however, be made to yield some behavioral data bearing upon the study of Dravidian kinship if we look to dynastic marriage as recorded in epigraphy and chronicles. Few though these instances be, their interest is nevertheless considerable; for kingship is the politics of kinship, and the strategic manipulations to which the Dravidian system can be put for political ends are shown in the historical record as in a series of laboratory experiments. Because cross-cousin marriage implements a tendency to perpetuate affinity between two groups, its capacity to articulate the ordering of relationships within a political elite is of a fairly high degree. The variety of such orderings, especially when marriage patterns are considered in relation to variant rules of succession to the throne, is too great to be expounded on this occasion. In regard to the contrast between Dravidian and Indo-Aryan kinship, we may simply state that survey of the historical record of dynastic marriages shows that cross-cousin marriage occurs only within the present confines of the Dravidian area (Sātavāhanas; Ikṣvākus; Rāṣṭrakūṭas and Kalacuris; Cōḷas and Veṅgī; Sinhalese kings; and, in a certain sense, the medieval kingdoms of Kerala), and that the uses of marriage in North India follow different strategies, under its very different, Indo-Aryan, constraints.

Thus far we have invoked the two contrastive concepts, Dravidian and Indo-Aryan, of the triad we claim to be the minimal conceptual equipment by which the Dravidian can be separated from the non-Dravidian. Having investigated narrative literature and the epigraphic and chronicle sources of dynastic marriage, we turn to the Sanskrit lawbooks (Dharmaśāstra), the centerpiece of most existing scholarship on kinship in ancient India. In doing so we will have to ring in the third of our triad, the idea of an Indian culture of kinship which transcends the genetically Dravidian and Indo-Aryan cultures.

To do so is something of a departure from the usual treatment of kinship in the Dharmaśāstra, which tends to fix it firmly within the Indo-Aryan system. This conventional wisdom is not wholly wrong, especially when we consider the Veda, of which the Dharmaśāstra is in its own estimation a kind of codifying extension. We have shown in the work referred to above that the Veda makes no indubitable reference to cross-cousin marriage. Yet, linguistic evidence renders it likely that the early, North Indian composers of this literature had resident Dravidians in their midst. That they made no reference to cross-cousin marriage is probably to be explained by the pronounced xenophobia of the custodians of Vedic lore, rather than an absence of Dravidians in early North India. Moreover, the Veda is in nature liturgical, not ethnographic; and even if the Aryans had had an ethnographer's interest in demotic customs repugnant to them, their very language would have proven an obstacle to the comprehension of the Dravidian system, equally as bad as English in that regard. It is not until the *Baudhāyana Dharma Sūtra* that Sanskrit literature takes note of cross-cousin marriage, and by this time it is considered a regional peculiarity of the Deccan (the Dākṣiṇātyas), subject to a northerner's disapproval.[14] This text is a watershed, however, for it testifies that Deccani Brahmins were by this time marrying their cross-cousins, as they continue to do to this day, and it inaugurates the debate within the Dharmaśāstra by Brahmin jurists of North and South as to the propriety of the custom. This dispute never reached a consensus: the Dharmaśāstra as a whole does not speak with one voice on the matter, and in practice the pious of each region follows what by its own lights is its *dharma*, exogamy of close kinsmen in the North, cross-cousin marriage in the South.

In respect of the marriageability of kin, then, the Dharmaśāstra taken as a whole fails to resolve the matter in favor of the one genetic system or the other, nor does it establish a rule which supersedes both. Nevertheless, there is an aspect of marriage in which a consensus is reached whose validity is not limited to a part of India under the doctrine of regional custom (*deśa-dharma*) and which therefore constitutes an Indian culture of kinship. I mean the conception of marriage as the gift of a maiden, or what I would like to call "the *kanyādāna* complex."

The śāstric theory of exchange makes a radical distinction between worldly and religious gifts. Worldly gifts are those made with an obvious, "visible" motive such that an expectation of reciprocal benefit attaches to the act of giving. Such gifts are no better than buying and selling, of "giving for a price." Only those gifts for which there is no visible return can be presumed to bear an invisibly engendered fruit. Such a gift, when made to a disinterested, superior being is a religious gift (*dharma-dāna*). Its mark is the absence of an obvious reciprocity. A *quid pro quo* does exist, but it is transcendental. The causal nexus between the religious gift and its fruit is unseen (*adṛṣta*) or, as it is more usually put, the fruit itself is invisible (*adṛṣtaphala*) in that the meritorious effects of the gift do not immediately accrue to the giver and may not do so until the next life.

The śāstric ideal of marriage as the gift of a maiden is derived from this theory as a special case, and the elements of the *kanyādāna* complex are the workings-out of its implications. Marriage by gift begins by presuming the superiority of the groom's people vis-à-vis the bride's people. It continues by injecting into the marriage ceremony a ritual of giving whereby the bride is given by her guardian (in principle, her father) into the groom's keeping, utterly severing the connection between the bride and her family and transforming her into an extension of the groom and his family. Thus, marriage by gift is also a rite of initiation into another kinship group for a woman, and a sacrament which creates an indissoluble bond between husband and wife, rendering divorce and widow remarriage impossible. By virtue of this transformation of women upon marriage, the married and the unmarried are differently classified from the patrilineal perspective which *kanyādāna* assumes. Women born within the lineage (*gotrajā, kulajā*) become "women given away" (*prattā*) upon marriage, a class whose counterparts are the "brides of the lineage" (*kula-vadhū*). Finally, *kanyādāna* ends by perpetuating the asymmetry between two parties to the transaction, for after marriage hospitality, gifts and deference must flow always and only from the bride's people to the groom's people. For the wife-givers to accept the smallest return would constitute taking visible "payment" for their daughter, destroying the invisible merit of the gift and making it no better than a commercial transaction. Givers must not be takers in the transcendental commerce; and, we may add, takers being by definition the superiors of givers, the *kanyādāna* complex carries with it a tendency to hypergamy.

It is reasonably certain that the basic idea of marriage as gift has an ancient Indo-Aryan and even an Indo-European pedigree, though we cannot say whether earliest Dravidian culture also sponsored such a conception. However that may be, the ideal of *kanyādāna* is developed by the jurists into something quite different from the assimilation of marriage to gift-giving widely reported in historical and ethnographic materials. For *kanyādāna* deliberately sets aside the wisdom of the many (worldly reciprocity) in favor of the higher truth of the elect (transcendental reciprocity), and acquires through the prestige of the Dharmaśāstra a pan-Indian ambit. The ethnographic record resounds with the overtones of this rich śāstric concept (here presented in but the simplest of terms). Unmistakable echoes may be found in ethnography from Kashmir to Jaffna,[15] in variations made to harmonize as best they may with other elements, including the prevailing rules of marriage, of the local kinship system. To the Indo-Aryan system of kinship, the *kanyādāna* complex adds a number of things, including a prohibition on sister-exchange in marriage (which is not itself forbidden by the Indo-Aryan exogamy of close kin), often honored in the breach.[16] To the Dravidian system it adds a preference for cross-cousin marriage in the matrilateral direction (MBD) as a means of avoiding direct reciprocity, also often given only lip service.[17] Since it derives from the learned culture of the Brahmin jurists, the effects of the *kanyādāna* complex are more frequently encountered among the upper castes. But (and this is the main point) it is not limited by regional or genetic culture boundaries. It constitutes an Indian culture of kinship. The consequence for method is plain: if we are to know the nature of the Dravidian kinship system, we must be able to identify, and exclude, the effects of the *kanyādāna* complex in the ethnography of contemporary Dravidians.[18]

The excision of Indo-Aryan and Indian features from the data is but one side of the study of Dravidian kinship. The other is to bring the variations represented by particular Dravidian systems into an ordered relation to one another. It is at this point that understanding the Dravidian system through a single "type case" presumed to be representative loses the conditional validity it enjoyed in the contrastive phase of the investigation. The task is necessarily "data-extensive," so much so that I cannot embark on it here. It will have to suffice simply to state that this second half of the program is as indispensable as the first is to a knowledge of Dravidian kinship.

Programmatic remarks would be superfluous if the several participants were agreed on the program. But the spate of work on kinship in India, inspired by Lévi-Strauss and led by Dumont, fine as it is, has on the whole been lacking in historical depth and skimpy in the historical side of its conceptualization. A recent attempt by Carter to synthesize the ethnographic record sets out from the dictum of Dumont and Pocock that "India is one" and, with an assist from the *kanyādāna* complex, finds a fundamental unity in Indian kinship, North and South.[19] Starting out from the proposition that "India is many," the ethnography could as easily be made to show the opposite. Neither proposition is wrong, nor does the truth lie somewhere in the middle. As I have tried to show, both models, the divergent and the convergent, need one another for their own completion, and both are needed for a complete apprehension of the data.

NOTES

1. This is in the nature of a report on work in progress to be entitled *The Frontiers of Dravidian Kinship*. The summary generalizations made in this paper will be elaborated and documented therein. Research toward the book has at different points enjoyed support from The National Endowment for the Humanities, The American Council of Learned Societies, The American Institute of Indian Studies, and The Horace Rackham Graduate School of The University of Michigan, here gratefully acknowledged.
2. M. B. Emeneau, "India as a Linguistic Area," in *Collected Papers*, Linguistic Department Publication no. 8, Annamalai University (Annamalainagar, 1967).
3. Colin P. Masica, *Defining a Linguistic Area* (Chicago: University of Chicago Press, 1976).
4. Franklin C. Southworth, "Detecting Prior Creolization: An Analysis of the Historical Origins of Marathi," in *Pidginization and Creolization of Languages*, ed. Dell Hymes (London: Cambridge University Press, 1971), pp. 255-74. See also, in the same volume, John J. Gumperz and Robert Wilson, "Convergence and Creolization: A Case from the Indo-Aryan/Dravidian Border," pp. 151-68.
5. Franklin C. Southworth, "Linguistic Stratigraphy of North India," *International Journal of Dravidian Linguistics* 3, no. 2 (1974).
6. A. M. Shah, in *The Household Dimension of the Family in India* (Berkeley and Los Angeles: University of California Press, 1973), has devised a method of measuring behavioral conformity to what he calls "the principal of the co-residence of patrikin and their wives," which takes the demographic possibility of joint residence into account in each instance. This might well provide a model for the assessment of the effect of Dravidian marriage rules on behavior.
7. Lewis Henry Morgan, *Systems of Consanguinity and Affinity of the Human Family*, Smithsonian Contributions to Knowledge no. 218 (Washington, D.C.: Smithsonian Institution, 1870).
8. Irawati Karve, *Kinship Organization in India*, 2nd ed. (Bombay: Asia Publishing House, 1965).
9. Irawati Karve, *Kinship Organization*, and "Kinship Terminology and Kinship Usages of the Marāṭhā Country," *Bulletin of the Deccan College Research Institute* 1 (1940):327-89; 2(1941):9-33.
10. A. T. Carter, "A Comparative Analysis of Systems of Kinship and Marriage in South Asia," *Proceedings of the Royal Anthropological Institute of Great Britain and Ireland*, 1973, pp. 29-54, with an excellent bibliography of current anthropological literature.
11. H. R. Trivedi, "Some Aspects of Kinship Terminology among the Mers of Saurashtra," *Journal of the Maharaja Sayajirao University of Baroda* 3, no. 1 (1954):157-68.
12. Southworth, "Detecting Prior Creolization."
13. Thomas R. Trautmann, "Consanguineous Marriage in Pali Literature," *Journal of the American Oriental Society* 93 (1973):158-80 (whence the story of Ajātasattu and Pasenadi), and "Cross-Cousin Marriage in Ancient North India? " *Kinship and History in South Asia*, ed. Trautmann, Michigan Papers on South and Southeast Asia no. 7 (Ann Arbor: Center for South and Southeast Asian Studies, 1974).
14. *Baudhāyana Dharma Sūtra* 1.1.2.1ff.

15. T. N. Madan, *Family and Kinship: A Study of the Pandits of Rural Kashmir* (Bombay: Asia Publishing House, 1965); Kenneth David, "Until Marriage Do Us Part: A Cultural Account of Jaffna Categories for Kinsmen," *Man*, n.s. 8, no. 4 (1973): 521-35.
16. Madan, p. 115: "The Pandits agree that reciprocal marriages offend against the basic notion of marriage being the ritual gift of a daughter to her chosen husband. Nothing, it is said, should be accepted in return for such a gift. But whereas a minority of the Pandits, usually those belonging to the aristocratic families, criticize reciprocal marriages as ritually and socially improper, the majority justify them on grounds of expediency and social survival."
17. E. Kathleen Gough, "Brahman Kinship in a Tamil Village," *American Anthropologist* 58, no. 5 (1956):826-53: "Because of these differences in the status of cross-cousins and of affines, Brahman youths say that they prefer matrilateral as opposed to patrilateral cross-cousin marriage. For a man respects his sister's affines and patronizes his wife's relatives, and a man respects his father's sister's husband and father's sister's son. If he marries his mother's brother's daughter, then his wife's kinsmen (mother's brother, mother's brother's son), whom he may now patronize, are people with whom his prior relationship was similarly patronizing. If he marries his father's sister's daughter, then his wife's kinsmen (father's sister's husband, father's sister's son) are individuals whom he once respected, but who should now respect him. Matrilateral cross-cousin marriage therefore reinforces already existing asymmetrical relationships, whereas patrilateral cross-cousin marriage (and also marriage to the elder sister's daughter) reverses such relationships. Nevertheless, in spite of their stated preference for matrilateral cross-cousin marriage, Kumbapettai Brahmans in fact practise both types with equal frequency" (p. 844).
18. From this perspective, the indigenous Jaffna Tamil theory of kinship in the fine article by Kenneth David ("Until Marriage Do Us Part") contains elements which are non-Dravidian in that they derive from the *kanyādāna* complex.
19. Carter, "A Comparative Analysis of Systems of Kinship and Marriage"; Louis Dumont and David Pocock, "For a Sociology of India," *Contributions to Indian Sociology* 1 (1957):7-22.

LINGUISTIC PREHISTORY: THE DRAVIDIAN SITUATION

David W. McAlpin
University of Pennsylvania

The first part of this paper is a summary of the evidence indicating that Elamite, a major language of ancient West Asia, is cognate with the Dravidian family of languages. This is primarily an updated version of data published elsewhere.[1] It will be shown that while many details remain to be worked out, the existence of a Proto-Elamo-Dravidian stage is the only tenable hypothesis. The second part builds from this hypothesis of a genetic connection between Dravidian and Elamite and adds information from the vocabularies of the protolanguages and from the modern distribution of Dravidian speakers. From all of this, several new views of the position of the Dravidians in South Asian prehistory are inferred.

Elam occupied what is now southern Iran, primarily in the Zagros mountains extending from Mesopotamia into Baluchistan, in the period beginning in the fourth millennium B.C. until it was ultimately absorbed into the Achaemenid Persian empire. Elamite was written in two different scripts. The first, called Proto-Elamite, was in use from the fourth millennium B.C. (shortly after the beginning of writing in Sumer) to around 2200 B.C. It has not been deciphered and is assumed to be Elamite due to its distribution and undisturbed overlap with the later Elamite script. In form this older script is very similar to the Indus Valley script. Around 2500 B.C. Elam adopted and adapted the cuneiform script of Mesopotamia. The stages of Elamite in cuneiform are Old Elamite, a single document from around 2200 B.C.; Middle Elamite, the largely monolingual inscriptions primarily from Susa and Choga Zambil from ca. 1300 B.C. to ca. 640 B.C.; and Achaemenid Elamite, used as an official bureaucratic language of the Persian empire from the fifth and fourth centuries B.C. Achaemenid Elamite has two major varieties, Royal Achaemenid Elamite which was used in official inscriptions, particularly the great Behistun inscription, and the Persepolis tablets consisting of many hastily written memoranda and records. Both varieties of Achaemenid Elamite tend to be bilingual with Old Persian or Akkadian. Achaemenid Elamite has been the key to all work done on Elamite, although it is highly contaminated with Old Persian.

Partially due to historical accident and partially due to the fact that Achaemenid Elamite has by far the best attestation for the meaning of its words, my work began with Achaemenid Elamite. This base has since been expanded considerably with a number of Middle Elamite sources.[2] However, in spite of more than doubling the available corpus, there have had to be only minor changes in the set of phonological correspondences set out in 1974 (McAlpin 1974:93-95); see Appendix A for an updated version. The major additions have been the addition of a phoneme */h/ for Proto-Elamo-Dravidian and the splitting of the Proto-Elamo-Dravidian dental series into dental and postdental series, reflecting the dental-retroflex contrast in Dravidian. The indications of Dravidian retroflexes corresponding to Elamite *r* plus consonant clusters have not been borne out and this direction has been dropped.

This work on etyma and phonological correspondences has been largely restricted to the initial syllable (C)VC. For Dravidian (and seemingly for Elamite), this initial syllable is commonly the verb root to which a derivational augment of -V(C) is often added. Since it is also usually stressed, and prefixing of any sort is rare, this initial syllable is by far the most stable element phonologically in the languages involved. Even for nouns, the initial monosyllabic root is normal, although multiple derivational augments are more common. Vowel length for Proto-Elamo-Dravidian has been ignored since it is not indicated in Elamite and is so highly structured in Dravidian as to be a likely innovation.

In this work Elamite has always been the limiting factor. At present, there are fewer than 250 lexical roots [initial (C)VC(V)] with a well-described phonology and a usable meaning. This is in contrast to the more than five thousand entries in the *Dravidian Etymological Dictionary* (DED) and its supplements. If we examine the cognation rate for these usable initial forms where the CVC are consistent with the phonological correspondences and the meaning is clear, several interesting statistics are generated. In the original *Language* article, using only Achaemenid Elamite sources, the rate of cognates to usable Achaemenid Elamite words was about 25 percent. Today, with Elamite vowel variation better understood[3] and with meanings and origins clarified with Middle Elamite data, the cognation rate for Achaemenid Elamite attested words is almost 40 percent. In Middle Elamite roots meeting the same requirements and using strict correspondences, the cognation rate is 50 percent (73 out of 149). For the unique Middle Elamite bilingual text the rate climbs to 75 percent (18 out of 24) for lexical roots. This is comparable to cognation rates within a branch of the Indo-European language family and higher than between English and German. This high rate is partly the result of using the most conservative part of the language. Rates are considerably lower when only nouns are examined. However, the overall rate and the direction of the rate, i.e., higher between older and hence closer stages of the languages, argue very strongly that Elamite and Dravidian are cognate for the simple reason that no other hypothesis better explains the nature of the data. Borrowing at such a high rate for verbs, but not for nouns is extremely unlikely, and such rates for similar vocabulary are beyond chance.

However, with the morphological correspondences the situation is less sanguine. The basic problem is the paucity of morphology. There are very few basic forms and these tend to consist of a single consonant and an often ambiguous vowel. Chance becomes a major factor. Elamite morphology can be easily summarized on one sheet of paper. Dravidian morphology, while fairly clear in overall structure, is currently poorly understood when any detail is attempted at a Proto-Dravidian level. Current work at several points holds promise for some sort of breakthrough with the morphology.

Nevertheless, there are some striking fits in the morphology. The second person pronouns are a good example (see table 1). Both languages attest a basic form of *ni* for 'you' (Old Elamite has *ni* for the later *nu*). In itself, this is insignificant; chance is simply too great. In addition, the non-nominative (oblique, accusative) forms end in *-n* and the plurals in *-m* for both languages. Elamite accusatives are restricted to the pronouns, and obliques in *-n* are normal and most commonly found in the Dravidian pronouns. For both groups of languages plurals in *-m* are unusual and restricted to the pronouns. What is significant is not the base form *ni*, the non-nominative in *-n*, or the plural in *-m*, but that all three occur and shift together even when they are not common endings in the languages involved. Also note the forms for the first person plural pronouns: Elamite *nuku*, acc. *nukun*; Proto-Dravidian *yām*, obl. *yam* (exclusive), *nām*, obl. *nam* (inclusive). Another related example is from the nonpast paradigm of the verbs (see table 2). Note the striking similarity of the Old Tamil forms and the Elamite forms. However, pay close attention to the forms for 'we' (inclusive) and 'you' (1pin, 2s, 2p) in Old Tamil, Konda, Kui, and Kurux. Note that all the forms have a *t* (or its immediate reflex such as Kui *-s-* and Kurux *-d-*) as does the Elamite second person ending. In other words, every form with a second person component (the Elamite first person plural pronoun is taken to be derived from an inclusive

TABLE 1

SECOND PERSON PRONOUNS

Second Person Pronouns	Middle Elamite	*PED	*PDr	Old Tamil
Singular				
Nominative	*nu (<ni)*	*ni*	*nī(ṉ)*	*nī*
Oblique	*nun*	*nin*	*niṉ*	*niṉ/uṉ*
Plural				
Nominative	*num*	*nim*	*nīm*	*nīm/nīr*
Oblique	*numun*	*nimən*	*nim*	*num/um*

TABLE 2

SELECTED NONPAST PARADIGMS

Group	South Dravidian	Central Dravidian				North Dravidian	Proto-Dravidian	Elamite	
Language	Old Tamil	Konda	Kui	Gondi	Naiki	Kurux (f)		AE	ME
Tense	nonpast	nonpast	future	future	present/future	present	nonpast	nonpast	nonpast
1s	*-∅-ku*	*-n-a*	*-∅-i*	*-k-ā*	*-t-an*	*-∅-en*	*-N-kə*	*-n-kə*	*-n-kə*
1pex	*-∅-kum*	*-n-ap*	*-n-amu*	*-k-ōm*	*-t-am*	*-∅-em*	*-N-kum*	*-n-un*	
1pin	*-∅-tum*	*-n-aṭ*	*-n-asu*	*-k-āṭ*		-d-*at*	*-N-taṭ*		
2s	*-∅-ti*	*-n-i(d)*	*-d-i*	*-k-ī*	*-t-i*	*-d-i*	*-N-ti*	*-n-ti*	*-n-ti*
2p	*-∅-tir*	*-n-ider*	*-d-eru*	*-k-īṭ*	*-t-ir*	*-d-ay*	*-N-tir*	*(-n-ti?)*	
3sm	*-m-aṉ*	*-n-anr̠*	*-n-an*	*-ān-ūr*	*-t-en*	—	*-N-aṉr̠ə*	*-n-ra*	*-n-rə*
3sn	*-um*	*-n-ad*	*-n-e*	*-ār*	*-t-un*	*-∅-i*	*-N(-atə)*	*-n*	*-n*
3pmf	*-m-ar*	*-n-ar*	*-n-eru*	*-ān-īr*	*-t-er*	*-n-ay*	*-N-ar*		
3pn	*-∅-pa*	*-n-e*	*-n-u*	*-ān-ūŋ*	*-t-e*	*-∅-i*	*-N-pa*	*-m-pə*	*-n-pə*

Note: Forms given are tense marker plus personal ending.

Abbreviations are as follows: 1, first person; 2, second person; 3, third person; s, singular; p, plural; ex, exclusive; in, inclusive; m, masculine; f, female, feminine; n, neuter, nonmasculine. AE = Achaemenid Elamite; ME = Middle Elamite. *N* = (*u*)m/n. *ə* = variable or indeterminate vowel.

For discussion and more details, see McAlpin 1975:107.

form) begins with an *n* if word initial and with a *t* if a suffix. While the details remain to be worked out, such a relationship is beyond pure chance. Elamite and Dravidian, unlike Indo-European, do not have elaborate paradigms to make morphological relationships clear. What must be found are patterns which are beyond chance, consisting of elements which alone could easily be due to chance. While table 2 may seem short and ad hoc, the morphological endings given there for Elamite are about one quarter of the available verbal morphology.

The semantic content of Proto-Dravidian vocabulary for agriculture and animal husbandry has some very interesting patterns. There is a fairly complete set of terms for general agriculture including 'plowing' (*ur̤u* DED 592), 'threshing floor' (*kalam* DED 1160), 'agricultural field' (*vayal* DED 4298, *key* DED 1629), and 'reap' (*koy* DED 1763). However, there are *no* Proto-Dravidian terms for any specific crop. All such terms are limited to one subbranch or another. There are specific terms for domesticated animals: 'cow' (*āy* DED 283), 'calf' (*kan̠r̠u* DED 1187), and 'goat/sheep' (*yāṭu* DED 4229). These terms are especially well developed for caprids and bovines. The vocabulary is that of a transhumant society where herding dominates or is at least the most stable continuing factor. Moreover, the connection is decidedly West Asian in its details, looking to a wheat-barley-goat-sheep-cattle complex as opposed to a Southeast Asian(and currently dominant) rice-water buffalo-chicken complex. The poor adaptability of wheat and barley to the Deccan and South India and their subsequent abandonment explains the lack of Proto-Dravidian crop names. This abandonment of cereal agriculture by groups with a West Asian culture is attested in the archaeological record. Elamite has an elaborate set of herding terms, some of which are cognate with Proto-Dravidian, but no agricultural terms are attested.

Certain etyma in Proto-Elamo-Dravidian give some clues to the culture involved and to the direction of semantic shift. Animals and objects in Elamite have a tendency to show up in South Indian caste names for the caste traditionally associated with the Elamite referent; for example, PED **ăs* 'herd, cattle', RAE *aš* 'herd, cattle as a possession', PDr. **āy* 'cow', Tamil *āy* 'cowherd (caste)' (DED 283); PED **hiṭ* 'to herd (goats)', ME *hit* 'herd', AE *hidu* 'goat', Tamil *iṭai* 'herdsman caste (of goats)', Brahui *hiḍing* 'to gather, herd' (DED 382); and PED **uppaṯ* 'brick', ME *upat* 'brick(work)', Kannada *uppāṟa* 'bricklayer', Telugu *uppara* 'caste of tank diggers' (DED 537). A very informative etymon is PED **tal̤l* 'to push in', ME *tallu-*, AE *talli-* 'to write', PSDr. **tal̤l* 'to push (in)' (DED 2559). While the semantics fits beautifully for the cuneiform Elamite, it clearly shows that separation was preliterate. Dravidian words for 'write' generally come from words meaning 'paint' or 'draw',(cf. DED 725, 1533, 4304). Another informative etymon is PED **šeṯ* 'to pay tax or tribute', ME *šerum* 'tribute', AE *šura-* 'to present', PDr. **teṟ* 'to pay tax', Tamil *tiṟai* 'tribute' (DED 2833). Taken together these indicate that the preseparation society was preliterate but well into complex social organization beyond the hunting and gathering stage; note 'herd', 'brick', 'pay tax'.

Two sets of words pose problems. The first is AE *martukkaš* 'portion of herd paid to herdsman for his services', Tamil *maṭakku* 'to engage as a servant or agent', Kannada *maḍaṅgu* 'to procure, hire'. Here the length of the form, the nature of the phonological correspondences (*ṟt* to *ṭ*, while very plausible, has not been supported by other evidence), and the closeness of the meanings is probably too good to be true. It seems to be a loanword. Either as an etymon or as a loanword it shows a sophisticated level of economic interaction. The other set concerns the South Dravidian word for 'horse', *kutiray*. Burrow has clearly shown that the Proto-Dravidian word for *horse* must be related to Old Tamil *ivuḷi* and Brahui *hulli.*[4] Elamite has *kuti* for 'to bear, carry' and the regular form for 'bearer' is *kutira*. It seems certain that this word was borrowed into South Dravidian for the domesticated horse (*Equus caballus*) with *ivuḷi* being kept for the native wild horse (*Equus hemionus*). This argument is strengthened by the fact that the formative *-ra(y)* cannot be explained in terms of Dravidian morphology; the addition of *y* to an *a*-final word would be automatic.

The modern distribution of Dravidian speakers points to some interesting conclusions. There is no evidence of an ancient penetration of Sri Lanka by Tamils. The fact that the Aryan Sinhalese were able to outflank them as the dominant group implies that any Tamil occupations were coastal and in small numbers. Given the ease of crossing the Palk Strait, this lack of Tamil occupation is very odd if the Tamils were aboriginal to South India. There is little to indicate that Dravidians were anciently in eastern India. The Kurux (and by implication the closely related Malto), according to their own traditions, have moved up the valley of the Narbada in historic times. While considerably influenced by the surrounding Munda and Indo-Aryan speakers, Kurux and Malto show differing influences. Dravidian has two outlier languages, Brahui and Koraga. Brahui is spoken in the Brahui Hills centering on Kalat, south of Quetta in Pakistan. It is divergent in many ways from common Dravidian. While considered to be related to Kurux and Malto in North Dravidian, the main reason for grouping them together (the *k* to *x* shift) has recently been brought into doubt.[5] Koraga (not to be confused with Koḍagu [Coorg]) is spoken by a small group of untouchables in North Kanara district on the west coast. While swamped with Kannada loans, its morphology is distinctly not South Dravidian and most closely resembles Kurux. It should probably be treated as a separate group for the time being.

If we take one of the standard family tree diagrams and superimpose it on a map of South Asia, several interesting relationships are brought to light.[6] The South Dravidian group (Tamil-Koḍugu, Kannada, and [?] Tulu) has the trunk of the tree clearly pointing north through Karnataka. Kurux and Malto look back to the west, down the valley of the Narbada. For Central Dravidian, with the major exception of Gondi, closely related groups cluster in the east or south and divergent groups in the west. In general, odd groups and isolates (Brahui, Tulu, Kodaga) are in the west, closely related groups in the east or south. The *Stammbaum* seems to point to Gujarat and on to Baluchistan. Thus, the pattern of distribution supports the concept of a fairly recent expansion of Dravidians into the Indian peninsula through Gujarat with possible forerunners (such as Koraga ?).

If we accept the argument that Elamite and Dravidian are cognate or at least that this is a hypothesis which has reached a *prima facie* level of argument, then several points can be made about the Dravidians, their origins, and their possible relationships with the Indo-Aryans:

1. Given the nature of the modern distribution of Dravidian speakers and the supporting evidence from family-tree relationships, we must conclude that the Dravidians came from the west, are not aboriginal to the Indian peninsula (Deccan and South India), and in fact, must have entered it relatively late (second millennium B.C.) in prehistory.
2. Given the nature of their vocabulary, they were almost certainly transhumants practicing both herding and agriculture, with herding the more unbroken tradition.
3. Given the high percentage of cognates, the cultural nature of these cognate terms, and the historical existence of Elam, then the separation came relatively late (ca. 5000 B.C.?) and took place in West Asia.
4. Dravidian speakers moved through the Indus valley during the formation and height of the Harappan civilization and must have played some part in it.

Thus, the Dravidians, like the Aryans, were a group that entered South Asia from the west. They were moving to occupy the Indian peninsula at about the same time the Aryans were moving into the Panjab. These are essentially parallel movements of peoples.

These examples are very brief and do not include all of the details of form or meaning. Groups A and B give the total corpus of etyma with initial *š*, which is of particular interest since *š* does not occur in Dravidian. There are two variants. In group A, initial *š* in Elamite corresponds to initial *t* in Dravidian. In all these cases the second consonant is an alveolar (or retroflex ?) liquid, i.e., PED **r̤, *l,* or **ṯ*. In group B, initial *š* in Elamite corresponds to a vowel initial word in Dravidian, but this vowel is always long. Here the second consonant is anything except an alveolar liquid. This type of consistent phonological patterning in a way which would not be expected in loanwords is normal when two languages are cognate, but under no other circumstances.

Groups C and D give the etyma which contrast intervocalically: the normal *r* and the alveolar *ṯ* (which would have been a tap in this environment). Middle Elamite collapses the two together showing no contrast and having a single *r* as the reflex for both. However, significantly Achaemenid Elamite will normally spell the reflex of **r* with two *r*'s (commonly using signs for syllables closed in *-r* to do so), but always the reflex of **ṯ* with one. The two phonemes commonly fall together in Dravidian languages but contrast actively in some dialects of Tamil, Malayalam, and Konda among others. In all cases the two phonemes are phonetically very similar. The overall pattern is one of two similar phonemes that have independently fallen together repeatedly. Thus, Achaemenid Elamite has the contrast weakly while Middle Elamite does not. This indicates that Middle Elamite is not the direct ancestor of Achaemenid Elamite. Similarly Malayalam, Literary Tamil, and Jaffna Tamil do, but continental colloquial Tamil does not. This is a pattern of inherited rather than borrowed phonology. Also, in Dravidian the contrast is so fine phonetically that it has never been borrowed into a non-Dravidian language.

APPENDIX A
PHONOLOGICAL CORRESPONDENCES

	*PED	*PEl	*PDr.	PED environment
1.	*a*	*a*	*a*	#_C, #C_C, VC_(C)
2.	*i*	*i*	*i*	#_C, #C_C, VC_
3.	*u*	*u*	*u*	#_C, #C_C,
4a.	*e*	*e*	*e*	#_C, #C_C
4b.	*e*	*e*	*i*	VC_(C)
5.	*o*	*u*	*o*	#_C, #C_C
6a.	*h*	*h*	*Ø*	#_V
6b.	*h*	*h*	*k,v,Ø*	V_(V)
7.	*w*	*HU*	*v*	#_V
8.	*y*	*Ø*	*y*	#_V
9a.	*k*	*k*	*k*	#_V, V_#
9b.	*k*	*h,k*	*k*	#V_V, #_V*l*
10.	*kk*	*kk*	*kk*	V_
11.	*nk*	*nk*	*ŋk*	V_
12.	*c*	*c,s*	*c*	#_V
13.	*cc*	*cc*	*cc*	V_
14.	*ňc*	*ns*	*ñc*	V_
15a.	šV	šV	V̄	#_C See Appendix B.
15b.	*š*	*š*	*t*	#_V ⟦*r, l, ṯ*⟧
15c.	*š*	*š*	*y*	V_
16.	*t*	*t*	*t*	#_V, V_(V)
17.	*tt*	*tt*	*tt*	V_(V)
18.	*ṭ*	*t,tt*	*ṭ*	V_(V)
19a.	*n*	*n*	*n*	#_V
19b.	*n*	*n*	*ṉ*	V_(V)
20.	*nn*	*nn*	*nn*	V_(V)
21a.	*p*	*p*	*p*	#_V, C_V
21b.	*p*	*p*	*v*	V_V
22.	*pp*	*p*	*pp*	V_V
23.	*mp*	*p*	*mp*	V_
24.	*m*	*m*	*m*	#_V, V_V Elamite script does not
25.	*v*	*m*	*v*	#_V contrast *m̲* and *v̲*.
26a.	*r*	*r,rr*	*r*	V_V See Appendix B.

26b.	*r*	*r*	*r*	V_#	
27a.	*ṯ*	*r*	*ṟ*	V_V	*ṟ*=Dravidian alveolar stop/tap
27b.	*ṯ*	*t*	*ṟ*	V_#	
28.	*l*	*l*	*l*	V_(V)	
29.	*ḷ*	*ll,EL*	*ḷ*	V_(V)	
30.	*r*	*r,l*	*r*	V_	

C = any consonant
V = any vowel, V̄ = long vowel
#= word boundary, space; #_ = initial; _# = final
HU and *EL* refer to cuneiform signs.

APPENDIX B
SAMPLE ETYMA

	*PED	Elamite (ME, AE)	Dravidian (*=PDr.)
A 1.	*šar̤-* 'be low'	*šara* 'below, under'	*tār̤- 'be/fall low'
2.	*sar̤-* 'shoot, stalk'	*šaliha* 'leg (?)'	PSDr. **tār̤* 'leg; stem, stalk'
		săli 'twig, branch (?)'	**tar̤-* 'to sprout; twig'
3.	*šal-* 'head, top'	*šalu* 'high social class'	**tal-ay* 'head, top'
4.	*šeṯ-* 'pay tax'	*šerum* 'tribute'	**teṟ-* 'pay tribute'
		šura- 'to present'	
5.	*šaṯ-* 'cut (off)'	*šari-* 'cut, hew'	**taṟ-* 'cut (off/down)'
		šara- 'cut, apportion'	
B 6.	*šakk* 'sprout'	*šak, šak* 'son'	PCDr. **ākk-* 'leaf, sprout'
7.	*šak* 'be equivalent'	*šak* 'counterpart'	**āk-* 'to be, become'
8.	*šin-* 'arrive'	*šinni-* 'approach, arrive'	**īṉ-* 'bear, yean'
		šinnu- 'come'	
9.	*šar-* 'collect'	*šarra-* 'collect (?)'	**ār-* 'collect, gather'
C 1.	*par* 'young one'	*par* 'descendants'	**pār-* 'child, young'
2.	*par-* 'look at'	*para-* 'supervise'	PSDr. **pār-* 'look at, watch'
3.	*pari-* 'go away'	*pari-* 'go'	**pari-* 'run (away)'
		pari- 'go to, issue'	
4.	*ere-* 'burn, blaze'	*erentim* 'baked brick'	**eri-* 'burn, blaze'
5.	*cari-* 'slide down'	*sarra-* 'clear away, demolish'	**cari-* 'slip and fall'
		sari- 'destroy'	
6.	*kari* 'young animal'	*karri, kariri* 'kid'	**karu* 'fetus, young animal'
7.	*vari-* 'fix, hold'	*mari-* 'seize, grasp'	**vari-* 'bind, tie, fix'
		marri- 'seize, hold'	
	(See also B9)		
D 1.	*paṯi-* 'pull, drag'	*pari-* 'pull, draw, drag'	**paṟi-* 'pull (out)'

2. *peṯa-* 'speak'	*pera-, bera-* 'read'	**paṟay-* 'speak, say'
3. *aṯaš* 'storeroom'	*araš* 'possession'	**aṟay* 'room, chamber'
	araš 'granary (?)'	
4. *iṯ(ə)š-* 'great'	*riša-* 'large'	**iṟay* 'anyone great'
	irša- 'great, large'	
5. *uṯ-* 'consider'	*uri-* 'believe'	**uṟ-* 'consider, think'
6. *tuṯu-* 'mention, say'	*turu-* 'speak, order'	**tuṟu-* 'slander, cite'
	tiri- 'speak, say'	

(See also A4-5)

NOTES

1. See McAlpin 1974 and 1975 for details.
2. These include Reiner; Stève 1962 and its translation; Lambert; and Stève 1967. Other sources for Middle Elamite include König. The main source for Achaemenid Elamite is Hallock.
3. Elamite is somewhat ambivalent in its attestation of the vowels *i* and *u*. Compared to Proto- and Old Elamite, Middle Elamite often has *u* where *i* is original (OE *ni*, ME *nu* 'you'). Compared to all foregoing stages, Achaemenid Elamite commonly has *i* where *u* is previously attested; for example, the following Middle Elamite, Achaemenid Elamite pairs: *turu, tiri* 'speak'; *puktə, pikti* 'help'; *hute, iddu* 'distribute'. Given the inherent vagaries of cuneiform, it is hard to tell if this is due to the script or the phonology.
4. See Burrow 1972.
5. Recent work published by Das on Malto makes it clear that this language has a true uvular *q* rather than the fricative *x* as a reflex of PDr. **k*. Thus, it is probable that closely related Kurux independently and recently innovated the shift of **k (*q?)* to *x* rather than having this as an old change shared with Brahui.
6. This use of family-tree relationships should not be taken too seriously. The main point is that it can be done without difficulty. At the moment there is a considerable flux in the ideas about how the subgroups are related. It makes little difference which of the current models is used here. I personally suspect that any attempt to provide a framework over the obvious subgroups (such as Tamil-Malayalam-Toda-Kota-Koḍagu) is premature and probably futile.

REFERENCES

Burrow, Thomas. 1972. "The Primitive Dravidian Word for the Horse." *International Journal of Dravidian Linguistics* 1:18-25.

Burrow, Thomas and Murray B. Emeneau. 1960. *A Dravidian Etymological Dictionary.* Oxford: Oxford University Press.

Das, A. Sisir Kumar. 1973. *Structure of Malto.* Annamalainagar, India: Annamalai University.

Hallock, Richard T. 1969. *Persepolis Fortification Tablets.* Oriental Institute Publication no. 92. Chicago: University of Chicago Press.

König, F. W. 1965. *Die elamischen Königsinschriften.* Graz: Archiv für Orientforschung.

Lambert, Maurice. 1965. "Les inscriptions élamites de Tchoga-Zanbil." *Iranica Antiqua* 5:18-38.

McAlpin, David W. 1974. "Towards Proto-Elamo-Dravidian." *Language* 50:89-101.

———. 1975. "Elamite and Dravidian: Further Evidence of Relationship." *Current Anthropology* 16:105-15.

Reiner, Erica. 1969. "The Elamite Languages." In *Altkleinasiatische Sprachen (Handbuch der Orientalistik,* sec. 1, vol. 2, pts. 1-2, no. 2), edited by B. Spuler, pp. 54-116. Leiden: E. J. Brill.

Stève, M.-J. 1962. "Textes élamites de Tchoga-Zanbil." *Iranica Antiqua* 2:22-76; 3:102-23.

———. 1967. "Textes élamites et accadiens de Tchoga Zanbil." In *Tchoga Zanbil (Dur-Untash),* vol. 3. Mémoires de la Délégation Archéologique en Iran, tome 61. Paris: Librairie Orientaliste Paul Geuthner.

LEXICAL EVIDENCE FOR EARLY CONTACTS BETWEEN INDO-ARYAN AND DRAVIDIAN

Franklin C. Southworth
University of Pennsylvania

SUMMARY. On the basis of earlier work by Burrow, Emeneau, and others, plus some new materials, various early loanwords between Indo-Aryan and Dravidian are identified (some of which may originate in other languages). This evidence is interpreted to indicate an extended period of contact in the pre-Ṛgvedic period, under circumstances not involving technological, cultural, or military domination of one group by the other. The evidence of linguistic features in the Ṛgveda suggests that at the time it was composed, the Aryans were in a transitional stage between a period in which they maintained autonomy in their dealings with neighboring groups and a period in which they gradually began to merge with other local groups (Dravidians and others). There is also clear evidence of the presence of other important ethnic groups, speaking other languages, in the area of contact, but their identity is not known. Both Indo-Aryan and Dravidian borrowed terms for local flora and fauna, and possibly a few agricultural terms, from these groups, though the Dravidians were acquainted with grain cultivation from an earlier time. The possibility that the ruling group in the Indus Valley civilization was Dravidian-speaking is discussed, along with the possibility that the contact with Aryans took place in the Indus Valley during the late Harappan period.
Contents: (1) Introduction, (2) The Lexical Evidence, (3) A Survey of Botanical Terms, (4) Phonological Assumptions, (5) Conclusions. *Appendices* (A) Early Indo-Aryan Borrowings from Dravidian; (B) Early Loans in Dravidian from Indo-Aryan; (C) Shared Lexical Items of Uncertain Origin; (D) Terms for Flora Shared by Dravidian and Indo-Aryan.

1. INTRODUCTION

Considerable work has already been done on Indo-Aryan borrowings from

Dravidian, Munda, and other South Asian languages (see works by Przyluski, Bloch, Kuiper, Burrow, and Emeneau in the bibliography). If it is necessary to justify a new treatment of the subject at this time, we can point to a number of considerations. Since that earlier work, several great dictionaries have been completed: Turner's *Comparative Dictionary of the Indo-Aryan Languages*, Burrow and Emeneau's *A Dravidian Etymological Dictionary* and *A Dravidian Etymological Dictionary–Supplement*, and Mayrhofer's *Kurzgefasstes etymologisches Wörterbuch des Altindischen.* In addition, knowledge of the Munda languages and their relationships with languages outside India are on much firmer ground than they were at the time of Przyluski's and Kuiper's work (see, for example, Zide and Zide, 1973, 1976). Furthermore, it has been shown (at least to the author's satisfaction) that the Dravidian family is not indigenous to India (see McAlpin), and this throws a new light on the lexical materials shared by Indo-Aryan and Dravidian, since the possibility of borrowing by both families from a third (indigenous) source needs to be given serious consideration. The author's interest in this subject is part of a general study of the "linguistic archaeology" of India, and an attempt to put together conclusions drawn from various kinds of linguistic evidence.[1]

Burrow and others, in their work on non-Aryan lexical elements in early Indo-Aryan, were concerned primarily to show the possibility or probability of the existence of borrowing, particularly in the oldest Indo-Aryan texts. Ultimately, we hope to do something more than this, namely, to show the kinds of contact which can be inferred from this evidence of linguistic borrowing. Along with other kinds of evidence, it may ultimately be possible to reconstruct the social circumstances and the linguistic effects of the earliest period of contact between Dravidian and Indo-Aryan. This paper is proposed as a step in this direction; however, there will be many more steps before that goal is reached. If we examine only those lexical items shared by Indo-Aryan and Dravidian, which I propose to do here, we find many problems. For one thing, there is disagreement among the experts as to the source of many of these terms, as will be pointed out below. For another, there are still many gaps in the materials, particularly with regard to the attestation of words in Dravidian.

For the present purpose, I propose to examine those lexical items shared by Dravidian and Indo-Aryan which appear to belong to the earliest period of contact. On the Indo-Aryan side, this means that they should be attested in the Vedic literature, preferably in the *Ṛgveda*. I will assume that the *Ṛgveda* as we have it represents the earliest period of Indo-Aryan habitation in the subcontinent, and that it can be localized in the northwestern part of the subcontinent, i.e., in the Panjab.[2] I hope to show evidence for an intimate relationship between the groups speaking Indo-Aryan and Dravidian at (or prior to) that time, and other evidence to show that there was a subsequent change in the linguistic situation, probably reflecting a significant alteration of the relationship between these two groups.

On the Dravidian side, in order to demonstrate that a lexical item is early, we have to show that its distribution within Dravidian makes it likely that it belongs to an early stage of the development of the Dravidian family. This raises certain problems, which I have discussed elsewhere (Southworth 1976). Briefly, there is no clear agreement on the basic subgroups of Dravidian, though the separateness of North Dravidian (Brahui, Malto, and Kurukh) is generally accepted, and therefore any words with cognates in one of these languages and any other language (eliminating possible borrowings between Malto or Kurukh and nearby Central Dravidian languages) can safely be reconstructed for Proto-Dravidian. Since, however, the material for the North Dravidian languages is rather thin, additional material of respectable antiquity may also be used if we include items occurring in one of the four languages, Kolami, Naiki, Parji, and Gadaba (see Krishnamurti 1975), which are also attested in South Dravidian (Tamil, Malayalam, Kodagu, Toda, or Kota), since these groups appear to have been separate from each other for perhaps a millennium or more.[3]

2. THE LEXICAL EVIDENCE

I have attempted to organize the loanwords belonging to the earliest period of Dravidian-Aryan contact into three groups: (a) probable borrowings from Dravidian into Indo-Aryan (2.1), (b) probable borrowings from Indo-Aryan into Dravidian (2.2), and (c) a category of words which seem to be too similar for accident and appear to be early in both families, but which are of indeterminate origin–either Dravidian, Indo-Aryan, or some other source (2.3). One of the problems I have encountered in trying to sort the words into these three categories is that there is a temptation to place all the words in the third category, except, of course, those very few having solid Indo-European or Dravidian etymologies. For the present, however, I have allowed myself to be guided by specialists who have more experience with these materials than I–except, of course, where these distinguished gentlemen disagree with each other.

2.1 For Dravidian loans in early Indo-Aryan, we have primarily the work of Burrow (1946, 1947). He has listed twenty-six words, all clearly attested in the *Ṛgveda*, for which he claims Dravidian origin. Emeneau has supported several of these. Mayrhofer has challenged eight of them, and Thieme has challenged three (including one also challenged by Mayrhofer). Mayrhofer has agreed with the *possibility* of Dravidian origin in nine cases. Eliminating those which have been *seriously* challenged, as well as a few which look unconvincing to me, we have the following nineteen cases for which Dravidian origin seems to be at least as plausible as any other (detailed information is contained in the appendices under the appropriate letter and number):

1. Words relating to technology
   - A-1. *kuṇḍa-* 'pot, hole, pit' – Ta. *kuṇṭam* 'cavity, pit'
   - A-2. *kūṭa-* 'mallet, hammer' (cf. *kuṭṭayati*) – Ta. *koṭṭu-* 'beat'; *kuṭṭu-* 'strike'
   - A-3. *daṇḍa-* 'stick, club' – Mal. *taṇṭa* '(fore)arm'
   - A-4. *ulūkhala-* 'mortar' – Ta. *ulakkai* 'pestle'

2. Words for flora and fauna
   - A-5. *phala-* 'fruit' – Ta. *paẓu-* 'ripen' *paẓam* 'ripe fruit'
   - A-6. *naḍa/naḷa-* 'reed' – Ka. *naḷḷu* 'a reed'
   - A-7. *mayūra-* 'peacock' – Ta. *maññai, mayil* 'peacock'

3. Body parts, bodily deformities
   - A-8. *kulpha-* 'ankle' – Ta. *kuḷampu* 'hoof'
   - A-9. *ukha-* 'part of thigh' – Ta. *ukkam* 'waist'; *ukkalai* 'hips'
   - A-10. *vriś-* 'finger' – Ta. *viral* 'finger, toe' Go. *wirinj-* 'do'
   - A-11. *kāṇa-* 'blind in one eye' – Ta. *kāṇ-* 'see'; *kāṇ-a-* (neg. stem) 'not seeing' (cf. *kaṇ* 'eye')
   - A-12. *kuṇāru-* 'having a crooked or withered arm' – Mal. *kuṇṭan-* 'cripple' (cf. Ta. *kōṇ* 'crookedness')

4. Features of nature
   - A-13. *kulāya-* 'nest' – Ta. *kūṭu* 'nest, etc.'
   - A-14. *bila-* 'hole, cave' – Ta. *viḷ-* 'open out'; *viḷavu* 'cleft, crack'
   - A-15. *piṇḍa-* 'lump, clod' – Ka. *peṭṭe*; Tu. *heṇṭe* 'clod'

5. Food
   A-16. *karambha-* 'a mixture of flour or meal with curds' – Ta. *kuẓampu-* 'be mixed, etc; mixture, curry'

6. Other
   A-17. *kaṭu(ka)-* 'bitter' – Ta. *kaṭu-* 'pain, sting, be pungent, etc.'; *kaṭuku* 'mustard'
   A-18. *bala-* 'strength' – Ta. *val* 'strong, skillful'; *vallu-* 'be able'

2.2. On the other side, Dravidian borrowings from Indo-Aryan, the main source is Emeneau and Burrow, *Dravidian Borrowings from Indo-Aryan* (DBIA), which is basically a list of materials which were excluded from the *Dravidian Etymological Dictionary* (DED) as borrowings. The main list includes 336 items. In addition, they mention 54 cases which were included in the DED, but which they later felt should (probably) have been listed as borrowings from Indo-Aryan. There are also 16 entries in the DED which involve some words borrowed from Indo-Aryan, but which the authors feel may be "reverse borrowings," i.e., the original source of these words is (or may be) Dravidian. Finally, there are another 16 DED entries which represent probable original Dravidian material, but involve some Indo-Aryan "influence" on semantic and/or phonological developments.

Most of the materials in DBIA are attested only in the four southern literary languages and thus do not offer adequate evidence for being very early borrowings. In addition, a number of words can be clearly regarded as later borrowings on phonological grounds: for example, Ka. *mika, miga, mige* 'wild beast, antelope' appears to be from Pkt. *miga-* rather than from Skt. *mṛga-*. Similarly, Ta. *mērai* 'boundary, limit' (with related forms in Malayalam, Kannada, Tulu, Telugu, Kolami) appears to be from a modern Indo-Aryan form like Marathi *mer* 'edge, border', rather than directly from Skt. *maryādā* (which appears in literary Tamil as *mariyātā* 'respect, etc.'). From this whole lot, I have selected out those which appear in Vedic or early post-Vedic sources and which are found in Dravidian not only in the southern literary languages but also in some of the nonliterary languages (eliminating those cases where the latter have clearly borrowed from the former). By this process I am left with the following thirteen items:

1. Words relating to technology
   B-1. Ta. *accu* 'axle' – *akṣa-* (RV)
   B-2. Ta. *kancam* 'bell-metal' – *kaṃsa-* 'metal cup' (AV); 'bell-metal' (Pat.)

B-3. Ta. *kaṭṭai* 'wood'	– *kāṣṭha-* (SBr.)
B-4. Ta. *kampaḷi* 'blanket, covering'	– *kambala(ka)-* (AV)
B-5. Ta. *ālai* 'shed, etc.'	– *śālā-* (AV)
B-6. Ta. *(c)ūci* 'needle'	– *sūci-* (RV)
B-7. Ta. *āṇi* 'nail'	– *āṇi-* (RV)
B-8. Ta. *tōṇi* 'boat'	– *drōṇa-* 'trough' (RV)

2. Agricultural terms

B-9. Ta. *kāṇṭam* 'stem, stalk'	– *kāṇḍa-* (AV)
B-10. *cāmai* 'millet'	– *śyāmaka-* (VS)

3. Terms for fauna

B-11. Te. *gadda* 'kite'	– *gṛdhra-* 'greedy, vulture' (AV)

4. Social structure

B-12. Ta. *turai* 'chief'	– *dhurya-* 'foremost' (AV); (later 'leader, chief')

5. Other

B-13. Ta. *pakkam* 'side'	– *pakṣa-* 'wing, side' (RV)

Regarding the semantic content of these two lists, there is not much that can be said. For one thing, they are too short. Apart from that, both contain technological terms, and terms for flora and fauna. We cannot make too much out of the fact that there appears to be a word relating to social hierarchy in the second list and not in the first; my reconstruction of Proto-Dravidian cultural vocabulary (in preparation) contains at least one such word, and McAlpin has shown a possible case in Proto-Elamo-Dravidian also. It is perhaps interesting that these two lists both seem to suggest a rather wide range of cultural contacts, and that they do *not* show the typical (or perhaps stereotypical) one-sided borrowing relationship expected in a "colonial" situation, with words for technology and high culture mostly going in one direction and words for local flora and fauna mostly in the other (cf. English and Hindi, for example).

2.3. Coming to the third category of words, we have here a number of items (most of them from Burrow's work, with a few contributed by me) which clearly suggest early connections between Indo-Aryan and Dravidian, though we cannot easily determine the direction of borrowing. Even allowing for the possibility that some of these items may be chance resemblances, this list still strongly suggests to me that there was a high degree of contact between these two groups at the earliest period for which we have records, and possibly before.

The following two cases involve verbs which are widespread and of high frequency in most languages of both families. Though the first of these has probable Indo-European cognates, it may be significant that it is the *-l-* form rather than the *-r-* form which has persisted in the meaning 'go, etc.' in almost all the modern Indo-Aryan languages.

C-1.	*carati-* (RV), *calati-* (MBh.) 'moves, goes away, etc.' (cf. Hindi *car-* 'graze', *cal-* 'move, walk, go, etc.')	– Ta. *cel-* 'go, flow, pass, be suitable, etc.'
C-2.	*paṭhati-* 'repeats aloud' (TAr.); 'reads' (Mn.)	– Ta. *pāṭu-* 'sing, chant, etc.'; *pāṭṭu-* 'song'

The following three items are from Burrow, who has suggested that in all three cases the semantics of the Dravidian forms lead to the belief that they may be primary:

C-3.	*nagara-* 'town' (TAr.)	– Ta. *nakar-* 'house, abode, mansion, temple, palace, town, city'
C-4.	*vithura-* 'staggering, tottering' (RV)	– Ta. *vitappu-* 'trembling, agitation, haste'; *vitir-* 'shake, shiver'
C-5.	*vaśi-* 'knife, axe, adze, chisel' (RV)	– Ta. *vai-* 'sharpness'; *vaci-* 'point, edge'; Te. *vasi-* 'nail, thorn'

The following case may possibly be the result of an accidental resemblance, but it should be noted that the Dravidian verb appearing here is the ordinary and most common word for 'die' in most Dravidian languages, occurring in all branches, and therefore unquestionably the word for 'die' in Proto-Dravidian:

C-6.	*śava-* 'corpse' (RV)	– Ta. *cā-* 'die'; Ko. *ca·v-* 'corpse'

The following case is hard to evaluate, but probably there is some connection between the Dravidian and Indo-Aryan words. (Incidentally, this animal may have been known to both groups before their arrival in the subcontinent.)

C-7. *gardabha-* 'ass' (RV) – Ta. *kaẓutai-* 'do'

The following cases suggest the possibility of cultural contact in the area of religion or the supernatural:

C-8. *piśāca-* 'demon' (RV) (*piśāci-* [AV]) – Ta. *pēy-* 'devil, goblin, fiend; madness, frenzy, etc.'

C-9. *māyā-* 'supernatural power, skill' (RV); 'illusion'(SBr.) – Ta. *maya-* 'mistake, misunderstand'; *mayakku-* 'bewilder, confuse, fascinate, charm, etc.'; see further meanings in Appendix C, (9)

Sanskrit *māyā-*, in the later religious literature, became the word for the illusoriness of the material world. The earliest meaning, which appears in the *Ṛgveda*, was 'supernatural power' or 'skill', presumably related to notions of magic as manifested by human or nonhuman agents. This meaning may also underlie some of the words cited in DED 3852, such as Mal. *mayakkuka* 'to perplex, delude, fascinate'; Ka. *maccu/meccu* 'a decoy powder' (also 'illusion, deception'); Te. *maidu* 'an enchanting powder' (also 'deception, delusion'); Malto *méca* 'an intoxicating beverage....' The DED contains two other possibly related entries: 3835 (Ta. *mata-* 'be furious, wanton, intoxicated, bewildered', etc.) and 4297 (Ta. *vayam* 'desire'; *vayā* 'desire...longings of pregnant women, etc.'). A possibility to be considered here is that the Dravidian words may have influenced the semantic development of the Indo-Aryan word.

The following item is perhaps the most significant of those which I present here:

C-10. *tanū-* 'body, person, self' (RV) (also used as reflexive pronoun) – Ta. *tāṉ/taṉ-* 'oneself'

We do not often find languages borrowing pronouns, though it does occasionally happen. All of the cases known to me have occurred in situations of extreme linguistic displacement, such as those typical of pidginized languages. This, however, appears very close to such a case, although it seems difficult to determine the direction of borrowing. The word is deeply embedded in the structure of Dravidian, being found in almost all the languages (including

Brahui), as well as showing an alternation in the length of the stem vowels which occurs in other pronouns (see Krishnamurti 1968). Furthermore, the same element has been recognized by Emeneau in the terms for younger brother (*tampi*) and younger sister (*tankai*) which are attested in early Tamil (see note 6; also Emeneau 1953). On the Indo-Aryan side, the word appears in the *Ṛgveda*; and there is, furthermore, an Avestan *tanū* with the same meanings, also used as a reflexive, as well as an Old Persian *tanūš* 'body; self'. (The Persian *tan* 'body' may possibly be the source of Hindi-Urdu *tan* 'body', rather than the Sanskrit *tanū*.) Though there is no clear Indo-European etymology for this word, it is hard to imagine the Indo-Iranianists accepting it as a loan from Dravidian. And it would be unreasonable to expect Dravidianists to concede it as a borrowing from Indo-Aryan.[4] The possibility of classing it as an accidental resemblance seems to be precluded by the closeness in form and meaning. One could perhaps argue for the possibility that Indo-Iranian had a word for 'body' which accidentally resembled a Dravidian pronoun meaning 'self', and that the Indo-Iranian word came to be used as a reflexive pronoun under the influence of the Dravidian word. (Note that Sanskrit *ātman-* 'self' had a similar history, cf. Marathi *āplā* 'one's own', *āpaṇ* 'you' (formal), Hindi-Urdu *apnā* 'one's own', *āp* 'you'.) Even such a possibility would, however, indicate a very close relationship between Indo-Aryan and Dravidian at a very early period.

3. A SURVEY OF BOTANICAL TERMS

In this section I pursue a different approach to the question of early contact between Indo-Aryan and Dravidian. Since, according to McAlpin's work, it now seems likely (or at least possible) that the speakers of Dravidian languages were fairly recent arrivals in the subcontinent,[5] we must consider the possibility that words shared by Dravidian and Indo-Aryan might have come from a *third* language family, i.e., from languages spoken by a pre-Dravidian group of inhabitants. In the case of local flora and fauna, this possibility becomes a probability. In order to explore this question in some detail, I have examined one category of items–botanical terms–which are shared by Indo-Aryan and Dravidian. I make no claim of exhaustiveness, since my sampling procedure has been to use everything I could find in the work of Emeneau and Burrow, as well as items reported from the work of Przyluski (not available to me at the time of writing). Appendix D, in which these examples are listed, contains fifty-four items, covering the following categories:

1. Trees (20)

2. Cereals (9)
3. Edible gourds, etc. (6)
4. Spices, etc. (7)
5. Beans and pulses (5)
6. Other (7)

As to the original source for these, in the past many have been ascribed to Munda, or to a family known as "Austroasiatic," which in the early days included what we now know as Austroasiatic plus Austronesian or Malayo-Polynesian, and possibly others. As far as Munda is concerned, the recent work of Zide and Zide on Proto-Munda agricultural terms produces only about five items which can be associated with these Indo-Aryan/Dravidian comparisons; two of these are animals: the peacock, **mara* (compare Skt. *mayūra-*, also *marūka-*, Drav. *mayil*, etc.); and the cat, for which they reconstruct **pusi*. Only three botanical terms seem to relate: **kodaXj* 'horsegram, etc.' (cf. Drav. *kulattha,* etc. [D-42]), *ərig* 'millet' (D-26), and **sarg/sarj* 'sal tree' (cf. Skt. *sarja-* [D-16]). Perhaps we should also mention Proto-Munda **vid* 'sowing seed' (cf. Drav. **vit(t)*, Skt. *bīja-*), see Southworth 1975.

As Burrow (1958) has pointed out, there is no reason to believe that Munda speakers ever came farther west than those parts of Orissa, Bihar, Madhya Pradesh, and eastern Maharashtra where they are now found, whereas it is likely that the linguistic source of most of the botanical terms I have mentioned was a language or group of languages existing in western or north-western India. As to what it could have been, we have only the slightest hints so far. Masica's work (1976) on typological similarities suggests that we should look to Central Asia or to East Africa. Other evidence also points to Africa, at least as an area of contact: words similar to our words for "rice" occur in Somali and in Malagasy (Madagascar). We also find several words in Proto-Austronesian which resemble words found in Dravidian and Indo-Aryan, including words for rice, fruit, cotton, and possibly some others (Southworth 1975). Finally, there are a number of agricultural terms shared by Dravidian and Indo-Aryan, as noted by Masica in his paper for this conference. Several such terms have been included here in Appendix C:

C-11. *khala-* 'threshing floor'	– Ta. *kalam, kaḷaṉ* 'place, open space, threshing floor, battle-field'
C-12. *lāngala-* 'plow' (RV) (Bengali *lāngal, nāngal*)	– Ta. *nāncil-* 'plow'
C-13. *sīra-* 'plow' (RV)	– Ta. *(c)ēr-* 'plow, etc.'

C-14. *kūṭa-* 'plowshare' lex. – Ta. *koẓu-* 'bar of metal, plowshare'

4. PHONOLOGICAL ASSUMPTIONS

In the following section, I attempt to make explicit the major assumptions regarding the phonology of loanwords, particularly Old Indo-Aryan borrowings from Dravidian, which are implied in the foregoing and which have been implicit in much earlier work on this subject.

4.1. Where Old Indo-Aryan shows a cluster of consonants corresponding to a geminate consonant (or occasionally a single consonant) in Dravidian, it has been usual to assume that the Old Indo-Aryan form is the original form and that the Dravidian forms have been simplified (or borrowed from a simplified Middle Indo-Aryan form). In some cases, however (such as Old Indo-Aryan *mukta-* 'pearl', C-15), it seems more likely that the Dravidian form is original and that the Old Indo-Aryan form is a "Sanskritization" of a form with geminate consonant.

For some of these cases, we may envisage a further possibility–namely, that the development of the geminate from an older consonant cluster took place *within Dravidian*. (McAlpin's comparison with Elamite contains some hints of such a development, e.g., the *-rt-* of Middle Elamite *martukkaš* 'portion of goods paid for services' and the *-ṭ-* of Tamil *maṭank* 'hire'.) Possible examples of this in the materials presented here are: *agasti-* (D-2), *sarjā-* (D-16), *kuṣmāṇḍa-* (D-28), *cirbhaṭa-* (D-29), and *śarkarā-* (D-30); note that the Dravidian forms here, if indeed they are cognate with the Old Indo-Aryan forms, show both stages of development, *-r(a)k-* and *-kk-*).

In this connection, it may not be inappropriate to point out that Dravidian and Middle Indo-Aryan appear to have undergone several parallel developments, including the assimilation of consonant clusters, the spirantization or loss of single intervocalic stops, and the development of retroflex consonants (which must be reconstructed in Proto-Dravidian but do not appear in Elamite). It is possible that further research will show that these developments were not independent of each other. For the moment, let me say only that such a conclusion would not be inconsistent with one of the main points I am trying to demonstrate here, namely, that contact between Indo-Aryan (or Indo-Iranian) and Dravidian probably began to take place before the main period of settlement of Indo-Aryan speakers in the subcontinent.

4.2. The following phonological changes and phonological relationships within Dravidian are relevant to the present discussion:

1. *c-* ⟶ zero frequently in Tamil, Malayalam, Toda, Kota, Kannada,

Kodagu, Tulu, and Telugu (Emeneau 1970:58).
2. *c-* ⟶ *t-* in Toda, and occasionally in Kota, Kannada, Tulu, and other languages (Emeneau 1970:58).
3. Except for the Sanskritized varieties of the literary Dravidian languages, there is no contrast in Dravidian between a palatal affricate (*c*) and a sibilant (*ś, ṣ, s*). In some languages, affricate and sibilant are in an allophonic relationship.
4. *k-* ⟶ *c-* before a front vowel under most circumstances in Tamil, Malayalam, and Telugu (Emeneau 1970:50).
5. Stops are generally voiced following a nasal consonant and between vowels.

4.3. The Greek *z* in *zínziber* 'ginger' (D-40), *óryzon* 'rice' (D-26), and in Muzíris (the name of a seaport on the west coast of India which appears in inscriptions as Muciri, Muyiri) appears to correspond to a Dravidian *c*, presumably as the closest available Greek equivalent (though in one or more of these cases there may have been an Arabic intermediary, cf. Arabic *ruz* 'rice'). Note also the Greek form *oríndes*, where *-nd-* possibly corresponds to Iranian *-nj-*. The Greek *ó-* in *óryzon, óryza* most likely represents the Dravidian *va-*, Greek having no closer equivalent of *v-*.

4.4. In some cases Dravidian initial stops correspond to Old Indo-Aryan aspirated stops, e.g., in *phala-* (A-5), *khala-* (C-12). If the Dravidian forms are considered as original in these cases, the aspiration remains unexplained. It is possible that some North Dravidian language had aspirated stops; note the *x*⟵PDr. **k-* which occurs in Brahui (Emeneau 1970:51). Other possibilities include the existence of aspirated consonants in some pre-Dravidian language, or, in individual cases, "Sanskritization" or folk etymology.

4.5. A few items in the compared materials show a change of (apparently original) *l-* to *n-*, both in Indo-Aryan and Dravidian: *lāngala-* 'plow' (C-11), *laśuna-* 'garlic' (D-38), *nimbū-* (D-10); medially in *panasa-* (D-12). This change appears frequently in certain areas of Indo-Aryan, particularly in the "tribal belt" which extends from the Bhil area across Madhya Pradesh and northern Maharashtra into Orissa and Bengal. The possibility that this phonological phenomenon represents an old linguistic substratum will be discussed in a forthcoming article.

4.6. A number of the Indo-Aryan items listed show some forms with *ḍ* and some with *l* (or *ḷ*) in the various Modern Indo-Aryan languages, and a few show such variation even in Old Indo-Aryan: e.g., *naḍa-* (A-16), *guḍa-* (D-36), *tāla-* (D-7). Such cases may well be the result of borrowings containing a phonological item with no close correspondences in Old Indo-Aryan, such as Dravidian *ẓ*.

5. CONCLUSIONS

The materials presented in section 2 above indicate that Indo-Aryan and Dravidian speakers must have been in contact with each other for some time before the composition of the *Ṛgveda*. Assuming the position that it was composed in the period 1500-1000 B.C., then the period of contact must be placed around the middle of the second millennium B.C. at the latest. One of the examples given above (OIA *tanū-*, Drav. *tāṉ/taṉ* [C-10]) strongly suggests a much earlier period of contact. The Dravidian forms are clearly inherited from Proto-Dravidian, and very possibly go back to Proto-Elamo-Dravidian.[6] Thus, it seems most probable that this word was borrowed from Dravidian (or conceivably from Proto-Elamo-Dravidian) into Indo-Iranian, before the breakup of this group into Aryan and Iranian. (Admitting the possibility that the borrowing went the other way, from Indo-Iranian into Dravidian, would put the period of contact even farther back, according to current estimates.) It is conceivable, but unlikely, that there was continuous contact between Indo-Aryans and Dravidians from the Indo-Iranian period up to the time of the composition of the *Ṛgveda*, and thus OIA *tanū-* may be a residue of a very early and distinct period of contact. Since the other words presented in section 2 do not have known Iranian cognates, it can be presumed that most of them entered Old Indo-Aryan after the breakup of Indo-Iranian. The area in which this contact can be presumed to have taken place would include the Indus Valley and perhaps the mountainous area to the west of it.[7]

Since the majority of the words given in section 2 have survived in Modern Indo-Aryan and, indeed, since most are well-represented in all branches of Modern Indo-Aryan,[8] it can be presumed that the contact with Dravidian involved the group of Old Indo-Aryan speakers in the Panjab as a whole, before the beginning of the movement toward the east and south of the subcontinent. Further, since almost all of these examples have cognates in South Dravidian and are fairly well-represented in the other branches of Dravidian currently found in peninsular India (our K, T, C, P [see note 3]), there is clearly continuity between the Dravidian group which was in contact with the Indo-Aryans at the time of the *Ṛgveda* and the speakers of Dravidian languages currently in South and Central India. Thus, this contact presumably involved both Dravidian and Indo-Aryan speakers at a time when they were still fairly compact, undivided groups (though there is some question concerning the extent of North Dravidian involvement [see note 14]).

The contact which produced these borrowings must have been a rather prolonged one, probably persisting over several centuries. This is indicated by the nature of the words borrowed, which include not only the usual technological terms (borrowed in both directions), but also some words of high-frequency general vocabulary, terms for body parts, and words relating to social structure (OIA *kula-* [A-19], Drav. *turai* [B-12]). No picture of technological, cultural, or military dominance by either side emerges from an examination of these words. Dravidian apparently borrowed, among others, terms relating to wheeled vehicles (see B-1, B-7), while Old Indo-Aryan borrowed various terms relating to household technology (A–1-4).

The question of agricultural technology would seem to be important here. The words listed in Appendix C relating to the plow and threshing (C–11-14) have been classed as of uncertain origin, since they have no certain etymologies in either branch. However, if we have to choose between Dravidian and Indo-Aryan, the likelihood is that these terms originated with the former, since there is fairly clear evidence for the presence of grain cultivation in the Proto-Dravidian period, possibly even in the Proto-Elamo-Dravidian period.[9] The words connected with OIA *lāngala-* 'plow' (C-12), however, apparently come from an indigenous source, since they have clear Austro-asiatic cognates. (Items B–9-10 are not attested in the *Ṛgveda* and may be later borrowings; possibly they should have been listed in Appendix D.)

The word *yava-* 'barley' is the only specific word for a cereal crop found in the *Ṛgveda*. Though the Aryans probably also knew wheat before reaching the subcontinent, the word for wheat, *godhūma-*, is problematic, and may well be a popular etymological transformation of some indigenous word. Note the Dravidian words like Brahui *xōlum*, Ta. *kōti*, etc. (see DBIA, item 123, p. 27). Note also that the Modern Indo-Aryan forms have three different vowels in the first syllable (Oriya *gohū̃*, Hindi-Urdu *gehū̃*, Marathi *gahū*), which suggests that we may be dealing with a composite form with a first element *go/ge/ga* and a second element *dum* or *dūm* (cf. Persian *gandum*), though we have as yet no notion of a source for such a word.

The Indus Valley civilization was primarily a wheat-eating culture. Rice husks are found in Lothal, a late Harappan site which is outside of the Indus Valley itself, and it seems plausible that rice became known only toward the end of the Harappan period, as the Harappan cities were collapsing and the population was moving southward and westward. One archaeologist, Walter Fairservis, has suggested that the abandonment of the Harappan city-sites was primarily the result of the exhaustion of the agricultural resources of the Indus Valley due to population expansion and ecological factors (Fairservis 1967). The movement southward represented by Lothal may have brought the Harappans into contact with rice-growing peoples. According to Sankalia, rice was clearly a means of subsistence in several of the post-Harappan chalcolithic cultures, especially in Bihar and Bengal (1974:133), but there is also evidence of rice in the Ahar or Banas culture in southeast Rajasthan (p. 137) and in the Navtadoli culture of the middle Narmada (p. 140). The linguistic evidence appears to suggest a possible connection between the Indus Valley and western India (Gujarat and Maharashtra) as far as rice is concerned. The Old Indo-Aryan term *vrīhi-* 'rice', which occurs in the *Atharvaveda*, survives in Modern Indo-Aryan only in some of the Kafir and Dardic languages to the north of the Indus and in Sinhalese, with possible cognates in Gujarat and Marathi (Guj. *varī* 'a particular kind of grain', Marathi *varī* 'the grain *Coix barbata'*, Pkt. *varaia-* 'a kind of rice', Turner, s.v., *varī-*). As noted in Appendix D (26), both Dravidian and Iranian (as well as Munda) have words which can hardly be separated from OIA *vrīhi-*.[10] A postulated **vari(n)c(i)* would explain most of these forms, except possibly the Munda form, which is also semantically distinct, since it refers to millet rather than rice; but, again, we have no notion as to the possible source of such a word.

The presence of other ethnic groups, speaking other languages, must be assumed for the period in question, as well as for later periods. The word *mayūra-* 'peacock' (A-7), though it may have entered Old Indo-Aryan from Dravidian, is most likely derived from an indigenous language. As noted above, the words for rice, as well as one of the words for plow (OIA *lāngala-*, etc.), also appear to be from another source. Going beyond our present data, numerous examples can be found to suggest early contact with language groups now unrepresented in the subcontinent. A single example will be noted here. The word for 'mother' in several of the Dardic languages, as well as in Nepali, Assamese, Bengali, Oriya, Gujarati, and Marathi (mostly belonging to Grierson's "outer group" of Indo-Aryan) is *āī* (or a similar form). The source of this is clearly the same as that of classical Tamil *āy* 'mother' (DED 308). These words are apparently connected with a widespread group of words found in Malayo-Polynesian (cf. Proto-Austronesian **bāji*, i.e., **bāyi* [Dempwolff 1938]) and elsewhere. The distribution of this word in Indo-Aryan suggests that it must have entered Old Indo-Aryan very early (presumably as a nursery word, and thus not likely to appear in religious texts), before the movement of Indo-Aryan speakers out of the Panjab. In Dravidian, this word is well-represented in all branches (though *ammā* [DED 154] is perhaps an older word) and thus, if it is a borrowing, it must be a very early one.

Many scholars have accepted Kuiper's argument that retroflex consonants and other structural features in the *Ṛgveda* (such as the gerund construction) are the result of contact with Dravidian speakers (Kuiper 1967). No one, to my knowledge, has yet considered the possibility that these features might have come into Dravidian through the same process, i.e., contact with languages which existed in South Asia when Dravidian speakers reached there. Now that it seems likely that the Dravidians came from the west a millennium or two before the Indo-Aryans, and in view of the evidence of terms for local flora, etc., apparently borrowed into both Dravidian and Indo-Aryan from the languages of the older inhabitants,[11] this possibility must be given serious consideration. (Note also the comments on parallel phonological developments in Indo-Aryan and Dravidian in 4.1 above.) While the evidence of loanwords is language-specific, the evidence of structural borrowing is not necessarily so. While the features used to argue the presence of a Dravidian substratum (e.g., by Kuiper 1967 and Southworth 1974) are present in Dravidian, they have not been shown to exist in Elamite. Therefore, it is possible that some of these features have their origin in an even earlier linguistic substratum.

What clues do we have to help in the identification of these early groups? I have noted in section 3 of this paper the reasons why I do not believe that Munda was one of the language groups contacted directly by Dravidians and Indo-Aryans in this early period, though Munda languages were clearly important later. One hint which may ultimately be of use is Masica's discovery that the "South Asian linguistic area" extends northward into Central Asia, suggesting long-term contact with northern peoples (Masica 1976); there is also a suggestion of a typological similarity with Amharic, an Ethiopian language. As yet we do not know the significance of these linguistic areas based on typological grammatical similarities, but clearly they deserve further study. Looking again at lexical evidence, Malayo-Polynesian shares cognate forms of a few of the words discussed above, notably OIA *phala-*, Drav. *paẓam*, etc. (A-5) (cf. Proto-Austronesian **paḷam* 'to ripen a fruit artificially' in Dempwolff 1938), and the words for rice (see the information given in D-28). These words, as well as the Somali *bariis* 'rice', are likely to have been borrowed by seafaring peoples as a result of later contact with Dravidian speakers, and therefore may not be of help in identifying peoples present in the Panjab in the middle of the second millennium B.C.

As Deshpande and others have pointed out, "Dravidian" structural features in the *Ṛgveda* appear with relatively low frequency in the earliest texts and increase markedly in the later literature.[12] I believe that the appearance of these linguistic features in the *Ṛgveda* reflects a period of transition between an earlier period of contact, in which the Aryans were largely distinct from neighboring groups (Dravidians and others), and a later period. This later period culminated, in many parts of the subcontinent, in a fusion between the original Aryan group and other groups into a new composite society–with, of course, local variations developing more and more over time–whose principal symbols of identity came to be Hinduism and the Aryan language.

I suggest that the first period (before the composition of the *Ṛgveda*) was characterized by regular but limited contact between Dravidian and Indo-Aryan speakers, probably leading to limited bilingualism. It is probable that there were numerous individuals in each group with a rudimentary (or pidgin-like) command of the other group's language and possibly a small number of genuine bilinguals (such as offspring of mixed sexual unions or marriages, individuals growing up in contact areas, etc.). The relationship between the groups no doubt involved some hostility, escalating at times to actual combat, but at the same time probably accommodated a variety of social contacts, including trade and other joint economic activities and marital exchanges (or at least interbreeding). What we find described in the Vedic texts is mainly the hostile aspects of these relationships, and the military successes of the Aryans against their foes, which are no doubt greatly exaggerated. The other side of the relationships, namely the social relationships I am assuming, is not mentioned in the texts but can be inferred from the evidence I have been discussing here. This type of contact, in fact, generally produces loan-words but does not produce the kind of structural convergence which we find later on.

The second period of contact, after the composition of the *Ṛgveda*, involved the gradual integration of Aryans (presumably already including some Aryanized Dravidians and others) into the system of village agriculture already existing in the Indus Valley and the extension of this system along with the new Aryan culture to the east and south. I have argued elsewhere that it is precisely the conditions of "village coexistence," in which groups of different ethnic backgrounds achieve a symbiosis whose basis is economic cooperation for agricultural production, which allow the typical South Asian structural convergence to occur (see Southworth 1974; also Southworth and Apte 1974, introduction). Where village landowners and village laborers belong to different linguistic groups, and where frequently there is a group of intermediaries (tenants, managers, merchants, etc.), the conditions are created for the unconscious transfer of structural (grammatical and phonological) features from one language to the other. Where the language of the elite group (landowners, military and religious elite) is the minority language, the predictable outcome is the spread of this language as a lingua franca, with simultaneous absorption of features from the majority language(s).[13] This is, I believe, the best explanation which can be offered for the dilemma presented by Masica (1976:183-84) regarding the almost complete absence of structural features of Indian languages in Southeast Asia, in spite of the prolonged cultural and "linguistic" influence (mainly evidenced by loanwords) exerted by India, in this region.

Recent work by Fairservis on the Harappan script has again raised the possibility of finding evidence to establish it as Dravidian. While there is nothing in the evidence presented here to link either the Indo-Aryans or the Dravidians with the Indus Valley civilization, it may be worth pointing out that the picture presented here is at least consistent with this possibility. The time period suggested above for the contact between Indo-Aryan and Dravidian (mid-second millennium B.C. or before) falls within the limits of the late Harappan period. Fairservis' suggestion that the "official" language of the Harappan civilization was Dravidian, implying that the Harappan elite spoke a Dravidian language, would be consistent with the influence of Dravidian on Indo-Aryan during this early period.[14] If this is true, however, we must infer that Indo-Aryans during this period had their main contact with *peripheral* areas of the Harappan civilization and not with the main population centers, since in the latter case the impact on their language would necessarily have been far greater. We may note in this context that two Old Indo-Aryan terms for 'town' or 'city' may be of Dravidian origin: *nagara-* (C-3) and *paṭṭana-* (Turner, s.v., and DED 3199), though neither of these occurs in the *Ṛgveda.* There is also a possible connection between OIA *pura-* 'fortress, town' (RV *pur-* 'stronghold') and the Dravidian verb *pura-* 'keep, protect, defend', etc. (DED 3515).

APPENDICES

Please note the following:

1. All Old Indo-Aryan (OIA) forms are from Turner (1966) unless otherwise noted.
2. Most of the Dravidian-Indo/Indo-Aryan comparisons are from Burrow (1945, 1946, and 1947), and Emeneau and Burrow (DBIA). The following items have been contributed by the present author: *carati* (C-1), *piśāci-* (C-8), *māyā-* (C-9), *tanū-* (C-10), *vrīhi-* (D-26), *śarkarā-* (D-39), *āmra-* (D-46).
3. Phonological relationships have been discussed in the body of the paper in section 4, Phonological Assumptions.
4. Source abbreviations are listed below. Language abbreviations appear in the note at the bottom of page 210.

Apast.	–	Āpastamba
AV	–	Atharvaveda
BHSk.	–	Buddhist Hybrid Sanskrit
Car.	–	Caraka
EWA	–	Mayrhofer 1953
Gaut.	–	Gautama's Dharmaśāstra
Gobh.	–	Gobhila
GrS	–	Gṛihya Sūtra
Hariv.	–	Harivaṃśa
Kapisth.	–	Kapiśṭhala Saṃhitā
Kas.	–	Kāśikā Vṛitti
Katy.	–	Kātyāyana
MBh.	–	Mahābhārata
Mn.	–	Manu's Lawbook
Nir.	–	Nirukta by Yāska
Npr.	–	Nighaṇṭuprakāsa
Pan.	–	Pāṇini
Pat.	–	Patañjali
R	–	Rāmāyaṇa
RV	–	Ṛgveda
SBr.	–	Śatapatha Brāhmaṇa
Susr.	–	Suśruta
TAr.	–	Taittirīya Āraṇyaka
Var.	–	Varāhamihira
VS	–	Vājasaneyi Saṃhitā

APPENDIX A
PROBABLE EARLY INDO-ARYAN BORROWINGS FROM DRAVIDIAN

TECHNOLOGY

1. *kuṇḍa-* 'pot, hole, pit' (RV) (EWA "wohl mit kuṭaḥ, kuḍikā, kūṭam und golaḥ aus dem Dravidischen")	DED 1389 Ta. *kuṇṭam* 'cavity, pit'; Kui. *kuṭṭ* 'pit' (SKTCP)*
2. *kuṭa-* 'mallet, hammer' (RV) (cf., *kuṭṭayati*) (EWA: "von unsicherer Herkunft; dravidische Ursprung...ist durchaus fraglich")	DED 1717 Ta. *koṭṭu* 'beat', Mal. *koṭṭi* 'hammer' (SKTCPN); DED 1391 Ta. *kuṭṭu* 'strike' (SKTCPN)
3. *daṇḍa-* 'stick, club' (RV) (EWA: an unresolved problem; Dravidian or Munda origin not excluded)	DED 2476 Mal. *taṇṭa* '(fore)arm; upper arm' (SCP); cf., DED 2479 Ta. *taṇṭi* 'try hard' (S)
4. *ulūkhala-* 'mortar' (RV) (Thieme [1955]: from **urū-khara-* 'having a broad *khara*'; (EWA: "wohl dravidisch oder einheimisch")	DED 580 Ta. *ulakkai* 'pestle' (SK)

FLORA AND FAUNA

5. *phala-* 'fruit' (RV) (EWA: "nicht sicher erklärt... trotz vedischer Bezeugung...ist... die Möglichkeit dravidischer Herkunft...zu erwägen")	DED 3299 Ta. *paẓu* 'ripen'; *paẓam* 'ripe fruit' (cf., *kāy* 'unripe fruit') (SKTCPN)

—

* Attestation in Dravidian: S = South Dravidian [Tamil (Ta.), Malayalam (Mal.), Kota (Ko.), Toda (To.), Kodagu (Kod.)]; K = Kannada (Ka.); T = Tulu (Tu.); C = Central Dravidian [Telugu (Te.), Gondi (Go.), Konda, Kui, Kuwi, Pengo, Manda]; P = Kolami (Kol.), Naiki, Parji, Gadaba (Ga.); N = North Dravidian [Kudukh (Kud.), Malto, Brahui]

6. *naḍa-* 'species of reed' (RV), *nala-* (Pan.) (EWA: possibly connected with Dravidian)	DED 2370 Ka. *nānal, naḷḷu* 'a reed' (SKC), DED 2391 Ta. *ñeḷ-* 'become hollow' (SKT)–all forms from orig. **ñ-*
7. *mayūra-* 'peacock' (RV) (EWA: definitely connected with the Dravidian words)	DED Ta. *maññai, mayil* 'peacock' (SKTCP)

BODY PARTS AND BODILY DEFORMITIES

8. *kulpha-* 'ankle' (RV) (EWA: "nicht sicher erklärt")	DED 1519 Ta. *kuḷampu* 'hoof' (SK)
9. *ukha-* 'part of thigh' (RV) (EWA: "vielleicht Dravidisch")	DED 481 *ukkam* 'waist', *ukkalai* 'hips' (ST)
10. *vriś-* 'finger' (RV) (EWA: "verfehlt ist Burrows Herleitung"–see Emeneau 1954: 286, note 21)	DED 4436 Ta. *viral* 'finger, toe'; Go. *wirinj* (SKTCP)–note that the Old Indo-Aryan form is closer in form to Central Dravidian than to South Dravidian
11. *kāṇa-* 'blind in one eye' (RV) (EWA calls Burrow's derivation "sehr erwägenswert," but unlikely due to Vedic attestation)	DED 1209 *kāṇ-* 'see' (SKTCPN, cf. DED 973 *kaṇ* 'eye'); neg. stem *kan-a-* 'not seeing'
12. *kuṇāru-* 'having a crooked or withered arm' (RV) (EWA: "wahrscheinlich dravidisch"–but cf. Emeneau 1954: 286, note 21)	DED 1408 Mal. *kuṇṭan* 'cripple', Kod. *kuṇṭ-* 'be lame' (SKTCP); cf. DED 1834 *kōṇ* 'crookedness', *kōṇu-* 'be bent' (SKTCP)

FEATURES OF NATURE

13. *kulāya-* 'nest' (RV) (EWA: uncertain)	DED 1563 Ta. *kuṭu* 'nest, etc.' (SKTCP); cf. DED 1562 Ta. *kūṭu-* 'meet, etc.' (SKTCPN)

14. *bila-* 'hole, cave' (RV) (EWA: "Nicht überzeugend erklärt; autochthone Herkunft [including Dravidian] ist nicht ausgeschlossen")

DED 4459 Ta. *viḷ-* 'open out', *viḷavu* 'cleft, crack' (STCPN)

15. *piṇḍa-* 'lump, clod' (RV) (EWA: "nicht überzeugend erklärt"–cf. "Khotansak. piṇḍaa-...arm pind aus dem iranischen")

DED 3606 Ka. *peṭṭe,* Tu. *heṇṭe* 'clod' (KTCP)

FOOD

16. *karambha-* 'mixture of flour or meal with curd' (RV)

DED 1510 Ta. *kuẓampu* 'be mixed, etc.; mixture, curry' (SK)

OTHER

17. *kaṭu(ka)-* 'bitter' (RV)

DED 952 Ta. *kaṭu-* 'pain, sting, be pungent, etc.', *kaṭuku* 'mustard' (SKTCN)

18. *bala-* 'strength' (RV) (EWA: Indo-European origin unquestionable)

DED 4317 Ta. *val* 'strong, skillful', *vallu-* 'be able' (SKTCPN)

(See Emeneau 1954; because of the widespread attestation in Dravidian and in view of the change from *v* to *b*, Dravidian origin seems at least plausible, in spite of the arguments of Thieme [1955] and EWA in favor of Indo-European origin–cf. Latin *dēbilis*, etc.)

19. *kula-* 'herd, flock, lineage' (RV) (EWA: Burrow "sehr ansprechend")

DED 1513 Ta. *kuẓu* 'assembly, flock, herd' (SKP); cf. DED 1562 Ta. *kūṭi-* 'come together' (SKTCPN)

20. *mukta-* 'pearl' (Mn.); according to Turner, Sanskritization of MIA *muttā*, from Dravidian (EWA accepts this as possible)

DED 4062 Ta. *muttu* 'pearl, tear, castor-bean, oil-seed...' (SKTC)

APPENDIX B
PROBABLE EARLY LOANS IN DRAVIDIAN FROM INDO-ARYAN

TECHNOLOGY

1. *accu* 'axle' (SKTCP) (7)*	*akṣa-* (RV)
2. *kancam* 'bell-metal' (SKTC) (67)	*kaṃśa-* 'metal cup' (AV), 'bell-metal' (Pat.)
3. *kaṭṭai* 'wood' (SKTC) (68)	*kāṣṭha-* (SBr.)
4. *kampaḷi* 'blanket/covering' (SKTCN) (76)	*kambala(ka)-* (AV)
5. *ālai* 'shed, etc.' (Mal. *ala* 'shed') (SKTCP) (165)	*śāla-* (AV) (Mal. *śāla*, as in *bhōjan-aśāla* 'dining hall', etc., borrowed from literary Skt.)
6. *(c)ūci* 'needle' (SKTCPN) (171)	*sūci-* (RV)
7. *āni* 'nail' (SKT) (DED 295)	*āṇi-* (RV) (cf. Latin *ulna*, Ger. *Lünse*, Eng. 'linch-pin')
8. *tōṇi* 'boat' (SKTC) (220)	*drōṇa-* 'boat, trough' (RV) (or **donga-* 'boat, trough?' see Turner 6641)

AGRICULTURE

9. *kāṇṭam* 'stem, stalk' (STC) (88)	*kāṇḍa-* (AV)
10. *cāmai* 'millet' (SKTC) (163)	*śyāmaka-* (VS)

FAUNA

11. Te. *gadda* 'kite' (CP) (83)	*gṛdhra-* 'greedy, vulture' (AV)

*Numbers refer to Emeneau and Burrow, 1962. Dravidian forms are Tamil unless otherwise indicated.

SOCIAL STRUCTURE

12. *turai* 'chief' (SKCP) (213) — *dhurya-* 'foremost' (AV); later 'leader, chief'

OTHER

13. *pakkam* 'side' (SKTCP) (233a) — *pakṣa-* 'wing, side' (RV) (but cf. DED 3154 Ta. *paku-* 'be divided, split'; *pakuti* 'portion' (SKTCPN); DED 3337 Ta. *pānku* 'side, neighborhood, etc.' [SKC])

APPENDIX C
SHARED LEXICAL ITEMS OF UNCERTAIN ORIGIN (DRAVIDIAN, INDO-ARYAN, OR OTHER)

1.	*carati* 'moves, goes away, etc.' (RV); *čalati* (MBh.) (EWA = aw. *cara*^{i}*ti*...vgl. gr. *pélomai*...alb. *sjet* wende, lat. *colere* bebauen, pflegen, aksl. *kolo* Rad)	DED 2286 Ta. *cel-* 'go, flow, pass, be suitable, etc.' (SKTCPN)
2.	*paṭhati* 'repeats aloud' (TAr.) 'reads' (Mn.) (EWA "wohl mi. aus *prathati* 'breitet aus' ..."; Burrow "nicht besser")	DED 3348 Ta. *pāṭu-* 'sing, chant, etc.'; *pāṭṭu* 'song' (SKCPN); cf. DED 3351 *pāṇ* 'song; caste of musicians' (STC)
3.	*nagara-* 'town' (TAr.) (EWA "wahrscheinlich dravidisch")	DED 2943 Ta. *nakar* 'house, abode, mansion, temple, palace, town, city' (STC)
4.	*vithura-* 'staggering, tottering' (RV) (EWA = aw. wiþura-...zu vyathate)	DED 4425 *vitappu* 'trembling, agitation, haste'; *vitir-* 'shake, quiver' (SKTC)
5.	*vāśi-* 'knife, axe, adze, chisel' (RV) (EWA "Zu oset. uæs "axe for cutting wood"← Iran. **vasa-*...– Eine dravid. Deutung des ved. Wortes bietet Burrow...")	DED 4568 Ta. *vai* 'sharpness'; *vaci* 'point, edge'; Te. *vasi* 'nail, thorn' (SKC)
6.	*śava-* 'corpse' (RV) (EWA "wahrscheinlich zu *śvayati* gehörig [vom Aufschwellen der Leichen] ; Thieme, *Lg.* 31,444... nicht vorzuziehen die Deutung aus dem Dravid.")	DED 2002 Ta. *cā-* 'die', Ko. *ca·v* 'corpse' (SKTCPN)
7.	*gardabha-* 'ass' (RV)	DED 1149 Ta. *kaẓutai* (SKTCP)

(EWA "zu *gard-* "aufschreien"... Unnötig und lautlich schwierig ist die Annahme dravidischer Herkunft")

8. *piśāci-* 'demon' (AV) (*piśaci-* [RV]) (EWA "Nicht überzeugend erklärt")

DED 3635 Ta. *pēy* 'devil, goblin, fiend; madness (as of a dog), frenzy, etc.'; *pē(y)cci* 'demoness, woman under possession of a demon' (SKTCP; ?N)

9. *māyā* 'supernatural power, skill' (RV) (EWA "Der Ermittelung eines sicheren Etymons...stehen... Schwierigkeiten entgegen")

DED 3852 Ta. *maya-* 'mistake, misunderstand'; *mayakku-* 'bewilder, confuse, puzzle, mystify, fascinate, allure, charm, mix up, unite, ruin, destroy, disturb, unsettle, make swoon; mental delusion, stupor, bewilderment, etc.'; Ka. *mayamu* 'bewilderment', *maccu* 'illusion, decoy powder'; Te. *maikamu* 'intoxication, etc.'; *maidu* 'deception, deceit, illusion, etc.'; Kud. *mãyã* 'malt prepared for making beer' (SKTCN); cf. also DED 3835, 4297

10. *tanū-* 'body, person, self' (RV); also used as reflexive pronoun (EWA = Avestan *tanū* 'body, person, self' (also reflexive pronoun); OPers. *tanūs* 'body, self'; Persian *tan* 'body'–" [gehört wahrscheinlich] zur Sippe von tanoti")

DED 2612 Ta. *tāṉ/taṉ-* 'oneself' (SKTCPN); cf. *tampi* '(one's own) younger brother', *tan-kai* '(one's own) younger sister' (Emeneau, 1953); Ta. *taṉiyā* 'alone, by oneself, on one's own' (cf. Urdu *tan-e-tanhā* 'alone, singly')

11. *khala-* 'threshing floor' (cf. *khalya-* 'being on the threshing floor' [VS], 'fit for a threshing floor' [Pan.]; *khalapū-* 'one who cleans

DED 1160 Ta. *kaḷam, kaḷaṉ* 'place, open space, threshing floor, battlefield' (SKTCPN)

the threshing floor' [Pan]) (EWA "nicht sicher erklärt")	
12. *lāngala-* 'plow' (RV) (Bengali *lāngal, nāngal*; Marathi *nāngar*) (EWA: "davon nicht zu trennende Wörter finden sich auch in der dravidischer...und in der austroasiatischer Sprachfamilie (khasi lyṅkor [*lēṅkol]); Munda-Sprachen ..."–most probably originally Austroasiatic)	DED 2368 Ta. *ñāncil, nāncil* 'plow'; Ka. *nēgal*, Ga. *nāngal* (from **ñān-kel/kil/kal*) (SKTCP)
13. *sīra-* 'plow' (RV) (*sīla-* Kapisth.) (Shina *siru* 'a plowing', Sindhi *sīra* 'long string by which bullocks are guided in the plow'; Assamese *xir* 'furrow, one plowing') (EWA "Mit sītā und sīmā zu verbinden"; cf. sītā Furche/furrow; sīmā Scheitel, Haarscheide/parting of the hair)	DED Ta. *ēr* 'plow, plow and team of oxen, yoke of oxen'; *cēr* id. (Jaffna) (SKCP)
14. *kūṭa-* 'part of a plow, its share' lex. (EWA "wohl dravidisch")	DED 1785 Ta. *koẓu* 'bar of metal, plowshare' (SKT)

APPENDIX D
TERMS FOR FLORA SHARED BY DRAVIDIAN AND INDO-ARYAN

Note: No attempt has been made to categorize these terms strictly according to botanical genera. The categories used below may have some relevance, however, to the *cultural use* made of the plants and their products.

TREES

1. *agaru-* 'fragrant aloe-tree and wood, *Aquilaria agallocha*' (lex.) (EWA "wohl dravidisch")	DED 14 Ta. *akil* 'eagle-wood, *Aquilaria agallocha*' (SKT)
2. *agasti-* 'the tree *Agasti grandiflorum*' (Susr.) (EWA "wohl dravidisch")	DED Ta. *akatti, accam, acci* 'West Indian pea-tree, *Sesbania grandiflora'* (SKTC)
3. *āmupa-* 'the cane *Bambusa spinosa*' lex. (Monier-Williams) (EWA "vielleicht dravidisch")	DED 144 Ta. *āmal* 'spiny bamboo; āmpal bamboo' (S)
4. *karavīra-* 'oleander, *Nerium odorum*' (MBh.) (EWA "wohl...aus einer dravidischen Quelle")	DED 977 Ta. *kaṇavīram, kaviram, kayiram* 'red oleander', Mal. *kaṇavīram 'Nerium odorum'* (SKC)
5. *candana-* 'sandalwood' (Nir.) (EWA "wohl dravidischen Ursprungs")	DED 2021 Ta. *cāttu* 'to daub, smear, anoint'; *cāntam* 'sandal'; *cāntu* 'sandal tree, sandal paste, etc.' (SKTC)
6. *cincā-* 'the tree *Tamarindus indica*' (Bhpr.) (cf. also *tintiḍī-* id. lex.) (EWA "...wohl aus dem Proto-Munda...Die...dravidischen Wörter ...dürften aus der selben Munda-Quelle stammen")	DED 2086 Ta. *cintam* 'tamarind tree', *intam* 'tamarind'; Malto *site* 'sour' (SCPN)

7. *tāla-* 'palmyra' (Mn.) (EWA "Vielleicht hängt...mit gleichbed. dravidischen Wörten wie kan. tāẓ, tel. tāḍu zusammen")	DED 2599 Ka. *tāẓ* 'palmyra or toddy palm, *Borassus flabelliformis*' (KTCPN)–some forms possibly reborrowed from Skt. *tāla-*
8. *tulasī-* 'the sacred basil plant' (BhP.) (EWA "wohl dravidisch")	DED 2761 Ta. *tuẓāy, tuḷaci, tuḷavam, tuḷavu* 'sacred basil, *Ocimum sanctum'* (SKTCP)–some forms possibly reborrowed from Skt. *tulasī*
9. *nimba-* 'the tree *Azadirachta indica*' (Gobh.) (Hindi *nīb, nī̃b, nīm;* Marathi *nī̃b, lī̃b)* (EWA "nicht genügend erklärt")	DED 4551 Ta. *vēmpu* 'neem', *margosa, 'Azadirachta indica*' (SKTC)
10. *nimbū-* 'the lime, *Citrus acida*' (lex.) (Hindi *nimbū, nī̃bū, nīmū, lī̃bū, līmū*) (EWA "wohl Sanskritisierung neuindischer Wörter wie hindī nī̃bū...die letztlich aus austrischer Quelle stammen dürften, vgl. muṇḍārī lembu")	DED 712 Ta. *elumiccai, elumiccankāy* 'sour lime, *Citrus medica acida*' (SK)
11. *pūga- 'Areca catechu*, its nut' (Susr.) (EWA "vielleicht dravidisch")	DED 3333 Te. *pō̃ka* 'the areca tree, *Areca catechu*; an areca nut' (STC)
12. *panasa-* 'the breadfruit tree, *Artocarpus integrifolia*' (MBh.), 'its fruit' (Susr.) (EWA "wegen der mi. und unbel. Nebenformen wird dravidischer, vielleicht letztlich austroasiatischer Ursprung vermutet")	DED 3290 Ta. *palavu, palā, pilā* 'jack-tree, *Artocarpus integrifolia*' (SKTCP)
13. *bilva-* 'the wood apple tree, *Aegle marmelos*' (AV) (EWA "vielleicht einheimischer	DED 4535 Ta. *veḷḷil, veḷḷiyam, viḷā, viḷam, viḷari, viḷavu, viḷātti* 'wood apple, *Feronia elephantum'*

Ursprungs...die verzweigten dravidischen Formen dürften gegenüber dem indoarischen Wort primär sein")	(SKC,?P)
14. *vambha-* 'a bamboo, etc.' lex. (Monier-Williams) (EWA "wohl Wiedergabe des dravidischen 'Bambus'-Wortes")	DED 4294 Ta. *vampu* 'curved bamboo pole of a palanquin'; Tu. *bambu* 'bamboo' (SKT) (cf. Malay *bambu*)
15. *vañjula-* 'name of various trees and plants including *Jonesia asoka* and *Calamus rotang*' (MBh.) (EWA "wohl ein einheimischer Pflanzenname; nicht zu trennen von tamil vanci...")	DED 4265 Ta. *vānci* 'common rattan of South India, *Calamus rotang* (and some other similar plants)' (S)
16. *sarja-* 'the tree, *Vatica robusta*' (MBh.) (EWA "Nicht klar; nach Burrow... dravidisch")	DED 288 Ta. *āccā* 'sal, *Shorea robusta*' (SK)
17. *hintāla-* 'the marshy date-palm, *Phoenix paludosa*' (Hariv.) (EWA "Schwierig...tāla- am wahrscheinlichsten dravidisch")	DED 459 Ta. *īntu* 'date-palm, *Phoenix dactylifera*, etc.'; Mal. *īntal 'P. farinifera'*; Kur. *kī̃ndā* 'palm tree, date tree' (SKTCPN)
18. *śāka-* 'the teak tree, *Tectona grandis'* (EWA "Wohl eine Lehnwortsippe")	DED 2842 Ta. *tēkku* 'teak, *Tectona grandis'* (SKCP)

18a. See item 46 below
18b. See item 54 below

CEREALS AND CEREAL GRASSES

19. *godhūma-* 'wheat' (VS) (Hindi *gohū̃, gehū̃, gahū̃*) cf. Avestan *gantumō*, Persian *gandum*	Burrow and Emeneau, 1962, item 123: Ta. *kōti*, Ka. *gōdi*, Tu. *gōd(h)i*, Go. *gohk*, Br. *xōlum*

	(EWA "Für das ai. Wort ist mit volksetymologisch Anlehnung an *gauḥ (go-)* und *dhūmaḥ* zu rechnen. Zu beachten ist aber auch brāhūī *xolum* [←*γolum] wohl eine Entlehnung aus dem indisch-iranischer Grenzgebiet"; EWA considers Bloch's argument of the variation in the initial syllable of this word being influenced by Dravidian words like Kannada *gōdi* "beachtlich")	
20.	*tinikā- 'Holcus sorghum'* (Npr.) (EWA "vielleicht dravidisch")	DED 2671 *tiṉai* 'Italian millet, *Setaria italica*, etc.' (SK)
21.	*nīvarā-* 'wild rice' (VS), *nīvāraka-* (Susr.) (EWA "vielleicht dravidisch")	DED 2991 Ta. *navarai* 'a kind of paddy'; Te. *nivari* 'Oryza' (STC)
22.	*munja-* 'the grass *Saccharum sara* or munja' (SBr.) (EWA "Nicht erklärt...die Sippe kan. mode...aus der Burrow... herleitete, wird aber jetzt als primär arisch erwogen")	DED 4026 Ta. *munci* 'reedy sugar-cane, *Saccharum arundinaceum"* (SKT)
23.	*yavanāla- 'Andropogon bicolor'* (Susr.) *yōnala-* (lex.) (cf. Bengali *janār* 'a kind of maize', Marathi *jondhaḷā* 'the grain *Holcus sorghum'*) (EWA: from *yavana-* Greek, Ionian, etc.)	DED 2359 Ta. *cōḷam, coṉṉal* 'maize, great millet, *Sorghum vulgare'*; Ka. *jōḷa* 'several species of millet'; Te. *jonna(lu)* 'millet'; Go. *jōnnang* 'juwar', *jonā* 'maize'; Ga. *jōnel* 'maize', *jonnēl* 'millet' (SKTCP)–cf. Brahui *cōṇḍ* 'lucerne (alfalfa)', Bray 2.88 (?)
24.	*varuka-* 'a species of inferior grain' (Susr. [Monier-Williams]) (EWA "wohl zu der dravid. Sippe von tamil varaku..."	DED 4300 Ta. *varaku* 'common millet, *Paspalum scrobiculatum;* poor man's millet, *P. crusgalli'* (SKC)

25. *vīraṇa-/viraṇa-* 'a fragrant grass, *Andropogon muricatus'* (MBh. [Monier-Williams]) (EWA "wohl nicht zu trennen von dravid. Wörten...wie tamil viẓal usw.")

DED Ta. *viẓal* 'darbha grass, a kind of sedge, cuscus *(Andropogon muricatus)'* (SKC)

26. *vrīhi-* 'rice' (AV) (Shina *brīu,* 'brīm, etc.'; Sinhalese *viya;* cf. *varī 'Asparagus racemosus', vara-* 'a kind of grain' lex., Marathi *varī* 'the grain, *Coix barbata'*) (EWA "ein Kulturwort von dem eine grössere zahl iranische Wörter [zor. pehl. blnč = *brinǰ, khotansak. rrīysu, neup. birinǰ, gurinǰ, afghan. wrižē, ormuri rīdzan, rēzan 'Reis'...und gr. oríndēs (ártos) 'Brot aus Reismehl', óryza, óryzon 'Reis'] nicht zu trennen sind")

DED 178 Ta. *ari* 'rice, ear of paddy'; *arici* 'rice without husk, any husked grain' (SKTC)–cf. Ta. *ēlav-arici* 'cardamom seed' (DED 768 Ta. *ēlam* 'cardamom'); DED 3790 Ga. *mānjik* 'rice (CP)'; DED 4306 Ta. *vari* 'paddy'; Parji *verci*; Go. *wanjī* 'rice' (SCP) (Brahui *brinj* 'rice' from Persian)–cf. Proto-Munda **ərig 'panicum miliare'* (Zide and Zide 1973); also Malagasy *vari, vare* 'rice'; Ngaju-Dayak *bari* 'boiled rice, food'; Somali *barìs* 'rice' (Southworth 1975); Elamite *bar* 'seed'

27. *śūka-* 'awn of grain' (R); *śungā* 'sheath or calyx of young bud (GrS); awn of barley, etc.' (lex.) (EWA "wohl in alte Sprache zurückreichend...Zu vergleichen mit aw. sūkā f., mp. sūčan, neup. sōzan Nadel, sōk Granne, kurd. šūzin dss.")

DED 2777 Ka. *tūngu/sūngu* 'the beard of barley, etc.' (basic meaning of this group of words, which occurs in all the Dravidian languages, is 'sleep, swing, hang, etc.')

VEGETABLES

28. *kuṣmāṇḍa-* 'the pumpkin gourd, *Beninkasa cerifera'* (MBh.) (EWA "wahrscheinlich austroasiatisch, aus dem Präfixform kuṣ- und einen nach austro-

DED 1455 Ta. *kumpaḷam* 'wax gourd; *kumaṭṭi, kommaṭṭi* 'a small watermelon, *Citrullus;* cucumber, *Cucumis trigonus'* (SKTCPN) asiatischen Sprachgesetzen mit bhaṭā usw. vermittelbaren -māṇḍa- zusammengesetzt")

29. *cirbhaṭa-* '*Cucumis utilissimus*' (Car.) (EWA: carbhaṭa "...wohl mit cirbhaṭah und cirbhiṭam Präfixform zu bhaṭā, also protomundiden Ursprungs; Kuiper 144")

DED 394 Ka. *ibbuḍlu-baḷḷi* 'the melon plant, *Cucumis melo*'; Tu. *ibbuḍlu* 'a kind of cucumber' (KT)

30. *tuṇḍikā-* '*Momordica monadelpha*' lex.; *tuṇḍikerī-* (Susr.) (EWA "vielleicht dravidisch")

DED 2880 Ka. *toṇḍe, toṇḍi,* etc. 'the gourd, *Momordica monadelpha*' (SKCP)

31. *paṭola-* 'the gourd, *Tricosanthes dioeca*; its fruit' (Susr.) (EWA "wohl dravidisch")

DED 3491 Ta. *puṭal(ai), puṭōl* 'snake gourd, *Tricosanthes anguina*' (SKTCP)

32. *murangī-* '*Moringa pterygosperma*' (Susr.) (EWA "wohl aus der dravid. Sippe von tamil murunkai...")

DED 4085 Ta. *murunkai* '*Moringa pterygosperma*, Indian horseradish tree' (SKTCP, ?N)

33. *vātingana-* 'the eggplant, *Solanum melongena*' (lex.; also *vanga-, vangana-*) (EWA "Fremdwörter, die wohl letztlich mit bhaṇṭakī zusammengehören"; cf. bhaṇṭakī "wohl ein unarischer Pflanzenname")

DED 4339 Ta. *vaẓutalai, vaẓutaṇai* 'brinjal, eggplant, *Solanum melongena*' (SKTCPN)

SPICES, ETC.

34. *elā-* 'cardamom' (Susr.) (EWA "wohl mit *elavālu* zusammengehörig"; cf. elavālu "unklar")

DED 768 Ta. *ēlam* 'cardamom plant, *Elettaria cardamomum*; cardamom' (SKTC)

35. *kustumbarī-* 'coriander' (Susr.) (cf. *tumburu-* 'fruit of *Diospyros embryopteris*, coriander' [Paṅ. Kas.]) (EWA kustumbarī, tumburuḥ "Unklare, wohl fremde Wortsippe")

DED 2732 Ta. *tumpi 'Diospyros tomentosa*; Ceylon ebony, *D. ebenum'; tumpili* 'Coromandel ebony, *D. melanoxylum*...' (SKCP)

36. *guḍa-* 'boiled sugarcane juice, molasses' (Katy.) (cf. *guḍa-* 'globe, ball' [MBh.], also *guḍikā-, gula-, guli-, gulikā-, guṭikā-, gola-*) (EWA "Nach Bagchi, pre-Aryan xxix zu den austroasiatischen Wörtern für "Zucker": Malay. *gula* usw.: ganz unsicher")

DED 1400 Ka. *guḍḍu, guḍḍi* 'eyeball, egg'; *guḍasu* 'anything round'; *guḍi* 'circle, halo' (KCP); DED 1414 Ta. *kuṇṭu* 'ball, anything circular and heavy, bullet, testicles of beasts' (SKTCP)

37. *marīca-* 'peppercorn' (Apast.) *marica-* (Susr.) (EWA "Wohl ein austroasiatisches LW (vgl. mon mrāk...), das im älterer Lautgestalt..auch in die dravid. Sprachen ausgestrahlt hat...ohne direkten Zusammenhang mit dem Ai.")

DED 3986 Ta. *miḷaku* 'black pepper, *Piper nigrum*' (SKT)

38. *laśuna-* 'garlic' (Gaut.) *rasona-* (Susr.) (EWA "Nicht geklärt; wahrscheinlich ein Kulturwort... [die These dravidischen Ursprungs] ist weniger überzeugend, zumal Kui und v. a. Malto viele Munda-Lehnwörter zeigen...")

Kui *lesuṛi* 'garlic', Malto *nasnu* (CN) –from Burrow 1968:297 (not in DED)

39. *śarkarā-* 'gravel, grit' (AV); 'candied sugar' (Hariv.), *śarkara-* in cmpd. (MBh.) (EWA undecided)

DED 2297 Ka. *ceruku* 'sugarcane'; Kol. *saragurak* (KCP); cf. DED 1876 Ta. *cakkai* 'jackfruit, jungle jack (from which a type of sugar is made)' (S)

40. *śṛngavera-* 'dried or fresh ginger' (Suśr.) (according to Turner, this is a popular etymology for Pali *singi-vera-* from Dravidian) (EWA "Fremdwort. Der Anklang an *śṛngam* ist nur einer...Volksetymologie zuzuschreiben...*vera-* vielmehr ein dravid. Wort...mi. *singi-*...tamil mal. inci...wohl letztlich ein ostasiatisches Kulturwort")

DED 363 Ta. *inci* 'ginger' (S) (from **cinki-*, with usual loss of *c-* and palatalization of *-k-*?); DED 4554 Ta. *vēr* 'root' (SKTCP); SDr. **cinci-vēr* is probably the source of Gk. *zinziber*, Eng. 'ginger', etc. (cf. Gk. *z* for Drav. *c* in Muziris for Muciri, the name of a west coast port, and in Gk. *óryzon, óryza* for SDr. **(v)arici*—see under *vrīhi-*)

BEANS, PULSES

41. **uḍidda-* 'a pulse' (Pali *udida-*, Hindi *uṛad*, etc., Marathi *udid)*

DED 594 Ta. *uẓuntu* 'black gram', *urad, 'Phaseolus mungo'* (SKTCP)

42. *kulattha-* 'the pulse, *Dolichos uniflorus*' (MBh.) (EWA "wohl dravidisch")

DED 1790 Ta. *koḷ* 'horse gram, *Dolichos uniflorus*' (STCP)

43. *kulmāṣa-* 'a sort of *Phaseolus*; a species of *Dolichos*' (lex.) (EWA "Im Vorderglied steckt wahrscheinlich dasselbe dravidische Wort wie in *kulatthaḥ*... dass der zweite Teil māṣa- "Bohne" sein soll...ist zu bezweifeln")

Burrow 1968:196: compounded of *kul-* (see *kulattha-*) and *māṣa-* 'bean (q.v.)'

44. *māṣa-* 'bean' (RV) (cf. also *masūra-* 'lentil' [VS]) (EWA "nicht überzeugend erklärt; wahrscheinlich ein Kultur- und Wanderwort")

DED 4195 Ta. *moccai* 'hyacinth bean, *Dolichos lablab*' (S)

45. *varaka-* '*Phaseolus trilobus*, a kind of rice' (EWA "wohl ein einheimischer Pflanzenname")

DED 224 Ta. *avarai* 'field bean, *Dolichos lablab*' (SKT)

OTHER

46. *āmra-* 'mango tree' (MBh.); its fruit (SBr.); cf. *mākanda-* 'mango tree'	DED 3919 Ta. *mā, mā(n)ti* 'mango', *mān-kāy* 'unripe mango', *mām-paẓam* 'ripe mango' (SKCP); cf. DED 3925 Ka. *māgu* 'to ripen fully, as fruit' (KTCP)
47. *kamala-* 'lotus' (R); cf. also *kuvalaya-* (MBh.) (EWA "wahrscheinlich aus dem Dravidischen")	DED 1574 Ta. *kūmpu* 'close, shut (as a flower)...' *kuvaḷai* 'blue nelumbo (which closes by day)'; Mal. *kumpuka* 'close'...*kuvaḷa* 'waterlily' (SK)
48. *tāmarasa-* 'red lotus' (MBh.) 'copper' lex. (EWA "wohl dravidisch")	DED 2583 Ta. *tāmarai* 'lotus, *Nelumbium speciosum*' (SKTCP)
49. *tila- 'Sesamum indicum'* (AV) (EWA "nicht erklärt, vielleicht unarisch")	DED 726 Ta. *eḷ, eṇ 'Sesamum indicum'* (SKT)
50. *tūla-* 'tuft of grass, etc.' (AV); 'cotton' (MBh.) (EWA "nicht überzeugend erklärt")	DED 2790 Ta. *tūval* 'feather, etc.', *tuy* 'cotton' (SKTCP)
51. *panji-* 'ball of cotton from which thread is spun' (lex. [Assamese *pā̃zi* 'wisp of cotton, roll of cotton or thread']); cf. *karpāśa-* 'the cotton plant' (Susr.) (EWA "S. die dravid. Sippe von Tamil *panci*...der letzte Ursprung scheint im Austroasiatischen zu liegen...Burrow, *BSOAS* 12:382")	DED 3173 Ta. *panci, pancu* 'cotton cloth, cotton cushion' (SK)
52. *mulālin/mulālī-* 'a species of edible lotus' (AV) (Monier-Williams;	DED 4100 *muḷai* 'sprout, etc.'; *muḷari* 'lotus'; Mal. *muḷa* 'germ,

see Turner s. v. *mṛṇāla-* 'edible lotus root' [MBh.])
(EWA "vermutlich fremden Ursprungs")

sprout, young plant' (SKTCN)

53. *mūrvā-* 'bowstring hemp, *Sanseviera rox.* (Var. Susr. [Monier-Williams])
(EWA: mūrvā, maurva- "wohl Fremdwörter")

DED 3857 Ta. *maral, maruḷ* 'bowstring hemp' (SK)

54. *nārikera-, nālikela-* (Susr.), *nārikela-* (MBh.), *nāḍīkerī-, nālīkera-* (BHSk.) 'coconut palm and fruit'
(EWA "Wohl ein einheimisches Wort"; Bloch [*BSOAS* 5:740] considers it a Dravidian compound of nāri + kēḷi 'coconut palm')

DED 3023 Ta. *nār* 'fiber, string, cord, rope'; *nāri* 'bowstring, fibrous covering at the bottom of a leaf stalk, as of a coconut palm' (SKTCP)

NOTES

1. This paper is based on research supported by the American Institute of Indian Studies and the American Council of Learned Societies, whose help I hereby gratefully acknowledge. I also wish to thank Joan P. Mencher and David McAlpin for their helpful comments on my work.
2. Deshpande, in his paper for this conference, has challenged the usual assumption that the Ṛgveda as we know it is identical to its original form. His analysis of this question is brilliant and extremely thorough, and his argument seems to me very plausible. As I understand it, however, he is concerned only with the *phonological* form of the text (particularly the retroflex consonants) and does not question the presence of Dravidian loanwords in the text. See section 5 below, and particularly note 12, for further discussion of this matter.
3. Because of the lack of agreement on the affiliations of certain languages, I have adopted a scheme which assumes provisionally six branches of Dravidian (see Southworth, 1976): S(outh Dravidian, i.e., Tamil, Malayālam, Kodagu, Toḍā, Koṭā); K(annaḍa); T(uḷu); C(entral Dravidian, i.e., Telugu, Goṇḍī, Konda, Kui, Kuwi, Pengo, Manda); P(arji, Gadaba, Naiki, Kolāmī); N(orth Dravidian, i.e., Kudukh, Malto, Brahui). The abbreviations S, K, T, C, P, and N are used to indicate the attestation of each item given in the appendices.
4. If it were a Dravidian borrowing from Indo-Aryan, it would have had to be borrowed at the time of Proto-Dravidian. Though this is not impossible, it would put the period of contact much earlier than previously supposed, perhaps as early as the fourth millennium B.C., and probably in an area quite distant from the subcontinent.
5. Even if the Elamo-Dravidian hypothesis is rejected, and the lexical similarities between Elamite and Dravidian are regarded as the results of borrowing, this would still require an assumption that (at least some) Dravidian speakers were in contact with Elamite speakers in Iran. In any case, my own view of the matter is that it is McAlpin's *morphological* evidence which makes the strongest case for the relationship of Elamite and Dravidian.
6. David McAlpin has drawn my attention to the following points relevant to this discussion: first of all, there exists a pronominal suffix *-ta* in Achaemenid Elamite (AE), occurring, for example, in *(u) attata* 'my father', in which *u* means 'I' or 'my' and *atta* means 'father' (Hallock 1962). Since there is, in addition, a more regular first person possessive suffix *-uri* (probably analyzable as *u-* 'I' + *-ri* 'possessive', cf. *-eri* 'third person possessive'), there is a distinct possibility that AE *-ta* means the same as Drav. *taṉ/taṉ-*, namely pronominal reference to a previously mentioned noun phrase (usually the subject of the sentence). The lack of *-n* in Achaemenid Elamite is parallel to the lack of final *-n* in the first and second pronouns (AE *ū, nū*), cf. Drav. *yān*, etc. (DED 4234), *nī(n)* (DED 3051). Note, in addition, the use of *ta(ṉ)* with kinship terms, as in *tampi* '(one's) younger brother', *tankai* '(one's) younger sister' (2.3 above), *tāy* '(one's) mother' (see 2.3). The comparison is not invalidated by the fact that the form in question occurs as a suffix in Elamite and as a prefix in Dravidian, since such variation is fairly common with possessive markers: compare, for example, Spanish *mi padre* and *padre mio* 'my father'.

7. Some evidence for the presence of Dravidian speakers in the Iranian plateau is provided by a number of place-names including the suffix *-ar* (cf. Drav. *(y)āru* 'river', DED 4233), e.g., "Haftar, a place where seven rivers mingle together" (Ramaswami Aiyar 1930:51), and *Mala* (cf. Drav. *mala*, etc., 'mountain', DED 3882). The possibility of additional Dravidian loanwords in Iranian deserves investigation. At present, the only items I might suggest are the demonstrative stems *i-* and *a-* (Old Persian *iyam* 'this', *a-* 'this', *ava-* 'that'), which are also found in Old Indo-Aryan and are also "typically" Dravidian (see DED 1, 351).
8. The few exceptions to this statement are the following: (1) items not attested in Modern Indo-Aryan: *kūṭa-* (except for a possible Assamese form) (A-2), *ukha-* (A-9), *vriś-* (A-10), *kulāya-* (A-13), *karambha-* (A-14), *dhurya-* (B-12), *vithura-* (C-4); (2) items marginally attested in Modern Indo-Aryan: *muktā-* (A-20), *kūṭa-* (only in Lahnda and Hindi) (C-14); (3) items found only in western Modern Indo-Aryan and Sinhalese: *piśāca-* (C-8), *māyā-* (plus a possible Old Bengali form) (C-9); and (4) items missing in western Modern Indo-Aryan: *āṇi-* (B-7).
9. There are at least three distinct verbs referring to winnowing which are reconstructable for Proto-Dravidian; see DED 1679 (attested in SKCPN), DED 2827 (SKTCN), DED 3123 (SCN). The word for rice discussed below (D-26) cannot be reconstructed for Proto-Dravidian in this meaning, but possibly can be reconstructed in the meaning 'seed' (note Kudukh *manjī* 'seed (in general)', DED 3790; also Ta. *arici*, etc., in the meaning 'seed' in such expressions as *ēlav-arici* 'cardamom seed', DED 768). One item related to grain cultivation has a possible Elamite cognate: AE *umi-* 'grind (grain)': Ta. *umi* 'husk, chaff', DED 548 (SKTCN), (see McAlpin 1974). A verb meaning 'to plow' (possibly originally 'root up') is attested in all branches (DED 592).
10. In Indo-Aryan, *vrīhi-* was replaced early by a number of other words, one of which –**cāmala-*/**cāvala-* (Hindi-Urdu *cāval*, etc. [Turner, s.v.])–has possible cognates in Tibeto-Burman (e.g., Newari *jā*) and in Southeast Asian languages, suggesting that the rice-growing cultures in the Ganges Valley obtained the term, and perhaps also the grain, from Tibeto-Burman-speaking peoples. (I have hypothesized elsewhere [1974] a Dravidian substratum for western and northwestern Indo-Aryan and a different substratum in the Ganges Valley and the east: *cāval* = Tibeto-Burman *cā* + *val*/*var* ← Drav. *vari*, etc.? Modern Indo-Aryan also has *-r-* forms, e.g., Bhoj. *cāur*, etc.)
11. Note that several of these terms show consistently different forms in Dravidian and Indo-Aryan; for example, the words for 'mango' (D-46) have initial *m-* in Dravidian but not in Indo-Aryan; the words for 'pepper' (D-37) have IA *-r-*, Drav. *-l-* or *-ḷ-*, etc. One of the words for 'plow' (C-12) has initial *l-* in most of Indo-Aryan (except for Bengali and Marathi), but initial *n-* in Tamil (see 4.5 above).
12. This argument about the transitional status of the Ṛgvedic period is not affected by Deshpande's claim that retroflex consonants were not present in the original form of the *Ṛgveda*. In fact, his analysis of the situation tends to confirm the notion that structural convergence between Indo-Aryan and other languages was beginning at this time. In evaluating this argument, it will be important to bear in mind the results of recent studies of linguistic change in progress, particularly the work of William Labov (see, especially, Labov 1972). These studies show clearly that linguistic innovations enter the language very gradually, first as variable rules affecting

only a limited number of environments, and later becoming more general. Furthermore, innovations generally appear first in the speech of members of a single subgroup of the society, and only later become generalized to the speech community as a whole. Thus, it can be assumed that retroflex consonants first began to appear in Old Indo-Aryan as optional allophonic variants of dentals in a few environments, perhaps first in the speech of individuals who also spoke a non-Aryan language. Later generations would have extended the scope of these variants, as has been shown repeatedly in Labov's studies. We do not know how long it should take for such a change to be generalized to the whole Aryan speech community, but it is possible that in a rather conservative society it could have taken a century, or even several centuries, for this innovation to pass from a variable feature in informal speech to an invariant feature in the ritual language of the *Ṛgveda*. Thus, rules for variable retroflexion, presumably derived from contact with non-Aryans, must have been part of what Labov calls the "grammar of the speech community" for generations, perhaps centuries, before their actual appearance in the spoken form of the Vedic hymns.

13. This later period presumably involved more and more the type of multilingualism which prevails in the subcontinent today, with widespread switching of languages, as well as the "compartmentalization" of languages into different social functions (intergroup versus intragroup, ritual versus secular, formal versus informal, etc.).
14. Note also that, of the Dravidian borrowings from Indo-Aryan listed in B-2, only a few can be shown to be very early. Only the following have cognates in North Dravidian: *kampaḷi* 'blanket/covering' (B-4), *(c)ūci* 'needle' (B-6); only the following have cognates in the Parji-Kolami group: *accu* 'axle' (B-1), *ālai* 'shed' (B-5), *gadda* 'kite' (B-11), *turai* 'chief' (B-12), *pakkam* 'side' (B-13). All of these are likely to have entered Dravidian before its dispersal into different parts of the subcontinent. (The relative paucity of North Dravidian cognates in these comparisons is apparently, in part, the result of the scantiness of materials for these languages, but may also be an indication that the speakers of North Dravidian languages had already begun to separate from the rest of the speakers of Proto-Dravidian during the period of contact with Indo-Aryan, and thus were only indirectly or marginally involved in this contact. This would suggest that the North Dravidian languages were the first to split off from Proto-Dravidian.

REFERENCES

Bloch, Jules. (See Levi.)

Burrow, Thomas. 1945. "Some Dravidian Words in Sanskrit." *Transactions of the Philological Society*; reprinted in Burrow, 1968.

———. 1946. "Some Loanwords in Sanskrit." *Transactions of the Philological Society*; reprinted in Burrow, 1968.

———. 1947. "Further Dravidian Words in Sanskrit." *Bulletin of the School of Oriental and African Studies* 12; reprinted in Burrow, 1968.

———. 1958. "Sanskrit and the Pre-Aryan Tribes and Languages." *Bulletin of the Ramakrishna Mission*, Calcutta; reprinted in Burrow, 1968.

———. 1968. *Collected Papers on Dravidian Linguistics.* Department of Linguistics publication no. 13, Annamalai University, Annamalainagar, South India.

Burrow, Thomas, and M. B. Emeneau. 1961. *A Dravidian Etymological Dictionary.* Oxford University Press.

———. 1968. *A Dravidian Etymological Dictionary–Supplement.* Oxford University Press.

Dempwolff, Otto. 1938. *Vergleichende Lautlehre des Austronesischen Wortschatzes.* Berlin: Verlag von Dietrich Reimer; reprinted 1969 by Kraus Reprint, Nendeln, Liechtenstein.

Emeneau, M. B. 1953. "Dravidian Kinship Terms." *Language* 29:339-53.

———. 1970. *Dravidian Comparative Phonology: A Sketch.* Annamalai University, Annamalainagar, South India.

Emeneau, M. B., and Thomas Burrow. 1962. *Dravidian Borrowings from Indo-Aryan.* Berkeley and Los Angeles: University of California Press.

Fairservis, Walter A., Jr. 1967. "The Origin, Character, and Decline of an Early Civilization." *American Museum Novitates* 2302:1-48.

———. Forthcoming. *The Consequences of Harappan as a Dravidian Language: A Problem in Archaeology and Linguistics.*

Hallock, R. T. 1962. "The Pronominal Suffixes in Achaemenid Elamite." *Journal of Near Eastern Studies* 21:53-56.

Kent, Roland G. 1950. *Old Persian: Grammar, Texts, Lexicon.* New Haven, Conn.: American Oriental Society.

Krishnamurti, Bh. 1968. "Dravidian Personal Pronouns." In *Studies in Indian Linguistics*, edited by Bh. Krishnamurti, pp. 189-205.

———. 1975. "Gender and Number in Proto-Dravidian." *International Journal of Dravidian Linguistics* (Trivandrum) 4, no. 2:238-50.

Krishnamurti, Bh., ed. 1968. *Studies in Indian Linguistics* (Professor M. B.

Emeneau *ṣaṣṭipūrti* volume). Poona: Linguistic Society of India, Deccan College.

Kuiper, F. B. J. 1948. *Proto-Munda Words in Sanskrit.* Amsterdam.

———. 1967. "The Genesis of a Linguistic Area." *Indo-Iranian Journal* 10: 81-102; reprinted in Southworth and Apte.

Labov, William. 1972. "The Social Setting of Linguistic Change." In *Sociolinguistic Patterns.* Philadelphia: University of Pennsylvania Press.

Levi, Sylvain; Jean Przyluski; and Jules Bloch. 1929. *Pre-Aryan and Pre-Dravidian in India.* Translated from the French by Prabodh Chandra Bagchi. Calcutta.

McAlpin, David W. 1974. "Toward Proto-Elamo-Dravidian." *Language* 50:89-101.

———. 1975. "Elamite and Dravidian: Further Evidence of Relationship." *Current Anthropology* 16, no. 1:93-104.

Masica, Colin P. 1976. *Defining a Linguistic Area: South Asia.* Chicago: University of Chicago Press.

Mayrhofer, Manfred. 1953-77. *Kurzgefasstes etymologisches Wörterbuch des Altindischen.* Heidelberg.

Polomé, Edgar C. 1975. "Linguistic Borrowing." In *Linguistic Borrowing,* edited by Herman H. van Olphen. Center for Asian Studies, University of Texas.

Przyluski, Jean. (See Levi.)

Ramaswami Aiyar, L. V. 1930. "Dravidic Place-Names in the Plateaux of Persia." *Quarterly Journal of the Mythic Society* 20:49-53.

Sankalia, H. D. 1974. *The Prehistory and Protohistory of India and Pakistan.* New Edition. Poona: Deccan College.

Southworth, Franklin C. 1971. "Detecting Prior Creolization: An Investigation of the Historical Origins of Marathi." In *Pidginization and Creolization of Languages,* edited by Dell Hymes. Cambridge University Press.

———. 1974. "Linguistic Stratigraphy of North India." In Southworth and Apte, pp. 201-23.

———. 1975. "Cereals in South Asian Prehistory: The Linguistic Evidence." In *Ecological Backgrounds of South Asian Prehistory,* edited by K. A. R. Kennedy and G. L. Possehl. Ithaca, N. Y.: South Asia Program, Cornell University.

———. 1976. "On Subgroups in Dravidian." *International Journal of Dravidian Linguistics* (Trivandrum) 5, no. 1:114-37.

Southworth, Franklin C., and M. L. Apte. 1974. *Contact and Convergence in South Asian Languages.* Special publication of the *International Journal of*

Dravidian Linguistics (Trivandrum).

Thieme, Paul. 1955. Review of *The Sanskrit Language*, by T. Burrow (Faber and Faber, London). *Language* 31:428-48.

Turner, Sir Ralph L. 1966. *Comparative Dictionary of the Indo-Aryan Languages.* London: Oxford University Press.

Zide, Arlene, and Norman Zide. 1973. "Semantic Reconstructions in Proto-Munda Cultural Vocabulary." *Indian Linguistics* 34:1-24.

———. 1976. "Proto-Munda Cultural Vocabulary: Evidence for Early Agriculture." In *Proceedings of the First International Austroasiatic Conference, Honolulu.*

GENESIS OF ṚGVEDIC RETROFLEXION
A HISTORICAL AND SOCIOLINGUISTIC INVESTIGATION

Madhav M. Deshpande
The University of Michigan

> The text of Ṛgveda, there is reason to suppose, is not quite the same as it was originally. Some Sūktas and Ṛks are found in the other Vedas, and there the readings in some cases are different. What the original readings were will have to be determined, if at all possible, by comparing the variation and taking a good many other facts into consideration. The way has been shown by Oldenberg, and it is quite open to any of us to follow it.
>
> Sir R. G. Bhandarkar
> *Collected Works*, vol. 1, p. 398

SUMMARY

1) A Perspective on the Problem;
2) Plurality of Ṛgvedic Recensions;
3) Recensional Variation: An Epistemological Problem;
4) *Aitareya-Āraṇyaka* (3.2.6): Its Implications;
5) Pre-Ṛgvedic Aryan-non-Aryan Bilingualism?;
6) Emergence of Retroflexion in Prehistoric Indo-Aryan;
7) *Brāhmīkaraṇa*: A Gradual Transformation;
8) Retroflexion and the Development of the Brāhmī Script;
9) Instability of Post-Vedic Retroflexion;
10) Irregular Retroflexion in the Vedic Recensions;
11) Retroflexion in the *Prātiśākhyas*;
12) Aspects of Dravidian Influence on Indo-Aryan;
13) Problems in the Reconstruction of the Ur-*Ṛgveda*;
14) Other Instances of Alleged Dravidian Influence;
15) Conclusions.

1. A PERSPECTIVE ON THE PROBLEM

1.1. Most modern scholars, if not all, accept that retroflex consonants already appear in the *Ṛgveda* and are seen increasingly in Middle Indo-Aryan. The question for most of these scholars is not whether there is retroflexion in the *Ṛgveda*, but how one is to explain its undisputed presence there. In this paper, I would like to deal with the prior question: Was there any retroflexion in the Ur-*Ṛgveda*? If there was no retroflexion in the Ur-*Ṛgveda*, how is it that the text of the *Ṛgveda* as we now have it has retroflexion? Before I deal with this question, however, it is important to survey existing views on the question of Ṛgvedic retroflexion.

For some, retroflexion is an independent "well-motivated" process that began in pre-Vedic Indo-Aryan. Others argue that retroflexion in Indo-Aryan is a result of contacts with Dravidians and/or Mundas, and that such influential contacts must have occurred in pre-Vedic times. Bloch (1965:325) says: "As to the distinction between dentals and cerebrals we have seen that it depends on the adaptation and crystallization of a series of alterations due at first to the action of the pre-historic Aryan *sh* sounds." But he does place a good deal of emphasis on the adaptational aspect of this phenomenon: "The Indo-Aryan innovation is best explained in terms of the use of the two classes in the indigenous languages. This is without doubt the most decisive fact in deciding the earliest Sanskrit texts to be purely Indian" (1965:56).

1.2. While Katre (1944:129) thinks that "the action of either Dravidian or Munda substratum is subordinate to the action of the Indo-Aryan" itself, other scholars tend to place equal, if not more, emphasis on the "action of the substratum." Such a trend has been developed in the recent work of Kuiper and Emeneau. Emeneau outlines his main thesis as follows: "The fact, however, that the later in Indo-Aryan linguistic history we go, the greater is the incidence of retroflex consonants and the further fact that most of the Dravidian languages and the proto-Dravidian itself have this type of consonant in abundance, can only lead to the conclusion that the later Indo-Aryan developments are due to a borrowing of indigenous speech habits through bilingualism, and to the well-grounded suspicion that even the early development of retroflexes from certain Indo-European consonant clusters results from the same historic cause."[1] Even if "well-grounded," the theory is still a matter of "suspicion" as far as the early stages of Indo-Aryan are concerned. Kuiper (1967:90) raises some important historical-theoretical questions concerning Emeneau's "well-grounded suspicion," but finally accepts it.

1.3. Kuiper points out that there are retroflexes in the *Ṛgveda* which are reflexes of certain Indo-European consonantal clusters, and that there are also some retroflexes in a small number of words of "evidently foreign origin," and explains the contribution of these retroflexed foreign words to the development of retroflexion in Vedic Sanskrit as follows: "It may seem natural to assume that in the same way, pre-historic Indo-Aryan, bilingual speakers who recognized a phonemic contrast between dentals and retroflexes in the foreign language, came to interpret the allophones of proto-Indo-Aryan in terms of the foreign phonetic system. The loanwords with retroflexes which–at least in my interpretation of Ṛgvedic evidence–they must have introduced into Indo-Aryan may have contributed considerably to the spread of this novel phonemic distinction among the speakers of early Indo-Aryan" (1967:89-90). Kuiper agrees with Emeneau in concluding that pre-Dravidian and pre-Indo-Aryan bilingualism provided conditions which allowed pre-Indo-Aryan allophones to be redistributed as retroflex phonemes. But the fact that there are already retroflexes in the present text of the *Ṛgveda* prompted Kuiper (1967:97) to derive a "historical implication that the period between the arrival of the Indo-Aryans in the subcontinent and the composition of the oldest Vedic hymns must have been much longer than was previously thought." He also refers to the difference between the "older and more recent" parts of the *Ṛgveda* to explain the gradual increase in the occurrence of these "innovations of Indo-Aryan" (1967:93). Relying on the existence of retroflexion and non-Aryan loanwords in the *Ṛgveda* and on the fact that the Dāsas and Dasyus of the *Ṛgveda* are known to the Iranians as Dāhae and Dahyu, Chatterji (1951:159) claims that the Aryans "did not find any appreciable difference in the non-Aryan people they encountered in India from the non-Aryan people they knew in Eastern Iran. It is also equally likely that racial and cultural fusion (including linguistic influencing) had commenced between the Aryans and the Dāsa-Dasyu people outside the soil of India itself–in Iran in all likelihood."

1.4. Emeneau (1974:92) refers to Kuiper (1967) and says that this article "spelled out some of the theoretical and chronological implications of the occurrence of retroflex consonants...in the Ṛgveda, including other matters, that we must accept pre-Dravidian influence upon pre-Indo-Aryan to explain these full-fledged Ṛgvedic occurrences." The surveys of previous work in Southworth (1974) and Hock (1975) show that no scholar has as yet doubted the existence of retroflexion in the *Ṛgveda*. Therefore, it is no wonder that Southworth and Apte (1974:14) remark: "The close contact and wide-spread bilingualism among Indo-Aryan and Dravidian speaking groups in the Vedic period seems well-established by the evidence presented by Kuiper and Emeneau."

Turner has discussed the problem of retroflexion in Indo-Aryan at some length. He takes for granted the existence of retroflexion in the *Ṛgveda*, and also partly seems to favor the substratum argument (see Turner 1975:226, 240-41, 244, 365). Turner (1924) makes an important distinction between "common Indo-Aryan cerebralization" and "dialectal cerebralization," and tries to reconstruct "the history of the chief waves of cerebralization." Though Turner does not look at the existing Vedic retroflexion as a result of successive modifications of a given oral text under the influence of these waves of cerebralization, he does show that cerebralization is not a monolithic event in the history of Indo-Aryan. He thinks that retroflexion in Indo-Aryan is a combined result of the influence of the Dravidian substratum and of a tendency inherent in Indo-Aryan. According to Grammont (*Mémoires de la Société de Linguistique de Paris*, vol. 19, pp. 254, 267, 277), the origin of cerebralization in Indo-Aryan must be attributed to this general tendency in Indo-Aryan to relax the pronunciation in favor of articulation in the neighborhood of the palatal arch, a general tendency which, he thinks, is also responsible for other sound changes in Indo-Aryan. One can certainly question the origin of such a tendency in Indo-Aryan. Is it a genetic development within a branch of Indo-European? If so, why is it so unique? Is it possible that the origin of this tendency lies somewhere in the influence of India as a linguistic area? These are quite important, but as yet unanswered, questions. Ivanov and Toporov (1968:48-49) offer some interesting diachronic remarks on Sanskrit retroflexion, but their discussion is by no means conclusive.

1.5. So far I have presented the "other side." In the present paper I aim to shake up the strong conviction that retroflex consonants form part of the original *Ṛgveda* and to show that they were most probably not a "full-fledged Ṛgvedic occurrence." What was acquired during the long process of preredactional oral transmission has been ascribed by these scholars to the original compositions of the *Ṛgveda*. The Ṛgvedic evidence produced by these scholars is clearly from only one of the postredactional versions of the *Ṛgveda* and is not sufficient to let us draw directly any conclusions concerning the original compositions of the *Ṛgveda*. Along with these scholars, I had myself accepted the occurrence of retroflex consonants in the *Ṛgveda* and had used it as an argument in some of my previous work (Deshpande 1975*c*: 207). However, since then I have come to quite different conclusions. Though I realize fully that I cannot prove my case beyond the shadow of a doubt and that I cannot produce evidence from those lost original texts of the *Ṛgveda*, I hope that my arguments are at least sufficient to raise serious doubts concerning the existence of retroflex phonemes in the Ur-*Ṛgveda*, if not to prove their nonexistence.

1.6. My conclusions, though unorthodox, are by no means entirely new. Grierson (1929) has given a fascinating account of how the Kashmiri text of *Lallā-vākyāni*, originally composed in the latter half of the fourteenth century, has been preserved orally to the present day without ever having been written down. Grierson (1929:74) points out that "save for a few forms that have remained unchanged...her verses are in what is practically modern Kashmiri." However, the text of the *Mahānayaprakāśa* was composed in the fifteenth century and was written down at the time it was composed, and hence its language is preserved without any further change. Grierson describes the "unconscious" change taking place in a precodification oral tradition: "Each hymn [of *Lallā-vākyāni*] was handed down from teacher to pupil through five centuries, care being taken to preserve the text unchanged. But during all this time the language was insensibly changing, and, as there was no written record of the originals in the form in which they were first uttered, the language of the hymns insensibly changed at the same time. The reciters, it is hardly necessary to point out, were unaware of the change of language that was going on. In each generation that was very slight, and was not noticeable, but the total of the changes at the end of five centuries was very great indeed....It was so gradual that no one was ever aware that any change was taking place at all" (1929:75). Grierson clearly perceived that the same must have happened in the case of the Vedic texts before they were codified by the redactors. He says: "Unfortunately, for the Veda, we have nothing corresponding to the *Mahānayaprakāśa*, i.e. nothing written, and fixed in writing, at about the time that the oldest Vedic hymns were composed, so that we are unable to gauge the difference between the original form of the hymns and the form given to us by the Vyāsa (i.e. the redactor); but the parallel case of the *Mahānayaprakāśa*, is instructive, and shows us that the difference must have been great. In other words, the Ṛg-veda, as we have it now, is couched in a modernized form of the language in which the oldest hymns were originally composed" (1929:76-77).

2. PLURALITY OF ṚGVEDIC RECENSIONS

2.1. In most recent discussions, a historical fact of utmost importance is often overlooked, namely that the text of the *Ṛgveda* that we have today is not necessarily the original *Ṛgveda*. What we have is only one recension (*saṁhitā*) of the *Ṛgveda* compiled several centuries after the hymns were composed by the Ṛgvedic sages. After the hymns were composed over a period of several generations of sages, they remained for a long time as a kind of floating oral literature preserved through family traditions. At a later time, about 700-800 B.C., several compilers or editors collected these hymns, arranged them according to certain principles, and prepared various editions, along with corresponding "word texts" (*pada-pāṭha*), by analyzing the words of the orally preserved hymns. The available recension of the *Ṛgveda* is ascribed to the compiler-sage Śākalya and his school. Śākalya is quoted by Pāṇini,[2] the *Ṛk-Prātiśākhya*,[3] and texts such as the *Aitareya* and *Śāṅkhāyana Āraṇyaka*s,[4] and could not possibly have been a mythical figure.

2.2. Other recensions of the *Ṛgveda* did exist but are lost today. We hear of the Bāṣkala recension which had a few more hymns than Śākalya's recension. The *Ṛk-Prātiśākhya* and the *Śaiśirīya-Śikṣā* belong to the Śaiśirīya recension.[5] Having studied the treatment of *Abhinihita Sandhi* in the *Ṛgveda* in the *Ṛk-Prātiśākhya* by Śaunaka, Rastogi (1957:29) suspects that "possibly Śaunaka had a text before him which was not totally identical to the extant one." The *Śāṅkhāyana Āraṇyaka* belongs to the Śāṅkhāyana tradition. There are a few mantras in this text which cannot be traced to Śākalya's recension and belong most probably to the Śāṅkhāyana recension of the *Ṛgveda.*[6] The *Aitareya* and *Śāṅkhāyana Āraṇyaka*s refer to the Māṇḍūkeya recension which preceded Śākalya's recension and differed from it in certain respects.[7] Patañjali speaks of the well made recension (*sukṛtā saṁhitā*) of Śākalya but also says that there are twenty-one different recensions of the *Ṛgveda.*[8] Pointing to a hymn of three verses and three verses of three other hymns which do not have their *pada-pāṭha* prepared by Śākalya, Ghosh (1951:231) claims that "hymns and verses could have been added to the *Ṛk-Saṁhitā* even after the date of Śākalya." We also know of other redactors of the *Ṛgveda* such as Rathītara (Śākapūṇi) and Bharadvāja Bāṣkali (Bishnupada Bhattacharya 1958:12).

2.3. Several Indologists have expressed doubts as to the originality of the present text of the *Ṛgveda*. Bloch (1970:1-2) remarks: "The editors of the Ṛgveda, as we have it, have partially adapted to their own dialects various religious texts composed in another dialect." Oldenberg (1962:28) acknowledges that "the study of Śaunaka's work [that is, the *Ṛk-Prātiśākhya*] affords us the proof that *from that time on* [author's emphasis] the Vedic hymns, protected by the united care of grammatical and religious respect for letters, have suffered no further appreciable corruptions." However, worth noting are his comments on the preredaction textual transmission: "In some cases, isolated details of the additions of prior epochs were caught and clung to with felicitous acumen; in others, no hesitation was had in wiping out of existence entire domains of old and genuine phenomena to suit half-correct theories, so that the most patient ingenuity of modern science will only be able to restore in part what has been lost" (1962:27). Oldenberg (1962:26) reminds us that "the collection was re-corrected on repeated occasions. It is conceivable enough that thus the original structure, yes, even the existence itself of special hymns was often injured, effaced, or destroyed." Basing his conclusions on metrical evidence, Macdonell (1916:14) inferred that there must have been a period of transition between the original composition and the final redaction of the *Ṛgveda* by Śākalya. Meillet (1912-13) has discussed the changes effected by the editors of the *Ṛgveda* with respect to *h* (>*bh* and *dh*) and *r* (>*l*) in accordance with their dialect which preserved the distinction between Indo-European **r* and **l*.[9] Bloch (1970:2) rightly observes that the editors "could not, however, touch the grammatical forms without seriously modifying the aspect of the religious language borrowed by them." *Thus, most of the changes which occurred during the early "natural" oral transmission were euphonic and phonetic and were mostly unconscious changes, not deliberate alterations.* Recently, Esteller has devoted a number of publications to the question of the reconstruction of the original *Rgveda.*[10] He calls the text of Śākalya a "palimpsest," a written-over text, and remarks: "The bamboo-curtain of a Ṛgveda-Saṁhitā palimpsest was woven twenty-five centuries ago by the skillful and well-meaning but deformingly reforming, updatingly defacing (and thus palimpsesting) paṇḍita-mentality of the Saṁhitā-kāra agency in the Śākala-śākhā tradition" (1968:16; 1969:17). It is quite natural that not every scholar would agree with Esteller, for example Abhyankar (1969). Particularly when he alleges that the redactors made "conscious" grammatical changes and changes in the word order, etc., we must reject his views. For a critique of Esteller's theories, see Mehendale (1975).

3. RECENSIONAL VARIATION: AN EPISTEMOLOGICAL PROBLEM

3.1. We must, at this stage, face up to certain important epistemological questions. It must be said that all our knowledge about the *Ṛgveda* rests primarily on the recension of Śākalya as we have it preserved today. To what extent can we say that Śākalya's text exactly represents the phonology of the original *Ṛgveda*?

Let us consider a simple example. The *Ṛgveda* as we have it changes intervocalic *ḍ* and *ḍh* into *ḷ* and *ḷh*. The retroflex *ḷ* is not known to the classical Sanskrit. Many scholars have considered *ḷ* as forming a genuine part of the original *Ṛgveda*. However, Bloch (1970:156), with his characteristic caution, says: "Does it go back directly to the Vedic language? We dare not affirm it." Concerning the *l*/*ḷ* variation in Prakrits, he remarks: "Paiśācī is the only dialect which is shown as normally converting the intervocalic Skt. *l* into *ḷ*. But it should also be noted that the rules concerning the same date from Hemacandra, that is to say from a very late epoch. The texts, written in other dialects, do not have a uniform sign. Thus, as could be expected, the meridional manuscripts have *ḷ*, while those of the North keep *l*" (1970:154). Burrow (1971:556) refers to the continuation of *ḷ* into Pāli. However, that also could very well be a result of Dravidian influence on the Sinhalese text-transmission of Pāli, and we do not know whether the "Indian Pāli" had this sound before being transported to Ceylon. In this connection, then, it is important to note Vaidya's remarks concerning the text-transmission of the *Ṛgveda* as we know it. He points out that the Ṛgvedic Brahmins at present are to be chiefly met with in the Deccan and the Koṅkaṇ and in some parts of southern India. The *Ṛgveda* is the most important and the oldest of all the Vedas, and yet its adherents are so few and found only to the south of the Vindhyas. Vaidya (1930:56) attributes the existence of the retroflex sounds *ḷ* and *ḷh* in the present text of the *Ṛgveda* to this predominantly southern (or rather Dravidian) tradition of oral transmission and suggests that these sounds "are not to be found in the recitation of the Black Yajurveda and probably not in the recitation of the other Śākhās of the Ṛgveda itself now extinct."[11] I value Vaidya's remarks more as a caution. I shall try to show later that substitution of the sounds *ḷ* and *ḷh* in the available recension of the *Ṛgveda* for intervocalic *ḍ* and *ḍh* originated most probably in the oral traditions in northeastern India and did not exist in the Ur-*Ṛgveda*.

3.2. How far can we say that the distribution of retroflex sounds and their statistics in the Śākalya text represent the reality of the original *Ṛgveda*? Let us consider the example of different recensions of the Yajurveda which are fortunately available to us. As Hoffmann (1960:176-77) shows, the Maitrāyaṇī text has the reading *páṇyāt páṇyatarā*, while the Kāṭhaka text reads *pányāt pányatarā*. One may note that the Kāṭhaka text itself has *páṇyāt páṇyatarā* beside *pányāt pányatarā* without cerebrals (Bloomfield and Edgerton:vol. 2, p. 87). This helps us realize that in a chaste epistemology we must begin with all these variant readings of different recensions and then reconstruct the original reading if we can. The important point is that the original—the prerecensional original—is not given to us but must be reconstructed from what *is* given to us. After comparing a few passages from the Kāṭhaka, Kapiṣṭhala-Kaṭha and Maitrāyaṇī recensions, Kuiper (1958:350) concludes: "The parallel texts [Kāṭhaka and Kapiṣṭhala-Kaṭha] leave no doubt that *krūḍayati* is a variant of the rather rare verb *kūḍayati* or *kūḷayati*, for which the Maitrāyaṇī version has substituted the current synonym *vidahati*." This example brings forth various different issues. We not only have phonological alternation, but occasionally a recension substitutes a "current synonym" for an archaic expression. By the same token, it is perfectly logical to argue that after a lapse of several hundred years, the received product of the precodification oral tradition may exhibit rather more "current" phonological features.

3.3. Comparing the identical hymns in the Śaunakīya and the Paippālada recensions of the *Atharvaveda*, one finds the same principle of recensional variation:[12]

1. *tanvo adya dadhātu me* (*Ś-AV*, 1.1.1)
2. *tanvāmadhyā dadhātu me* (*P-AV*, 1.6.1)
3. *vidmo ṣvasya mātaram* (*Ś-AV*, 1.2.1)
4. *vidmo hyasya mātaram* (*P-AV*, 1.3.1)
5. *apo devīrupa hvaye* (*Ś-AV*, 1.4.3)
6. *apo devīrupa bruve* (*P-AV*, 1.2.3)

Thus, we cannot consider either of the two recensions as automatically representing the original *Atharvaveda*. With respect to this variation, Acharya (1971:97) says: "As has been rightly pointed out by Hoffmann (IIJ, XI, 1968, pp. 1-10), these variations should be regarded as authentic in as much as they are taken to form the peculiarities of the particular *śākhā* to which they belong." Quite instructive is Edgerton's (1936:507-8) discussion of the two recensions of the *Saddharma-puṇḍarīka*.

3.4. Coming back to the *Ṛgveda*, we have the biggest hurdle to overcome. The fact that one recension is all that we have creates an illusion that this is *THE Ṛgveda*. However, even the existing exegetical literature on the *Ṛgveda* indicates that there must have been serious differences in various text-traditions. Apart from differences in wording (as we have seen in the two recensions of the *Atharvaveda*), the different recensions and oral traditions must have differed in the pronunciation of sounds, too. Uvaṭa, the commentator of the *Ṛk-Prātiśākhya*, says that while some traditions pronounced an *anusvāra* in the sequence *māṁśćatve*, other traditions pronounced a nasal vowel, i.e., *mā̃śćatve*.[13] As I have discussed elsewhere, the *anusvāra* varied from a voiced consonant-or-vowel pronunciation to an unvoiced nasal fricative according to the testimony of the *Ṛk-Prātiśākhya* itself.[14] The *Ṛk-Prātiśākhya* (13.15-16) refers to the variation in the pronunciation of the diphthongs *e, o, ai* and *au* in the different schools of reciters.[15] It is extremely important to note that the so-called dental series *t, th, d, dh, n* is in fact *danta-mūlīya* 'produced at the roots of the teeth' or alveolar, according to the *Ṛk-Prātiśākhya* (1.9), while for all other known traditions, including Pāṇini, these are dental (*dantya*) sounds. The *Prātiśākhya*s vary on the pronunciation of *r, ṛ,* the *k*-series and several other sounds. It may be noted that the *Ṛk-Prātiśākhya* (1.11) quotes the view of Vedamitra that *ḍ* and *ḍh* were in fact palato-velars (*jihvā-mūlaṁ tālu ca*)[16] and not retroflexes. This brings these sounds closer to the Iranian *źd* and *źdh*. The more we study these variations, the more ignorance we must confess concerning our knowledge of the exact original sound system of the Vedic texts. In terms of our epistemology, whatever Vedic literature is given to us is already in the form of various sectarian recensions of a relatively later period, a period in which variation of pronunciation existed among different regions and different Vedic schools. We do not have a presectarian recension of any of the Vedic texts, let alone the prerecensional original compositions of the Vedic poets.

3.5. The strength of retroflexion in Indo-Aryan has always varied in different periods of Indian linguistic history and in different regional and social dialects. Based on a study of modern Indian languages, Southworth (1974:211-12) concludes that the strength of retroflexion was greater in the northwest and in the South and that it was weaker in the northeastern regions. However, that may not have been the case for all periods of Indian linguistic history. Patañjali shows that the local Prakrit had words like *goṇī, yarvāṇa, tarvāṇa, āṇapayati, diṇṇa*, etc., for the Sanskrit words *gauḥ, yad vā naḥ, tad vā naḥ, ājñāpayati* and *datta.*[17] These are examples from the eastern part of the country during the immediate post-Mauryan period. Looking at the Aśokan inscriptions, one finds that the eastern region shows a higher frequency of cerebrals as compared to the western region. Bloch (1970:6) points out that *r* plus dental gives a dental in the west, and a cerebral in the east, but while we find "*ṇ* in the west, in the east there is no cerebral *ṇ* nor a palatal *ñ*." This is confirmed by the extensive work of Mehendale, who says: "The dentals under the influence of *r* or *ṛ* are cerebralised in all inscriptions of Aśoka, save those in the West (only *rdh* is cerebralised so early as that in the West). The influence is observed in the West mostly from the beginning of the Christian era. The dentals *t* and *th* in combination with *ṣ* are, however, cerebralised at all places since the earliest times" (1948:xxiii); and, "It will be observed that the Western dialect is the least affected by cerebralisation" (1948:18).

3.6. Even within the same region of northwestern India, there were variations. Thus, while the Prakrit Dhammapada knows the distinction between *n* and *ṇ*, Konow (1936:607) remarks: "It is, however, remarkable that the

Kurram casket inscription which contains a quotation of a canonical passage written in practically the same language as Dhp. [i.e., Dharmapada] , has no trace of the Dhp. distinction between *n* and *ṇ*. We are left with the impression that Dhp. in this respect represents a normalization which may be due to the influence of another literary Prakrit, or belongs to a limited territory within the area, where the treatment of *n* was different." While the Aśokan inscriptions do show a regional variation in the strength of retroflexion, one may contrast the treatment of literary Prakrits by the Prakrit grammarians. The cerebralization of dentals under the influence of *r, ṛ* or a sibilant is noticed by the grammarians as a feature common to all Prakrits, without any dialectal variation (Mehendale 1948:xxxi).

3.7. Very often the orthography of documents is misleading. With respect to literary Prakrits, Ghatage (1941:23) points out: "By a convention the editors write *ṇ* everywhere in purely Mahārāṣṭrī works. But the practice of the Jaina scribes to write initially *n* is followed in editing works in AMg [i.e., Ardhamāgadhī] and Jain Mahārāṣṭrī. It has been suggested that initial *n* became alveolar and was felt by some as dental and by others as cerebral." In the Kharoṣṭhī inscriptions "*n* is cerebralised both initially and medially... *n* is also preserved in many cases" (Mehendale 1948:304). With respect to this variation, Konow (1929:ciii-civ) writes: "The impression left by this state of affairs is that intervocalic *ṇ* and *n* had the same sound, at least over the great part of the territory, and that the sound was probably a cerebral. The significance of the two letters was consequently lost sight of, the traditional writing acting as a check on the development of a consistent orthography." This is quite comparable to Grierson's (1906:18) remarks on the modern Paiśācī languages: "Cerebral and dental mutes appear to be interchangeable.... So far as I can ascertain...there is no real distinction between these two classes of mutes, and there is only one class...a semi-cerebral....To some, these sounds appeared to be dentals and were recorded as such; and to others they appeared to be cerebrals and were recorded as such....Identical words are quite frequently recorded with cerebral letters by one and with dental letters by the other."

3.8. Along with these perceptual and orthographic problems, we must also bear in mind certain other difficulties. We find that one passage of *Samayasāra* has the reading *hodi* (<*bhavati*), while the other has *havadi.*[18] The meter is not affected by either reading. This is also true of retaining or dropping the intervocalic voiced stops and of inserting or not inserting the euphonic weak *y*. For example, while the printed text of Kundakunda's *Pañcāstikāya* (verse 49) reads *egattappasādhagam* (<*ekatvaprasādhakam*), the commentary

Tātparyavṛtti of Jayasenācārya has the reading: *eyattapasāhagam*. The morphology of the two readings is the same, but they represent two different phonological states. Similar other variants are: text *pagāsagā*, commentary *payāsagā* (verse 51); text *padhāṇā*, commentary *pahāṇā* (verse 53); text *hoi*, commentary *havadi* (verse 54); *bhaṇidam*, commentary *bhaṇiyam* (verse 54).[19] These are variations of the "same" text. These are all phonological variations of the kind which does not seriously affect the morphological or the syntactic content of the text or its metrical form, and hence they seem to have been tolerated with ease by the reciters, scribes, and readers. But this creates an intolerable situation for a critical historical understanding of what the exact phonology of the original text might have been, and such a picture of the original phonology often remains a matter for scholastic reconstruction. What is important is the fact that such variations as those mentioned above did exist and were treated as a matter of little concern, and were not normally viewed as seriously altering the basic text.

3.9. In the oral transmission of the Vedic texts, there are two important historical periods. The first is the period of their composition and scattered retention by the early Vedic families. This is a "natural" period of oral transmission. The second is the scholastic period of recension-making and also of the growing formalism concerning the magical potency of the exact pronunciation. The text of the Vedic compositions must have been quite fluid, in both the synchronic and diachronic sense, in the prerecensional oral traditions. Otherwise we would not be able to explain the vast differences between the various recensions of the Vedic texts. But the postrecensional period of oral transmission must be clearly distinguished from this early fluid state. In this later period, monumental intellectual efforts have been made to preserve the recensions intact in the form given them by the various sectarian schools. These schools devised meticulous methods of oral recitation like the *pada-pāṭha* and textual permutation-combinations (*vikṛti-pāṭha*). Particular sectarian phonetic treatises were written to "freeze" the then existing sectarian pronunciation. These traditions of formal recitation have been kept up until recent times, and they maintained an "idealized text" more or less intact. I call it an idealized text because, in fact, the pronunciation of the same Vedic text in Kashmir, Bengal, and Tamilnadu was never the same. Regional variation in Sanskrit pronunciation has been ably described by Chatterji (1960*a*). I shall take up the concept of fluidity of the preredactional oral traditions later in detail.

4. *AITAREYA-ĀRAṆYAKA* (3.2.6): ITS IMPLICATIONS

4.1. Scholars who attempt reconstructions of the original *Ṛgveda* have not paid much attention to discussions of the various redactors and editors of the *Ṛgveda* found in the *Aitareya* and *Śāṅkhāyana Āraṇyakas.* Though it is true that a large number of these discussions on the notion of *saṁhitā* are somewhat mystical and mythological, there are still a very significant number of linguistic discussions. The participants in these discussions, such as Śūravīra Māṇḍūkeya, Hrasva Māṇḍūkeya, Mākṣavya, Śākalya, and others, clearly represent the first known generation of scientific linguistic thinkers and are quoted directly as respected authorities by the *Prātiśākhya*s and by Pāṇini.[20] We cannot underestimate the value of their linguistic speculations simply because they also engaged in the study of mystical and theological aspects of speech. Discussions such as those of "colors," "deities," and "castes" of sounds and other linguistic items are found even in the *Prātiśākhya*s. What follows is an examination of certain passages related to the question of retroflexion found in these texts.

4.2. How far are the retroflexes in the existing *Ṛgveda* historically authentic? In my view, they are authentic only in that they represent the sounds in the text as it was preserved in the Śākala school at the time of the formation of this particular recension. Beyond this point we are entering the field of reconstruction. If we know that at a certain point there had been doubts and differences concerning Ṛgvedic retroflexion, then we should be less categorical about ascribing retroflexion existing in the present text to the original. Such an indication is to be found in the *Aitareya-Āraṇyaka* (3.2.6 [Keith: 256-57]):

> Now Kṛṣṇahārīta proclaims this secret doctrine, as it were, regarding speech to him. Prajāpati, the year, after creating creatures, burst. He put himself together by means of the meters, therefore it is the *Saṁhitā.* Of that *Saṁhitā* the letter *ṇ* is the strength, the letter *ṣ*, the breath, the self. He who knows the verses in the *Saṁhitā* and the letters *ṇ* and *ṣ*, he knows the *Saṁhitā* with its breath and its strength....*IF HE IS IN DOUBT WHETHER TO SAY IT WITH AN Ṇ OR WITHOUT AN Ṇ, LET HIM SAY IT WITH AN Ṇ. IF HE IS IN DOUBT WHETHER TO SAY IT WITH AN Ṣ OR WITHOUT AN Ṣ, LET HIM SAY IT WITH AN Ṣ.*
>
> *HRASVA MĀṆḌŪKEYA SAYS: "IF WE REPEAT THE VERSES ACCORDING TO THE SAṀHITĀ, AND IF WE RECITE*

> *(ACCORDING TO) THE TEACHING OF MĀṆḌŪKEYA, THEN THE LETTERS Ṇ AND Ṣ ARE OBTAINED FOR US."*
>
> *STHAVIRA ŚĀKALYA SAYS: "IF WE REPEAT THE VERSES ACCORDING TO THE SAṀHITĀ, AND IF WE RECITE (ACCORDING TO) THE TEACHING OF MĀṆḌŪKEYA, THEN THE LETTERS Ṇ AND Ṣ ARE OBTAINED FOR US."*

This is an extremely important passage. Regarding the doctrine, which is repeated twice, Keith (p. 257, fn. 9) comments: "The sayings are identical and apparently this is intended to denote that the doctrine received universal acceptance." I do not quite agree with Keith's interpretation. The passage does indeed emphasize and preach the doctrine of *ṇ* and *ṣ*, but it also implies at the same time that there were others who did not accept this doctrine and doubted the correctness of this practice.

4.3. The word *saṁhitā* could theoretically mean either a *sandhi* "joint, euphonic combination, juncture," or it could mean the whole "continuous, undivided" text, as contrasted with the later scholastic *pada-pāṭha*. If the word *saṁhitā* refers only to the "joints," then the passage would refer only to *ṇ* and *ṣ* produced at the joints or boundaries of contiguous words. This would imply that while Śākalya and Māṇḍūkeya recensions read *mo ṣu ṇaḥ* (<*mā* + *u* + *su* + *naḥ*), there were other traditions which doubted the existence of *ṇ* and *ṣ* in such cases and perhaps read **mo su naḥ*. However, in this interpretation of *saṁhitā*, the dispute would not refer to those instances of *ṇ* and *ṣ* which are in some sense "internal" or intrinsic to the words and do not depend on word junctures. However, whether internal or external, the sounds *ṇ* and *ṣ* in the present *Ṛgveda* passage *mo ṣu ṇaḥ* and in words like *viṣṇave* or *vidatheṣu* are produced by the same basic historical rules which cover both the internal and external *ṣ* and *ṇ*. The word *saṁhitā* is frequently used for "whole" texts, and we know that Śākalya and Māṇḍūkeya collected these "continuous texts" and then subjected them to a scholastic analysis. The analytical "word-text" was not given by the early oral tradition. The creation of the "word-text" is the very first attempt to analyze and explain the orally received songs. As I shall demonstrate later, during the preredaction period, these Vedic texts were passed down as unanalyzed sequences and were split into words later by scholars like Śākalya. But the historically significant fact that different redactors disagreed even on the words in a given sequence clearly indicates the manner in which these "continuous texts" were transmitted. Many phonetic changes took place in these continuous sequences at a time when there was no clear awareness of word boundaries, and hence the distinction between "internal" and "external" is somewhat irrelevant with respect to pre-*pada-pāṭha* oral transmission. For instance, it seems that the original sequence **āpṛṇosi* diverged later into *āpṛṇosi* and *āpṛṇoṣi*. Then the sequence *āpṛṇosi* was analyzed as *āpṛṇaḥ* + *asi*, and the sequence *āpṛṇoṣi* was looked upon as a single verbal form from the root *pṛ-* (*Vedic Variants*, vol. 2, p. 152).[21] In my view the above passage gives an indication of how the phonologies of orally preserved continuous texts had diverged. But even in the limited interpretation of *saṁhitā* as "juncture," the passage indicates that there were people who considered the *saṁhitā* text to be **mo su naḥ* rather than *mo ṣu ṇaḥ*. I shall demonstrate later that this latter kind of retroflexion is irregular even in the existing Vedic recensions.

4.4. We have to examine this passage carefully. Contrary to Keith's suggestion, I see in this passage an indication that even at this stage, there were some people who suspected that the original *Ṛgveda* might have been *aṇakāra* "without *ṇ*" and *aṣakāra* "without *ṣ*." The very phrase "*if* we say [i.e., follow in recitation] the teaching of Māṇḍūkeya, *then* the letters *ṇ* and *ṣ* are obtained for us" seems to indicate that if the teaching of Māṇḍūkeya was not followed, then these sounds were not obtained in the *Ṛgveda*. This would be parallel to the statement: "If we accept the Maitrāyaṇī tradition, then the forms *páṇyāt páṇyatarā* are *saṇakāra* 'with *ṇ*,' but if we follow the tradition of the Kāṭhaka reciters, these forms could be *aṇakāra* 'without *ṇ*'." Thus, the presence or absence of *ṇ* is not absolute with respect to the Ur text of the *Yajurveda* but is definitely a recension-specific phenomenon. Kuiper (1958: 350) claims that *krūḍayati* of the Kāṭhaka text is replaced by the "current synonym" *vidahati* in the Maitrāyaṇī text. One could similarly argue that the nonretroflexed forms *pányāt pányatarā* of the Kāṭhaka text (which occur beside the retroflexed forms *páṇyāt páṇyatarā*) are replaced by the more current retroflexed forms in the Maitrāyaṇī text. Thus one could claim the following probable development: The Ur-*Yajurveda* had **pányāt pányatarā*. By the time of the Kāṭhaka recension, retroflexion had made its way into the oral tradition but was still quite unstable. Thus, the Kāṭhaka text has retroflexed forms beside nonretroflexed forms. By the time the Maitrāyaṇī recension was codified, or in the region where it was codified, the process of cerebralization had advanced further, and hence the Maitrāyaṇī text shows only the retroflexed forms. I am, by no means, claiming that this was the actual development. The example simply shows the possibility and perhaps the necessity of such a reconstruction.

4.5. The *Aitareya-Āraṇyaka* passage indicates that not every school accepted the teachings of the Māṇḍūkeya tradition. At any rate, the *Aitareya-Āraṇyaka* was known to Pāṇini, who also quotes Śākalya (Keith:intro., p. 25; p. 73). The Māṇḍūkeya tradition preceded Śākalya, who accepted its prescription of *ṇ* and *ṣ* in the recitation of the *Ṛgveda*. We must recognize the fact that whatever the statistics of any retroflex sound that we collect from Śākalya's text, they do not directly represent the Ur text of the *Ṛgveda*. They only reflect the phonology of Śākalya's recension.

4.6. What is the intention in saying that *ṇ* is the strength and *ṣ* is the breath of the *saṁhitā*? I have discussed this issue in another article (Deshpande 1976:177, fn. 12). Briefly stated, we may ask why only these sounds posed a doubt in the minds of some of the reciters. The answer to this question requires a careful study of the *Prātiśākhya*s and the Indo-Iranian sources of the Sanskrit retroflexes. The only retroflex sounds known to the *Prātiśākhya*s are the retroflex series *ṭ, ṭh, ḍ, ḍh,* and *ṇ*, and the sibilant *ṣ*. Occurrence of *ḷ* and *ḷh* as intervocalic allophones of *ḍ* and *ḍh* in the present text of the *Ṛgveda* very well could be a recension-specific phenomenon, as is certainly the case with the different recensions of the *Yajurveda.*[22] The vowel *ṛ* is not retroflex, but either *jihvāmūlīya* 'produced at the root of the tongue' (velar or uvular?) or alveolar; and *r* is either dental or alveolar.[23] It seems quite conceivable that *r* and *ṛ* (that is, *ərə*), which are also found in Iranian, continued from Proto-Indo-Iranian to the *Prātiśākhya* period in their non-retroflex form. We see that *ṇ* and *ṣ* are relatively more unpredictable in their distribution, while *ṭ, ṭh, ḍ, ḍh* are more stable by this time. One conceivable reason for this is that sounds such as *ḍ* and *ḍh* are often reflexes of the Proto-Indo-Iranian clusters such as **źd* and **źdh*. Since **ź* did not exist in later Indo-Aryan, there was no question of confusing *ḍ* and *ḍh* with any existing **ź* clusters. Similarly, the operation of Fortunatov's Law reducing IE **l* plus dental to a Sanskrit retroflex was complete by the pre-*Prātiśākhya* period, leaving only very few examples of such clusters behind, e.g., Vedic *gáldā-* beside *gárdā-*. However, *n>ṇ* and *s>ṣ* are changes which have numerous exceptions and spontaneous occurrences (see section 9.1-5). Though the statement of the *Aitareya-Āraṇyaka* directly relates only to the sounds *ṇ* and *ṣ* (which are peculiarly involved in mechanical metrical retroflexion), the historical source of this concern must be related to the entire question of retroflexion at an earlier period of the language. It seems difficult for me to accept a stage in the history of ancient Indo-Aryan at which the phonemes *ṭ, ṭh, ḍ* and *ḍh* had emerged but *ṇ* did not exist, since the shifts caused by principles like Fortunatov's Law should apply equally to *ṇ*. Though the Prakrit languages show different stages in the distribution of *ṇ* in different times and regions, it is hard to separate the general emergence of *ṇ* from that of the other retroflex consonants. The case of *ṣ* is slightly different, since there are many Prakrits known to us which had other retroflexes but did not have *ṣ*. This sound is found only in the northwestern Prakrits and Dardic. Emergence of *ṣ* is predominantly due to a partial modification of the Indo-European *ruki* rule in Sanskrit, and apparently did not cover all the Indo-Aryan dialects. These points will be discussed in detail later.

4.7. If at a late period, such as that of the *Aitareya-Āraṇyaka* (about 700 B.C.), retroflexion of *ṇ* and *ṣ* was being debated among various schools of Ṛgvedic recitation, what kind of a phonetic picture can we reconstruct for the Ur-*Ṛgveda*? The methodological problems in such an attempt are numerous. We not only have to follow a method similar to "internal reconstruction," but perhaps must also go beyond it, since we are dealing with purely Aryan compositions in a form which was fixed and handed down to us after Aryan-non-Aryan convergence was well advanced. Thus, we have to figure out the impact of such convergence on the oral text transmission and try to eliminate those features which are most probably results of this convergence. It is difficult for me to accept the view that the retroflex phonemes existed in the Ur-*Ṛgveda* composed before the Aryan-non-Aryan convergence, and that several centuries later, when in fact Aryan-non-Aryan convergence was well developed, a dispute arose among the traditional reciters about the authenticity of these sounds. Theoretically, either we have to accept the hypothesis that retroflexion existed in the Ur-*Ṛgveda*, and then was lost or retained in different recensions, or we accept a nonretroflexed Ur-*Ṛgveda* with the development of retroflexion in particular recensions and the retention of a less retroflexed or nonretroflex text by certain "conservative" schools of Vedic recitation.

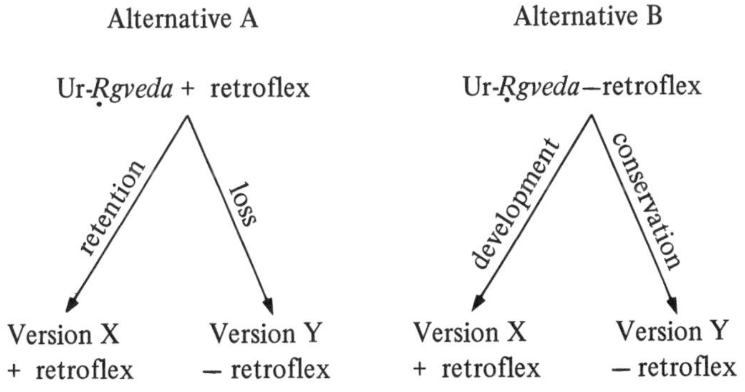

Of these two alternatives, alternative B is more logical and suits the historical situation in India as we know it from various sources. It also resembles previous attempts by Mehendale (1968:96-97, 101) to reconstruct certain "pre-Sanskrit" stages. In his analysis Mehendale depends primarily on the formal linguistic method of "internal reconstruction," and hence calls the reconstructed stage "pre-Sanskrit." In my view, we have the additional sociolinguistic complexity of Aryan-non-Aryan convergence to consider, and I find that his "pre-Sanskrit" stage often closely resembles my concept of "preconvergence" Sanskrit in which the original *Ṛgveda* was composed.

4.8. In the period between the composition of the hymns (1500-1200 B.C.) and the work of the compilers of various recensions (about 700 B.C.), the retroflex sounds had developed in Sanskrit and had become an organic part of it. Since the Vedic hymns were being preserved and transmitted orally, often without awareness of word boundaries in continuous sequences, the phonology of the language of the reciters naturally had an impact on the transmitted recensions. We may compare this with the different pronunciations of Pāli texts in different countries of Southeast Asia. Thus, at a later time the dispute arose quite naturally as to whether the orally transmitted texts should or should not, and did or did not, have these retroflex sounds, the "innovations of Indo-Aryan" as Bloch calls them. Known variations in the different recensions of the *Atharvaveda, Yajurveda*, and even within the text of the *Ṛgveda* as we have it, are definitely a result of this natural instability of oral literature before it is codified. I shall discuss examples of such variation later on.

4.9. It is extremely important to note that the present recension of the *Ṛgveda* is based on the northeastern recension of the Māṇḍūkeya tradition which had established itself in Magadha. The Aryan character of groups like the family of Māṇḍūkeyas is a matter of suspicion (see Kosambi 1947 and 1950). There is even some question concerning the origin of the Aitareya and the Kauṣītaki traditions. While the tradition considers Aitareya to be the son of a slave woman, there is a possibility that the founder of the Kauṣītaki tradition was a purified *vrātya*, a non-Vedic Aryan (see Banerjea 1963: 164ff). We also know from other sources that there were severe disputes over the question of retroflexion in Magadha in ancient times. Rājaśekhara informs us in his *Kāvyamīmāṁsā* (*Gaekwad's Oriental Series* edition, Baroda, 1916, p. 50) that the king of Magadha, Śiśunāga banned retroflex sounds in his harem. Specifically he banned the following eight sounds: *ṭ, ṭh, ḍ, ḍh, ś, ṣ, h,* and *kṣ*. It has been suggested that Śiśunāga was a non-Indo-Aryan person. Deb (1922 and 1925) argues that he was an Elamite, while A. Banerji Shastri

(1936-37) contends that he was a Nāga prince. Whatever the origin of the Śiśunāgas, it is extrememly significant that there were poignant disputes over retroflexion in Magadha even up to the fifth century B.C.

5. PRE-ṚGVEDIC ARYAN-NON-ARYAN BILINGUALISM?

5.1. The postulation of the Ur-*Ṛgveda* without any retroflexes may at first seem to be a radical departure. However, if we reinterpret the facts known about the *Ṛgveda* and its transmission–as well as the history of the development of religion, mythology, and social structures–in the light of what we have learned from studies of contemporary bilingualism, then we find support for such a hypothesis.

5.2. We cannot deny that the incoming Aryans came in contact with certain non-Aryan people in India. There is ample evidence for such contacts. Though in most cases the Ṛgvedic Aryans are seen as generally hating the non-Aryans (i.e., the Dāsas, Dasyus, and Paṇis), occasionally we find that some Aryans did enter into political and military alliances with some non-Aryans, as evidenced by the War of Ten Kings. We may also agree that some of the Vedic sages like Kavaṣa Ailūṣa had non-Aryan sounding names and were a sort of "converted" non-Aryan (cf. Kuiper 1967:87). Moreover, one may perhaps agree with Kosambi (1965:82-83) that the unorthodox birth-account of Vasiṣṭha indicates his non-Aryan origin. One may perhaps also accept that there is grafting of an Austroasiatic myth onto one of the Indra myths (Kuiper 1967:87). On rare occasions, the Ṛgvedic poets praise gifts from certain non-Aryan kings like Bṛbu. I am not sure exactly how to interpret and evaluate these "sporadic reports" of Aryan-non-Aryan contacts, but even if one were to accept them all as reflecting historical facts, the general picture in the *Ṛgveda* is still one of Vedic Aryans in this early period hating non-Aryans and despising their religion and speech. Apart from "implications" and "assumptions," there is not the slightest evidence in the *Ṛgveda* of any large-scale bilingualism or social or religious convergence of Vedic Aryans with non-Aryans. For a critique of Kosambi's views on such early non-Aryan influence in the *Ṛgveda*, see Brough (1953:xiv ff.).

5.3. Emeneau (1974:93) not only proposes that there was "extensive bilingualism," but that "Sanskrit was handed down at some early period by a majority of speakers who learned it as a second language, their first language being Dravidian. In their first language, there were contrasting dentals and retroflexes; in Sanskrit, or we had better say pre-Indo-Aryan, there were only dentals and some allophones of dentals 'backed' toward the Dravidian retroflex position. Assignment of these backed allophones to their own Dravidian retroflexes was easy for native Dravidians." Emeneau himself begins this statement with "we must postulate," and it must be said that there is no positive evidence to turn this postulation into a historical assertion, particularly with respect to the period of the composition of the *Ṛgveda. It is impossible to believe that the composers of the Ṛgveda had Sanskrit as their second language and had some Dravidian language as their first language.*

5.4. However, the linguistic "process" suggested by Emeneau is quite significant, and I shall try to demonstrate in this paper that this process must have taken place in the text transmission of the *Ṛgveda*, rather than prior to the original composition of the Vedic hymns. Emeneau himself and others have adduced strong evidence for the socioreligious and linguistic convergence of the Indo-Aryans with indigenous populations at a somewhat later period.

5.5 Brown (1953:131) describes the Vedic Aryans as being "more like their linguistic and religious kinsmen, the Iranians, than like their eastern Indian contemporaries." Even by the time of the composition of the *Ṛgveda*, the Vedic Aryans had hardly moved to the east of the *sapta-sindhu* "land-of-the-seven-rivers" region, i.e., Panjab. Chakladar (1928, 1961-62) claims that the Vedic culture originated in the eastern region and that the Ṛgvedic Aryans had "occupied" the eastern lands during the composition of the *Ṛgveda*. This is absolutely untenable. The attitude of the Vedic Aryans toward the non-Aryans as seen in the *Ṛgveda* is also very significant. The general attitude is characterized by a strong hatred toward the non-Aryans, whether they are Paṇis, Śabaras, or Dāsas; very rarely are there any references to them as friends.[24] The battles with the non-Aryans are called *Dasyu-hattyā* 'slaughter of the Dasyus'.[25] The non-Aryans are hated for being *mūra-deva* 'with dummy gods', *śiśna-deva* 'phallus-worshippers', *adeva* 'godless', etc., and are particularly accused of being *mṛdhra-vācaḥ* 'with obstructed speech'.[26] It is unreasonable to think that such attitudes prevailed when the Aryans entered India and yet did not continue up to the composition of the *Ṛgveda.* These are the attitudes of the Ṛgvedic poets themselves. How could the Ṛgvedic poets expressing these attitudes be Sanskrit-speaking Dravidians, assuming that some of the non-Aryans mentioned in the *Ṛgveda* are in fact Dravidians?

5.6. This does not contradict the existence of several words in the *Ṛgveda* which can only be explained as loanwords from Dravidian and Munda languages. The loanwords do indicate contact with non-Aryan peoples, something known even from Ṛgvedic descriptions and which cannot be doubted. But at the same time, these loanwords are not sufficient to indicate the degree of intensity of Dravidian or Munda influence on the Vedic language which Kuiper would like to see in them. Even if one accepts the entire lists of Ṛgvedic loanwords provided by Kuiper and Burrow,[27] the total number of these words in the *Ṛgveda* is still not as great as the number of Indo-Aryan loanwords in Tamil or in Southeast Asian languages. S. Vaidyanathan has put together a list of Indo-Aryan loanwords in old Tamil, and not only do those words show clear signs of Tamilization, but the oldest Tamil grammar, *Tolkāppiyam*, has explicit rules for changing Sanskrit sounds into Tamil sounds.[28] Rarely did Tamil sounds change because of Indo-Aryan loanwords. Ganesan (1971:152) has discussed in detail the sound changes involved in Sanskrit loanwords in Tamil. He remarks: "This [Tamil] phonemic system, which has been fairly well stabilised by the corresponding phonemic orthographic system, makes substantial changes inevitable in words which are borrowed from other languages, especially from a language like Sanskrit, which has a much different phonemic system. Practically whenever a word is borrowed, a phonological change is almost obligatory and the word gets a new form." (Also see Miranda 1977:264).

5.7. Ananthanarayana (1970:66) basically accepts the concept of bilingualism as proposed by Emeneau and Kuiper but derives a slightly different conclusion: "It is suggested that in the first period of this contact bilinguals were recruited chiefly from the native population. Support for such an assumption is provided in the greater number of Sanskrit loans as opposed to an insignificantly small number of Dravidian words in Sanskrit." This would mean that more Dravidians accepted Aryan words than Aryans accepted Dravidian words. This also suggests that the initiative for adoption was more prominent on the part of the native non-Aryan than on the part of the incoming Aryans.

5.8. Kuiper's account of the specific role of bilingualism in the development of retroflexion is somewhat less convincing. He says that the Aryans–bilingual Aryans–recognized a phonemic contrast between dentals and retroflexes in the *foreign language*, and then they–the Aryan bilinguals–interpreted allophones of their Aryan language in terms of the *foreign phonemic system*. Early Aryans, even if there were some bilingual Aryans, most probably did not reinterpret allophones of their own Aryan language in terms of a *foreign phonemic system*. On the contrary, they would have adapted foreign loanwords to their own native Aryan phonology. Kuiper himself (1958: 351) says that there were such "Sanskritizations": "Sanskritization of foreign words by substitution of *tr, dr* (or *rt, rd*) for *ṭ, ḍ* is well attested in the classical language." He (1958:352) carries this tendency further into the *Ṛgveda*: "The explanation of *kartá-* as a Sanskritization of *kāṭá-* would seem to be rather the only one that is phonetically admissible according to our present knowledge." If one accepts Kuiper's explanation of *kartá-<kāṭá-*, which is by no means certain,[29] it would appear that the Ṛgvedic Aryans did think of *rt* as being more native to the Aryan tongue, and *ṭ* as being somewhat foreign. (I would agree with this inference but would consider *kāṭá-* in the *Ṛgveda* as being a post-*Ṛgveda* development in the oral tradition at a period when *rt* and *ṭ* were both a part of the "native system of the redactors.")

5.9. Further support for the implausibility of Kuiper's view may be gained by examining the British treatment of retroflexes in loanwords from Indian languages. "It is no wonder," says G. S. Rao (1954:39), "that he (i.e., an Englishman) wrote and spoke each Indian word as he heard it with his English ears." He points out (p. 47) that "the laws of English phonetic usage operated in the transition of Indian words into English." The British had to use hundreds of local Indian words in English. However, they did not pick up the retroflex sounds, but rather approximated them to other English sounds. Thus, the Marāṭhī place name *puṇe* became "Poona" and *khaḍkī* came to be called "Kirkee." Similarly, the presence of non-Aryan loanwords in the *Ṛgveda* is insufficient to indicate that the intensity of contact with the non-Aryans was sufficient to cause phonetic and phonemic alterations in the Aryan language in that early period. W. J. Gedney's extensive work on "Indic Loan-words in Thai" also indicates that, despite the existence of hundreds of loanwords and a living tradition of Pāli texts, the Thai language did not adopt Indian sounds and that the same is true of Cambodian and Burmese.[30] It may be noted that several words in the *Ṛgveda* claimed by Southworth to be Dravidian loanwords have no retroflexes in their Ṛgvedic form, but their supposed Dravidian cognates do have retroflexes.[31] This appears to me to be the expected direction of change.

5.10. On the other hand, a study of Indian English and English loanwords in Indian languages reveals the other side of the process. When native speakers of Indian languages heard English with their "Indian ears," English alveolars were naturally felt to be closer to Indian retroflexes and were approximated to Indian retroflexes. For example, English 'table' becomes *ṭebal* in Marāṭhī. Also compare other English words in Marāṭhī: 'government' *gavharnmeṇṭ*, 'bottle' *bāṭlī*, 'taxi' *ṭæksī*, 'post' *posṭ*, etc. T. Grahame Bailey (1938:109) says: "The modern Indian hearing alveolar *t* and *d* considers them cerebrals." Thus, the adoption by Indian speakers of English as a second language has caused changes in English in India, but hundreds of loanwords in British English from Indian languages have not altered the phonemic structure of English as spoken by the British. "The historic statement of the problem of loan phonology is that a speaker of L_T, in perceiving and reproducing the sounds of L_S, substitutes for them those that he takes to be 'closest' in his own language" (Lovins 1974:240).

5.11. However, Emeneau recognized this problem. Instead of saying that Aryans interpreted allophones of Proto-Indo-Aryan in terms of the foreign Dravidian phonemic system, he considers it more logical to assume that the Dravidians interpreted allophones of Proto-Indo-Aryan in terms of their native phonemic system in the process of adopting the foreign Aryan language. In his excellent paper "Bilingualism and Structural Borrowing," as early as 1962, Emeneau (1962*a*:434) points out that "the evident Dravidianization of Sanskrit in some of its structural features must lead to the partial conclusion that a sufficient number or proportion of certain generations of Sanskrit speakers learned their Sanskrit from persons whose original Dravidian linguistic traits were translated into Indo-Aryan and who provided the model for succeeding generations." Ananthanarayana (pp. 60, 67) essentially agrees with Emeneau and points out that, numerically, more Dravidians than Aryans must have participated in the transmission of the Aryan language, and he refers to the example of retroflexes in Indian English.

5.12. In his 1962 article, Emeneau proposed an essentially correct "sociolinguistic process" for the development of retroflexion in Sanskrit, but he was not sure of the exact chronology or of the intensity of this process with reference to the early Vedic texts. Were Dravidians participating in a significant proportion in the use of Sanskrit in the pre-Vedic times? In 1962 Emeneau (1962*a*:434) was not sure: "Nothing is known of the Indian social and political structure into which the Sanskrit-speaking invaders made their way or of the changes brought about by incursion, or of the numbers of the invaders, or even how many bands were involved; was there intermarriage of the invaders and the aborigines, or concubinage, or the use of aboriginal nurses? And above all, who were the bilinguals—a significant number of the invaders or of the aborigines or of both? We shall never know the answers to these questions in detail." In 1974, making essentially the same sociolinguistic argument, Emeneau (1974:92) claims more confidently that such a process must have taken place before the composition of the *Ṛgveda*, and agrees with Kuiper that retroflexion in the existing *Ṛgveda* is an indication of pre-Ṛgvedic Dravidianization of the Aryan language.

5.13. In my view, this is the beginning of confusion. I entirely agree with Emeneau that retroflexion in the existing *Ṛgveda* can and must be explained by the Dravidianization of the Aryan language. However, the fact that the present text of the *Ṛgveda* has retroflexion does not at all prove that there must have been retroflexion in the original compositions of the *Ṛgveda*, and hence does not prove that the original compositions of the *Ṛgveda* must also be posterior to Aryan-Dravidian convergence. The totality of evidence provided by Kuiper for pre-Ṛgvedic "convergence" is, in my opinion, still insufficient to prove that the original *Ṛgveda* was composed by Sanskrit-speaking Dravidians. Even two hundred loanwords, if we accept the entire list of Kuiper, a few non-Aryan sounding names, and an Austroasiatic myth grafted onto the Indra myth, do not prove that the composers of the *Ṛgveda* were already Aryanized Dravidians. Kuiper (1967:87) mentions the Vedic sage Kavaṣa Ailūṣa as a non-Aryan accepted by the Aryans. However, this is not a norm. The *Aitareya-Brāhmaṇa* (2.8.1) shows that initially the Vedic Aryans rejected him by saying: "How could this bastard born of a *dāsī*, a cheat who is not a brahmin be initiated into the sacrifice with us." He was accepted only when he "saw" a hymn. The Southeast Asian languages would definitely compete and fare better in all these respects. Those languages have hundreds of Indic loanwords, entire Hindu and Buddhist religious and cultural systems, and also the living continuity of Pāli texts, and yet these languages did not develop retroflexion. This is a very strong counterexample to Kuiper's claims.

5.14. The difference between the sages who composed the original hymns of the *Ṛgveda* and the editor-redactors of the later Vedic recensions is quite considerable. Oldenberg (1973:39) points out that "in the ancient times for instance, the Aryans of the Northwestern part of further India had not yet entered deep into the borderland by the use of force and were still the brothers and almost neighbours of the Zarathustrian Aryas of Iran, or rather of the Aryans who were opponents of Zarathustra. The situation changed in later times. Hinduism spread all along the peninsula with the Aryan character ever weakening, with the blood of the natives mingling in their blood stream in a never-ceasing continuity and with an infinite series of shades of complexion, ranging from the fair to the dark, observable in the populace....It will not do to mix up the old times with the modern times." He further differentiates the Ṛgvedic Aryans from the later bearers of the Hindu culture: "The linguistic affinities between the Veda and the Avesta...have been compared with the dialectal refinements of the inscriptions of Aśoka; or, if we, on the other hand, compare the Vedic gods with the Avestic gods, or if we compare the Vedic sacrifice, the priests and the special designations of priests with their counterparts in the Avesta, and then, on the other side, if we observe what revolutionary changes have been introduced in the gods and in the sacrifices by the cult of Viṣṇu or Śiva...and how the externals as well as the inner meanings of religion have been profoundly changed...we can say that there has been here a development corresponding to that between the script of the Aśokan rock-edicts and the present Devanāgarī script" (Oldenberg 1973:34-40). Nothing that Kuiper has come up with can change the picture thus depicted by Oldenberg and turn the composers of the original Vedic hymns into Sanskrit-speaking Dravidians.

5.15. In order to be able to evaluate the arguments put forward by Kuiper to establish "bilingualism" between the Vedic Aryans and Dravidians, we must take into account a recent analysis of bilingualism by Nadkarni (1975: 681), who points out that "structural borrowing at all levels of language, including syntax (the so-called 'deepest' level), can take place irrespective of the factor of social prestige, but solely as a consequence of 'intensive and extensive' bilingualism with a certain time-depth....By 'extensive' bilingualism, I mean a situation in which bilingualism is coextensive with the entire community, as in the case of K[annad] S[arasvat] Ko[nkani] speakers. By 'intensive' bilingualism, I mean a situation in which a community whose mother tongue is language A is not merely conversant with language B, but actually uses it for a wide range of purposes in the course of normal, everyday living. Extensive bilingualism, in particular, seems necessary for structural borrowing to be stabilized, since it renders all the members of the community more or less equally receptive to influences and traits of the non-native language–which, first randomly, and gradually more and more regularly, find their way into their mother tongue. A linguistic innovation has a strong chance of stabilizing itself in a language if it attracts no notice, and therefore no resistance from speakers, particularly in the early stages. This is possible only in situations of extensive bilingualism."

5.16. A more recent study of Konkani loan-phonology by Miranda (1977: 264) asserts: "Konkani dialects in the Dravidian area have been under the influence of the local Dravidian languages not only with respect to vocabulary but also with respect to phonology and syntax. However, they have succeeded to a large extent in molding the Dravidian loan words to their own phonological and morphological patterns." This is an important conclusion. With Nadkarni's precise definitions and with Miranda's conclusions, we must question Kuiper's theory of loan-phonology in the *Ṛgveda*. We must say that the non-Aryan languages were not only not prestige languages for the Aryans, but that the Aryans, by referring to their obscure language (*mṛdhra-vācaḥ*) as they did, hated the non-Aryans. There is no evidence that there existed "extensive" or "intensive" bilingualism with the non-Aryans. Kuiper's data can at best indicate "sporadic" bilingualism, but is utterly insufficient to indicate "extensive" or "intensive" bilingualism as defined by Nadkarni.

Without making distinctions between the different kinds of bilingualism and the differences in their impact, the concept of bilingualism as used by Kuiper not only remains vague but leads to misleading conclusions which are not supported by the cases of loan-phonology referred to earlier.

5.17. The Ṛgvedic Aryans were always conscious of the Aryan-non-Aryan distinction (*ārya-varṇa* versus *dāsa-varṇa*). This unity among the Aryans does not have to be total racial unity, since the Indo-Europeans must have mixed with the local populations of Iran and other countries before they reached India. This unity is more a matter of cultural perception. However, things changed in later times. The original Vedic Aryans settled in northwestern India and gradually expanded to the east and to the south. The original non-Aryan population underwent Aryanization, and the non-Aryan religion and culture were gradually "Sanskritized."[32] Eventually the earlier distinctions lost their value.

5.18. Already in the *Brāhmaṇa* texts, we hear of dark-complexioned Brahmins proving themselves academically superior to the fair-complexioned Brahmins (Chatterji 1962:69-70). The author of the *Mahābhārata* is the dark-complexioned (*kṛṣṇa*) Vyāsa, who is also the progenitor of the Kauravas and Pāṇḍavas, and has himself a non-Aryan mother. It is to him that the Indian tradition attributes the beginning of the process of editing and redacting the Vedas. With the prominence of Kṛṣṇa, the "dark" Lord, the *Mahābhārata* shows the emergence of dark Aryanized non-Aryan personalities in religious and political life.[33]

5.19. The Māṇḍūkeya tradition had reached Magadha in the east by the time Śākalya compiled his recension.[34] Looking at this drastically different sociolinguistic situation, it is not at all surprising to see that the reciters of the *Ṛgveda* at this late "postconvergence" period were influenced by the retroflexion in their own post-Vedic speech. What is in fact more surprising is that, even after such a long time, there were at least some people who doubted the existence of retroflexion in the original text of the *Ṛgveda*.

5.20. Based on the references in the *Brāhmaṇa* and *Āraṇyaka* literature, we may be able to speculate on the possible reasons for this divergence of opinion on the authenticity of retroflexion in Sanskrit. As the Indo-Aryans entered India and moved eastward, it seems that some of them always thought of the "good old days" in the "golden age in the western homelands," while others gradually accepted the changes that were taking place in their life while they were moving eastward. Thus, in terms of purity of speech, some Aryans kept looking back to the northwestern trails from which they had come. This is clearly supported by the *Brāhmaṇa* statements that those who want to learn the best speech go to the north(west), since the best known speech is spoken in the north(west).[35]

5.21. On the other hand, there were traditions such as that of Māṇḍūkeya, which had moved eastward as far as Magadha, and which were fighting for the recognition of "new" or "more eastern" features such as retroflexion as a part of the orally transmitted *Ṛgveda.*[36] We know now that Śākalya accepted the tradition of the Māṇḍūkeyas in the matter of retroflexion; and hence, in the text of the *Ṛgveda* as we have it today, the retroflex sounds are there as an integral part of it. It is also important to note that Śākalya did not accept all the conventions of the Māṇḍūkeyas and introduced some new changes. The text of the Māṇḍūkeya recension of the *Ṛgveda* was perhaps somewhat "closer" to the original *Ṛgveda* than was Śākalya's recension.[37] Figure 1 shows the geography of these shifts.

6. EMERGENCE OF RETROFLEXION IN PREHISTORIC INDO-ARYAN

6.1. The fact that the pre-Śākalya tradition of the Māṇḍūkeyas, upon which Śākalya relied for his retroflex sounds, had already reached Magadha in the east, and the fact that the *Kauṣītaki-Brāhmaṇa* (7.6) considers the northwestern dialect to be relatively purer are of great significance to the linguistic history of ancient India. At this point, one has to consider the theory of successive migrations of Aryans into India. As I shall demonstrate, this theory is quite relevant to the historical development of retroflexion in Indo-Aryan.

6.2. Hoernle (*A Grammar of the Eastern Hindi*, 1880, pp. xxx-xxxii) postulated the existence of two early Aryan groups in North India, the Māgadhan and the Śaurasenī, representing two waves of Indo-European language speakers, of which the Māgadhans were the older. This idea was supported by Grierson (*Imperial Gazetteer of India,* vol. 1, pp. 353-59) and given an ethnological footing by Risley (*The People of India*, London, 1915, p. 55). In addition to social institutions and languages, the shape of the skull, according to Chanda (1916:59) shows that "the Indo-Aryans of the outer countries originally came from an ethnic stock that was different from the stock from which the Vedic Aryans originated."[38] However, Chanda's "inner" and "outer" are different. For him the second wave of post-Vedic Aryans bypassed the "inner Vedic Aryans" and went into the "outer" regions. For Chakladar (1928, 1961-62), the second wave of post-Vedic Aryans pushed the Vedic Aryans into the "outer" lands and itself occupied the "inner" lands. To me, Burrow's conception of the west to east movement of the two waves of Aryans seems to be more reasonable than the other theories. Oldenberg also supported and elaborated this idea and pointed out that "probably

FIGURE 1

GEOGRAPHICAL LOCATIONS OF THE ORIGINAL *ṚGVEDA* AND LATER RECENSIONS

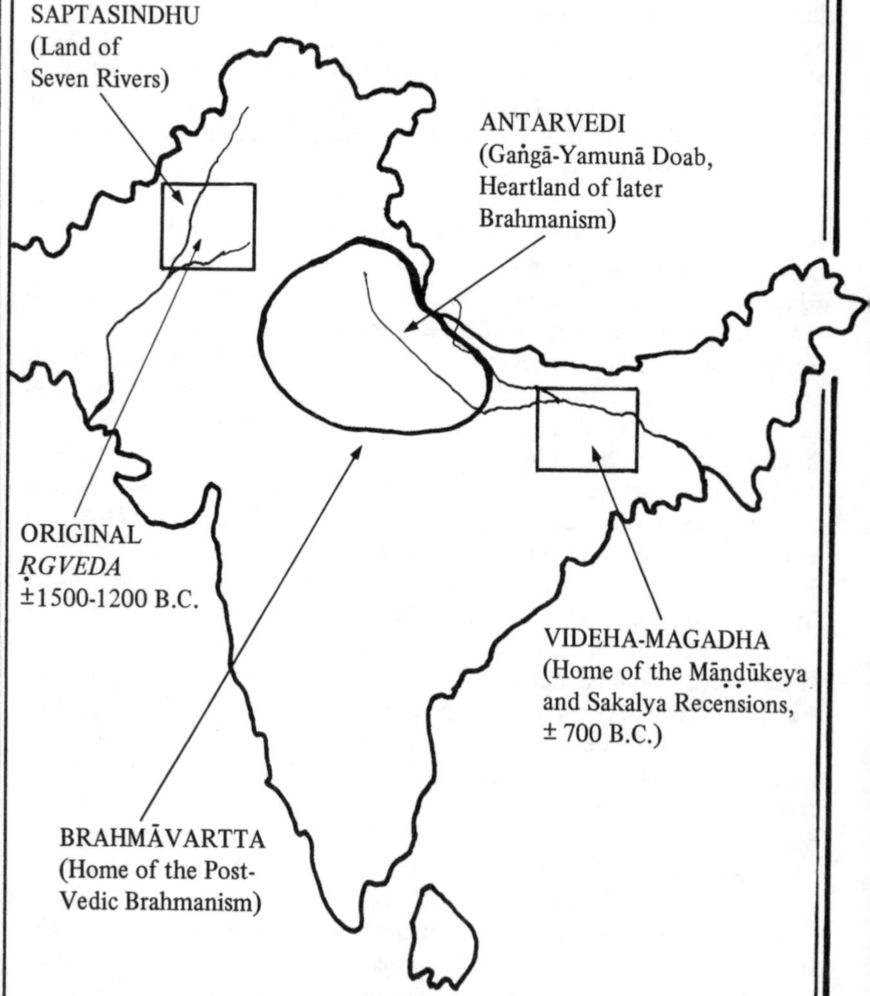

the first immigrants, and, therefore, the farthest forward to the east...are those tribes...the Aṅga and Magadha, the Videha, the Kosala and Kāśī."[39] He (1882:9) also claims that it was the second wave that produced the Vedas. This theme has been linguistically upheld by Meillet who shows that the Vedic dialect, like the Iranian, is an *r*-only dialect in which the Indo-European **l* merged into *r*, but the dialect of the redactors of the Vedas was an *r* and *l* dialect, where the original Indo-European **r* and **l* were retained; the redactors of the Vedic texts have put this *l* back into some of the Vedic words, where the original Vedic dialect had an *r* (Meillet 1912-13; Bloch 1970:2). In later Prakrits we clearly see the eastern Prakrit, Māgadhī, developing into a pure *l*-only dialect; whereas the western and particularly the northwestern dialects, almost devoid of *l*, represent the early *r*-only dialect (Mehendale 1948:297).

6.3. The difference between the *r*-only dialect, the *r-l* dialect (and possibly an *l*-only dialect) is quite significant. Burrow (1972:535), in a recent study, says that "the *r*-dialect prominent in the early Ṛgveda shares a common change (of *s*>*ś*) with Iranian. It is unlikely to have undergone this change independently and consequently we must assume that it took place when a group of Indo-Aryan migrants were still in contact with Iranians....On the other hand, those Indo-Aryans who preserved the distinction between *r* and *l* had already departed to India, and so they were unaffected by it. The speakers of the *r*-dialect were the latest comers on the Indian scene and there ensued a mixture of the two dialects."

6.4. The significance of the *r-l* dialect moving earlier into the interior of India and eventually on to eastern areas like Magadha (where dialectally all *r*>*l*) is further enhanced by its connection with the operation of Fortunatov's Law. The law states that in the group IE **l* + dental in Sanskrit, the *l* is dropped and the dental is changed to a cerebral (cf. Skt. *paṭa-* 'cloth', OSlav. *platino*, Russ. *polotno*). Here an original Indo-European cluster yields a single retroflex, while *r* + dental in Middle Indo-Aryan always results in a cluster, dental as well as retroflex (cf. Skt. *vartate*, Pkt. *vaṭṭai* beside *vattai*) (Burrow 1972:531). The particular connection of Fortunatov's Law with *l*-clusters means that this Law cannot apply in dialects, such as Iranian and Ṛgvedic Sanskrit, where every IE **l*>*r*. Burrow (1972:531) has admirably defended Fortunatov's Law against all the objections raised by different scholars and has tried to date the beginning of its operation on the basis of the Ṛgvedic word *gáldā-* 'dripping, flow', beside the *r*-dialect form *gárdā-* The fact that *gáldā-* is still found in the *Ṛgveda*, while later Sanskrit has the derived root *gaḍ*, implies, according to Burrow (1972:542), that "the change according to

Fortunatov's Law took place during the period of early Ṛgveda, so that it was possible for one form antedating that change to be preserved in that collection."

6.5. One could argue in a slightly different way. The Ṛgvedic dialect, as pointed out by Meillet and by Burrow himself, is an *r*-only dialect, like the Iranian, and hence was not logically subject to Fortunatov's Law. Thus, the retroflexes in the existing *Ṛgveda*, which can only be accounted for by Fortunatov's Law, may be viewed as a part of "normalization" by the later redactors belonging to the *r-l* dialect in tandem with the replacement of the Ur-Vedic *r* by *l* from their own dialect. This further separates the Ur-*Ṛgveda* dialect from the direct impact of Fortunatov's Law.

6.6. The fact that the *r*-only dialect of the northwest and the *r-l* dialect (and possibly the *l*-only dialect) of the northeast underwent different developments with respect to retroflexion can be demonstrated by referring to the early inscriptional Prakrits. In particular, Mehendale's monumental *Historical Grammar of Inscriptional Prakrits* throws a flood of light on this problem. It must be remembered that the major portion of northern India, until this time, had not been invaded by any people other than Indo-Iranians, and hence the linguistic development reflected up to this period is very much an affair of Indo-Iranian and the pre-Aryan languages of India. Mehendale (1948:18) points out that the cerebralization of dentals in the environment of *r* is predominant in the eastern inscriptions, but "it will be observed that the western dialect is the least affected by cerebralisation." Bloch (1970:6) and Burrow (1936:419, 421) also emphasize this point. Burrow (1936:421) further points out that even within the northwestern region, the Niya Prakrit in the further west preserved *r* + dental clusters better than the northwestern Aśokan inscriptions. He concludes that phonologically the language of Niya presents a pronouncedly more archaic aspect than that of Aśoka, namely, by better preserving consonant combinations such as *rt, rdh,* etc.(Burrow 1936: 422). Extremely significant is Burrow's final conclusion:

> Obviously we cannot derive the Niya Prakrit from the language of Aśoka, and the most natural conclusion to draw from the fact that phonetically it is better preserved is that its home is to be sought further to the west. Because it seems clearer (then as now) that the more remote a language was in the direction of the North-West the less liable it was to phonetic decay (1936:422).

In a strange way, Burrow's conclusion reads like a translation of the passage from the *Kauṣītaki-Brāhmaṇa* (7.6) discussed earlier.

6.7. It is thus clear that Fortunatov's Law primarily applied to the *r-l* dialect (or the *l*-only dialect) of pre-Vedic Aryans who later moved into eastern India and not to the *r*-only dialect of Iranians and Vedic Aryans of northwestern India. Oldenberg discusses in detail the question of the non-Vedic eastern Aryans and says that they confronted the non-Aryans long before the Vedic Aryans did.[40] At this point a discussion of the *Vrātya* Aryans becomes quite relevant. For a detailed discussion of the *Vrātya*s and their eventual assimilation into the later Aryanized society, I shall only refer to the treatment by K. A. Nilakanta Sastri (1967),[41] but I shall quote an important observation by Kimura (1927:26ff.): "The Vrātyas being Aryans outside the Vedic circle always fought against the Vedic Aryans. Therefore, their sympathy naturally tended towards other tribes beside the Vedic Aryans." The *Baudhāyana Dharma-sūtra* (1.1.32-33) gives us a clear idea of how the "Vedic Aryans" viewed the "mixed Aryans" of the "outer" regions: "The inhabitants of Ānartta, of Aṅga, of Magadha, of Saurāṣṭra, of the Deccan, of Upavṛt, of Sind, and the Sauvīras are of mixed origin. He who has visited the countries of the Āraṭṭas, Kāraskaras, Puṇḍras, Sauvīras, Vaṅgas, Kaliṅgas [or] Pranūnas shall offer a Punastoma or Sarvapṛṣṭhī sacrifice [for purification]." Thus the early Aryan dialect of the *Vrātya*s came into closer contact with non-Aryans and this gives us a necessary sociolinguistic motivation for the operation of Fortunatov's law in their dialect. But it must be remembered that this development is essentially different from the history of the Vedic *r*-dialect. In later times, there occurred an obvious dialectal mixture which is reflected in classical Sanskrit.

6.8. The evidence of Prakrit inscriptions is significant in another respect as well. It has been claimed by Burrow (1971:557), quite rightly, that "the cerebral sibilant *ṣ* is differentiated from the other cerebrals in that its ultimate origin goes back to a much earlier date. The development of *s* to *ś* (whence Indo-Aryan *ṣ*) is common to Indo-Aryan and Iranian." It may be observed that despite a few cases of *ṣ* as a spontaneous retroflex (cf. Burrow 1971: 557) and a few cases to be derived by Fortunatov's Law (Burrow 1971:543-44), the sound *ṣ* in Sanskrit is primarily an extension of the Indo-Iranian palatal *ś*, itself derived from the Indo-European **s* by the *ruki* rule, and is generally not in any way connected with Fortunatov's Law. This law applies to the *l* dialect of the pre-Vedic eastern Aryans, while the development of the Indo-European **s* into the Indo-Iranian *ś* by the *ruki* rule, essentially a development within the Indo-Iranian *r* dialect, is preserved in the northwestern inscriptional Prakrits.

6.9. It has been pointed out by many a scholar that of all the Prakrits, only those of the northwest preserve the triple distinction between *ś*, *ṣ* and *s*.[42] It may be hard to determine whether or not the phonetic development of [*ṣ*] by an extension of the *ruki* rule had already taken place by the time of the Ur-*Ṛgveda*. It seems more probable that the western *r*-dialect of the Vedic Aryans had allophones of *s* and *ś* which were reinterpreted later, after the dialect mixture, as a separate phoneme *ṣ* parallel to the retroflexes *ṭ*, *ḍ*, etc., derived by Fortunatov's Law in the eastern dialect. In the same way, the later Sanskrit rule of *n*>*ṇ* due to preceding *r*, *ṛ* or *ṣ* may have its origin in the western dialect. This may be one of the reasons why the early western Prakrit inscriptions have *rt*, *rd*, etc., for eastern *ṭ*, *ḍ*, etc., but have *ṇ* corresponding to eastern *n* (Bloch 1970:6).

6.10. However, at the time of the composition of the original *Ṛgveda*, the western dialect of the Vedic Aryans most probably had nothing more than cerebral allophones of *ś* and *n*, and also perhaps of *t*, *d*, etc., in clusters with *ś*, which were later identified with eastern retroflexes and interpreted as phonemes by the later mixed population. Thus, *ṣ* in the word *deveṣu* comes from an extension of the *ruki* rule in the western Aryan dialect, while *ṣ* in *bhāṣate* is the result of the operation of Fortunatov's Law from an Indo-European cluster **ls*, cf. Lith. *balsa*- 'voice'. While in early stages of Indo-Aryan these two instances of *ṣ* seem to have had two different origins in two different dialects, in later Sanskrit they are interpreted as belonging to the same phoneme.

6.11. A study of inscriptional Prakrits also helps us clear another problem with respect to the existing recension of the *Ṛgveda*. This is the problem of the origin of the retroflex sounds *ḷ* and *ḷh* for intervocalic *ḍ* and *ḍh* in Śākalya's recension of the *Ṛgveda*. Most scholars take for granted the existence of these sounds in the *Ṛgveda*. I have already referred to Vaidya's view that these sounds developed in the southern (Dravidian) recitational traditions. I disagree with this view. I think that like other eastern retroflexes, *ḷ* developed when the Ṛgvedic recitational traditions moved eastward in North India. Evidence to support this possibility comes from inscriptional Prakrits. Mehendale (1948:11) points out that, in inscriptional Prakrits, the "change *-ḍ->-ḷ-* occurs in the non-Western groups." His detailed statement is as follows:

> Medially the change *-ḍ->-ḷ-* or *-l-* is found in the East and North (and perhaps in the Center) in the days of Aśoka. It is next noticed in the Western inscriptions in the 1st cent. A.D. and in the Southern group in the 2nd cent. A.D. The change, therefore, seems to have gone from E (and N)→C→W→S (1948:272-73).

This is an extremely important statement. This shows that the change of *-ḍ-* to *-ḷ-* did not occur in the northwestern regions of India at the time of Aśoka or later. Pāṇini, who comes from the northwest and precedes Aśoka by about two centuries, does not have the sound *ḷ* in his Sanskrit. It is also a matter of great significance that his rules concerning the Vedic language do not have any indication of the existence of the sound *ḷ* in the Vedic texts known to him. In fact, in his rules like P.6.3.113 (*sāḍhye sāḍhvā sāḍheti nigame*) and P.8.3.54 (*iḍāyā vā*), he refers to Vedic usages such as *sāḍha* and *iḍā* without *ḷh* and *ḷ* for the intervocalic *ḍh* and *ḍ*, but the commentators like Bhaṭṭojī Dīkṣita quote the examples *sāḷhā* and *iḷā* (*Siddhānta-Kaumudī*:340, 348). It is a matter of great surprise that Thieme does not notice this point in his *Pāṇini and the Veda*. Pāṇini obviously knew Śākalya's *pada-pāṭha*, and hence it is quite surprising to find him not recording the existence of *ḷ* in that text. The *Ṛgveda-Prātiśākhya* also does not ascribe the sounds *ḷ* and *ḷh* to Śākalya, but it attributes them to Vedamitra (see note 16). Is it then conceivable that the version of Śākalya's *Ṛgveda* available to Pāṇini did not contain the sounds *ḷ* and *ḷh*? I think that we cannot simply brush aside this possibility.

However, accepting the other possibility that Śākalya's recension could indeed have had the sounds *ḷ* and *ḷh*, we may be able to explain the probable origin of these sounds in the eastern recitational traditions. It is quite possible that the Śākalyas had the sounds *ḷ* and *ḷh* in their own dialect and the question whether they unconsciously introduced these sounds in the orally preserved texts is a legitimate question (see note 16). Yaska is not too far removed from the *pada-kāras* like Śākalya, and he often doubts their *pada*-divisions and proposes his own. Mehendale (1965:13) has given a very convincing argument to prove that Yāska had the sounds *ḷ* and *ḷh* in his own dialect:

> In *Nirukta* 7.16, Yāska cites Rv. 1.1.2 and in *N.* 8.8 he cites Rv. 10.110.3. In both these verses occurs the word *īḍyaḥ* which shows *ḍ* since it does not occur between the two vowels. But while paraphrasing it in his commentary, Yāska uses the form *īḷitavyaḥ* with *ḷ* since here it occurs between two vowels. Had Yāska not used *ḷ* in his speech, he would have paraphrased the Vedic word by *īḍitavyaḥ*.

If this argument is valid, and I think it is, then one may advance a similar argument to indicate a possibility that Śākalya's own dialect also had the sounds *ḷ* and *ḷh*. Sköld has indicated that Śākalya's word text for the *Ṛgveda* word *viḍvagam* (1.118.9) is *viḷu-agam* (see note 16). This raises a strong possibility that Śākalya's own dialect had these sounds. The *Aitareya-Āraṇyaka* passage discussed earlier shows that the Śākalya tradition followed the Māgadhan tradition of the Māṇḍūkeyas. The *Bṛhadāraṇyaka Upaniṣad* (3.1-9) has clear indications that Brahmins from the Kuru-Pañcāla region in north-central India were migrating to the eastern regions like Videha, and that a Vidagdha Śākalya was at the court of the king Janaka of Videha. Though the question of identity of this Vidagdha Śākalya with the Sthavira Śākalya of the *Aitareya-Āraṇyaka* and the redactor of the *Ṛgveda* is a matter of dispute (see *Aitareya-Āraṇyaka*, Keith:239ff; and *Vedic Index of Names and Subjects*, Macdonell and Keith:vol. 2, 368-69), the available information is quite sufficient to place the Śākalya tradition in the eastern regions of Videha and Magadha. Considering the above arguments it seems quite unlikely that the Ur-*Ṛgveda* of the northwestern region had the sounds *ḷ* and *ḷh*. Even in later times, there must have been other recensions of the *Ṛgveda* which did not have the change of *-ḍ-* and *-ḍh-* to *-ḷ-* and *-ḷh-*. For instance, while the available recension of the *Ṛgveda* (10.90.5a) reads *tasmād virāḷajāyata*, the *Yajurveda* version of the same hymn in the Mādhyandina recension (31.5a) reads *tasmād virāḍajāyata*. Is it not conceivable that the Mādhyandina reading represents a pre-Śākalya stage in the evolution of the Ṛgvedic oral traditions?

6.12. My interpretation of the phonological details of the early Prakrit inscriptions by itself would not have been sufficient for understanding possible early developments of Sanskrit sounds. But, whatever we know about Vedic, pre-Vedic, and Iranian from other independent sources fits amazingly well with the regional distribution of sounds in the early North Indian Prakrit inscriptions. One may reasonably suspect that this is not due to accident but is the result of natural developments. It seems interesting that the inscriptional Prakrits known from the third century B.C. should reflect a natural development of what we know to have been true of pre-Vedic and Vedic Indo-Aryans, and Iranians of a much earlier period. One of the reasons could very well be that after the arrival of the Indo-Aryans, this region was not seriously disturbed by any peoples other than Iranians until the invasion of Alexander the Great. Figure 2 sums up the results of the preceding discussion of the development of Indo-Aryan retroflexes.

7. *BRĀHMĪKARAṆA*: A GRADUAL TRANSFORMATION

7.1. The passage which is quoted from the *Aitareya-Āraṇyaka* also appears with slight differences in the *Śāṅkhāyana-Āraṇyaka* (8.11). It contains a significant additional statement which throws some new light on the process of

FIGURE 2

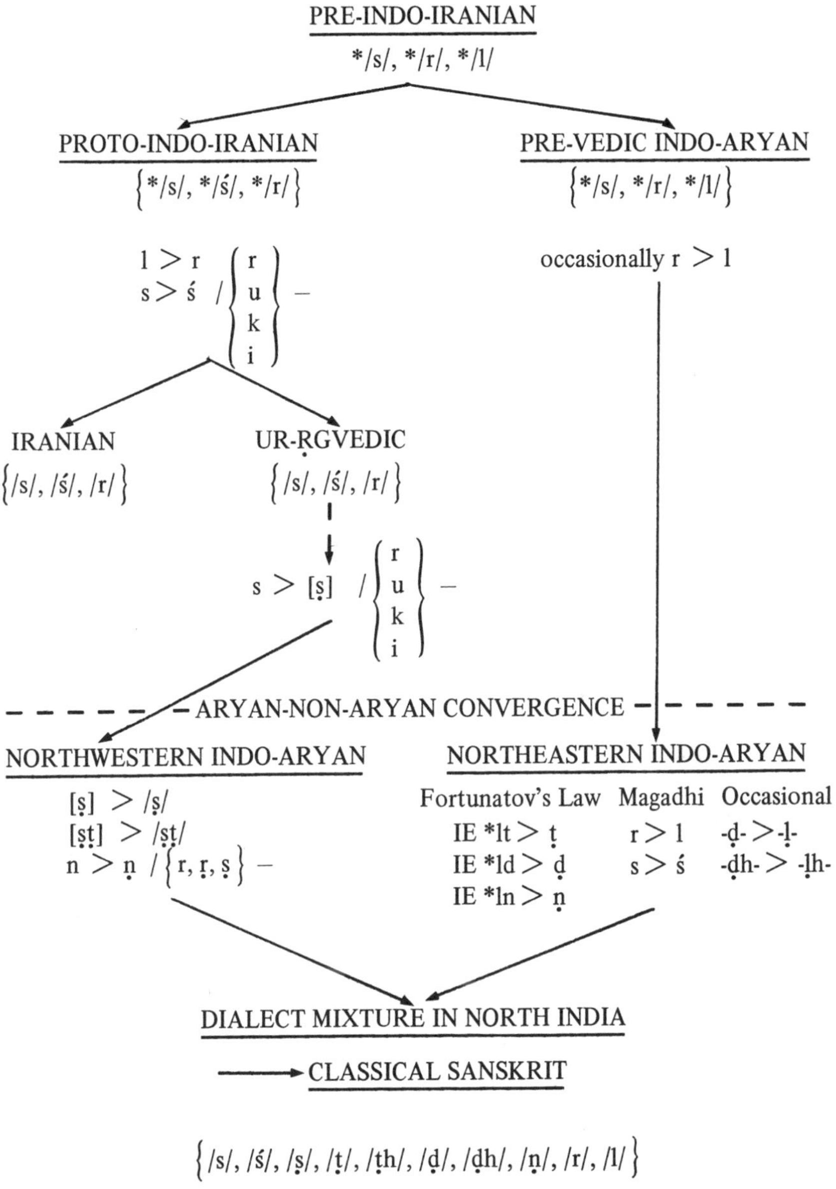
PRE-INDO-IRANIAN
*/s/, */r/, */l/
PROTO-INDO-IRANIAN
{*/s/, */ś/, */r/}
l > r
s > ś / {r, u, k, i} –
PRE-VEDIC INDO-ARYAN
{*/s/, */r/, */l/}
occasionally r > l
IRANIAN
{/s/, /ś/, /r/}
UR-ṚGVEDIC
{/s/, /ś/, /r/}
s > [ṣ] / {r, u, k, i} –
ARYAN-NON-ARYAN CONVERGENCE
NORTHWESTERN INDO-ARYAN
[ṣ] > /ṣ/
[ṣṭ] > /ṣṭ/
n > ṇ / {r, ṛ, ṣ} –
NORTHEASTERN INDO-ARYAN
Fortunatov's Law
IE *lt > ṭ
IE *ld > ḍ
IE *ln > ṇ
Magadhi
r > l
s > ś
Occasional
-ḍ- > -ḷ-
-ḍh- > -ḷh-
DIALECT MIXTURE IN NORTH INDIA
CLASSICAL SANSKRIT
{/s/, /ś/, /ṣ/, /ṭ/, /ṭh/, /ḍ/, /ḍh/, /ṇ/, /r/, /l/}

editing and redacting the older texts that had just begun in this period. After saying that some people have doubts about the existence of *ṇ* and *ṣ* in the *Saṁhitā*, and after advising that these sounds must be pronounced—as is done in the traditions of Māṇḍūkeya and Śākalya—the *Śāṅkhāyana-Āraṇyaka* (8.11, p. 315) says:

> *SIMILARLY, ONE SHOULD RECITE WHATEVER ELSE THERE IS, NAMELY ANY SPEECH, HISTORICAL TRADITIONS AND PURĀṆA-TEXTS, ONLY AFTER HAVING THEM TRANSFORMED INTO THE BRĀHMA [SYSTEM].*[43]

What is the process that is signified by the gerund *brāhmīkṛtya*? The compound verb *brāhmī-kṛ*, according to the standard rules of Sanskrit, should refer to a process of transforming something which is not *brāhma* into something which is *brāhma.*[44] The word *brahman* is often used in the contexts where its identity with *vāk* 'speech' is clearly expressed (*Aitareya-Āraṇyaka*: 1.1.1, 1.3.1, 1.5.1, etc.). The concrete manifestation of this *brahman* = *vāk* = 'speech' is seen by the *Aitareya-Āraṇyaka* (2.3.6) in terms of individual sounds such as stops (*sparśa*) and sibilants (*ūṣman*). This text uses developed phonetic terms such as *svara* 'vowel', *vyañjana* 'consonant', *sparśa* 'stop', *ūṣman* 'sibilant' and *antaḥsthā* 'semi-vowel'. The term *antaḥsthā* 'semi-vowel', which literally means 'standing in between [vowels and consonants?]' (cf. Pāṇini's *Śivasūtras*), possibly suggests that the formation of an ordered alphabet had already taken place (*Aitareya-Āraṇyaka*: Index 5). The *Aitareya-Āraṇyaka* actually uses the term *akṣara-samāmnāya*, which is the standard technical term for "ordered alphabet" in systematic works on Sanskrit phonetics and grammar.[45] This standardized alphabet, *akṣara-samāmnāya*, is called *brahma-rāśi* 'collection of *brahman* = speech' by the *Prātiśākhyas* and later by Patañjali.[46]

7.2. Thus, the gerund *brāhmī-kṛtya* most probably stands for the gradual process of "normalization" or "standardization" of the older oral texts in accordance with the norms of the Gangetic basin. The connection of this word with the name *brahmāvartta* for the Gangetic basin may be strongly suspected. This region becomes the home of standard speech by the time of the *Āraṇyakas*, in contrast to the northwestern frontier of India which was the homeland of the Ṛgvedic Aryans. Even Yāska seems to use the word *ārya* in a somewhat regional sense, i.e., inhabitants of *Āryāvartta* (often called *Brahmāvartta*), whose linguistic habits he distinguishes from those of *Kamboja* 'Eastern Iran, Western Punjab', *Surāṣṭra*, etc.[47] Patañjali also discusses the concept of standard speech, and defines it as the speech of the learned Brahmins of *Āryāvartta.*[48] Thus, it may be said that in the early centuries of the first millennium B.C. there took place in north-central India a gradual process of *brāhmīkaraṇa* 'normalization and standardization' of the older oral texts in accordance with the norms of *Brahmāvartta*. The location of this region also explains how, by this time, there had occurred a mixture of north-western and northeastern dialects in an essentially north-central region.

7.3. This process of "normalization" or "standardization" of orally preserved ancient texts is quite similar to what happened to the originals of the Sangam works which were composed in Ancient Tamil during the first three centuries after Christ, but which had their language altered and are now found in Cen-Tamiẓ redactions which must date from about 600 A.D. and later. Chatterji, who talks about this normalization, also speaks of a similar normalizing transformation in the case of the Vedic literature from its composition to its present preserved form and mentions several other cases of such transformations in the process of oral transmission.[49]

8. RETROFLEXION AND THE DEVELOPMENT OF THE BRĀHMĪ SCRIPT

8.1. In the context of the process of *brāhmī-karaṇa*, it is important to look at the origin and development of the Brāhmī script. Bühler (1895:84-85) has convincingly demonstrated the derivation of the Brāhmī script from Phoenician signs, and recently this has been supported by Dani and Mahadevan.[50]

8.2. The highly probable Phoenician origin of the Brāhmī script raises some interesting questions. The *Ṛgveda* speaks of a non-Aryan community called Paṇi, which is hated by the Aryans for being foolish, faithless, having obstructed speech and not worshipping the Aryan gods like Indra. But at the same time they are described as being well-established merchants who were rich and went in caravans and who undertook sea voyages for trading and gain (Rahurkar 1974:43ff.). Some scholars have identified the Paṇis of the *Ṛgveda* with the Phoenicians (Rahurkar:45-46; S. R. Rao 1972-73:6). At present, there is not sufficient evidence to establish such an identification, but the plausibility of the identification cannot be easily denied. In any case, the Phoenician language did not have retroflexion and hence could not have affected Aryan speech directly in that respect. The Phoenician language does have a contrast of emphatic and nonemphatic dental stops and sibilants, but the development of the Brāhmī script shows that Indians did not look upon these emphatic dentals as retroflexes.

8.3. It is interesting to see how the retroflex Sanskrit sounds could have gradually been represented through modification of the Phoenician signs for dentals. Sir Alexander Cunningham remarks that "it seems not improbable that this old Indian alphabet, when it was framed or adopted, did not possess any retroflex letters."[51] The Phoenician *Samech* is the origin of the signs for both *s* and *ṣ* in the Brāhmī script. Bühler (1895:66) points out that a single sign probably served in the beginning to express both *s* and *ṣ* and that two separate signs were developed later out of this original representative of the Phoenician *Samech*. Similarly, the signs for the sounds *ṭ, ṭh, ḍ, ḍh* and *ṇ* in the Brāhmī script are derived from the dental signs in the Phoenician alphabet (Bühler:73). While the Brāhmī *ḍ* comes from *d* (*dh* Phoenician *daleth*), the sign for retroflex *ḷ* is a further modification of the sign for *ḍ* (Bühler: 77). The following chart shows the derivation of the Brāhmī retroflex signs (Bühler:82-83):

Phoenician		Brāhmī		Brāhmī Derivatives
Daleth	→	*dh*	→	*d, ḍ* {*ḍh*, *ḷ*}
Theth	→	*th*	→	*ṭh, ṭ*
Nun	→	*n*	→	*ṇ*
Samech	→	*ṣ* (Bhattiprolu type)	→	*s, ṣ*

Even if we do not believe in the Phoenician origin of the Brāhmī script, still the relatedness of its retroflex and dental signs is quite significant in itself.

8.4. The fact that the same sign was earlier used for *s* and *ṣ* and that two different signs were later developed from this common sign is quite interesting. As the Sanskrit grammarians teach, the sound *s* changes to *ṣ* under the influence of the preceding *i, u, ṛ, e, ai, o, au, k*-series, *r*, or *l*.[52] It is quite possible that originally *ṣ* was looked upon only as an allophone of *s* and was not distinguished from *s* in writing. Gradually as *ṣ* became phonemically different from the original *s* through changes in its distribution, *s* and *ṣ* came to be distinguished in writing. The derivation of the Brāhmī *ṣ* from *s* perhaps goes hand in hand with the phonemic evolution of *ṣ* from *s*. The derivation of the Brāhmī sign for *ḷ* from *ḍ* may indicate a similar evolution.[53] Bühler has amply demonstrated that Indian grammarians and phoneticians must have been involved in the formation of the Brahmi script. Since the formation of an *akṣara-samāmnāya* 'standard alphabet' had already taken place before the *Aitareya-* and *Śāṅkhāyana-Āraṇyakas* and since this very *Śāṅkhāyana-Āraṇyaka* speaks of the process of *brāhmī-karaṇa*, we may be able to conclude with some justification that the process of *brāhmī-karaṇa* referred to here was the gradual process of "normalizing" and "standardizing" the orally preserved ancient texts and involved the phonetic and orthographic realignment of the older texts.

8.5. In terms of the development of ancient Indian scripts and retroflexion, it may be interesting to refer to S. R. Rao's recent attempts to decipher the Harappan script. While most of the recent Western attempts (cf. Parpola 1975) presume that the Harappan language is an old Dravidian language, S. R. Rao's alphabetical interpretation of the late Harappan inscriptions is interesting in that, according to his findings, the Harappan script, like the later Brāhmī script, is derived from the Phoenician alphabet, and the Harappan language turns out for him to be a form of (pre-Vedic?) Indo-Aryan. According to him, there are no signs for the retroflex sounds *ṭ, ṭh, ḍ, ḍh,* and *ṇ*, but there are signs for the sounds *r, ṛ,* and *l*.[54] This, surprisingly, resembles the phonetic system of the pre-Vedic Indo-Aryans which I have already discussed.

I claim to be a perfect nonexpert with respect to ancient scripts and cannot possibly evaluate the validity of S. R. Rao's decipherments. At least there is a chance that, if S. R. Rao is right, there did exist an Aryan language in India, closely allied to the known Vedic language, and yet did not have any retroflexion. This is at least a possibility, and at the very least a check against instinctively reading a form of Dravidian into the Harappan inscriptions, as is being done quite frequently in recent years.[55]

9. INSTABILITY OF POST-VEDIC RETROFLEXION

9.1. Coming down to post-Vedic times, one finds that the sounds *ṇ* and *ṣ* continue to be intriguing even after the time of Śākalya. Pāṇini, who refers to Śākalya as an authority, has rules dealing with *ṇ* and *ṣ*, in particular, which show us that these sounds were still among the least predictable in Sanskrit. The whole distinction of *ṇopadeśa* and *ṣopadeśa* verbs in Pāṇini testifies to this complexity.[56] In simple terms, the distinction worked in this way: the sound *n* of roots sometimes changed to *ṇ* after *r, ṛ,* and *ṣ* in the prefix (*upasarga*), but sometimes it did not change. Pāṇini knew where the change took place and where it did not, but he could not find any general phonological or morphological condition that would distinguish these two classes of verbs from each other. In fact, he had to identify every such item which underwent such a change individually. For example: *nṛtyati/pranṛtyati*, but *namati/praṇamati*. The same situation existed in roots with *s*. This either changed to *ṣ* or remained *s*. For example: *sīdati/viṣīdati*, but *sarpati/visarpati*. Even Patañjali could provide only a partial generalization for these cases.[57]

9.2. An instance of "right" and "wrong" speech given by Patañjali shows that retroflexion was fluid in the speech of even upper-caste learned people. He narrates the story of two sages who were called Yarvāṇa and Tarvāṇa (MB: vol. 1, sec. 1, p. 56). They were so called because instead of pronouncing the Sanskrit sequences *yad vā naḥ* and *tad vā naḥ* correctly, they used to pronounce these as *yarvāṇa* and *tarvāṇa* in everyday speech, but as *yad vā naḥ* and *tad vā naḥ* when they were either teaching or sacrificing. This story illustrates how, in these post-Vedic times, there was a situation where even the learned Brahmins were involved in diaglossia.

9.3. In order to explicate further the relationship of retroflexes to dentals and palatals in Sanskrit, it may be observed that there is a hierarchy of phonological features. The following examples illustrate the presence and absence of such hierarchies. In Sanskrit, a voiced stop, followed by an unvoiced consonant, becomes unvoiced, e.g., *dt*>*tt*. However, an unvoiced stop, followed by a voiced consonant, becomes voiced, e.g., *td*>*dd*. This general rule, which operates only in the specified direction, indicates that the features of [+ voice] and [– voice] are of equal strength in the context of assimilation. On the other hand, the dental, palatal, and retroflex sounds show a clear hierarchy. Pāṇini's rule 8.4.40 (*stoḥ ścunā ścuḥ*) says that a dental stop or sibilant is replaced by the corresponding palatal stop or sibilant *if followed or preceded by* a palatal stop or sibilant, e.g., *tat* + *ca*>*tacca*.[58] A palatal never becomes a dental. Pāṇini's rule 8.4.41 (*ṣṭunā ṣṭuḥ*) says that a dental stop or sibilant is replaced by the corresponding retroflex stop or sibilant *if followed or preceded by* a retroflex stop or sibilant, e.g., *rāmas ṭīkām*>*rāmaṣṭīkām*, *ṣaṭ nagaryaḥ*>*ṣaṇṇagaryaḥ*. A retroflex consonant never becomes dental. Similarly, there are rules to change palatals into retroflex consonants, e.g., *viś* + *ta*>*viṣṭa*, *rāj* + *bhiḥ*>*rāḍbhiḥ*, but no retroflex consonant is ever changed into a palatal. This gives us a hierarchy of dental>palatal>retroflex, such that there are no changes in the reverse direction.

9.4. The first half of this hierarchy is to some extent part of the Indo-Iranian heritage, while retroflexion is the added "marked" higher feature of Indian origin. Acutally the Indo-European *ruki* rule which yields the Indo-Iranian *ś* from the Indo-European **s* has been partly extended in Sanskrit to *ṣ*. The *ruki* rule says that the Indo-European **s* is changed to *ś*, if preceded by *r, u, k,* or *i*. This particular rule ceases to be productive in Indo-Aryan, except as an extension to the derivation of retroflex *ṣ*. Pāṇini's rules 8.3.57 and 8.3.59 (*iṇkoḥ, ādeśa-pratyayayoḥ*) say that *s* which is either a substitute or a part of an affix is replaced by *ṣ*, if it is preceded by *i, u, ṛ, ḷ, e, o, ai, au, h*, semi-vowels, or one of the *k*-series, e.g., *deve + su >deveṣu.* The statement of the rule by Pāṇini is basically the same as the *ruki* rule if we understand the following relationships between different conditioning sounds:

$$ s > \underset{\cdot}{s} \; / \; \left\{ \begin{array}{c} r \\ u \\ k \\ i \end{array} \right\} \; - \quad \begin{array}{l} r \text{ covers } \underset{\cdot}{r} \text{ (and perhaps } \underset{\cdot}{l}, l \text{)} \\ u \text{ covers } o, au, \text{ and } v \\ k \text{ covers the } k\text{-series of stops} \\ i \text{ covers } e, ai, \text{ and } y \end{array} $$

For several of these conditioning sounds, there are no examples found in Sanskrit, and in the Pāṇinian group-symbols *i-Ṇ* and *kU*, several "unused" sounds are included. But the basic structure is the same as the *ruki* rule. This shift of the same basic *ruki* rule to retroflexion, a partial shift producing a split between *ś* and *ṣ*, shows the process of realigning the original Indo-Iranian nonretroflex sounds in terms of Dravidian influence on Indo-Aryan. This shift was by no means either complete or regular even by the time of Pāṇini (8.3.57ff).

Indo-European **s*

Indo-Iranian **s, *ś*

Iranian **s, *ś*   Ur-Vedic **s, *ś*

*s, *ś, [**ṣ*]

Recensional Vedic
after Aryan-Dravidian
Convergence
/s/, /ś/, /ṣ/

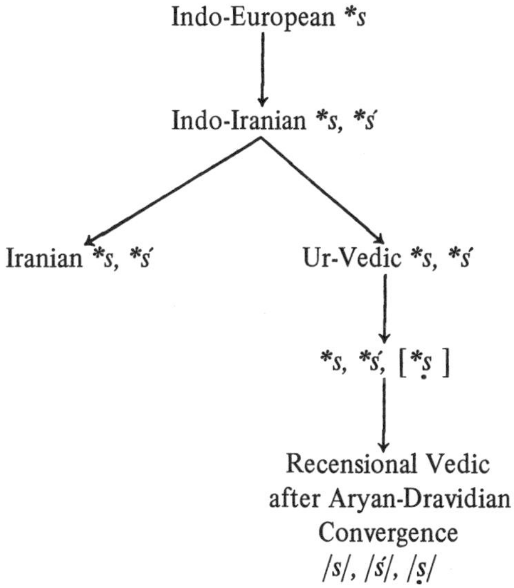

9.5. Though Hans Hock (1975:101-2) points out that retroflexion is "a natural, phonetically well-motivated phenomenon, found, at least dialectally, in the majority of the sub-branches of Indo-European," I would still agree with Kuiper (1967*a*:104) that "the assumption of retroflex phonemes for proto-Indo-Iranian is fully unwarranted. In old Iranian such retroflexes are entirely lacking, and in Indo-Aryan the genesis of these phonemes is in all likelihood a comparatively late process which must have taken place in the separate branch owing to foreign influence in the Indian linguistic area." At the same time, it must be emphasized that such foreign influence cannot be evidenced for the *Ṛgveda* (also see Hock:113-14) apart from some loan-words. Extension of the *ruki* rule to yield retroflex *ṣ* marks the beginning of *ṣ* in Sanskrit, but this extension had not begun by the time of the Ur-*Ṛgveda*. As we shall see in the following sections, the same must be true of Fortunatov's Law and Burrow's "spontaneous cerebrals" (Burrow 1972).

10. IRREGULAR RETROFLEXION IN THE VEDIC RECENSIONS

10.1. An examination of the present text of the *Ṛgveda* reveals certain aspects of retroflexion in that text which could have come about only through unconscious shifts and mechanical nonlinguistic application of the retroflexion rules by the early preredaction reciters and preservers of the Vedic texts. A few examples will suffice to clarify this point.

10.2. In classical Sanskrit as codified by Pāṇini, the change of *n* to *ṇ* and *s* to *ṣ* is specifically limited to occurrences of both the conditioning sound and the substituendum *n* or *s* within the same *pada* 'inflected word'. For instance, we have **rāmena>rāmeṇa* because both *r* and *n* are parts of the same inflected word; but we cannot have the sequence of the two words *tatra na* changed to **tatra ṇa*, because the sounds *r* and *n* belong to two different inflected items. The same is true of the change of *s* to *ṣ* when preceded by *iṆ* sounds (all vowels [except *a* and *ā*], *h*, and semi-vowels) and the *k*-series of stops. For instance, in *rāme* + *su* the sound *s* changes to *ṣ* and we get *rāmeṣu*; but we cannot get this change in cases like the sequence *rāme supte*, where *e* in one word is followed by *s* in another word. Thus, these rules in the normal language are not simply conditioned by the "absolute sound sequence," but by further morphological considerations. This seems to be quite natural; for instance, the Indo-European *ruki* rule is conditioned by sound sequence and morphology both, and not simply by the sound sequence alone.

10.3. However, if we look at the present text of the *Ṛgveda*, we find changes like the ones mentioned above taking place even when the conditioning sound belongs to a different word. All that seems to matter is the sound sequence within a metrical foot (*pāda*). A metrical foot is looked upon as if it is a continuous sequence, and the awareness of word boundaries is dispensed with in making changes like *n*>*ṇ* and *s*>*ṣ*. We find compounds in Vedic illustrating this kind of change, i.e., *agnī-ṣomau (agnī-somau)*.[59] One may perhaps understand the "psychological propinquity" involved in a compound, though this propinquity is not exhibited in classical Sanskrit. However, in Vedic even words which are uncompounded undergo changes of this type quite often, i.e., *mo ṣu ṇaḥ* (from *mā u su naḥ*).[60] Pāṇini himself is quite aware that the metrical foot, not the word, is the unit used as the basis of these changes (*antaḥ-pādam*).[61] If we were to say that this kind of change, based on metrical units and their assumed indivisibility rather than on word units, was quite normal in the real Vedic spoken language, then we are faced with a precarious situation. We would have to assume that the scope of retroflexion in the real spoken Vedic language was far greater than in classical Sanskrit. This would be quite contrary to the generally seen pattern of steadily increasing strength of retroflexion, along with the increasing intensity of the Aryan-Dravidian convergence.

10.4. To me it appears that this kind of retroflexion appearing in the preserved Vedic recensions must be ascribed to the effect of recitation. There was a gradual development of conditioned and spontaneous retroflexion in the spoken language of the reciters. The rules which in the real language were conditioned by particular sound sequences and limited in scope to the grammatical word were mechanically applied by these preserver-reciters to the orally preserved archaic texts wherever the sequence conditions were met. The metrical units of the Vedic recensions were viewed by the early reciters as undivided continuous units, and along with this notion of continuity the increasingly archaic nature of the texts helped such unconscious mechanical application of retroflexion rules. Ghatage (1962:93) says: "The sentence or word-group as the basis of Sandhi explains the change of *n* to *ṇ* and of *s* to *ṣ* even when the retroflex sound is found in another word, (*ni ṣasāda, pra ṇa āyūṁṣi*)." Without the sociohistorical background given above, Ghatage's statement is not an "explanation," but merely a statement of obvious facts.

10.5. Thus, a majority of the cases of retroflexion seen in the preserved Vedic texts must be ultimately ascribed to the gradual unconscious change in oral recitation. Such mechanical application of retroflexion rules was again not quite uniform.[62] That the emergence of retroflexion itself was not quite uniform can be seen from Pāṇini's retroflexion rules. Pāṇini himself notes that some of the retroflexion rules applied only as unconditioned options in certain Vedic texts. Thus, the same Vedic text shows *agnis tvā* and *agnis te,* but also *agniṣ ṭvā* and *agniṣ ṭe.*[63] Once personalities like Śākalya and Māṇḍūkeya had fixed the texts of their respective recensions, the orally preserved texts were as if quickly frozen with all the changes that had taken place so far, and then texts like *Prātiśākhyas* were composed to describe in detail the features of these "frozen" texts. Staal (1967:17) rightly points out that the *Prātiśākhyas* were "not interested in the Vedic language as such, *but in the utterances handed down*" by the oral tradition. However, phenomena like retroflexion had set in before the process of "text freezing" had begun. The same phenomenon is seen in the application of other *sandhi* rules in the preserved recensions.

10.6. In order to emphasize the point that the Ṛgvedic hymns were preserved for a long time as "continuous" archaic sequences and not as spoken sentences, I shall give a few examples which indicate that Śākalya, Yāska, and other ancient Vedic scholars who received the ancient "unanalyzed" continuous texts from the older oral traditions often could not agree on what the words were in a given sequence. All these instances are discussed by Bishnupada Bhattacharya (1958:9-23):

Ṛgveda Sequences

1. *vāyaḥ*	Śākalya	*/vā/yaḥ/*
	Yāska	*/vāyaḥ/*
2. *māsakṛt*	Śākalya	*/mā/sakṛt/*
	Yāska	*/māsa-kṛt/*
3. *mehanā*	Śākalya	*/mehanā/*
	Gārgya	*/mā/iha/nā/*
4. *tṛṣṇaje*	Śākalya	from *tṛṣṇa-ja-*
	Yāska	dative of *tṛṣṇaj-*

5. Śākalya's analysis: *katham/rasāyāḥ/antaraḥ/*
Yāska's analysis: *kathaṁ-rasā/yā/antaraḥ/*

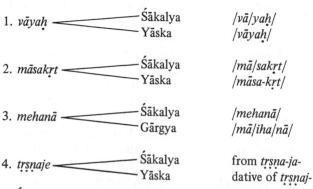

These examples show quite clearly that Śākalya, Yāska, Gārgya, and other ancient Vedic scholars were all dealing with orally preserved continuous texts and therefore the "words" in these "continuous texts" were essentially a matter of scholastic analysis and reconstruction. Twenty-eight pages of "false divisions and patchwords" in the second volume of *Vedic Variants* (3.66-94) substantially prove that preservation of the Vedic literature in the preredaction and preanalysis period was anything but perfect. All the austere methods of oral preservation like *krama-pāṭha, ghana-pāṭha*, etc., depend on the *pada-pāṭha* 'the word-text'.[64] But if Śākalya, Yāska, and Gārgya often could not agree with each other on what the exact words in the orally preserved continuous texts were, we can hardly imagine that the early oral traditions had the same austerity. Rather, they were very much "natural" ways of passing on an oral text from generation to generation. Therefore, the later austere methods could not have preserved what was lost before those methods themselves came into being.

10.7. Irregular, indeed, is retroflexion in the *Ṛgveda* sequence *mo ṣu ṇaḥ*. However, it is irregular not only with respect to the classical language, it is irregular within the *Ṛgveda* itself as it has been handed down to us. Below I shall mention instances of irregular "spontaneous" *n/ṇ* variation within identical texts. These cases are collected from *Vedic Variants* (vol. 2, pp. 444ff.).

Texts*			
RV, AV, TS, TB	*pra ṇo*	beside	*pra no*
SV, MS, AB	*pra ṇa*	beside	*pra na*
MS	*nakir ṇu*	beside	*nakir nu*
TS	*svar ṇa*	beside	*svar na*
KS	*indra eṇam*	beside	*indra enam*
VS, MS	*pari ṇo*	beside	*pari no*
MS	*uruṣyā ṇo*	beside	*uruṣyā no*

Similar cases of "spontaneous" *s/ṣ* variation occur (*Vedic Variants*:vol. 2, pp. 447ff.):

* *AB–Aitareya-Brāhmaṇa; ApS–Āpastamba-Śrautasūtra; AV–Atharvaveda; HG–Hiraṇyakeśi-Gṛhyasūtra; KS–Kāṭhaka-Saṁhitā; MS–Maitrāyaṇī-Saṁhitā; RV–Ṛgveda; SV–Sāmaveda; TA–Taittirīya-Āraṇyaka; TB–Taittirīya-Brāhmaṇa; TS–Taittirīya-Saṁhitā; VS–Vājasaneyī-Saṁhitā.*

Texts

RV	*dhanuṣ ṭanvanti*	beside	*dhanus tanvanti*
SV	*svasuṣ ṭamaḥ*	beside	*svasus tamaḥ*
TS	*agneṣ ṭvāsyena*	beside	*agnes tvāsyena*
KS, TA	*tābhiṣ ṭvām*	beside	*tābhis tvām*
SV	*prabhoṣ ṭe*	beside	*prabhos te*
TS, TB	*bṛhaspateṣ ṭvā*	beside	*bṛhaspates tvā*

These are only a few cases cited from the long lists of variants in *Vedic Variants*. The only explanation which Bloomfield and Edgerton (p. 444) could come up with is that "the greater degree of psychological propinquity between the alterant sound and *n*, the greater is the likelihood of lingualization." But free variation within the same texts and between different texts only suggests that this "psychological propinquity" was very much a matter of the reciters' psychology and unconscious phonological inclinations.

10.8. We also have occasional free variation in certain other retroflexes in the Vedic texts (*Vedic Variants*:vol. 2, pp. 87ff):

Texts

SV	*avatasya*	beside	*avaṭasya*
HG	*manthakālo*	beside	*maṇḍakālo*
KS	*panyāt panyatarā*	beside	*paṇyāt paṇyatarā*
ApS	*padbhiḥ*	beside	*paḍbhiḥ*
KS	*rāvat*	beside	*rāvaṭ*
KS	*vikirida*	beside	*vikiriḍa*

When it comes to such unconditional variation in the same text, Bloomfield and Edgerton (p. 444) remark: "The school tendencies which appear are capricious and unstable; one sometimes has a feeling as if Taittirīya texts, in particular, took a perverse delight in violating their own general principles." I believe I have given sufficient evidence to prove my point that the pre-redaction oral traditions were extremely irregular, imperfect, flexible and, therefore, ironically, more "natural" to ancient oral literature, and that a major amount of the phonetic "information" which we find in the existing Vedic recensions can hardly be considered to represent the original compositions.

10.9. This discussion agrees well with Burrow's excellent demonstration of the gradual increase of "spontaneous cerebrals" in Sanskrit. As Burrow

(1971:558-59) convincingly claims: "Spontaneous cerebralization has taken place in Sanskrit on quite a massive scale. Previously the view had been that cerebrals arose in Indo-Aryan only as a result of combinatory changes (though a few cases of spontaneous change had been admitted as exceptions), but it is now clear that this development has frequently taken place without the presence of any such influence." However, as Bloch (1970:128) points out, the spontaneous cerebrals are extremely rare, if any, in the *Ṛgveda*, but the "list starts getting longer the moment we reach the ancient most period of classical Prakrit." We can compare several *Ṛgveda* words with later Sanskrit words:

Ṛgveda	Classical Sanskrit
dī-	*ḍī-*
āti-	*āṭi-*
atati	*aṭati*
cat-	*caṭ-*
udumbara	*uḍumbara*
methī	*meḍhi*
nada	*naḍa*
suvenī	*suveṇī*
bhanati	*bhaṇati*

As Abhyankar points out, the Taittirīya reciters occasionally pronounce *ṇ* in the place of *n* "without any reason" (cf. *enāḥ/eṇāḥ* and *agniḥ/agṇiḥ*), and that this practice was noticed by Bhartṛhari as early as 400 A.D.[65] This process of unconscious "traditional" and spontaneous cerebralization was noticed by Patañjali (MB:vol. 1, sec. 1, p. 62) when he said that one must make a complete listing of all nominal stems so that one may know the correct pronunciation and not mispronounce the correct words *śaśa* and *palāśa* as **ṣaṣa* and **palāṣa*.

10.10. As Emeneau (1974:97) points out, Burrow's spontaneous cerebrals can be best explained on the sociolinguistic assumption of the increasing adaptation of Indo-Aryan by native Dravidian speakers to their own phonological system. This process is much more evident in the development of Prakrits, and Ananthanarayana (p. 67) rightly says that "retroflex consonants become much more frequent in the Prakrits as compared to Sanskrit which may have happened due to deeper contact of Dravidian with them." A gradual conversion of a large Kannada-speaking region to Marathi, without any shifting of the original Dravidian population, has been discussed by Joshi in his exciting book *Marhāṭī Saṁskṛti: Kā̃hī̃ Samasyā* [Marāṭhī culture: some problems], with an English subtitle: "A New Approach to the Dravidian Problem" (Poona, 1952).

11. RETROFLEXION IN THE *PRĀTIŚĀKHYA*S

11.1. As has been noted earlier, no *Prātiśākhya*s consider *r* and *ṛ* to be retroflex sounds (*mūrdhanya*), and to find them classified as retroflexes we have to come down to such late texts as the *Pāṇinīya-Śikṣā.*[66] What is of interest is the fact that even those texts which do not classify *r* and *ṛ* as retroflexes still have the rule which says that a dental *n* becomes retroflex *ṇ* if preceded by *r* and *ṛ*. If we look at the late texts such as the *Pāṇinīya-Śikṣā*, where *r* and *ṛ* are explicitly classified as retroflexes, the rule

$$\text{(A) dental } n > \text{ṇ} \;\; / \;\; \left\{ \begin{array}{ll} r & \\ \text{ṛ} & \text{all three retroflexes} \\ \text{ṣ} & \end{array} \right\} \;\; \text{—}$$

appears to be a phonologically *natural rule* of contiguous or noncontiguous assimilation as the case may be.[67] But if we look at the older classifications of *r* and *ṛ* in the *Prātiśākhya*s, the rule does not seem to be as natural as it appears in later times. The *Ṛgveda-Prātiśākhya* (1.8, 10) classifies *ṛ* as a *jihvā-mūlīya* 'produced at the root of the tongue (velar or perhaps uvular?)', and *r* as *danta-mūlīya* 'produced at the root of the teeth (alveolar)'. Thus, the rule for the *Ṛgveda-Prātiśākhya*, considering that the *t*-series for the *Ṛgveda-Prātiśākhya* is alveolar, may be stated as follows:

$$\text{(B) alveolar } n > \text{retroflex ṇ} \;\; / \;\; \left\{ \begin{array}{l} \text{velar ṛ} \\ \\ \text{alveolar } r \end{array} \right\} \;\; \text{—}$$

The *Ṛktantra* (2.1.4, 7, 8) classifies *ṛ* as a *jihvā-mūlīya* 'velar', and *r* as either a *dantya* 'dental' or *danta-mūlīya* 'alveolar' sound. The *Taittirīya-Prātiśākhya* (2.18, 41) classifies *ṛ* as being produced at the upper back gums and jaws, while *r* is an alveolar. For the *Śaunakīyā Caturādhyāyikā* (1.20, 28) and *Vājasaneyī-Prātiśākhya* (1.65, 68), *ṛ* is velar and *r* is alveolar. However, for all these texts, the *t*-series is a dental series, in contrast to the *Ṛgveda-Prātiśākhya*. Thus, we may write a rule to cover all these classifications:

$$\text{(C) dental } n{>}\text{retroflex } \d{n} \;\;/\;\; \left\{\begin{array}{l}\text{velar } \d{r}\\ \text{upper back gums } \d{r}\\ \text{dental } r\\ \text{alveolar } r\end{array}\right\} \;\; -$$

11.2. Looking at all these nonretroflex classifications of the sounds *r* and *ṛ*, and the fact that all of these texts do have the rule prescribing the change of *n*>*ṇ*, one must conclude that this is phonologically an unnatural process, at least on the surface. How can a nonretroflex sound such as *r* or *ṛ* cause the change of a dental *n* to a retroflex *ṇ*? We may hypothesize that even though different texts do not exactly consider *r* and *ṛ* to be retroflexes, still there must be something in common between a strict retroflex sound and alveolars and velars. It may be that in all variant classifications of *r* and *ṛ*, there is some degree of tongue-raising involved, if not retroflexing in the strict sense, and this tongue-raising may be considered to be the factor leading to the change of *n* to *ṇ*. Thus, this case of assimilation may be natural not so much in terms of "the point of articulation," but in terms of a somewhat similar manner of tongue-raising producing a somewhat similar acoustic quality.

11.3. This point needs some elaboration. In the ancient Sanskrit phonetic texts, we find that the Indian phoneticians considered articulatory process, as well as acoustic quality, while explaining interrelations of sounds. According to them, there was definitely something common to *r* and *ṛ*, despite the difference of the point of articulation as described by them. This common factor is designated as *ra-śruti* 'sound heard as *r*' by Patañjali.[68] Similarly, the consonant *l* and the vowel *ḷ* were said to have a common *la-śruti* 'sound heard as *l*'.[69] The term *śruti* 'heard sound' makes it clear that these statements refer to the acoustic common factor between *r* and *ṛ*, and *l* and *ḷ*. These statements of Patañjali are based on the older statements of the *Prātiśākhya*s where the constitution of the vowel *ṛ* is explained as *ərə*, a sequence of a vocoid plus a consonantal *r* followed by a vocoid. For instance, a text such as the *Ṛgveda-Prātiśākhya* (13.14) classifies *ṛ* as a velar vowel, and *r* as an alveolar consonant, but it maintains at the same time that *ṛ* contains an *r*. (The mutual relationship of the Sanskrit velar *ṛ* and alveolar *r* might have been similar to the premodern Polish velar and palatal *l*. But the "velar *l*" of Polish is [w]–it has no lateral color at all anymore–and the "palatal *l*" is [l]–it no longer has any palatality.) The close relationship between *r* and *ṛ* may explain the common functional load of these two sounds in conditioning the change of *n* to *ṇ*.

11.4. It is important to realize that despite the variations in the phonetic classifications of *r* and *ṛ* in different texts, these sounds had the same functional load in all the known grammatical systems of Sanskrit, and this functional load was shared in common with the sibilant *ṣ*, which is classified by all the known Sanskrit phonetic treatises as a retroflex. Thus, we may say that there was all along a kind of phonological retroflexion shared by *r, ṛ,* and *ṣ* in all the known grammatical texts, despite the differences in exact phonetic classifications. As far as the change of *n* to *ṇ* was concerned, this phonological retroflexion was the most dominant factor.

11.5. This "phonological retroflexion" may be viewed in a functional sense in that all three sounds *r, ṛ,* and *ṣ* are "cerebralizers," if not all cerebrals themselves in the view of the *Prātiśākhyas*. In later texts such as the *Pāṇinīya-Śikṣā*, both *r* and *ṛ*, along with *ṣ* are classified as retroflexes, and thus all of them become "cerebralizers" and cerebrals. This "development" may be viewed as a phonetic development, but at the same time one may speculate that the phonological behavior of these sounds–their phonological or functional retroflexion–may have at least partially contributed to this phonetic shift. Thus, we find that the phonological requirements in Pāṇinian grammar are greatly facilitated if we assume that *r* and *ṛ* had the same point-of-articulation classification (Bare 1976:171). We may trace the development of retroflexion in *r* and *ṛ* in the following sequence:[70]

Indo-Iranian
**r, *ṛ (*ərə)*
(not cerebrals)
↓
Ur-Ṛgvedic
**r, *ṛ*
(not cerebrals)
↓
Prātiśākhyas
r, ṛ
(not cerebrals, but cerebralizers)
↓
Pāṇinīya-Śikṣā
r, ṛ
(cerebrals and cerebralizers)

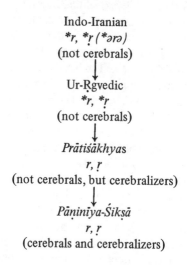

11.6. The phonetic description of *r* and *ṛ* in the *Prātiśākhyas* is perhaps more significant in understanding the history of retroflexion than it first appears. Fortunatov's Law connects the Indo-European clusters of *l plus dental with Sanskrit retroflexes, but in the later periods of Indo-Aryan, we find r and ṛ emerging as cerebralizers and have to connect clusters like *rt, rd, rn* with *ṭṭ, ḍḍ, ṇṇ,* and *ṭ, ḍ,* and *ṇ* in later Indo-Aryan. Emeneau speculates that in Proto-Indo-Aryan there were "backed" allophones of dentals, which were interpreted as retroflexes by the mixed Aryan-Dravidian bilinguals. If we observe closely the *Prātiśākhya* description of *r* and *ṛ*, we can see a phonetic motivation for Emeneau's comment in the role of these sounds as "cerebralizers." The sound *r* is rarely classified as dental. It is mostly alveolar. The vowel *ṛ* is mostly velar, and occasionally alveolar. Thus, both of these sounds may be described as "backed" with respect to dentals. This may phonetically explain why sequences such as *rt, rd, rn,* etc., would develop an assimilatory "backward" pull. Thus, a cluster of an alveolar *r* and dental *t* could easily produce an alveolar *t*. This alveolar stage would then be interpreted by the Aryan-Dravidian bilinguals as retroflexion. According to the *Ṛgveda-Prātiśākhya* (1.9), the *t*-series is not dental, but alveolar. It is true that the dental/alveolar variation is not phonemic, but it clearly provides documentary evidence for the existence of what Emeneau calls the "backed" allophones of dentals. The Indo-Iranian clusters like *źd* and *śt* may be viewed in the same light, where the palatals *ź* and *ś* must have exerted a similar "backing" influence on *t* and *d*.

12. ASPECTS OF DRAVIDIAN INFLUENCE ON INDO-ARYAN

12.1. With respect to the influence exerted on the early Aryan speech by the Dravidian languages of North India, I shall touch upon a point which has been left out of consideration by many previous studies. Referring to *Tolkāppiyam* (*Piṟappiyal*, verse 9), P. S. Subramanya Sastri (1930:13) remarks: "These two sounds *ṭ* and *ṇ* are alveolar according to Tolkāppiyaṉar, but at present they are pronounced by rounding the tongue and allowing it to touch the uppermost part of the hard palate exactly in the same way as *ṭ* and *ṇ* are pronounced in Sanskrit. Hence, it is worth investigation whether the Sanskrit *ṭ* and *ṇ* were borrowed from the Dravidian languages." He argues that retroflexes in Sanskrit are independent of Dravidian influence and that Fortunatov's Law could have worked independently in producing Sanskrit retroflexes (1934:58-60). He quotes Jesperson in support of this "natural development" theory, and takes the existence of retroflexes for granted in the *Ṛgveda*. With this he argues that the *Ṛgveda*, even though it has retroflexes, was composed before Sanskrit had been influenced by Dravidian languages. This argument presents interesting problems which are worth notice.

12.2. If all Dravidian languages had a triple contrast of dental/alveolar/retroflex, e.g., *t, ṯ, ṭ,* then at first it would appear unnatural that Dravidian influence would accelerate the change of Proto-Indo-Aryan dental *t, d, n,* or even *rt, rd, rn* to retroflex *ṭ, ḍ,* and *ṇ.* It would seem more natural that a dental *t*, under the influence of *r*, would shift to an alveolar *ṯ*. Thus, we might expect in Sanskrit, under Dravidian influence, an alveolar series, rather than a retroflex series.

However, Subramanya Sastri's argument is based only on one interpretation of Tamil, and does not take into account other Dravidian languages. In fact, while discussing Dravidian influence on the early phases of Indo-Aryan, consideration of Tamil is somewhat irrelevant, as early Indo-Aryan was definitely not affected by a southern Dravidian language, but must have been affected by northern Dravidian languages. Even a casual glance at the tables of phonetic correspondences given by Burrow and Emeneau (1961: xii-xiii) and Andronov (1970:38-39) show us an astonishing picture of Dravidian alveolar sounds. The northern Dravidian languages, i.e., Brahui, Malto, and Kurukh have no alveolar sounds. Among the central and south-central Dravidian languages, only Old Kannada, Old Telugu, Gondi, and Konda have a single alveolar sound, i.e., *ṟ*, while the other languages have no alveolar sounds. Toda in the south has the maximum number of alveolar sounds, i.e., *ṯ, ḏ, ṟ, s̱, ẕ,* and *ṉ*, while Malayalam and Kolami have only some: *ṯ, ḏ, ṟ,* and *ṉ*. Kolami does not have *ṟ*. Old Tamil had the alveolar sounds *ṯ, ḏ, ṟ,* and *ṉ*, but Andronov (1970:34) points out that "in Modern Tamil alveolar sounds (and phonemes) as well as the liquid retroflex sonant *ẓ* do not exist."

12.3. We have no clear historical evidence that the southern Dravidians of modern times are the ancient northern Dravidians pushed downwards by the Aryans. Brahui, Kurukh and Malto share some common innovations, and Emeneau (1962*c*:62ff.) argues for the existence of a northern Dravidian family which included these languages. "Having also words in common not known from other Dravidian languages, they may be considered as remnants of a large north Dravidian dialect area, which was subsequently overlaid and assimilated by the Aryans" (Porpola 1975:191). Thus, it seems natural to assume that the Aryans confronted and gradually intermingled with the northern Dravidians who did not have alveolar consonants, but, like all Dravidians, had markedly retroflex consonants.

12.4. This is quite interesting. Existence of alveolar *ṟ* in some of the central Dravidian languages may explain to some extent why the Sanskrit *ṟ* of the *Prātiśākhya* period could vary from dental to alveolar, and could stay an alveolar for some time, despite the emergence of *ṭ, ṭh, ḍ, ḍh,* and *ṇ*. The central Dravidian languages, Old Kannada and Old Telugu show retroflex *ṭ*, *ḍ*, *r*, and *ṇ*, but they do have the alveolar *ṟ* as well. However, under the influence of the existence of retroflex *r* in all the Dravidian languages, and internal phonemic leveling, this alveolar *ṟ* of the *Prātiśākhya* period seems to have shifted later to the retroflex *r*, as is seen in the *Pāṇinīya-Śikṣā* and other later treatises. In the development of retroflexes from dentals, there must have been an alveolar or "backed dental" stage, but this stage must have been quite unstable, since the northern Dravidian languages did not have alveolars. The existence of this unstable alveolar Sanskrit series is further supported by the fact that the *Ṛgveda-Prātiśākhya* considers the *t*-series to be alveolar rather than dental. This variation is clearly allophonic, but its existence as recorded by the *Ṛgveda-Prātiśākhya* is significant nonetheless.

12.5. Northern Dravidian languages do not have *ṣ*, and it is absent from Old Kannada, Old Telugu, and Old Tamil. This makes it harder to link emergence of *ṣ* in Sanskrit with any direct Dravidian influence. This corroborates the view expressed by Burrow (1971:554) and Ivanov and Toporov (1968: 49) that the development of *ṣ* in Sanskrit, by a special modification of the *ruki* rule was a somewhat different process from the emergence of *ṭ*, *ṭh*, *ḍ*, *ḍh*, and *ṇ*. However, later phonemicization of *ṣ* is indirectly connected with the general leveling of all retroflex sounds. Thus, northern Dravidian languages substantially explain the phonetic and phonemic transformations of the ancient Indo-Aryan. Since northern and central Dravidian languages show the most influence by Indo-Aryan (Zvelebil and Švarný 1955:379-80), we may look to these languages for early Dravidian influence on Indo-Aryan, rather than to the remote languages of extreme South India.

12.6. With respect to the argument given above in this section, Professor Emeneau suggests (in a personal communication) that Proto-Dravidian had a set of alveolars and most probably even the early North Dravidian languages had alveolars at the time they met the Indo-Aryans. Not being a Dravidianist myself, I can only gratefully accept Professor Emeneau's suggestion, without any further questions. If this is indeed the case, it would lead to a reconsideration of the explanation given.

One could argue that in a situation of language contact, the phonetic or phonemic polarities are more distinctly noticeable than the intermediate positions. Thus, it is quite conceivable that Dravidians perceiving the Aryan language viewed dentals and their backed allophones in terms of this polarity principle. Therefore, the "backed" allophones of dentals shifted to the polar position of retroflexion rather than stabilizing at the intermediate position of alveolars. Eventually, as the dental-retroflex polarity became dominant in

Indo-Aryan, the Dravidian languages in the North, which were encircled by Indo-Aryan, themselves adopted this dominant polarity, and hence the North Dravidian alveolars were eventually lost. As an example of this polarity principle, one may point out that despite the presence of alveolars in the South Dravidian languages today, the English alveolars are still perceived and pronounced by the speakers of these languages as retroflexes. This is the only explanation I can come up with at present. This explanation fits very well with the concept of "maximal differentiation" advocated by André Martinet (1966:191-92).

I have retained my previous explanation simply because both of these explanations are, coming from a non-Dravidianist as they do, no more than suggestions.

13. PROBLEMS IN THE RECONSTRUCTION OF THE UR-*ṚGVEDA*

13.1. Though it may be concluded with a fair degree of probability that the language of the Ur-*Ṛgveda* could not have been far removed from the ancient Iranian, the process of actual linguistic reconstruction is full of extreme difficulties, some of which we may never be able to overcome. Chatterji (1960:58-59) says that the present text of the *Ṛgveda* (1.1.1a) *agnim īḷe purohitam* may have been originally *agnim iźdai purazdhitam.* Going back from *ḷ* or *ḍ* to **źd* takes us from a single consonant to a cluster. This would also lead us to assume shortening of *i*. Thus, it is important to realize that restoring the nonretroflex originals of the Ur-*Ṛgveda* would also perhaps require vocalic changes, if we go all the way back to the Proto-Indo-Iranian clusters. Fortunately, this does not alter the number of syllables in the text and hence would not harm the metrical form. We must also realize that the sound change from **źd* to *ḍ* or *ḷ* is not a direct change of one sound into another but implies a whole range from **źd* to *ḍ* or *ḷ*. It seems probable that the cluster **źd* would pass through a phase of being reduced to a geminate or an emphatic single consonant before being reduced to a single retroflex *ḍ* or *ḷ*. Śākalya's own word-text *duḥ-dabha* for the *Ṛgveda dūḷabha* (7.86.4c), shows that he is aware of a probable development such as *dur-dabha*>*dūḍabha*>*dūḷabha*. It is quite possible that the Ur-*Ṛgveda* had some kind of geminates or emphatic backed allophones of dentals. However, in the present state of our knowledge, we cannot be more precise about the exact nature of these Ur-*Ṛgveda* sounds. Mehendale (1963:41) shows that a palatal pronunciation of the retroflex *ṣ* continued dialectally in Sanskrit even during the period of the Upaniṣads. This makes the prospects of an exact reconstruction quite difficult.

13.2. I shall discuss only a few problems in the linguistic reconstruction of the original nonretroflex sounds. For instance, if we remove *ṣ* from the text of the present *Ṛgveda*, where do we go back to? The retroflex *ṣ* in Sanskrit corresponds to various sounds in different Prakrits, e.g., to *s* in Pāli (Skt. *puruṣa*/Pāli *purisa*); to *ś* in Māgadhī (*puliśe*); to *kh* in some branches of Yajurveda (*purukhaḥ*), and to *ch* (Skt. *ṣaṭ*/Pāli *cha*). This may indicate the complexity of the problem. Alfred Master's description of *ṣ* and its features raises complex historical problems. He remarks: "Now *ṣ* is a cerebral by convention only. It is, like *r*, a cerebralizer, rather than a cerebral and has been differentiated from the palatal *ś*, its fellow hush-sound, partly for graphical, partly for phonetic reasons. So we find *aṣṭau* 'eight', but *aśītiḥ* 'eighty', *pṛṣṭa* 'asked', and *praśna* 'question'. The phoneme is not carried into Middle Indian and for *ṣaṣ* we find *cha*, which seems to show that *ṣ* is a graphic variant of *kṣ*, regular predecessor of *ch* or *kh* in Middle Indian. The later confusion of *ṣ* and *kh*, both phonetically and graphically (the Gujarati *akṣara* for *kh* is a form of Nāgarī *ṣ*) points to the same conclusion" (Master 1960: 261). Existence of *ṣ* in the ancient northwestern inscriptional and noninscriptional Prakrits complicates the issue of *ṣ* to a great extent. The sound *ṣ* is distinctly preserved in the Niya Prakrit, in the Prakrit Dhammapada, in northwestern Aśokan dialects and in Dardic languages (Konow 1936:609; Burrow 1936:419). Niya Prakrit, which presents a pronouncedly more archaic aspect than the northwestern Aśokan dialect, better preserves the cluster *rṣ* (Burrow 1936:422). Like Niya Prakrit, occasionally later Kharoṣṭhī inscriptions of the northwestern region have *ṣ* even in those contexts, where Sanskrit shows *ś* or *s*, e.g., *śr*>*ṣ* in *ṣamana* (from *śramaṇa*); in Niya, *śmaśru*>*maṣu* and *śrayate*>*ṣayati*; the Kharoṣṭhī Dhammapada shows it, and also a similar treatment of *sr* in which *anavaṣutacitasa* is equated with *anavasruta* (Burrow 1936:422).

13.3 Mehendale's occasional reconstructions of some of the "pre-Sanskrit" stages also raise some interesting issues. He says: "I had suggested that such an extension of I [nternal] R [econstruction] can be done on the basis of Sanskrit past passive participle morpheme, where we can see the alternation *t*/*ṭ* (*ga-ta*/*tuṣ-ṭa*). On internal evidence this *ṭ* can be reconstructed as **t*, because *t* never occurs after *ṣ* in Sanskrit....But once this is done, we make use of this information and always remember the possibility of reconstructing *ṭ* as *t* in other non-alternating items where *t* occurs in the same environment (after *ṣ*) in which it alternates with *t* in the paradigm. Hence, the possibility of reconstructing Sk. *aṣṭa-* as **aṣta* should not be lost sight of when we are comparing Sanskrit with Avesta which shows the cognate *ašta*" (1968:88). Referring to the forms *gata-* and *tuṣṭa*, he says, "We have every right to assume that the morpheme of the pre-Sanskrit stage had the phonetic shape **ta*, and not **ṭa.* The implication of our choice is that in the history of Sanskrit **naṣta>naṣṭa,* and not **gaṭa>gata.* In this illustration, I do not think anyone will feel satisfied if we were to say that from the Sanskrit alternation *t/ṭ,* it should be possible to reconstruct 'one original morpheme, *ṭa*' " (1968:96-97).

13.4. I largely agree with Mehendale's analysis, but would like to point out some differences. I would rather consider his "pre-Sanskrit" stage as closely corresponding to what I think to be the state of the original compositions of the *Ṛgveda*. Another point is that I doubt if one can reconstruct forms like **tuṣta* and **naṣta*, as different from the Indo-Iranian **tušta* and **našta*, implying that there was a stage in the history of Indo-Aryan when the phonemic contrast between *ś* and *ṣ* had developed, but the phonemic contrast between *t* and *ṭ* had not developed. In my opinion, the initial allophonic divergence between *ś* and *ṣ* on the one hand, and *t* and *ṭ* on the other, leading eventually to a phonemic split, went on quite side by side.

13.5. Mehendale has another interesting discussion of the emergence of *ṣ* from *s*. He says: "In Sanskrit, *s* alternates with *ṣ*, some of the environments being when the former is preceded by *i, u, e, o*. The first two of these vowels have closeness as the common feature, but while *i* is a front vowel, *u* is a back vowel. The first and the third are both front, but *i* is close while *e* is an open vowel. Now on some other evidence if it is possible to reconstruct Sk. *e* and *o* as **ai* and **au*, then we discover closeness as a feature common to all the four (*i, u, ai* and *au*) environments. Therefore it should be possible for us to say that the change **s>ṣ* is two stages removed from the attested stage, while **ai>e* is one stage removed" (1968:101). This is an interesting discussion and would indicate one possible way of reconstructing a pre-*ṣ* stage in the prehistory of Sanskrit. It shows the possibility of certain vocalic changes being necessary for such a reconstruction. I shall not go into a detailed discussion of Mehendale's analysis at this point, but I may point out that he is taking into account only the vowels in the *ruki* rule and that basically the *ruki* rule yields a palatal *ś* from Indo-European **s*, and that this rule is partially extended in Sanskrit to *ṣ*. Even within Sanskrit, the rule as stated by Pāṇini (8.3.57, 58) incorporates more conditioning sounds than just *i, u, e*, and *o* (cf. the examples: **dik-su>dikṣu, *pitṛ-su>pitṛṣu, *a-kār-sī-t>akārṣīt*). The question as to how, if at all, the sounds *i, u, r*, and *k* can be considered a natural class has been the subject of considerable investigation by Anderson (1968) and Zwicky (1970), although no entirely satisfactory solution has as yet emerged from this.[71]

14. OTHER INSTANCES OF ALLEGED DRAVIDIAN INFLUENCE

14.1. If the retroflex sounds do belong to a post-Ṛgvedic period, this would lead to a reconsideration of other elements such as gerunds and particular uses of *iti* 'thus', which are ascribed by some scholars to Dravidian influence (Kuiper 1967). There is no reason to rule out all foreign influences from the original speech of the Ṛgvedic poets. The very fact that there are loanwords in the *Ṛgveda* obviously indicates that there was some give and take even at that early period. However, as discussed in this paper, there is no evidence for extensive pre-Ṛgvedic convergence with non-Aryans. This opens up several new possibilities for consideration. If the Ṛgvedic gerunds and the use of *iti* cannot be traced back to extensive pre-Ṛgvedic convergence, what kinds of contacts may be considered to be sufficient for such borrowings of new patterns? Could these elements be traced back to some other source?

14.2. In fact, in both the cases, i.e., gerunds and the use of *iti*, we are not even talking about large-scale lexical borrowing. Kuiper (1967:91) himself notes that the word *iti* is an inherited word.[72] Similarly, in the case of gerunds in the *Ṛgveda*, we have to accept that they are not borrowed lexical items, but are developments of "inherited" roots, or, as Kantor and Jeffers (1976:44) point out, the Sanskrit gerund-endings reflect "regrammatized instrumental (*-tvā, -yă̆, -tyă̆*) or locative (*tvī*) verbal noun suffixes, and that they are to be associated etymologically with Old Indic infinitives in *-tu, -ti,* and *-i*." In this case, one would be seeking an explanation of a development of an "inherited" set of items in terms of "foreign influence."

14.3. Can we say on the basis of any general principles that the contact with the non-Aryans which was insufficient to produce large-scale phonological changes could have been sufficient to promote new morphological and syntactic developments of inherited items? Weinreich (1953) has studied such theoretical issues concerning languages in contact.[73] However, the total inventory of known linguistic and extralinguistic facts about early Aryan-Dravidian contacts is not sufficient to let us derive any conclusions which are in any real sense beyond doubt. Kuiper (1967:90) himself has raised several important doubts concerning the extension of methods based on later periods of history to early periods of prehistory. It may be noted that several scholars have expressed their disbelief concerning Dravidian influence in the development of Sanskrit gerunds.[74] A better approach here would be to investigate whether Ṛgvedic gerunds are rare and/or used differently than in Dravidian.

14.4. While considering retroflexion in Sanskrit and the question of Dravidian influence on early Indo-Aryan phonology, another instance ascribed by some scholars to Dravidian influence deserves mention. Chattopadhyaya (1974:194ff.) says that in the days of Pāṇini the short *a* in Sanskrit was an open (*vivṛta*) sound like long *ā*, and that in post-Pāṇinian times this open short *a* became a close short *a* due to Dravidian influence. I have discussed this question in detail elsewhere (Deshpande 1975*c*) and have shown that there is no evidence to indicate that Sanskrit short *a* was an open sound in the days of Pāṇini and none to indicate that Dravidian influence on Sanskrit began only after Pāṇini. From the evidence in the *Aitareya-Āraṇyaka*, we know that retroflexion had already made its way into standardized Sanskrit speech before Śākalya, who precedes Pāṇini. Thus, if the Sanskrit short *a* became close due to Dravidian influence, it would probably have become close before the time of Śākalya. Actually, Macdonell (1916:14) claims that short *a* was open at the time of the composition of the *Ṛgveda*, but had become close by the time the Vedic recensions were put together. This may, then, parallel the case of retroflexion. However, the evidence presented by Macdonell is not quite conclusive for a determination of the change in phonetic quality of *a*, and there is no evidence yet to conclude that North Indian Proto-Dravidian had indeed a close short *a*. If Old Tamil is any indication, according to *Tolkāppiyam*, there is no quality distinction between Old Tamil *a* and *ā* (Subbiah 1968:253). Max Walleser (1927:195ff.), on the other hand, argues that the short *a* in Sanskrit has always been close, and he connects it with the Indo-European schwa (ə). If that is the case, we have no reason to suspect Dravidian influence in this respect.

15. CONCLUSIONS

15.1. In conclusion, it must be emphasized that the aim of this paper is not to discount the contacts of non-Aryans with Aryans in Ṛgvedic times; but we must carefully differentiate between contacts, conflicts, confrontations, coexistence, and convergence. In the *Ṛgveda* we have evidence for contacts, conflicts, and confrontations with non-Aryans, but certainly there is no evidence for convergence with them. The Aryan speech at this time could not have been phonologically affected by foreign speeches. I think that Emeneau (1974) has come up with the correct linguistic process. Later speakers of Sanskrit, a mixed Aryan-non-Aryan community, interpreted allophones of Proto-Indo-Aryan in terms of their native Dravidian system. However, the convergence of Aryan-non-Aryan peoples required to support this process can be evidenced not for the Ṛgvedic times, but only for later times, and Emeneau himself, among others, has given significant evidence for later convergence in terms of the development of caste terminology.[75]

15.2. Even after accepting the arguments for Dravidian linguistic influence at the time of the *Ṛgveda*, Trautmann (1974:84) shows that the ancient North Indian literature does not show signs of cross-cousin marriage, which is a marked feature of Dravidian communities: "...had cross-cousin marriage obtained among the dominant Aryan group, its literature would have so testified." Thus, the Indo-Aryans did not borrow everything that was Dravidian from the first day of their arrival in India, and it is quite reasonable to assume that the non-Aryan influence on the language and culture of the early Indo-Aryans was not of equal strength at all times. Weinreich (1953:67) discusses various views concerning relationships of foreign influence in different linguistic domains such as vocabulary, sound system, morphology, syntax, proper names, etc., and points out that it is still very premature to say that we can predict priorities and proportions of influences among these various domains in a given situation of language contact.[76]

15.3. This discussion makes us aware of the fact that explaining the emergence of a feature like retroflexion involves many complex elements, and no simplistic solutions will work. After stating that "Indic acquires Dravidian retroflex apicals," Bailey and Gardens (1974:16) remark: "To analyse such typical cases in the history of languages as natural sound changes would of course be as theoretically profitless as to formulate umlauted German noun plurals or apophonic English verbs (e.g., *sing, sang, sung*) in terms of natural phonological rules." This indicates that features which are due to linguistic convergence cannot be reconstructed as part of texts belonging to a preconvergence stage, and it also warns us against pure genetic explanations of such features. Though features like retroflexion are unnatural from the point of view of genetic evolution within the Indo-Aryan language family, recent studies indicate that such features can be explained in terms of naturalness of loan phonology. Lovins (1974:240, 244) explains that the historic statement of the problem of loan phonology is that a speaker of a given language, in perceiving and reproducing the sounds of a foreign language, substitutes for them those that he takes to be "closest" in his own language. This further suggests that a feature like retroflexion, not genetically evolved, is a product of the process of *phonetic approximation* (cf. Lovins:240) of the phonic material of a given nonretroflexed language by the speakers of a retroflexed language. Thus, even in theory, it is hard to assume that speakers of a nonretroflexed language adopted the foreign feature of retroflexion without its phonetic approximation to their own system. Thus, to explain the development of retroflexion, we have to posit a sociolinguistic process of adaptation of a nonretroflexed Indo-Aryan tongue by the speakers of a retroflexed language. In the early stages, the principle of *phonetic approximation* must have affected the linguistic perception as well as the linguistic production of these people who adopted a nonretroflexed language as their second language. This process of linguistic adaptation guided by the principle of phonetic approximation can, then, be used to explain what happens in a preliterate oral tradition.

The orthodox Indian tradition has greatly respected the relationship of a teacher and his disciple and has continued to believe that nothing ever changed in this oral transmission. It is believed that the oral text has been handed down from one generation to the next without any changes. However, we must view a preliterate oral tradition with a fresh linguistic and analytical approach. We must distinguish a "pseudo-connection" from a "real connection" between two successive synchronic states of a preliterate oral text. For this purpose, we may compare the model of linguistic change given by Andersen (1973:767):

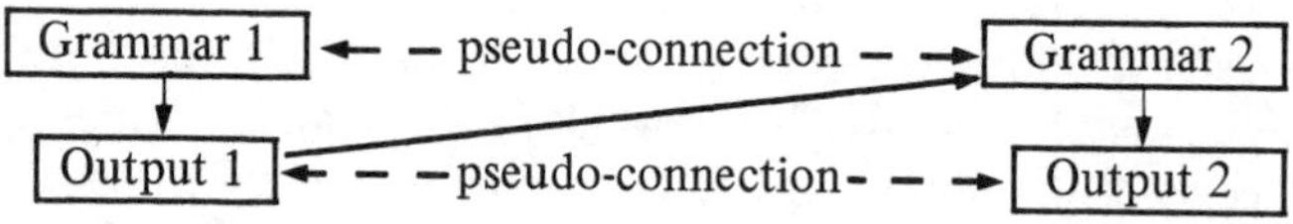

With respect to this model, Ebert (1976:ix) says: "The crucial process in language transmission–and the one that plays a central role in language change–is the learner's formulation of his grammar (Grammar 2) on the basis of the output of speakers from whom he learns (Output 1). An analysis of Output 1 by the learner which differs from Grammar 1 can lead to an observable change in usage."

By using this analysis of language change, we may construct a model for gradual change in a text orally transmitted from a teacher to a student in a preliterate society. The following is an attempted model:

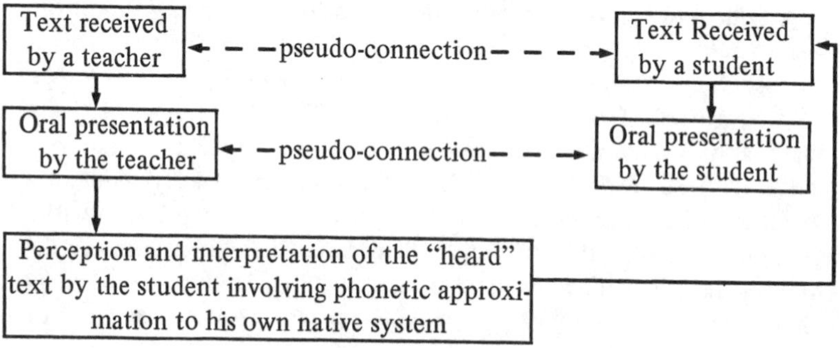

We must realize that only such dynamic models will explain the actual complex processes involved in the development of the nongenetic features like retroflexion in orally transmitted Indo-Aryan texts. With the above model in view, we may further sharpen our analytical tools.

Lovins (1974:244) talks about how context-sensitive processes determine one's perception of one's own native language and also of foreign sounds: "When we speak, we apply allophonic processes 'forwards' to produce contextual variants; when we listen to someone else, we apply them 'backwards' to relate the allophones to their associated phonemes....Likewise, in listening to unfamiliar foreign sounds, we try to relate what we hear to possible surface forms in our own language. These surface forms may already be acceptable underlying representations, or related to such by backwards-derivation of an allophonic process." Thus, one can say that when a teacher recites a "received text," he is applying allophonic processes "forwards" to produce an oral text. When a disciple hears this oral text, he applies the allophonic processes "backwards" to relate the heard allophones to "appropriate" phonemes in his own phonological system. When he recites the text, he applies allophonic processes "forwards" to the "received text." This received text must now, obviously, exist in full conformity with the disciple's native phonological system. Similarly, his "forwards" application of allophonic processes to produce an oral text must also be in full conformity with his native phonological system. Thus, if there is any difference between the native phonological systems of the teacher and the disciple, these underlying differences, plus the differences in the "forwards-and-backwards" application of allophonic processes, must lead to a gradual change in the transmitted oral text. This theoretical framework explains in a most clear manner the inner functioning of a preliterate oral tradition. Figure 3 is an attempt to schematize the nature of a preliterate oral tradition.

15.4. Having basically accepted Emeneau's "process" for the development of retroflexion, we may clearly distinguish between language contact that allows borrowing of vocabulary, but not transfer of phonemic contrasts, and contact which generates such contrasts. How far can we say that the Vedic Aryans, who originally did not have retroflexion in their language, developed this feature through contacts with non-Aryans whom they conquered, hated, dominated, and segregated? There are abundant examples which show that even culturally and politically dominating speakers of retroflexed languages could not transmit retroflexion to speakers of languages without retroflexion. For example, the Cambodians were culturally and politically dominated by an Indian empire. Through these Hindu and Buddhist contacts, the Old

FIGURE 3

MODEL OF AN ORAL TRADITION

"A student of the previous generation becomes a teacher of the next."

$(S\text{-}T)_1 \longrightarrow (S\text{-}T)_2 \longrightarrow (S\text{-}T)_3 \longrightarrow (S\text{-}T)_n$

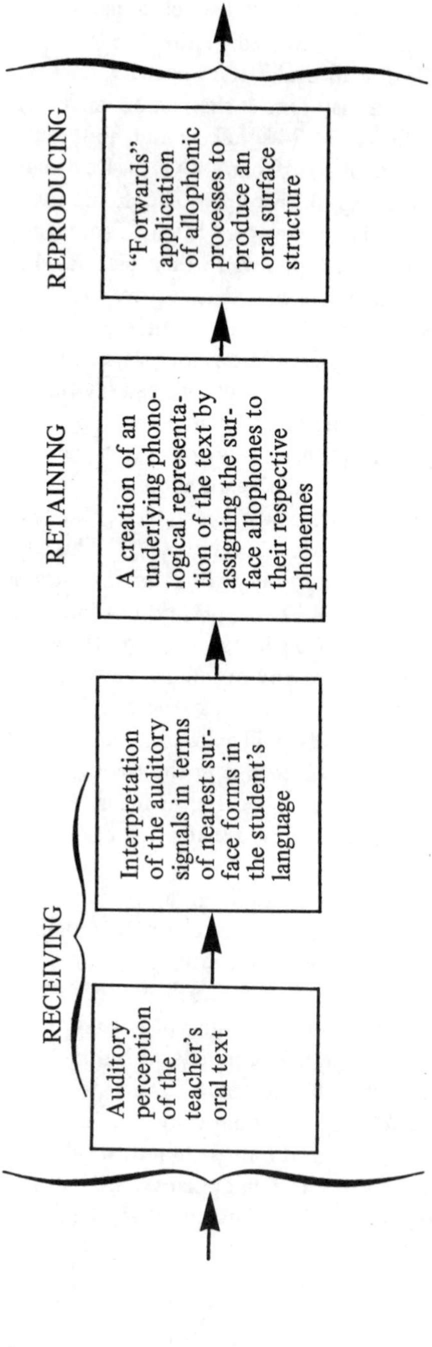
RECEIVING
RETAINING
REPRODUCING
Auditory perception of the teacher's oral text
Interpretation of the auditory signals in terms of nearest surface forms in the student's language
A creation of an underlying phonological representation of the text by assigning the surface allophones to their respective phonemes
"Forwards" application of allophonic processes to produce an oral surface structure

(S-T) = A student of one generation who becomes a teacher of the next.

Cambodian language borrowed a large number of Sanskrit/Pāli words. The Cambodians also adopted several aspects of Indian culture, but not retroflexion. In Old and Modern Cambodian, the Sanskrit and Pāli retroflexes are reduced to dentals.[77] The same phenomenon takes place in Old and Modern Siamese.[78] Burmese does have separate characters for retroflex sounds, which are used only in writing Pāli words, but the Burmese pronounce them exactly as the corresponding alveolars.[79] Assamese, an Indo-Aryan language which is historically almost a dialect of Bengali, shows convergence of dentals and retroflexes into alveolars, an event which can be explained as the result of the predominance of a Tibeto-Burman substratum in the Assamese population.[80]

15.5. Thus, simple contacts and even cultural and political domination do not seem to have caused the development of retroflexion in a nonretroflexed language. On the other hand, with respect to the occurrence of some retroflex sounds in eastern Iranian languages like Pašto, Parachi, and Ormuṛi, one can speak of Indian linguistic influence. Geiger and Kuhn (1895-1901:206-7) consider this point under "Fremde Elemente im Afghanischen," and speak of the influence of Sindhi. Morgenstierne speaks of Indic, and particularly Dardic, influence on Pašto.[81] Bloch (1965:56) thinks that "the presence of cerebrals in Afghan probably points to an Indian substratum," and a Dravidian element may be suspected on the basis of the nearby presence of Brahui.

15.6. In the case of Sanskrit, the origin of retroflexion lies not so much in the Aryans' borrowing this trait from Dravidians in early times as in Dravidians' adapting Aryan speech to their native phonology. As we can see from the cultural history of India, by the time of the *Brāhmaṇa* period, the speakers of the Sanskrit language were not pure Vedic Aryans but were already a mixed people. The development of the caste system shows to what extent the non-Aryan elements were Aryanized in the historical development of Hinduism.[82] Non-Aryans and non-Vedic Aryans were raised to the status of Brahmins and Kṣatriyas, and the Ṛgvedic enemies such as Paṇis seem to have been absorbed into the Vaiśya caste.[83] This makes one wonder if the descendants of the original Aryans were numerically not a minority in this mixed Aryanized society (Panikkar 1961:31). In the words of Dandekar (1967: 28-29): "In the long and continual history of Hinduism, the age of the Veda must be said to have occurred more or less as an interlude."

15.7. In classical Hinduism, the pre-Aryan Proto-Hinduism regained its strength in an Aryanized form, so much so that the Vedic gods like Indra and Varuṇa and their elaborate fire-sacrifices almost became extinct, while Kṛṣṇa, Śiva, and a host of other gods and goddesses came to dominate the field, with the claim that they still represented the essence of the Vedas.[84] This process gradually changed the constitution of the Sanskrit-speaking community in such a way that the ethnic non-Aryan segment of this Aryanized community steadily increased in proportion. In such circumstances, speakers of Sanskrit were essentially bilinguals, with Sanskrit as their second language, and a local language as their first language. The particular process involved in the development of retroflexion as described by Emeneau applies clearly to this post-Ṛgvedic period. Steadily increasing retroflexion in Indo-Aryan is a significant index of this sociolinguistic and religious transformation of the Sanskrit-speaking community. However, to the speech of the Ṛgvedic poets, retroflexion was most probably still a foreign habit.

NOTES

1. Emeneau, *Collected Papers*, 1967:159. For details of the convergence theory, see Southworth and Apte 1974, Southworth 1974, and Hock 1975.
2. Pāṇini 8.3.19, 6.1.128, and 1.1.16.
3. *RPR* 1.16, 1.19, 2.44, 3.7, 3.13, 4.2, 4.5, 6.7-8, 11.10-11, 11.31 and 13.12 (numbers refer to chapter and verse respectively).
4. *Aitareya-Āraṇyaka* 3.1.1, 3.2.1, 3.2.6; and *Śāṅkhāyana-Āraṇyaka* 7.3, 7.16 and 8.1-2.
5. *RPR, Vargadvaya*, verse 7.
6. Introduction to *Śāṅkhāyana-Āraṇyaka*, Ānandāśrama Sanskrit Series, no. 90 (Poona, 1922).
7. "The passage may indicate [cf. also *Śāṅkhāyana-Śrauta-Sūtra*, 4.10.3, where Śākalya is younger apparently than Māṇḍūkeya] that the Māṇḍūkeya Śākhā had its Saṁhitā text before Śākalya produced the *Pada-Pāṭha*, which is quite likely" (Keith, *Aitareya-Āraṇyaka*, p. 257, fn. 9).
8. *MB*:vol. 1, sec. 1, pp. 292-93 and p. 54.
9. See also Bloch 1970:2.
10. See Dandekar 1961:vol. 2, pp. 3-4.
11. See also note 16.
12. S. B. Pandit (*Atharvaveda* [Bombay, 1895], vol. 1, Introduction, p. 6) records an informative account of his dealings with an *AV* reciter: "He was more shocked that the several MSS of that Veda...exhibited numerous varieties of reading, and still more horrified when he found that the text he knew by heart...was the worse for the improvements. His great anxiety at first was that the text I was going to publish should not show that his pāṭha was incorrect...though he little hoped the Vaidikas would exchange their corruptions for our corrections."
13. Uvaṭa on *RPR* 13.10. On *RPR* 10.7, he says that some reciters pronounce *ṅ* in the place of an *anusvāra*.
14. *RPR* 1.2 refers to *anusvāra* as an unvoiced sibilant, but 13.3 excludes it from sibilants, and 13.5 considers it to be a voiced nasal sound; see Deshpande 1976.
15. Also see James Bare 1976:26-27.
16. Hannes Sköld (1926:44ff.) refers to Vedamitra's view and says that if Vedamitra's description of *ḍ* and *ḍh* as palato-velars is correct, then their intervocalic replacements, namely *ḷ* and *ḷh*, could not be retroflexes. "But the description in all points coincides with that of that *l* of Lithuanian, of the Turkish and Slav languages, which is described as a 'guttural *l*' and the existence of which can be traced in Latin and Old Armenian" (p. 45). Sköld (p. 45) argues that the *ḍ/ḷ* and *ḍh/ḷh* alternation as upheld by Vedamitra and by Śākalya's text was not accepted by the *RPR* itself. His conclusion (p. 46) is interesting: "The development of *ḷ* is posterior to the Saṁhitā text....Is the *ḷ* introduced by the Śākalas?" He points out that for the word *vīḍvagam* in *RV* 1.118.9, the word text of Śākalya gives *vīḷu-agam*. Also see section 6.11 of this paper.
17. The Prakrit word *goṇī* for Skt. *gauḥ* is found in *MB*:vol. 1, sec. 1, p. 42. Other Prakrit expressions noted by Patañjali are: *yarvāṇa* and *tarvāṇa* (*MB*:vol. 1, sec. 1, p. 56), *āṇavayati* (*MB*:vol. 1, sec. 2, p. 125), *vaṭṭati* and *vaḍḍhayati* (ibid.), and *diṇṇa* (ibid., sec. 1, p. 74).

18. The *Samayasāra* of Kundakunda, edited by J. L. Jaini (Lucknow, 1930). The verse 1.3 has *hodi* (Skt. *bhavati*), while the verse 1.13 has *havadi*. Metrically both the forms are of equal quantity. This makes one wonder if one of these forms was not a scribal error for the other, or if in the oral tradition the difference between *hodi* and *havadi* was simply metrically irrelevant.
19. *Pañcāstikāya*, Rāyacandra Jaina Śāstramālā, 3rd ed. (1969) vol. 7.
20. Śākalya has been quoted by Pāṇini (see note 2), and he along with others has been quoted by the *RPR*.
21. Another example (Bloomfield and Edgerton:vol. 2, p. 152) is the *Sāmaveda* variation of *made suśipram* with *madeṣu śipram*. On the variation *āpṛṇo'si/āpṛṇoṣi*, Bloomfield and Edgerton (vol. 2, p. 152) remark: "The latter is corrupt." For similar spontaneous variation of *s/ṣ*, see Bloomfield and Edgerton, pp. 149ff.
22. See note 16. The *VPR* (8.45) explicitly states that the Mādhyandina recension of the *YV* does not have the sounds *ḷ* and *ḷh* and that only the Kāṇva recension has these sounds. While the former is a North Indian tradition, the latter is a South Indian tradition. The commentaries of Uvaṭa and Anantabhaṭṭa on the *VPR* (3.87; 3.91, etc.) make it quite clear that the Kāṇva recension has decidedly more retroflexion than the Mādhyandina recension.
23. The *RPR* (1.8, 10) classifies *ṛ* as a *jihvāmūlīya* 'produced at the root of the tongue', and *r* as either *dantamūlīya* 'produced at the root of teeth' or *barsvya* 'alveolar'. The *VPR* (1.65, 68) classifies *ṛ* as a tongue-root sound and *r* as a dental. The *SCA* (1.20, 28) holds the same view. For the *TPR* (2.18, 41), *ṛ* and *r* are both alveolars.
24. The only favorable references are to some political alliances made by the Aryan enemies of the king Sudās with non-Aryans (*RV* 7.18-19), and a reference to the non-Aryan king Bṛbu who gave gifts to Aryan poets (*RV* 6.45.31-33).
25. *RV* 1.51.5-6, 1.103.4, 10.95.7, 10.99.7, and 10.105.11. It is extremely important to recognize that all of these references to *dasyu-hattyā* are found in those parts of the *RV* which are traditionally regarded to be late parts of that text. This would most probably mean that even by the time of the late parts of the *RV*, the attitudes of the Vedic Aryans had not significantly changed, and they still regarded the *dasyus* as those who deserve to be killed by Indra.
26. Other important descriptions are *ayajyavaḥ* 'non-sacrificers' and *anindrāḥ* 'those who do not believe in Indra'.
27. Burrow (1967:311) refers to twenty-five Dravidian loans in the *RV* and says that "it is not many, compared with the number in later Sanskrit." Kuiper (1955) lists many more non-Aryan loans in the *RV*, but many of these are debatable.
28. Vaidyanathan 1971. The rules for Tamilization of Sanskrit words are found in *Tolkāppiyam-Collatikāram*. For general rules for the Tamilization of Sanskrit words, see Vaidyanathan 1958, and Ganeshsundaram and Vaidyanathan 1958.
29. Bloch (1965:58) thinks that *kāṭá-* is derived from *kartá-*. Referring to Bartholomae's attempt to connect *kāṭá-* and *kartá-*, Burrow (1972:544) comments: "The connection of *kāṭá-* with *kartá-* is anything but certain, it could have a spontaneous cerebral and be connected with *kāṭu-* 'hole' along with which it is listed in Nighaṇṭu 3, 23."
30. W. J. Gedney, *Indic Loan-Words in Spoken Thai* (Ph.D. dissertation, Yale University, 1947). For details of nativization of Indic loanwords in Southeast Asia, see notes 77-79.

31. I refer to the following Sanskrit words, claimed to be Dravidian loanwords in the *RV* by Professor Southworth:

Skt. *phala-* 'fruit'	<	DED 3299 *paẓu* 'ripen'
Skt. *kulpha-* 'ankle'	<	DED 1519 Ta. *kuḷampu* 'hoof'
Skt. *kulāya-* 'nest'	<	DED 1563 Ta. *kūṭu* 'nest'
Skt. *bila-* 'hole, cave'	<	DED 4459 Ta. *viḷ* 'open out'
Skt. *kula-* 'herd, flock'	<	DED 1513 Ta. *kuẓu* 'assembly' or DED 1562 Ta. *kūṭi* 'come together'

32. For a religio-historical perspective, see Dandekar 1967:29ff. Emeneau (1974) discusses Sanskrit caste terminology and its bearing on borrowing from the Dravidian social structure. Also see Srinivas 1966:1-45, and Chatterji 1962.
33. Chatterji 1962:70-71. Also see Nilakanta Sastri 1967:48ff. Burrow (*Collected Papers*, 1968:312) points out "that the great majority (of Dravidian words in Sanskrit) have become established by the time of the epic poems, Mahābhārata and Rāmāyaṇa, and of these a large proportion are first quoted from these texts." Evidence gathered by Emeneau (1974:112) for social convergence on the basis of caste terminology also begins with lists of caste terms in the Mahābhārata. Also see Hart 1975:277ff.
34. *Śāṇkhāyana-Āraṇyaka* 7.13 refers to the views of Madhyama Māṇḍūkeya Magadhavāsin Prātibodhīputra. He is the "middle" Māṇḍūkeya residing in Magadha. For other early Brahmanic traditions in the east, see Chakladar 1928.
35. *Kauṣītaki-Brāhmaṇa* 7.6. See Keith, *Ṛgveda-Brāhmaṇas*, Harvard Oriental Series, no. 25 (1920):387. Also see Chatterji 1960:50. Chakladar (1928) holds that the first Aryan migration produced the Vedas, but that these Vedic Aryans were pushed into the "outer" regions by the second wave. His views are based on tenuous interpretations of the Vedic evidence, and I plan to deal with them separately.
36. See note 34.
37. Macdonell (1916:14, 22-23) shows that where Śākalya's recension of the *RV* shows a merging of the two vowels and a resulting loss of a syllable, needed by the meter, we must restore the two original vowels. The *Aitareya-Āraṇyaka* (3.1.5) gives indications that the text of the Māṇḍūkeya recension in fact kept these vowels separate and was thus closer to the original than Śākalya's text. See Keith's note on the *Aitareya-Āraṇyaka*, p. 244.
38. For a more comprehensive study, see Rakshit 1966.
39. Oldenberg 1882:9. He points out that the river Sadānīrā was the dividing line between the Vedic Aryans and the outlandic Aryans. The sacrificial fire had not crossed to the east of the river Sadānīrā (ibid., pp. 10-11).
40. Oldenberg (1882:394) says: "Thus we have here a distinction between those stocks, who felt themselves to be qualified champions of Aryan culture, and those who were Aryans, it is true, but were not regarded as equally accredited partakers in this culture. Momenta of many kinds may have co-operated to bring about and enhance this difference. Association with non-Aryan elements, to which the stocks that had migrated to the greatest distances were especially exposed, may have been at the same time in play."
41. Also see Banerjea 1963:81ff.

42. Mehendale 1948:297; Konow 1936:609; and Burrow 1936:419.
43. *atha vāg itihāsa-purāṇam yac cānyat kiñcid brāhmī-kṛtyevādhīyīta, tad apy evam eva vidyāt|*
44. This is expressed by the grammarians with the term *abhūta-tad-bhāva* 'transforming *x* into something which it is not'.
45. *Aitareya-Āraṇyaka* 3.2.3 uses the word *akṣara-samāmnāya* and says: "That which we call the person of the meters is the collection of letters. Its essence is the letter *a*." In 2.3.8, we have the assertion *a iti brahma* 'Brahman is named *a*'. In 2.3.6, *a* is said to represent speech as a whole. This clarifies the relation between the concepts of *vāk, brahman*, and *akṣara-samāmnāya.*
46. *VPR* 8.1.32 refers to *varṇa-samāmnāya* and calls it *brahma-rāśi*; also *RT* 1.4 and *MB*:vol. 1, sec. 1, p. 102.
47. *NR* 1.127-28; *MB*:vol. 1, sec. 1, p. 54.
48. *MB*, on P.6.3.109, vol. 2, p. 884.
49. Chatterji 1956:24-27. On page 26, he says: "Such a state of things is nothing new or remarkable in the history of literature–viz., of literary composition in one form, and an earlier one, and preservation and transmission in another and a later form of the language. The Vedas were probably compiled in the 10th century B.C., but some at least of the Vedic hymns were composed several centuries earlier and were continued from generation to generation by oral tradition, and these were unquestionably first composed in an older form of the speech than what we find in the compiled text, which is our received text."
50. Chatterji (1960:52-54) doubts the Phoenician origin of the Brāhmī script and suggests that it was adopted from the ancient Sindh-Panjab script of the non-Aryans. However, recently Dani (1963) has reasserted Bühler's theory, and it has also been accepted by Mahadevan (1970 and 1960), who shows that Brāhmī was later adapted for ancient Tamil.
51. Bühler 1895:2-3. Though Cunningham thought that the Brāhmī script was of purely Indian origin, he remarks: "Similarly, the series of cerebral letters, which was also wanting originally in Tibetan, was afterwards supplied by the invention of new letters, which are simply the five dental letters reversed. This is not exactly the case with the cerebral letters of the Ariano-Pāli alphabet, but their forms differ so slightly from those of the dentals, that it seems highly probable that they must have been a late addition to the original alphabetical scheme" (*Corpus Inscriptionum Indicarum*, vol. 1, introduction; p. 49; reprinted by Indological Book House, Banaras, 1961).
52. Pāṇini 8.3.57 (*iṇ-koḥ*).
53. "In the lingual *ḷa*, derived from the round *ḍ* a small semi-circle has been added to indicate the change of the phonetic value. Here also, I believe, we may recognize the influence of the grammarians or phoneticists. For the sounds *ḍa* and *ḷa* are frequently interchanged in the same word. Thus we find already in the Vedas regularly a *ḷa* for a *ḍa* between two vowels, as in *īḷe* for *īḍe*" (Bühler 1895:77).
54. "The absence of first two nasals *ṅ, ñ* and 'retroflex' or 'cerebral' consonants, namely *ṭ, ṭh, ḍ, ḍh* and *ṇ*, and the presence of *g, th, d* and *b*, which do not occur in Tamil, clearly show that the Late Harappan language is closer to the Indo-European than to the Dravidian group of languages" (S. R. Rao 1972-73:9).

55. Parpola (1975) assumes that the Indus Valley language is a form of ancient Dravidian. I think Thieme (1955:439) rightly points out that "it is easy to agree with Emeneau that 'the assumption that the language of the Indus Valley documents was Dravidian is clearly not fantastic' (*Proc. Amer. Phil. Soc.*, 98. 283 [1954]); the trouble is that the assumption that it was *NOT* is clearly not fantastic either."

56. P.6.1.64 (*dhātv-ādeḥ ṣaḥ saḥ*) and P.6.1.65 (*ṇo naḥ*). The rules P.8.3.56ff. and P.8.4.14ff. indicate the complexity of the problem. Referring to the question of unclear morpheme boundaries, Brough points out that we can have "*pūrvāhṇaḥ*, but *durahnaḥ*, without option, whereas in other examples the option may be permitted: *surāpāṇam, surāpānam*. In spite of the struggle to reduce this complicated situation to a series of rules, the junction of *upasarga*s seems to have been particularly resistant to systematic formulation." With respect to Pāṇini 8.4.1ff., he adds: "Many of the rules were doubtless valid, but it may be suspected that some of them are useful to the same extent as the advice given to schoolboys in elementary textbooks of Latin, that 'most names of rivers and many names of mountains are masculine' " (Brough 1962:107).

57. *MB*, on P.6.1.64-65, vol. 2, p. 715. Patañjali provides partial generalizations for *ṣopadeśa* and *ṇopadeśa* categories, with lists of additions and exceptions. All *n*-initial verbs are *ṇopadeśa* verbs, except *nṛt, nand, nard, nakk, nāṭ, nāth, nādh*, and *nṝ*. All *s*-initial verbs, with a post-initial vowel or a dental consonant, are *ṣopadeśa* verbs, except *sṛp, sṛj, stṝ, styā, sek*, and *sṛ*, but including *smi, svad, svid, svañj*, and *svap*. For a discussion of the implication in this passage that Patañjali considered *v* to be a pure labial sound, see Deshpande 1975*a*:54.

58. In practice, we do not find a word-final *ś* followed by a word-initial *s*. The final *ś* changes either to *k* or *ṭ*. For the development of final *ś*, see Kuiper 1967*a*.

59. The change *s*>*ṣ* of this kind is no longer productive in classical Sanskrit. It is found only in archaic survivals.

60. *RV* 1.173.12. Bloomfield's *Vedic Concordance* (p. 723) provides many more occurrences of *mo ṣu* in different texts. Other examples are *āsu ṣmā ṇaḥ* (*RV* 6.44.18), and *parīto ṣiñcata* (*RV* 9.107.1). Abhyankar (1974:55) calls the change of *sma* to *ṣma* in the above passage an irregular change.

61. P.8.3.101 (*yuṣmat-tat-tatakṣuḥṣv antaḥpādam*) has the condition *antaḥpādam* 'within the same metrical foot', and several following rules are governed by this condition. See the *Kāśikā-vṛtti* on these rules for Vedic examples.

62. This refers to the precodification period, when the Vedic hymns were a floating oral literature. Esteller (1969:9) says: "This will appear all the more convincing and decisive if we recollect that we are dealing with compositions in an archaic-literary style of a language that is beginning a period of rapid evolution–owing to a swift expansion and the influence of a pre-Aryan linguistic substratum." Also see Chatterji 1960:52. For a possible explanation of unevenness in these developments, see Lovins 1974:242.

63. The *Kāśikā-vṛtti* on P.8.3.102ff. quotes important examples of irregular retroflexion in the *Taittirīya-Saṁhitā: agniṣṭat* (1.1.14.5) and *agnistat* (3.2.5.4). Abhyankar (1974:35) notes that the *Taittirīya* reciters occasionally pronounce *ṇ* in the place of *n* without any reason: *enāḥ/eṇāḥ*, and *agniḥ/agṇiḥ*. He also points out that this practice is already noticed by Bhartṛhari (about 400 A.D.). Kuiper (1965:77ff.) notes the development of similar secondary retroflex variants from dentals in

Munda. Hoffmann (1960:176-77) refers to the variation in the Maitrāyaṇī and the Kaṭha versions of the *YV*.

64. If the words in a given sequence are *xyz*, then the later permutation-combinations could be produced giving us patterns like *xy, yz; xyyxxy, yzzyyz*, etc. But all these variations depend on first having the "continuous" text split into *x, y*, and *z*. If an editor-redactor felt that a certain sequence as a whole was a single word and was not to be split into *x, y*, and *z*, then there cannot be further variations based on *x, y*, and *z*.
65. See note 63.
66. *Pāṇinīya-Śikṣā*, verse 17. Also see note 23.
67. P.8.4.2 (*aṭ-ku-pv-āṅ-nuṁ-vyavāye' pi*) gives the conditions for noncontiguous application of the retroflexion rule. For a recent study of the noncontiguous aspect of this process, see Dasgupta (1972:118ff.).
68. *raśruter laśrutir bhavati, MB*:vol. 1, sec. 1, p. 84. For details, see Deshpande 1975*b*: 22-26.
69. Ibid.
70. This compares well with Emeneau's suggestion (1974:93) concerning the "backed" allophones of dentals which he suggests were later interpreted in terms of retroflexes by the mixed speakers.
71. Henning Anderson, "IE *s after *i, u, r, k* in Baltic and Slavic," *Acta Linguistica Hafniensia* 11(1968):171-90; Arnold Zwicky, "Greek-Letter Variables and the Sanskrit *ruki*-Class," *Linguistic Inquiry* 1(1970):549-55.
72. Also see Eric P. Hamp (1976:351-61), who has an insightful discussion of the *iti*-problem, where the role of the inherited item and the role of the *Sprachbund* have been presented in a balanced manner.
73. Also see Weinreich, Labov, and Herzog 1968; Hoijer 1948; and Dell Hymes 1964 and 1971.
74. Kuiper 1967:83.
75. Hock (1975:114) considers all the available evidence and concludes: "While it is thus unlikely that there was early convergence of Indo-Aryan with Dravidian, this should not be understood to imply that there is proof against such a convergence." Burrow (1955:387) cautiously says: "The main influence of Dravidian on Indo-Aryan was concentrated at a particular historical period, namely between the late Vedic period and the formation of the classical language." On the basis of comparisons of caste terminology in Sanskrit and Dravidian languages, Emeneau (1974: 113) argues that "the invading Aryans did not bring this social structure with them. They either met it in India and adopted it in their process of Indianization, or they and those they met in India developed it together to produce the India we know now." However, the elaborate lists of caste terms on which Emeneau's argument for convergence is based are first found in the *Mahābhārata* and not earlier. From a study of Agnicayana, Converse (1974) comes to the similar conclusion that convergence took place at a post-Ṛgvedic period. Hart (1975) arrives at similar conclusions through a study of the literary history of Indo-Aryan and Dravidian. He shows that the principle of poetic suggestion (*vyañjanā*) is of Dravidian origin, and that it makes its headway in Sanskrit literature after *Mahābhārata*, but is clearly seen in the *Rāmāyaṇa*. I have myself dealt with the question of the gradual increase of non-Brāhmaṇa and non-Aryan elements among the Brāhmaṇas in a post-Ṛgvedic period

in an article under preparation. In the case of Vyāsa, for instance, we find that his mother, grandmother, great-grandmother, and perhaps the great-great-grandmother were all at least non-Brāhmaṇa, if not also non-Aryan. But he was a Brāhmaṇa.

76. His discussion of the views held by Whitney, Pritzwald, and Dauzat on the relative strengths of the various linguistic domains is particularly illuminating.

77.

Sanskrit-Pāli		Old Cambodian		Modern Cambodian
t	>	*t* (voiceless)	>	*t* in clusters otherwise *d*.
th	>	*th* (voiceless)	>	*th*
d	>	*d* (voiced)	>	*t*
dh	>	*dh* (voiced)	>	*th*
n	>	*n* (voiceless?)	>	*n*
ṭ	>	*t* (voiceless)	>	*d*
ṭh	>	*th* (voiceless)	>	*th*
ḍ	>	*d* (voiced)	>	*d*
ḍh	>	*dh* (voiced)	>	*th*
ṇ	>	*n* (voiced)	>	*n*

I am indebted to Professor William Gedney for this information.

78.

Sanskrit-Pāli		Old Siamese		Modern Siamese
t,ṭ	>	*t* (voiceless)	>	*t*
th,ṭh	>	*th* (voiceless)	>	*th*
d,ḍ	>	*d* (voiced)	>	*th*
dh,ḍh	>	*d* (voiced)	>	*th*
n,ṇ	>	*n* (voiced)	>	*n*

This information is also provided by Professor William Gedney. The origin of retroflexion in Javanese is controversial, and the influence of Sanskrit and/or the existence of retroflexes *ṭ* and *ḍ* in Proto-Austronesian are hotly debated issues. See *Proto-Austronesian* by Otto C. Dahl (Lund, 1973), pp. 55ff.; and "Problems of Austronesian Comparative Philology," by André G. Haudricourt, in *Indo-Pacific Linguistic Studies*, pt. 1., edited by Milner-Henderson (Amsterdam, 1965). It is very difficult to say that Javanese "developed" retroflexion due to Sanskrit influence. It would be more appropriate to say that the Sanskrit influence strengthened the allophonic variation between dentals and alveolars, a variation which may have been originally stylistic or dialectal and which was also influenced by Malay loanwords with apical stops which were pronounced further back than the Javanese apical stops. Despite the use of the word "retroflex" with respect to Javanese *ḍ* and *ṭ* and **ṭ* and **ḍ* in Proto-Austronesian by Haudricourt and Dahl, there is actually no Sanskrit-like retroflexion in Javanese, but, rather, a contrast between dentals and alveolars. The retroflex signs in writing are due to the influence of Sanskrit, but have no corresponding phonetic value. The Sanskrit sounds have been definitely assimilated into the native phonology, e.g., the aspirate stops *ṭh* and *ḍh* are deaspirated and assimilated into alveolar *ṭ* and *ḍ*. Similarly, the nasal retroflex *ṇ* and sibilant *ṣ* of Sanskrit are assimilated into dental *n* and *s* respectively. Thus, we cannot look at Javanese as being very different from the normal pattern of assimilation of foreign sounds into components of the native phonology. I am thankful to Professor Alton Becker for clarifying for me the relationship between Sanskrit and Javanese.

79. J. A. Stewart, *Manual of Colloquial Burmese* (London, 1955), p. 6.
80. Banikanta Kakati, *Assamese, Its Formation and Development* (Gauhati, 1941), rev. 1962 by G. C. Goswami. On page 199, note 9, Goswami says: "The O.I.A. dental and cerebral series lost their original sound values and became alveolars, i.e., the point of articulation for the dentals is pushed back and for the cerebrals pushed forward" due to the Tibeto-Burman influence which had this leveling effect. See also P. C. Bhattacharya 1975:242; Southworth 1971:261, and 1974:206, 214-15.
81. Georg Morgenstierne, "Neu-Iranische Sprachen," in *Handbuch der Orientalistik, Iranistik* (Leiden-Köln, 1958), p. 169.
82. Emeneau 1974; K. A. Nilakanta Sastri 1967:48ff.; Srinivas 1966:1-45; Chatterji 1962:82ff.; and 1965:46ff.
83. Skt. *vaṇij* 'merchant' and *paṇya-* 'merchandise' are related to Vedic *paṇi*, the name of a non-Aryan trading tribe.
84. For instance, the *Bhagavad-Gītā* (15.15) mentions Krishna's claim that he is to be known from all the Vedas. Such statements can be found in almost all the Purāṇas. This kind of syncretism has been a hallmark of classical Hinduism.

REFERENCES

Abhyankar, K. V. 1974. *Veda-pada-pāṭha-carcā*. Bhandarkar Oriental Research Institute, Post Graduate and Research Department Series (Poona), no. 10.

———. 1969. "Accents in Sanskrit." *Annals of the Bhandarkar Oriental Research Institute* (Poona) 50.

Acharya, K. C. 1971. "Linguistic Remarks on Some Words in the 1st Kāṇḍa of the Paippalāda Saṁhitā of Atharvaveda." *Proceedings of the First All-India Conference of Linguists* (Poona).

Aitareya-Āraṇyaka. Edited and translated with notes, with parts of the *Śāṅkhāyana-Āraṇyaka*, by A. B. Keith. Oxford University Press, 1909; reprinted in 1969.

Allen, W. S. 1951. *Phonetics in Ancient India.* London Oriental Series, no. 1. London: Oxford University Press.

Ananthanarayana, H. S. 1970. "Prakrits and Dravidian Languages." *Proceedings of the Seminar in Prakrit Studies.* Poona: University of Poona.

Andersen, Henning. 1973. "Abductive and Deductive Change." *Language* 49.

Andronov, M. S. 1970. *Dravidian Languages.* Moscow: Nauka Publishing House.

———. 1963. "Lexico-Statistic Analysis of the Chronology of Disintegration of Proto-Dravidian." *Indo-Iranian Journal* 7.

Āpiśali-śikṣā-sūtrāṇi. Edited by Yudhishthir Mimamsak. Ajmer, Saṁvat 2024.

Bailey, C. J. N., and M. L. Gardens. 1974. "Naturalness in Historical Reconstruction and Changes That Are Not Natural." In *Natural Phonology*. Chicago: Chicago Linguistic Society.

Bailey, Grahame T. 1938. "The Development of English *t, d* in North-Indian Languages." In *Studies in North Indian Languages.* London (originally in *BSOS* 4).

Banerjea, A. C. 1963. *Studies in the Brāhmaṇas.* Delhi: Motilal Banarasidass.

Banerji Shastri, A. 1936-37. "The Nāgas." *Annals of the Bhandarkar Oriental Research Institute.*

Bare, James. 1976. *Phonetics and Phonology in Pāṇini.* Natural Language Studies, no. 21. Ann Arbor: Phonetics Laboratory, University of Michigan.

Bhattacharya, Bishnupada. 1958. *Yāska's Nirukta and the Science of Etymology.* Calcutta.

Bhattacharya, P. C. 1975. "Sino-Tibetan (Boro), Assamese, Bengali and Indic Languages." *Indian Linguistics* 36, no. 4.

Bloch, Jules. 1934, 1965. *Indo-Aryan, From the Vedas to Modern Times.*

French original published in Paris, 1934; revised by the author and translated by Alfred Master, Paris, 1965.

———. 1920, 1970. *The Formation of the Marāṭhī Language.* French original published in Paris, 1920; translated into English by Dev Raj Chanana, Delhi, 1970.

Bloomfield, Maurice. 1906. *Vedic Concordance.* Cambridge: Harvard University Press.

Bloomfield, Maurice, and Franklin Edgerton. 1932. *Vedic Variants*, vol. 2. Philadelphia.

Brough, John. 1962. *The Gāndhārī Dharmapada.* London Oriental Series 7. London: Oxford University Press.

———. 1953. *The Early Brahmanical System of Gotra and Pravara.* Cambridge: Cambridge University Press.

Brown, Norman. 1953. *The United States and India and Pakistan.* Cambridge: Harvard University Press.

Bühler, Georg. 1895. *On the Origin of the Indian Brāhma Alphabet.* London.

Burrow, Thomas. 1936. "The Dialectal Position of the Niya Prakrit." In *Indian and Iranian Studies*, presented to George A. Grierson. London: University of London.

———. 1955. *The Sanskrit Language.* London: Faber and Faber.

———. 1968. *Collected Papers on Dravidian Linguistics.* Department of Linguistics publication no. 13, Annamalai University, Annamalainagar, South India.

———. 1971. "Spontaneous Cerebrals in Sanskrit." *BSOAS* 34.

———. 1972. "A Reconsideration of Fortunatov's Law." *BSOAS* 35.

Burrow, Thomas, and M. B. Emeneau. 1961. *A Dravidian Etymological Dictionary*. Oxford University Press.

Chakladar, H. C. 1928. "Eastern India and Āryāvarta." *IHQ* 4, no. 1. (Also refer to the posthumous publication: "Aryan Occupation of Eastern India." *Indian Studies, Past and Present* 3. Calcutta, 1961-62.)

Chanda, Ramaprasad. 1916. *The Indo-Aryan Races.* Bengal: Rajshahi; reprinted in *Indian Studies, Past and Present*, Calcutta, 1969.

Chatterji, S. K. 1965. *Dravidian.* Annamalainagar: Annamalai University.

———. 1962. *Indianism and the Indian Synthesis.* Calcutta: University of Calcutta.

———. 1960. *Indo-Aryan and Hindi.* Calcutta: Firma K. L. Mukhopadhyaya.

———. 1960*a*. "The Pronunciation of Sanskrit." *Indian Linguistics* 21.

———. 1956. "Old Tamil, Ancient Tamil and Primitive Dravidian." *Tamil Culture* 5, no. 2.

———. 1951. "Race-Movements and Pre-historic Culture." In *The Vedic Age*. Bombay: Bhāratīya Vidyā Bhavana.
———. 1936. "Purāṇa Legends and the Prakrit Tradition in New Indo-Aryan." In *Indian and Iranian Studies*, presented to George A. Grierson. London: University of London.
Chattopadhyaya, K. C. 1974. "Did Pāṇini Envisage "A" as a Close Vowel?" *Charudeva Shastri Felicitation Volume*. Delhi, 1974.
Converse, H. S. 1974. "The Agnicayana Rite: Indigenous Origin?" *History of Religions* 14, no. 2.
Dandekar, R. N. 1961. *Vedic Bibliography*. Poona: University of Poona.
———. 1967. *Some Aspects of the History of Hinduism*. Poona: University of Poona.
Dani, A. H. 1963. *Indian Paleography*. Oxford: Oxford University Press.
Dasgupta, Probal. 1972. "Coronality, Old Indo-Aryan Palatals, and Ṇatva." *Indian Linguistics* 33, no. 2.
Deb, H. K. 1925. "Rājaśekhara on Śiśunāga." *JAOS* 45.
———. 1922. "India and Elam." *JAOS* 42.
Deshpande, Madhav. 1978*a*. "History, Change and Permanence: A Classical Indian Perspective." To appear in *Contributions to South Asian Studies*, no. 1. Oxford University Press (1978?).
———. 1978*b*. *Socio-Linguistic Attitudes in India: An Historical Reconstruction*. A monograph to be published by Karoma Publishers, Ann Arbor, Michigan (1978?).
———. 1978*c*. "Some Aspects of Prehistoric Indo-Aryan." To appear in *Annals of the Bhandarkar Oriental Research Institute*, (Poona), Diamond Jubilee Volume (1978?).
———. Forthcoming. "Rājaśekhara on the Ethnic and Linguistic Geography of India." Paper presented at the 1978 Meeting of the American Oriental Society in Toronto.
———. Forthcoming. "Nation and Region: A Socio-Linguistic Perspective on Maharashtra." Paper presented at the conference *National Unity: The South Asian Experience*, organized by the University of Toronto, March 1978.
———. Forthcoming. *Aryans, Non-Aryans and Brahmins: A Study in Socio-Linguistic History*. In preparation.
———. 1976. "On the *Ṛk-Prātiśākhya* 13.5-6." *Indian Linguistics* 37.
———. 1975*a*. "Phonetics of *V* in Pāṇini." *Annals of the Bhandarkar Oriental Research Institute* 56.
———. 1975*b*. *Critical Studies in Indian Grammarians, I, The Theory of*

Homogeneity. The Michigan Series in South and Southeast Asian Languages and Linguistics, no. 2. Ann Arbor: Center for South and Southeast Asian Studies, The University of Michigan.

———. 1975*c*. "Phonetics of Short *A* in Sanskrit." *Indo-Iranian Journal* 17.

Ebert, R. P. 1976. Introduction to *Diachronic Syntax*. Chicago Linguistic Society.

Edgerton, Franklin. 1936. "The Prakrit Underlying Buddhistic Hybrid Sanskrit." In *Indian and Iranian Studies*, presented to George Grierson. London: University of London.

Emeneau, M. B. 1954. "Linguistic Prehistory of India." *Proceedings of the American Philosophical Society* 98.

———. 1956. "India as a Linguistic Area." *Language* 32.

———. 1962*a*. "Bilingualism and Structural Borrowing." *Proceedings of the American Philosophical Society* (Philadelphia) 106, no. 4.

———. 1962*b*. *Brahui and Dravidian Comparative Grammar*. Berkeley: University of California.

———. 1967. *Collected Papers (On Dravidian Linguistics, Ethnology and Folktales)*. Annamalainagar: Annamalai University.

———. 1971. "Dravidian and Indo-Aryan: The Indian Linguistic Area." *Symposium on Dravidian Civilization*. Austin, Texas.

———. 1974. "Indian Linguistic Area Revisited." *International Journal of Dravidian Linguistics* 3, no. 1.

Emeneau, M. B., and Thomas Burrow. 1962. *Dravidian Borrowings from Indo-Aryan.* Berkeley and Los Angeles: University of California Press.

Esteller, A. 1969. "The Quest for the Original Ṛgveda." *Annals of the Bhandarkar Oriental Research Institute* 50.

———. 1968. "Problems in the Text-Critical Reconstruction of the Ṛgveda-Palimpsest." *Annals of the Bhandarkar Oriental Research Institute* 48-49.

Fortunatov, Ph. 1881. "L + Dental im Altindischen." *Beiträge zur Kunde der Indo-Germanischen Sprachen* (Göttingen) 6.

Ganeshan, S. N. 1971. "Phonological Pattern of Tamil and Homonymy Due to Loanwords from Sanskrit." *Proceedings of the First All-India Conference of Linguists* (Poona).

Ganeshsundaram, P. C., and S. Vaidyanathan. 1958. "An Evaluation of Sanskrit Loan-words in Tamil from the Point of View of Nannūl." *Indian Linguistics* 1.

Geiger, W., and E. Kuhn. 1895-1901. *Grundriss der Iranischen Philologie* (Strassburg) 1.

Ghatage, A. M. 1962. *Historical Linguistics and Indo-Aryan Languages.*

Bombay: University of Bombay.
———. 1941. *Introduction to Ardhamagādhī.* Kolhapur.
Ghosh, Batakrishna. 1951. "Vedic Literature–General View." In *The Vedic Age.* Bombay: Bhāratīya Vidyā Bhavana.
Grierson, George Abraham. 1931. "On the Modern Indo-Aryan Vernaculars." *Indian Antiquary.*
———. 1929. "The Language of the Mahānayaprakāśa." *Memoirs of the Asiatic Society of Bengal* (Calcutta) 11, no. 2.
———. 1906. *The Piśāca Languages of North Western India.* London.
Hamp, Eric P. 1976. "Why Syntax Needs Phonology." In *Papers from the Parasession on Diachronic Syntax.* Chicago: Chicago Linguistic Society.
Hart, George L. 1975. *The Poems of Ancient Tamil.* Berkeley: University of California Press.
Hock, Hans Henrich. 1975. "Substratum Influence on (Ṛgvedic) Sanskrit?" *Studies in the Linguistic Sciences* 5, no. 2. Urbana: University of Illinois.
Hoffmann, Karl. 1960. "Review of Wackernagel's *Altindische Grammatik.*" *ZDMG* 110.
Hoijer, Harry. 1948. "Linguistic and Cultural Change." *Language* 24, no. 4.
Hymes, Dell, ed. 1971. *Pidginization and Creolization of Languages.* London: Cambridge University Press.
———, ed. 1964. *Language in Culture and Society.* New York: Harper and Row.
Ivanov, V. V., and V. N. Toporov. 1968. *Sanskrit.* Moscow: Nauka Publishing House.
Kantor, R. N., and R. J. Jeffers. 1976. "A History of the Sanskrit Gerund" (abstract). *Meeting Handbook*, Linguistic Society of America, 51st Annual Meeting, Philadelphia, 1976.
Kāśikā-Vṛtti. By Vāmana and Jayāditya. Sanskrit Academy Series, nos. 17 and 20. Hyderabad: Osmania University.
Katre, S. M. 1944. *Some Problems of Historical Linguistics in Indo-Aryan.* Bombay: University of Bombay. Reprinted by Deccan College, Poona, 1965.
Keith, A. B. See *Aitareya-Āraṇyaka.*
Kimura, Ryukan. 1927. *A Historical Study of the Terms Hīnayāna and Mahāyāna, and the Origins of Mahāyāna Buddhism.* Calcutta: University of Calcutta.
Konow, Sten. 1936. "Note on the Ancient North-Western Prakrit." In *Indian and Iranian Studies*, presented to George Grierson. London: University of London.

———. 1929. *Kharoṣṭhī Inscriptions.* Corpus Inscriptionum Indicarum (Calcutta) 2, pt. 1.

Kosambi, D. D. 1965. *Ancient India.* New York: Meridian.

———. 1950. "On the Origin of the Brahmin Gotras." *JBBRAS* 26.

———. 1947. "Early Brahmins and Brahmanism." *JBBRAS* 23.

Kuiper, F. B. J. 1948. *Proto-Munda Words in Sanskrit.* Amsterdam.

———. 1955. "Ṛgvedic Loanwords." In *Festschrift für W. Kirfel*, Studia Indologica, Bonner Orientalistische Studien, Neue Serie, Band 3.

———. 1958. "Ṛgvedic *Kīrín-* and *Kṝḷī-*." *Indian Linguistics* 1.

———. 1965. "Consonant Variation in Munda." In *Indo-Pacific Studies*, pt. 1, edited by Milner-Henderson. Amsterdam.

———. 1967*a*. "The Sanskrit Nominative Singular *Vīṭ*." *Indo-Iranian Journal* 10.

———. 1967. "The Genesis of a Linguistic Area." *Indo-Iranian Journal* 10: 81-102; reprinted in Southworth and Apte.

Lovins, J. B. 1974. "Why Loan Phonology is Natural Phonology?" In *Natural Phonology*. Chicago: Chicago Linguistic Society.

Macdonell, A. A. 1916. *A Vedic Grammar for Students.* Oxford University Press; reprinted in 1971.

Mahadevan, Iravatham. 1970. *"Tamil-Brāhmī Inscriptions."* Madras: State Department of Archaeology, Government of Tamilnadu.

———. 1968. "Tamil-Brāhmī Inscriptions of the Sangam Age." *Second International Conference–Seminar of Tamil Studies* (Madras).

Martinet, André. 1966. *Elements of General Linguistics.* Chicago: University of Chicago Press.

Master, Alfred. 1964. *A Grammar of Old Marāṭhī.* Oxford University Press.

———. 1960. "Initial Cerebrals in Indo-Aryan." In *P. K. Gode Commemorial Volume.* Poona: Oriental Book Agency.

MB, Vyākaraṇa-Mahābhāṣya, by Patañjali, with commentaries by Kaiyaṭa and Nāgeśa. In three volumes. Delhi: Motilal Banarasidass, 1967.

Mehendale, M. A. 1975. "The Ṛgveda-Saṁhitākāra and Father Esteller." *Bulletin of the Deccan College Research Institute* 35, nos. 1-2.

———. 1968. *Some Aspects of Indo-Aryan Linguistics*. Bombay: University of Bombay.

———. 1965. "The Use of *ḷ* in the Speech of Yāska." In *Nirukta Notes.* Poona: Deccan College.

———. 1963. "Upaniṣadic Etymologies." In *Munshi Felicitation Volume.* Bombay: Bhāratīya Vidyā Bhavana.

———. 1948. *Historical Grammar of Inscriptional Prakrits.* Poona: Deccan

College.
Meillet, Antoine. 1912-13. "Les Consonnes intervocaliques en Védique." *Indogermanische Forschungen* 31.
Miranda, Rocky V. 1977. "The Assimilation of Dravidian Loans to Konkani Phonological and Morphological Patterns." *Indo-Iranian Journal* 19, nos. 3-4.
Nadkarni, Mangesh V. 1975. "Bilingualism and Syntactic Change in Konkani." *Language* 51.
NR, Nirukta, by Yāska, with a commentary by Durgācārya. Ānandāśrama Sanskrit Series (Poona), no. 88, pts. 1-2, 1921.
Oldenberg, Hermann. 1896, 1973. *Vedic Research.* Original German published in *ZDMG* 50, 1896; translated by V. G. Paranjpe, Poona, 1973.
———. 1890, 1962. *Ancient India, Its Language and Religions.* Originally published in *Deutsche Randschau*, Berlin, 1890; Indian English edition, Calcutta, 1962.
———. 1890, 1882. *Buddha; His Life, His Doctrine, His Order.* Original German published in Berlin, 1890; English translation by Hoey (London, 1882).
Panikkar, K. M. 1961. *Hindu Society at Cross Roads.* Bombay: Asia Publishing House, 1955; 3rd rev. ed., 1961.
Pāṇinīya-Śikṣā. Critically edited in all its five recensions, with introduction, translation, and notes, by Manmohan Ghosh. Calcutta: University of Calcutta, 1938.
Parpola, Asko. 1975. "Tasks, Methods and Results in the Study of the Indus Script." *JRAS.*
Rahurkar, V. G. 1974. "Who Were the Paṇis?" *CASS Studies*, no. 2. Poona: University of Poona.
Rakshit, H. K. 1966. "The Brahmans of India, An Anthropometric Study." *Man in India* 46.
Rao, G. Subba. 1954. *Indian Words in English.* Oxford University Press.
Rao, S. R. 1972-73. "The Indus People Begin to Speak." *Journal of the Andhra Historical Research Society* 33.
Rastogi, Moti Lal. 1957. "Śaunaka and Abhinihita Sandhi in Ṛgveda." *Indian Linguistics,* Bagchi Memorial Volume.
RPR, Ṛk-Prātiśākhya, pt. 1. Edited by M. D. Sastri. Banaras, 1959.
RT, Ṛktantra. Ascribed to Śākaṭāyana, edited by Surya Kanta. Lahore, 1939; reprinted in Delhi, 1971.
Śāṅkhāyana-Āraṇyaka. See *Aitareya-Āraṇyaka.*
Sastri, Nilakanta K. A. 1967. *Cultural Contacts between Aryans and Dravi-*

dians. Bombay: P. C. Manaktala and Sons.

Sastri, Subramanya P. S. 1934. *History of Grammatical Theories in Tamil.* Madras.

———. 1930. *Tolkāppiyam*, vol. 1. English translation, Madras.

SCA, Śaunakīyā Caturādhyāyikā. Edited and translated by W. D. Whitney. New Haven, 1862.

Schwarzchild, L. A. 1973. "Initial Retroflex Consonants in Middle Indo-Aryan." *JAOS*, 93, no. 4.

Sharma, U. C. 1973. "The Dāśarājña War." *CASS Studies*, no. 1. Poona: University of Poona.

Sköld, Hannes. 1926. "Papers on Pāṇini and Indian Grammar in General." *Lunds Universitets Årsskrift* (Leipzig), N. F. Avd. 1, Band 21, N. 8.

Southworth, Franklin C. 1974. "Linguistic Stratigraphy of North India." *International Journal of Dravidian Linguistics* 3, no. 2.

———. 1971. "Detecting Prior Creolization: An Investigation of the Historical Origins of Marāṭhī." In Dell Hymes, ed., 1971.

Southworth, Franklin, and Mahadev Apte. 1974. Introduction to the *International Journal of Dravidian Linguistics* 3, no. 1.

Srinivas, M. N. 1966. *Social Change in Modern India.* Berkeley: University of California Press.

Staal, J. F. 1967. *Word Order in Sanskrit and Universal Grammar.* Foundations of Language (Amsterdam), Supplementary Series, no. 5.

Subbiah, Rama. 1968. "Tolkāppiyam and Phonetics." *Indo-Iranian Journal* 10.

Thieme, Paul. 1955. Review of Burrow's *The Sanskrit Language. Language.*

TPR, Taittirīya-Prātiśākhya. Edited and translated by W. D. Whitney. New Haven, 1868.

Trautmann, Thomas R. 1974. "Cross-Cousin Marriage in Ancient North India?" In *Kinship and History in South Asia,* Michigan Papers on South and Southeast Asia, no. 7. Ann Arbor: Center for South and Southeast Asian Studies, The University of Michigan.

Turner, R. L. 1975. *Collected Papers.* London: Oxford University Press.

———. 1924. "Cerebralization in Sindhi." *JRAS* 3.

Vaidya, C. V. 1930. *History of Sanskrit Literature.* Poona.

Vaidyanathan, S. 1971. *Indo-Aryan Loan-words in Old Tamil.* Madras.

———. 1958. "A Study of the Semantics of Sanskrit Loan-words in Modern Tamil." *Indian Linguistics* 1.

Vedic Variants. See Bloomfield, Maurice, and Franklin Edgerton.

VPR, Vājasaneyi-Prātiśākhya. Edited and translated by Indu Rastogi. Kashi

Sanskrit Series (Banaras), no. 179, 1967.

Walleser, Max. 1927. "Zur Aussprache von Skr. *a*." *Zeitschrift für Indologie und Iranistik* (Leipzig), Band 5.

Weinreich, Uriel. 1953. *Languages in Contact.* 3rd printing. Mouton, 1964.

Weinreich, Uriel; William Labov; and Maurice Herzog. 1968. *Empirical Foundations for a Theory of Language Change.* Austin: University of Texas Press.

Zvelebil, Kamil. 1972. "The Descent of the Dravidians." *International Journal of Dravidian Linguistics* 1, no. 2.

———. 1970. *Comparative Dravidian Phonology.* The Hague-Paris: Mouton.

Zvelebil, Kamil, and Švarný. 1955. "Remarks on the Articulation of the Cerebral Consonants." *Archiv Orientální* 23, pt. 3.